An Anthology of Spanish Poetry

An Anthology of
SPANISH
POETRY

From the Beginnings
to the Present Day
Including both Spain
and Spanish America

Compiled and edited by JOHN A. CROW

Louisiana State University Press / Baton Rouge and London / 1979

LIBRARY OF CONGRESS CATALOGING IN PUBLICATION DATA

Main entry under title:

861.008
A628c

An Anthology of Spanish poetry / compiled and edited by John A. Crow.
 1. Spanish poetry—Translations into English.
 2. English poetry—Translations from Spanish.   Baton Rouge: Louisiana
 3. Spanish poetry. I. Crow, John Armstrong.   State University, 1979.
PQ6267.E2 1979   861'.008   78-4619
ISBN 0-8071-0482-5 A628c
ISBN 0-8071-0483-3 pbk.
        220f.

*Translation it is that openeth the window, to
let in the light; that breaketh the shell, that we
may eat the kernel; that putteth aside the curtaine,
that we may looke into the most Holy place; that
removeth the cover of the well, that we may come by
the water.*

Preface to King James Version of the Bible, 1611

Contents

FIFTEENTH CENTURY

RENAISSANCE

Juan del Encina (1469–1529)

Gil Vicente (*ca.* 1470–1539)

Cristóbal de Castillejo (*ca.* 1490–1550)

Antonio de Villegas (*ca.* 1500–1551)

Pedro de Padilla (16th century)

Anonymous

Garcilaso de la Vega (1503–1536)

NEOCLASSIC PERIOD

Tomás de Iriarte (1750–1791)

ROMANTICISM

José Zorrilla (1817–1893)

Gustavo Adolfo Bécquer (1836–1870)

Rosalía de Castro (1837–1885)

Ramón de Campoamor (1817–1901)

MODERNISM

Manuel Gutiérrez Nájera (1859–1895)

Note on Translations

This anthology was compiled to give the reader of English a selection of the best poetry of Spain and Spanish America from the eleventh century to the present. The need for such a collection has long existed. Four Hispanic poets are nobel laureates—Gabriela Mistral, Juan Ramón Jiménez, Pablo Neruda, and Vincente Aleixandre—and many other poets writing in Spanish enjoy an international reputation. Several of these have been well translated individually, and there are limited anthologies that represent one period or geographic region; but no previous collection in English has covered the entire range of Hispanic poetry. A common tradition and many cross influences between Spain and Spanish America have produced a corpus of poetry that is best appreciated when viewed as a whole, not limited by the vicissitudes of epoch or geography. Many excellent anthologies in Spanish have already demonstrated this overall view.

The task of the translator today is hazardous and frequently unrewarding. It was not always so. Robert Southey, poet laureate of Britain during the Romantic period, wrote: "In the earliest ages of English poetry, the task of translation was thought as honorable as that of original composition."[1] Perhaps this attitude was one of the main reasons for the great number of fine translations made in England before and during Southey's lifetime.

In any case, the translator must walk a tightrope. If his translation is precise in every detail, it often loses in poetic quality. If it sacrifices precision for a superior poetic statement, the translator may be accused of having written his own poem, and should this be true he will certainly have strayed. On the other hand, if his translation is not a work of art in its own right, he has failed completely.

If the scholar-critic is truthful (but stuffy), he will say that poetry can properly be appreciated only in its original language. But this is an arrogance that would have denied us the King James Version of the Bible, the many excellent translations of Greek tragedy, Edward Fitzgerald's *Rubaiyat*, and English versions of Goethe's *Faust*, the *Iliad* and the *Odyssey*, Calderón, Baudelaire, Rilke, and Neruda. The most famous foreign works, very naturally, have been translated many times, and some translations are far superior to others. The reader deserves the best translation available, and this must have real literary merit if it is to be an acceptable version of the original.

This anthology presents the very best translations of Spanish poetry that have been made across the centuries, and to these I have added a few of my own. Among the translators are many renowned poets and others who, though not original poets, have achieved a particular distinction by turning poems of Hispanic writers into very beautiful English verse. Among the most successful translators of the seventeenth century were Sir Richard Fanshawe (for his versions of Góngora's sonnets), Thomas Stanley (for his translations from Montalbán), and Philip Ayres. In the late eighteenth and early nineteenth centuries, the Romantic poets, who had a special interest in foreign literatures, produced many excellent translations from the Spanish. Some of the finest were made by Archbishop Thomas Percy, Edward Fitzgerald, Percy Bysshe Shelley, Lord Byron (George Gordon Byron), John Hookham Frere, Sir John Bowring, John Gibson Lockhart, Robert Southey, Lord Holland (Henry Richard Vassal Fox), Henry Wadsworth Longfellow, and William Cullen Bryant. Among the well-known contemporary poets who have also produced some very beautiful translations from the

1. Robert Southey, *Letters Written During a Short Residence in Spain and Portugal* (Bristol, England: J. Cottle, 1797), iv.

Spanish are John Masefield, Roy Campbell, Rolfe Humphries, W. S. Merwin, H. R. Hays, Robert Bly, and Ben Belitt.

No translation has been included in this anthology merely for historic purposes; every English version was chosen on the basis of its quality as poetry. I believe that they all capture much of the magic and flavor of the originals, but the reader must be the final judge. As Longfellow wrote:

> I have but marked the place,
> But half the secret told,
> That, following this slight trace,
> Others may find the gold.[2]

2. Henry Wadsworth Longfellow, *The Poetical Works of Henry Wadsworth Longfellow* (New York: Houghton, Mifflin, 1882), 438. (Final quatrain of his poem "Prelude," which introduces his "Translations.")

Acknowledgments

I would like to express here my very special appreciation to the Del Amo Foundation for its generous grant, which has helped to make this anthology possible.

My gratitude for permissions to use and to translate many poems still under copyright is also great. I would like to thank Isabel García Lorca for the poems of her brother, the wives of César Vallejo and Miguel Hernández for the poems of these two poets, Francisco H. Pinzón Jiménez for the poems of Juan Ramón Jiménez, Manuel Álvarez de Lama for the poems of Antonio and Manuel Machado, Vincente Aleixandre, Rafael Alberti, Jorge Guillén, Gerardo Diego, Eugenio Florit, Dámaso Alonso, and Octavio Paz for permission to use their poems.

For permission to reprint translations, I am especially grateful to Robert Bly, H. R. Hays, John F. Nims, J. M. Cohen, Donald F. Fogelquist, W. S. Merwin, Doris Dana, Ben Belitt, Mary H. Parham, and Katharine E. Strathdee, whose beautiful English versions of Spanish poetry have given a precious quality to this book. To Else Albrecht-Carrié, permissions editor of New Directions Press, I am deeply indebted for her generous aid in granting permission to use poems of Pablo Neruda, Octavio Paz, and Federico García Lorca.

I would also like to acknowledge the following:
"Barcarole," "Autumn Returns," and "Born in the Woods," from Pablo Neruda, *Residence on Earth (Residencia en la tierra)*. Translated by Donald D. Walsh. Copyright © 1973 by Pablo Neruda and Donald D. Walsh. © Editorial Losada, S.A. Buenos Aires, 1958, 1961, 1962. Reprinted by permission of New Directions Publishing Corporation and Souvenir Press Ltd.

"The Broken Waterjar," from Octavio Paz, *Early Poems*. Copyright © 1959 by Octavio Paz and Lysander Kemp. All rights reserved. Reprinted by permission of New Directions Publishing Corporation.

Federico García Lorca, *Obras completas.* Copyright © Aguilar, S.A. de Ediciones, Madrid, 1954. All rights reserved. Reprinted by permission of New Directions Publishing Corporation, agents for the estate of F. García Lorca.

Translations by W. S. Merwin of Pablo Neruda's "Your Breast is Enough," and "Every Day You Play," from *Twenty Love Poems and a Song of Despair* reprinted by permission of Harold Ober Associates Incorporated. Copyright © 1969 by W. S. Merwin. Permission to reprint the originals of these two poems given by Jonathan Cape Limited and Grossman Publishers.

Permission to make new translations of Pablo Neruda's "Arte poética," "Oda con un lamento," and "No hay olvido," given by the Grove Press and Ben Belitt. Copyright © 1961 by Grove Press, Inc. Originals reprinted by permission of Ben Belitt.

John Masefield's translation of one sonnet by Francisco de Quevedo reprinted with permission of the Macmillan Publishing Co., Inc., from *Poems* by John Masefield. Copyright 1912 by Macmillan Publishing Co., Inc., renewed 1940 by John Masefield. Permission to reprint in the British Commonwealth given by The Society of Authors, as the literary representative of the estate of John Masefield.

Three translations by W. S. Merwin, from *Some Spanish Ballads* published by Doubleday & Co., Inc., Copyright © 1961 by W. S. Merwin, reprinted by permission of Harold Ober Associates Incorporated.

Permission to reprint two selections from *The Book of Good Love* by Juan Ruiz, translated by Elisha K. Kane, was generously given by the University of North Carolina Press, Chapel Hill.

Three selections from *Selected Poems* by Rafael Alberti, translated by Ben Belitt. Copyright © 1966 by the Regents of the University of California; reprinted by permission of the University of California Press.

English translations of two poems by Jorge Guillén, from *Cántico: A Selection* by Jorge Guillén. Copyright 1954, © 1957, 1959, 1960, 1961, 1965 by Jorge Guillén and Norman Thomas di Giovanni; reprinted by permission of Little, Brown and Co. in association with the Atlantic Monthly Press.

Originals and translations of "Una piadosa," "Ayudadores," "Emigrada judía," and "Una palabra," from *Selected Poems of Gabriela Mistral*, reprinted by permission of Joan Daves. Copyright © 1961, 1964, 1970, 1971 by Doris Dana. English translations of Mistral's poems "El ruego," "Los sonetos de la muerte," "El pensador de Rodin," from *Desolación*, made with the permission of Joan Daves and Doris Dana. Copyright © 1922 of Spanish poems by Instituto de las Españas.

Permission to use Spanish originals and to make translations of four poems from *La realidad y el deseo*, by Luis Cernuda, given by Fondo de Cultura Económica. Copyright © 1958, 1964, 1970 by Fondo de Cultura Económica.

Introduction
A Brief Survey of Hispanic Poetry

It is noteworthy that the earliest known Spanish literature is found in poems of love. This contradicts the long-held belief that the epic *Poem of the Cid,* written *ca.* A.D. 1140, was Spain's first literary expression. The much older lyric poems of love, called the *kharjas* (refrains), were unknown until 1948, when S. M. Stern published several of them in the journal *Al-Andalus.* Since then, similar poems have been found. Most of these are at least one hundred years older than the *Poem of the Cid,* and some of them may be as much as two hundred years older.

These brief refrains of love, which were added at the end of longer poems written in Hebrew and Arabic, employed Hebrew and Arabic letters; but they made no sense in either language. When phonetically transcribed, however, they produced a primitive Mozarabic Spanish, the language spoken by the Christians living under Moslem rule in Spain and the most widely spoken language in Spain during the tenth and eleventh centuries.

The *kharjas* were a kind of *cri de coeur,* and they may well have been taken directly from the folk poetry of the people. In the *kharjas* a girl of the lower class bewails the loss or absence of her lover. Because these refrains were spontaneously spoken or sung in the language of the streets, their sentiments were made to seem more true-to-life.

The Moslem Moors occupied a part of Spain for almost eight centuries (711 to A.D. 1492), and their influence throughout this period was profound in every aspect of life. By the year 1100 however, the reconquest of Spain by the Spanish Christians was well under way. Toledo had already fallen, and the Cid himself conquered Valencia, although eight years later it was retaken by the Moors. The War of the Reconquest was a religious war, not only to regain lost lands, but also to overcome the infidel. It followed an ebb-and-flow pattern, with pressure from the Christians becoming increasingly stronger as the centuries passed. Throughout the war there were long periods of truce during which Moors, Christians, and Jews all lived together in a tenuous peace. From this intermingling of three cultures. the Spain that we know emerged, unlike any other European country.

The *Poem of the Cid* catches the major impulses of those centuries in verses of stark splendor. It is by far the most realistic epic of European literature. The fantastic elements present in the *Song of Roland* of in *Beowulf,* for example, are found nowhere in the *Poem of the Cid.*

In the following century (1200–1300) the conquest gathered momentum. The language of Castile gained in dominion over the other languages of the peninsula, and a certain linguistic refinement is noted in the literature. In a form known as the *cuaderna vía,* rhymed quatrains (aaaa) in Alexandrine verse, Gonzalo de Berceo was already preaching the victorious gospel of Christ to the populace. His *Miracles of Our Lady* put the stories of older Latin texts into Castilian Spanish. The Age of Faith was beginning to flower in literature as the War of the Reconquest reached its height. In 1212 Alfonso VIII of Castile defeated the Moors at Navas de Tolosa, in 1230 León and Castile were united, in 1236 Ferdinand the Saint captured Córdoba, in 1248 Seville also fell, and the years 1252–1284 mark the reign of Alfonso X the Learned, known as the "king of the three religions."

By 1300 the momentum of the great crusade of the reconquest had temporarily subsided. Spanish Christians rested within the territories they had conquered in order to recoup their energies, and lovemaking, not war, became the focus. This new way of life was not the result of a conscious decision but simply reflected a change of spirit that emerged naturally from the long period of truce following a lengthy war.

Out of this web of history was produced "the most powerful book ever written in the Spanish language," the *Book of Good Love* by Juan Ruiz, the archpriest of Hita, an insignificant village in New Castile.[3] Ruiz' main verse form in this book was the *cuaderna vía*. His book is a wonderful medieval arabesque that brings together all the cultural roots of the Spanish Middle Ages. It mentions Ovid, Cato, Aristotle, the good knight Tristram and contains many biblical references and quotations; animal fables; and apologues, a type of story brought into Spain by the Moors. Proverbs abound in nearly every tale, and numerous songs to the Virgin are included, as well as much bawdiness. Ruiz also shows a great firsthand knowledge of the Moors and their ways, and he alludes frequently to Arabic music. The various episodes are linked together in a disjointed manner, on a flimsy frame having no beginning or end. The stir of life, though, is always present, and the lusty personality of the poet stands out against the rapidly moving pageant he has portrayed. The whole book wavers between sensual impulse and moral restraint, and in this fluctuation lies its tremendous human appeal.

The fifteenth century in Spain, often called the "portico of the Renaissance," was the last century of the war against the Moors. The country was readying itself for the final assault on Granada in 1492. Meanwhile, there was a great flourishing of courtly lyrics, and a large collection of them appeared in the *Cancionero de Baena* in 1445. Lyric poetry, which had already blossomed in Portuguese and in the Galician dialect, made the shift into Castilian. The collector of the Castilian poems was Juan Alfonso de Baena, a converted Jew, who dedicated the book to John II. The poems, which reflect the slightly artificial taste of the collector and the king, follow two main styles: the direct lyrical approach of the Galician-Portuguese school and the style of the more sophisticated Italian poetic tradition. The anthology contains 567 poems by fifty-four named poets, and about three dozen anonymous pieces. In it, the quality of the verse is inconsistent, and the simplicity of an earlier age has been replaced with refined and studied concepts which somehow take away the magic that gives poetry a soul.

The *Cancionero de Baena* to some extent surveys the lyrics of an age that produced a plethora of poets who were facile but not great. The Spanish Golden Age was not to begin until almost exactly a century later. And yet the *Cancionero de Baena* is a fascinating parade of fifteenth-century life. It presents knights in armor, nobles, ladies in brocade, monks in flowing vestments, Arab physicians, nuns of Seville and Toledo who vie with each other in beauty—an entire world living, moving, singing in light verse, asking for gifts and favors, proposing and resolving riddles as was the custom of the day.

The great poet of the fifteenth century was Jorge Manrique, famous for his *Ode on the Death of His Father*, generally referred to as his *Coplas* (verses), written in 1478. A solemn and majestic elegy, it is perhaps the best-known poem in Spanish literature and has been beautifully translated into English by Henry Wadsworth Longfellow. According to the English critic Gerald Brenan, Manrique's poem, like Thomas Gray's *Elegy in a Country Churchyard*, "consists of a string of commonplaces." But the *Coplas* are very good, Brenan concludes, "because under the stress of a strong emotion they condensed a great deal of floating sentiment and rhetoric into impeccable verse."[4]

Another poet of the fifteenth century, Íñigo López de Mendoza, marqués de Santillana (1398–1458), wrote some short lyrics about peasant girls and love that have a considerable charm. The marqués is also said to have added a string to the Spanish guitar; and he is the first author to mention the *romances*, or ballads of Spain, just then reaching their crest of public acclaim. He did not think very highly of these expressions of the popular genius. His library was perhaps the finest in Spain, and he was delighted to allow any man of letters to use it.

A third poet of the fifteenth century, Juan de Mena (1411–1456), produced reams of rhetorical verse. Following a visit to Italy, he introduced many embellishments into Spanish poetry in imitation of the Italians. He was also one of the first Spanish writers to feel what Matthew Arnold in his essay on Homer calls "the high seriousness of poetry and of the poet's vocation."[5]

Although Manrique's *Ode* and the marqués de

---

3. Américo Castro, *The Structure of Spanish History* (Princeton, N.J.: Princeton University Press, 1954), 452.
4. Gerald Brenan, *The Literature of the Spanish People* (New York: Meridian Books, 1957), 98.
5. Matthew Arnold, *On Translating Homer* (2 vols.; London: J. Murray, 1861), I, 16.

Santillana's lyrics are choice anthology pieces, the fifteenth century was really the epoch of the *romances*. These ballads, which probably began to appear in the thirteenth century, vary greatly in approach and style and, taken as a whole, form a corpus of literature that has no counterpart in any other European country. They cover a multitude of subjects, which by the late fourteenth century included nearly every aspect of Spanish life: history, love, warfare, border episodes, Jewish and Moorish lyrics and lamentations, amorous lyrics, tales of actual and legendary heroes, and more. The *romances*, hundreds of which are anonymous, were sung by wandering minstrels (*juglares*) to entertain the people, in castle halls, public squares, and other gathering places. Sir John Bowring, one of the English translators of the *romances* and the equally beautiful anonymous lyrics of the *cancioneros*, wrote: "The popular poetry of Spain is especially interesting because it is truly national. Its influence has, perhaps, served more than any other circumstance to preserve, from age to age, the peculiar characteristics of the Spanish nation."[6]

The *romances* of Spain outnumber those of any other country. They have sixteen-syllable lines that break in the middle and end in assonance, a form of semirhyme in which the vowels are the same while the consonants are not. In Spain, this became the characteristic verse form. Assonance was also used in popular Latin poetry, and it is common to the other romance languages of Europe, but not to English. When the ballads were collected and printed many years after their composition, they were generally (and still often are) printed in eight-syllable lines, which are much easier to fit on the page.

The famous *Cancionero general* of 1511 was a large collection of *romances*, many lyrical *villancicos*, and religious poems in the popular tradition. Numerous additional collections called *romanceros* appeared in the sixteenth and early seventeenth centuries. During the period of Romanticism in the first half of the nineteenth century, a more systematic effort was made to collect and to publish the ancient ballads. The writers of Spain's Golden Age all composed

romances, and the drama of that period was filled with them. Lope de Vega called them "Iliads without a Homer," and the English Romantic poets praised them lavishly and translated many of them into beautiful English verse.[7]

The year 1492 was a turning point in Western culture as well as in world history. For Spain it was truly a year of miracles. After nearly eight centuries of struggle against the Moslem invaders, the last Moorish stronghold in the land, Granada, surrendered to the Christian forces of Ferdinand and Isabella; the Jews, Spain's second largest minority, were expelled from the country after having lived there for fifteen hundred years; a Spanish Pope, Alexander Borgia, was elected in Rome; and, finally, America was discovered. Probably at no other time in Spain's long history would she have been capable of such a heroic effort. In 1492 also the first grammar of a romance language, the *Gramática castellana*, appeared. Written by the Spaniard Antonio de Nebrija, it was material evidence of Spain's linguistic unity.

In effect, at the turn of the fifteenth century, Spain embodied and fused within herself the feeling of cultural and religious unity of medieval days with the idea of statehood as conceived by the Renaissance and thus became the first politically unified nation of modern Europe. Inevitably the sense of national pride produced by this achievement was reflected in a great burgeoning of the arts.

Spain's cultural explosion did not follow immediately upon the heels of the epic year 1492. She first gathered her resources and energies for the great crusade of conquest, exploration, and colonization of the New World. This experience produced a whole new kind of literature about the recently discovered hemisphere and one Spanish critic, perhaps in an excess of nationalistic zeal, affirmed that "Cortés is the equal of any Da Vinci."[8]

In 1543, a few years after the expansion across the seas was well under way, an epochal book, *Las obras de Boscán y algunas de Garcilaso de la Vega (The Works of Boscán and a Few Selections of Garcilaso de la Vega)*, appeared in Spain. In this anthology, which was pub-

6. John Bowring, *Ancient Poetry and Romances of Spain* (London: Taylor and Hessey, 1824), iii.

7. Lope de Vega, *Laurel de Apolo*, in Vol. XXXVIII of "Biblioteca de autores españoles" (300 vols.; Madrid: M. Rivadeneyra, 1864–1880), 195.

8. Castro, *Structure of Spanish History*, 664.

lished after both poets were dead, Juan Boscán and Garcilaso de la Vega brought to Spain the Italian manner in poetry, which Boscán in his prefatory comments aptly characterized as "more serious, more artistic, and much superior" to the traditional Spanish courtly style. After breaking the barriers of geography and putting an end to the concept of a static universe, Spain was now ready to embark on her most glorious adventure in literature and the visual arts, the Spanish Golden Age, which, generally, covered a period of time from 1543 through 1680.

Outside the Spanish peninsula, the year 1543 was the focal point of a widespread revolution in the nature of man's thinking about the universe. In that year the Polish astronomer Nicolaus Copernicus published his far-reaching treatise *On the Revolution of Heavenly Bodies,* which revealed that the earth was not the center of our planetary system. In the same year the Dutch scientist Andreas Versalius published his equally revolutionary *On the Structure of the Human Body,* which prepared the way for modern anatomical knowledge.

The anthology of Boscán and Garcilaso opened new vistas for the many gifted writers of Spain and brought a new flexibility to Spanish verse. It popularized the eleven-syllable line and made it almost as important as the sixteen-syllable line (by then broken into two lines of eight syllables). The eleven-syllable line became the Spanish parallel of iambic pentameter in English and, when employed in blank verse, suggested the unrhymed hexameters of classical antiquity. The subject matter and aesthetic attitude of the poems in Boscán and Garcilaso's anthology are in the Renaissance tradition. There is a long sequence of ninety sonnets by Boscán on tortured love, and there are sonnets, elegies, Horatian odes, and Vergilian eclogues by Garcilaso. All of these were innovations in Spanish. Garcilaso's pastoral poems made him immensely popular. Replete with mythological motifs, they are melodious, sensuous, erotic evocations of melancholy, love, and idealzed classical landsapces. This new kind of verse indicated a clear shift in poetic sensibility, and was, as Elias Rivers has pointed out, "the foundation of a Renaissance tradition of poetry in Spain."[9]

During the following century and a half, Spanish poets produced some of the finest sonnets in European literature. Lope de Vega alone is reputed to have written more than 1,500 of them. The enrichment of Spanish poetry by Boscán and Garcilaso made possible its flowering in the baroque Golden Age, when a wide variety of styles appeared.

The two great religious poets of the sixteenth century, Fray Luis de León (1527–1591), and San Juan de la Cruz (1542–1591), had imbibed copiously at Garcilaso's magic spring. They produced much deeply emotional religious poetry that is unique in European literature. Some of the best of it is in Garcilaso's five-line *lira* stanza, in which lines of seven and eleven syllables alternate. San Juan de la Cruz is passionately mystical; Fray Luis is much more classical and restrained. Fray Luis also wrote some of the most beautiful nonreligious lyrics in the Spanish language. Both poets represent an escape from reality. As the contemporary poet and critic Pedro Salinas has said, "If Garcilaso and Góngora were great poets, Fray Luis de León and San Juan de la Cruz are equal to them in perfection and greatness and superior to them in ardor and spirituality."[10]

Fernando de Herrera (1534–1597), who headed the Sevillian school of poets, annotated the works of Garcilaso and deliberately carried on his tradition. The Sevillian school was characterized by its erudition and restraint. Herrera wrote several odes on heroic and patriotic themes and also left a series of sonnets and elegies in carefully chiseled lines. He was the main link between the poets of the early Renaissance and the great poets of the Baroque Period, especially Góngora.

Luis de Góngora, a writer steeped in classical lore, was the sophisticated poet of the Spanish Golden Age. In his longer baroque pieces, *Galatea, Fábula de Polifemo,* and the famous *Soledades,* or *Solitudes,* he dazzles his readers with a flood of mythological allusions and a vocabulary or recondite poetic images that embody his exaltation of reality. These poems of Góngora are difficult for the uninitiated to understand; indeed, in his own day Góngora was accused of being unintelligible.

The fact that a given poet (or any creative artist) is not easily understood does not imply either his

---

9. Elias L. Rivers (ed.), *Renaissance and Baroque Poetry of Spain* (New York: Charles Scribner's Sons, 1966), 18.

10. Pedro Salinas, *Reality and the Poet in Spanish Poetry* (Baltimore: Johns Hopkins Press, 1940), 101.

worth or lack of worth as an artist. Some poets collect, channel, and embody the folk spirit of their epochs and are promptly accalimed. The prime example of this in Spanish literature is Lope de Vega. But sometimes, as in the case of Góngora, the artist is ahead of his epoch, opening new vistas, making new discoveries, creating new harmonies. Such an artist will frequently infuriate the public, which has not been taught to understand this new use of the language. Nevertheless, the role of the artist as pathfinder is a historic and honored one. As Proust once sagely remarked, ''The last quartets of Beethoven created the public, which did not exist before, for the last quartets of Beethoven.''[11] If in his heavier moments Góngora was often regarded as the angel of darkness, he was at other moments also the angel of light. In addition to his abstruse pieces, he produced a great number of beautiful sonnets, ballads, and short lyrics in the popular style (*villancicos* and *letrillas*) that became immense favorites.

Francisco de Quevedo, another gifted poet of the Baroque Period, was also an outstanding sonneteer and wrote short lyrics that, despite their superior technical refinement, rivaled those of the old song books (*cancioneros*). His satiric and humorous pieces have a pungent, popular tone that is *sui generis*. Quevedo's poetry is deeply concerned with the fleeting quality of life and with man's tenuous position in a hostile universe.

Lope de Vega, Spain's most prolific dramatist, was also the Baroque Period's outstanding lyric poet in the popular vein. He is not as polished as Góngora in his style, but his facility is unparalleled, and some of his lyrics cannot be distinguished from the anonymous ballads and folk songs in the oral tradition. Lope also wrote over 1,500 sonnets and perhaps five hundred or six hundred plays, many of which contain ballads and songs of great lyric beauty.

Spanish Golden Age drama is noted for several other outstanding playwrights who were also excellent poets: Tirso de Molina, Juan Ruiz de Alarcón, Juan Pérez de Montalbán, and above all, Pedro Calderón de la Barca, highly praised by the German Romantics and by Shelley and Edward Fitzgerald, both of whom translated selections of Calderón into

English. Pérez de Montalbán, for his part, produced a number of charming poems that remind us of the seventeenth-century poets of the Caroline period in Britain. One of these, Thomas Stanley, made some noteworthy translations of Montalbán.

The Golden Age is often said to have ended in 1695 in the Spanish New World with the death of Sor Juana Inés de la Cruz, a Mexican nun, who produced the finest poetry of the colonial territories of Spain. Sor (Sister) Juana wrote much on religious themes, but she is best remembered for her sonnets and lyrics of love and loss, a type of poetry rarely associated with a nun. Of illegitimate birth, this beautiful young lady amazed the viceroy of Mexico and his entourage with her knowledge and facility for expression, and she became famous as the outstanding woman of her day. She was also the leading feminist of the colonial period and protested vehemently against the double standard that relegated women to a subordinate position in the society of those times.

There was a long hiatus in literary and artistic production in Spain after the Golden Age. The eighteenth century and the early part of the nineteenth century represent the lowest ebb of the Hispanic world. The political decline had begun in the 1600s, spurred on by the increasing degeneracy of the Hapsburg monarchs, and the road back up was long and steep. In 1700, a Bourbon, Philip V, was invited in from France to occupy the throne and to bring new life into the country, and the ideals of the French Enlightenment slowly filtered into the peninsula. Literature puttered around in a neoclassic mold, and no great writer emerged. In 1808 Spain was taken over by Napoleon, who placed his brother Joseph on the Spanish throne; shortly thereafter, the American colonies began their war of independence. In less than a decade, Spain lost the entire New World (except the Antilles), and the great Spanish empire ''on which the sun never set'' came to a sputtering end.

The Romantic movement in Spain gained momentum in the 1830s, somewhat later than in the other European countries. Several Romantic poets began to acclaim in sonorous verse the glorious past of their nation and to lament in martyred and melancholy tones an individual sense of anguish.

11. Marcel Proust, *Jean Santeuil* (3 vols.; Paris: Gallimard, 1952), II, 284.

Their patriotic and egocentric poetry was often very good, much like that of Lord Byron in Great Britain. The best Romantic poets were Angel de Saavedra, also known as the Duke of Rivas, José Zorrilla, and José de Espronceda. In Spanish America, José Echeverría of Argentina, José María Heredia of Cuba, Andrés Bello of Venezuela, and Manuel Acuña of Mexico kept the Romantic fire aglow; but they were not equal in merit to the Spaniards, though each of the Romantics gave a distinctive tonality to his romantic poetizations.

Perhaps the finest poet of the nineteenth century was Gustavo Adolfo Bécquer (1836–1870), a belated Spanish Romantic whose *Rimas* were not published until a year after his death. Bécquer produced a very small quantity of poetry of a very superior quality. His lyre had a single note: love and the loss of love. In brief, staccato, searing rhymes he sang the desperation of his bleeding heart. Suffering became with Bécquer an obsessive ritual, but his simple, direct, intense style and imagery are unique in Hispanic literature, and he became one of the most loved poets who ever wrote in Spanish.

In Spanish America there was a great burgeoning of poetry in the nineteenth century, after the colonies became independent nations. Romanticism and neoclassicism had numerous exponents, and in Argentina a very special kind of poetry arose. This *poesía gauchesca*, whose subject matter was the gaucho, produced many beautiful poems; the gaucho theme was responsible for some of the best Argentine prose works as well. The most famous gaucho poem is *Martín Fierro* (Part I, 1872; Part II, 1879) by José Hernández, and among the outstanding prose works that treat the gaucho are Domingo Faustino Sarmiento's *Facundo* (1845) and Ricardo Güiraldes' fine novel *Don Segundo Sombra* (1926).

In the late 1870s and early 1880s a new poetic movement was born—modernism. José Martí of Cuba and Manuel Guitérrez Nájera of Mexico were the first modernists, but they were quickly followed by Julián del Casal of Cuba, José Asunción Silva of Colombia, Rubén Darío of Nicaragua, and a host of others.

Darío brought modernism into focus, and he be-

came the leader and best-known poet in that style. Through him, modernism effected a complete renovation of Hispanic poetry. It was an artistic blending of many European influences: romanticism, parnassianism, and symbolism, on an American base. The last two movements were of French origin, and symbolism in particular became the strongest single source of inspiration for the new poetry. Darío assimilated the French symbolist style and brought it into the poetry of both Spanish America and Spain. Perhaps the main tenet of his poetic creed was the famous dictum of Paul Verlaine, "Music above all else, and after music, shade." [12] Darío made popular many new verse forms and revived many old forms that had fallen into disuse. In his first two key works, *Azul (Blue)*, 1888, and *Prosas profanas (Secular Lyrics)*, 1896, he exalted the symbolist cult of beauty and the art for art's sake aesthetic creed. In his later poetry he simplified his vocabulary and style and took a more human approach.

Darío was a poet of such striking genius that he immediately attracted the attention of the talented young writers of Spain. Miguel de Unamuno, Ramón María del Valle-Inclán, Antonio and Manuel Machado, and Juan Ramón Jiménez all praised him and responded to his music. The Generation of 1898, of which these poets were a part, represented modernism in Spain. Each poet of the group had his own distinctive style, but the common denominator of the Generation as a whole was that all its members asked and attempted to answer the questions, What is Spain? What does it mean to be a Spaniard? The self-probing was sharp and clean, and some of the finest poetry to come out of Spain was its expression. Of the group's two outstanding poets, Antonio Machado and Juan Ramón Jiménez, the latter won the Nobel Prize, though Machado was an equally great poet.

The writers who followed this group tried to break away from all of the established canons, and this resulted in various poetic styles such as ultraism, surrealism, experimentalism, vanguardism, cubism, integralism, creationism. There was widespread use of illogical syntax and images in the new poetry, which strove to penetrate and reveal the

---

12. *French Symbolist Poetry*, trans. C. F. MacIntyre (Berkeley and Los Angeles: University of California Press, 1958), 34. (The quotation is from Verlaine's poem "Art Poétique," which first appeared in *Paris-moderne*, 1848.)

subconscious. After the early flurry of the absurd had abated, a considerable amount of very beautiful poetry was written.

By the 1920s, in both Spain and Spanish America, a younger generation of very gifted poets came to the fore. In Spain, Federico García Lorca, Vicente Aleixandre, Luis Cernuda, Rafael Alberti, and Pedro Salinas were among the best known. Góngora was an idol to them, but they were also drawn to the ancient folk poetry of Spain. García Lorca achieved international fame by fusing these two currents within his own unique and intriguing personality. His execution by Franco partisans in the early weeks of the Spanish Civil War no doubt added a dramatic cubit to his stature, but even without this his genius was such that he could not have failed to leave his effect on all who followed him. He became an almost mythic hero to the young writers of Spanish America.

García Lorca was not the only poet of his generation to strike out in a new direction. Vincente Aleixandre, who won the Nobel Prize in 1977, adopted and popularized a very free and fluid verse form that seemed more English in tone than Spanish. Pedro Salinas, Jorge Guillén, and Dámaso Alonso, all professors of literature and poets as well, helped to bring about a remarkable renovation in poetic style. Gerardo Diego added focus and cross-fertilization by assemblying a noteworthy anthology of the best poems that had appeared between 1915 and 1931. These poet-professors gave new life to the ancient ballads and beautiful anonymous lyrics of the *cancioneros* and to the poetry of the great masters of the Golden Age by praising and quoting them in widely heralded lectures and commentaries, and by using the same styles in many of their own poems. In this way the Spanish poetic past, particularly the popular tradition, provided stimulus and nutriment just as it had centuries before for Lope de Vega and Góngora. Outside the popular tradition Góngora was the strongest single influence, but Lope de Vega, Garcilaso, Fray Luis de León, San Juan de la Cruz, and Herrera were not far behind. The poetry of Spain in the twentieth century truly enjoyed a second golden age as the old roots burgeoned anew.

In Spanish America, poets were going through a parallel experience. Pablo Neruda, Gabriela Mistral, César Vallejo, Ramón López Velarde, and José Gorostiza became almost as widely admired as their Spanish contemporaries. Neruda and Mistral, both from Chile, won the Nobel Prize. Gabriela was perhaps the most widely loved woman in the Hispanic world; her life of dedication and involvement brought her more fame than her pen. Neruda, a staunch Communist, occasionally allowed his social convictions to distort his poetry, but in the main he was faithful to poetic art, and at his best he is well-nigh incomparable. César Vallejo of Peru, who in 1938 died in poverty in Paris, wrote in a style so completely his own that he has no counterpart in Hispanic literature. His name was exalted by all lovers of poetry after his death.

Hispanic poetry was no longer regional. It had entered the mainstream of Western letters on both sides of the Atlantic and had produced a considerable number of poets of as much distinction as those who wrote in other languages—poets, for example, comparable to Rainer Maria Rilke. T. S. Eliot, Paul Valéry, Eugenio Montale, and William Butler Yeats.

The Hispanic Muse is still very much alive today, but her finest twentieth-century voices are now dead or very old. Among those who have gone, leaving no comparable figures to take their places, are Federico García Lorca, Juan Ramón Jiménez, Antonio Machado, Pablo Neruda, Gabriela Mistral, and César Vallejo. Younger poets, led by Octavio Paz of Mexico, have come into the vanguard. The new poetry, brilliant in imagery but often abstruse in content, reflects the torment and fragmentation of our day. How it will be judged fifty years from now is impossible to tell. We stand now at the end of an epoch and at the beginning of another. The future, as always, is promising but unpredictable.

In conclusion, I would like to add a brief personal note. It has been my good fortune to know personally several of the Hispanic poets of this century: Gabriela Mistral, Federico García Lorca, Antonio Machado, Juan Ramón Jiménez, Luis Cernuda, Dámaso Alonso, José Gorostiza, Eugenio Florit, and Jorge Carrera Andrade. The inspiration of these contacts was a very strong influence in the preparation of this anthology.

John A. Crow

MEDIEVAL POETRY

Saying good-bye to something
is the poet's way of making
it endure.

Mozarabic Songs

eleventh century

What shall I do? What will become of me?
Oh, my beloved,
Do not abandon me now!

My heart is going away from me,
Oh, God, when will it return?
So great is the grief for my beloved!
For he is ill, when will he be well?

So much love, so much love,
Oh, sweetheart, so much love;
Eyes that were gay are now ill,
And hurt most cruelly.

Oh, mother, what shall I do?
My beloved is at the door.

Kharjas

¿Qué farayu o qué serád de mibi?
Habibi,
non te tolgas de mibi.

Vayse meu corachón de mib,
¿ya, Rab, si se me tornarád?
¡Tan mal meu dolor li-l-habib!
Enfermo yed, ¿cuándo sanarád?

Tant' amare, tant' amáre,
habib, tant' amáre,
enfermaron uelios gaios,
e dolen tan male.

¿Qué faré, mamma?
Meu-l-habib est' ad yana.

ANONYMOUS TRANSLATOR

Poem of the Cid

ca. 1140

The *Poem of the Cid*, Spain's great epic, was composed near the year 1140, only forty years after the death of its hero. It is in lines of a varying number of syllables in assonance and rhyme, with a break in the middle. The story lacks the fantastic elements of many other national epics; it is told simply, with a certain laconic solemnity, but has occasional bursts of lyric beauty.

The Cid was a historic figure, and in this epic and in the ballads about him he is portrayed as the great Spanish warrior. He fought the Moors, but he also had many close Moorish friends and allies. He was not a crusader. When he conquered a Moslem city, he never interfered with the religion of the populace. In the poem he often calls on Saint James (Santiago), while the Moors call on Mohammed; but his battles against the Moors were more for booty and glory than for gaining converts. "Those who came with me on foot, are now well mounted," says one of the lines of the poem, thus characterizing the emerging Spanish society of *peones* (menials on foot), and *caballeros* (gentlemen, literally, "those who are mounted.").

The first page of the poem's manuscript is missing. The epic begins with the Cid leaving his home in Bivar for exile, because his enemies had turned the king, Alfonso VI, against him. He heads for Burgos with a small retinue, but he finds the doors of the houses in the town all locked, and he is denied refuge. A nine-year-old girl comes forth to explain why. The Cid then proceeds to the monastery of San Pedro, where his wife, Jimena, and his two small daughters are waiting. Here the Cid says good-bye to his family. During an extended period in exile, he wins many

3

victories, and finally the king relents and welcomes him home again. He is renowned everywhere as *el Cid Campeador*; the term *Cid* is from the Arabic *Sidi*, "leader, lord," and *Campeador* means "winner of battles."

Later, at King Alfonso's insistence, the Cid promises his daughters in marriage to the arrogant counts of Carrión, Diego and Fernando González. During the wedding festivities, a lion kept in the palace breaks his chain and enters the main hall. The counts of Carrión react in a cowardly manner, cringing behind the other guests. The Cid, disgusted, takes the lion by his chain and leads him back to the cage.

On the return trip to Carrión, the two counts seek revenge because of the affront, which they thought had been deliberately planned to humiliate them. When they reach the forest of Corpes, they strip their wives, lash them mercilessly, and abandon them to the wild animals. The two women are found by one of the Cid's relatives who had been sent to check on their safety, and the Cid is informed of the affair. He calls for a hearing before the king and demands retribution.

At Toledo, the king assembles parliament (Cortes), which both parties attend. The counts of Carrión are forced to return to the Cid his two fine swords and the dowry he had given them. But the Cid is not satisfied; he demands that there be a tourney to the death. The king grants the challengers the right to meet in combat, and three weeks later they all appear on the plains of Carrión, where the tourney is to take place. In the combat itself the Cid's three champions are Pedro Bermúdez, Martín Antolínez and Muño Gustioz. It is easy to recognize the counts of Carrión because of their common surname, González.

The Exile of the Cid

The Cid leaves his home in Bivar for exile.

His eyes flooding with bitter tears, the Cid concealed his face,
He turned his head for one last look at his sweet dwelling place;
He saw the heavy doors ajar, the postern gate unbolted,
Bare perches where his skins had hung, and where his falcons molted.
His heart was sad, he heaved a sigh, in measured words he said:
"O blessèd Father in the sky, Lord of the quick and dead,
See what my enemies have done to me; the King has been misled."
They spurred their mounts, then dropped the reins they had been holding tight,
Leaving Bivar a bird of hope flew singing on their right,
But near Burgos a baleful crow hove leftward into sight.
The Cid looked up, he grimly shrugged and turned his head aside,
"Take heart with me Alvar, old friend," these words he proudly cried,
"While we are now cast from the land where all our kin reside,
Castile will yet hail our return, or claim us when we've died."
The Cid rode into Burgos then with sixty lances strong,
And men and women sallied forth to greet the passing throng,

Destierro del Cid

De los sos ojos   tan fuertemientre llorando,
tornava la cabeça   e estávalos catando.
Vío puertas abiertas   e uços sin cañados,
alcándaras vázias   sin pielles e sin mantos
e sin falcones   e sin adtores mudados.
Sospiró mio Çid,   ca mucho avié grandes cuidados.
Fabló mio Çid   bien e tan mesurado:
"¡grado a ti señor padre,   que estás en alto!
"Esto me an buolto   mios enemigos malos."

Allí pienssan de aguijar,   allí sueltan las riendas.
A la exida de Bivar   ovieron la corneja diestra,
e entrando a Burgos   oviéronla siniestra.
Meçió mio Çid los ombros   y engrameó la tiesta:
"albricia, Álvar Fáñez,   ca echados somos de tierra!
"mas a grand ondra   tornaremos a Castiella."

Mio Çid Roy Díaz,   por Burgos entróve,
en sue conpaña   sessaenta pendones;
exien lo veer   mugieres e varones,
burgeses e burgessas,   por las finiestras sone,
plorando de los ojos,   tanto avien el dolore.
De las sus bocas   todos dizían una razóne:
"Dios, qué buen vassallo,   si oviesse buen señore!"

Conbidar le ien de grado,   mas ninguno non osava:
el rey don Alfonsso   tanto avie le grand saña.

While other townsfolk gazed at them from windows all
along,
They wept in anguish at the sight and cried with one
accord:
"God, what a vassal he would make, if he had a good
lord!"
They gladly would have sheltered him, but dared not
disregard
The edict that the King had sent, which all of them
abhorred.

A little girl of nine came out to where the Cid's horse
stood,
"O Campeador of honored sword, we'd open if we could;
Last night the king's decree arrived closing our doors to
you,
By herald and well sealed it came to prove its message
true,
And so we dare not open up despite our angry cries,
We'd lose our homes and our estates, even our very eyes.
Cid, do not trespass on our plight, if by mischance you
should,
Then you would wrong us grievously, and do yourself no
good,
But God attend you where you go, this much we all
implore!"
So spoke the girl and went inside and locked the heavy
door;
The Cid then knew his royal sire would favor him no
more.

Una niña de neuf años   a ojo se parava:
"Ya Campeador,   en buena çinxiestes espada!
"El rey lo ha vedado,   anoch dél entró su carta,
"con grant recabdo   e fuertemientre seellada.
"Non vos osariemos   abrir nin coger por nada;
"si non, perderiemos   los averes e las casas,
"e aun demás   los ojos de las caras.
"Çid, en el nuestro mal   vos non ganades nada;
"mas el Criador vos vala   con todas sus vertudes santas."
Esto la niña dixo   e tornós pora su cosa.
Ya lo vede el Çid   que del rey non avie gracia.

The Cid takes leave of his family who are waiting for him at the monastery of San Pedro.

The prayer and mass were spoken to start them on their
way,
They left the church and mounted, but how they longed
to stay,
The Cid embraced Jimena, his hand that round her lay
She lifted gently to her lips, and sobbed in her dismay,
He turned and kissed his daughters, and to them softly
said:
"May God the Father guard you, His grace upon you
shed,
At last the time to leave has come, the parting that I dread.
God willing we will meet again, but now our travails
start."
They wiped the tears away once more, but still grieved in
the heart,
Then like nail that leaves the flesh, they tore themselves
apart.

JOHN A. CROW

La oración fecha,   la missa acabada la an,
salieron de la eglesia,   ya quieren cavalgar.
El Çid a doña Ximena   ívala abraçar;
doña Ximena al Çid   la manol va besar,
llorando de los ojos,   que non sabe qué se far.
E él a las niñas   tornólas a catar:
"a Dios vos acomiendo   e al Padre spiral;
"agora nos partimos,   Dios sabe el ajuntar."
Llorando de los ojos,   que non vidiestres atal,
assís parten unos d'otros   commo la uña de la carne.

The Counts of Carrión

Los Ifantes de Carrión

The following selections are from the last part of the poem. They take place after the counts of Carrión have abandoned their wives (the Cid's daughters) in a wild forest. The Cid is speaking to the king, who is holding court in Toledo.

Justice and mercy, my Lord the King, I beseech you of your grace!	¡Merced, ya rey señor por amor de caridad!
I have yet a grievance left behind, which nothing can efface.	La rencura mayor non se me puede olbidar,
Let all men present in the court attend and judge the case,	oídme toda la cort e pésevos de mio mal;
Listen to what these Counts have done and pity my disgrace.	Ifantes de Carrión quem desondraron tan mal;
Dishonored as I find myself, I cannot be so base,	a menos de riebtos no los puedo dexar.'
But here before I leave them, to defy them to their face.	Dezid ¿qué vos mereçí ifantes de Carrión,
Say, Counts, how had I so deserved, in earnest or in jest,	en juego o en vero o en alguna razón?
Or on whatever plea you can defend it at your best,	Aquí lo mejoraré a juvizio de la cort.
That you should rend and tear the heartstrings from my breast?	¿A quém descubriestes las telas del coraçón?
I gave you at Valencia my daughters in your hand,	A la salida de Valencia mis fijas vos di yo,
I gave you wealth and honors, and treasure at command:	con muy grand ondra e averes a nombre;
Had you been weary of them, to cover your neglect,	cuando las non queriedes ya canes traidores,
You might have left them with me, in honor and respect.	¿por qué las sacávades de Valencia sus honores?
Why did you take them from me, dogs and traitors that you were?	¿A qué las firiestes a çinchas e a espolones?
In the forest of Corpes, why did you strip them there?	Solas las dexastes en el robredo de Corpes,
Why did you mangle them with whips? Why did you leave them bare	a las bestias fieras e a las aves del mont.
To the vultures and to the wolves, and to the wintry air?	Por quanto les fiziestes menos valedes vos.
The court will hear your answer, and judge what you have done	Si non recudedes véalo esta cort.
I say your name and honor henceforth are lost and gone.	

The counts of Carrión defend themselves by boasting of their royal pedigree and by lying about their courage. One of the Cid's men then recalls the episode of the lion in which their cowardice was revealed. He directs his words to Count Fernando Carrión who had just spoken.

You are so tall and handsome, but cowardly and weak,	¡E eres fermoso mas mal varragán!
Thou tongue without a hand, how can you dare to speak?	¿Lengua sin manos quómo osas fablar?
There's the story of the lion should never be forgot,	Di, Ferrando otorga esta razón:
Now let us hear, Fernando, what answer have you got?	¿None te viene en miente en Valencia lo del león,
The Cid was sleeping in his chair, with all his knights around,	quando durmió mio Çid y el león se desató?
The cry went forth along the hall. "The lion is unbound!"	E tú, Ferrando ¿qué fizist con el pavor?
What did you do, Fernando, like the coward that you were?	¡Metístet tras el escaño de mío Çid el Campeador!
You slunk behind the noble Cid, and crouched beneath his chair.	Metístet, Ferrando por o menos vales oy.
We pressed around the sleeping man to shield our Lord from harm,	Nos çercamos el escaño por curiar nuestro señor,
Till the good Cid awoke at last; he rose without alarm;	fasta do despertó mio Çid el que Valencia gañó;
He went to meet the lion with his mantle on his arm.	levantós del escaño e fos poral león;
The lion was abashed and shamed the noble Cid to meet,	el león premió la cabeça a mio Çid esperó,
He bowed his mane down to the earth, his muzzle at his feet.	dexóse prender al cuello e a la red le metió.
	Quando se tornó el buen Campeador,
	a sos vasallos viólos aderredor;
	demandó por sos yernos ¡ninguno non falló!
	Riébtot el cuerpo por malo e por traidor.

The Cid then by his neck and mane withdrew him to his
    den,
He closed the cage and then came back into the hall again;
He found his knights, his vassals, and all his valiant men;
He asked about his sons-in-law, they were neither of
    them there.
I defy you for a coward and the weakling that you were.

The king calls for the tourney, the markers are laid out, and the fighting begins. The king is speaking:

"Hear this, my Lords of Carrión! Attend to what I say!
You should have fought this battle upon a former day,
When we were at Toledo, but you would not agree;
And now the noble Cid has sent these stalwart champions
    three,
To fight in ancient Carrión, escorted here by me.
Be valiant in your fight today, do no foul play or wrong;
If any man attempt it, he shall not triumph long;
He never shall have rest or peace within my kingdom
    more."
The faithless Lords of Carrión are now repenting sore;
The Heralds and the King himself are foremost in the
    place,
They clear away the people from the guarded middle
    space;
They measure off the boundaries, the barriers they fix,
They point them out in order, and explain to all the six:
"If you are forced beyond the line where they are marked
    and traced,
You shall be held as conquered and beaten and
    disgraced."
Six lances length on either side an open space is laid,
They share the field between them, the sunshine and the
    shade.
Their office is performed, and from the battle space
The heralds now are all withdrawn and leave them face to
    face.
Here stand the warriors of the Cid, that noble champion,
Opposing on the other side, the Lords of Carrión.
Earnestly their minds are fixed each one upon his foe;
And then apace they take their place, anon the trumpets
    blow;
They stir their horses with the spur, they lay their lances
    low,
They hold their shields before their breasts, behind their
    saddle bow.
The skies are overcast above, the earth trembles below.
The people stand in silence now, all gazing on the show;
Bermúdez the first challenger first into combat sped,
He met Ferrán González, and charged him head to head;
They rush together with such rage that all men count
    them dead.
They strike each other on the shield, and with no thought
    of dread.
Ferrán González with his lance pierced through the shield
    outright,

"Oíd que vos digo,   ifantes de Carrione:
"esta lid en Toledo la fiziérades,   mas non quisiestes
    vose.
"Estos tres cava'leros   de mio Çid el Campeadore
"yo los adux a salvo   a tierras de Carrione.
"Aved vuestro derecho,   tuerto non querades vose,
"ca qui tuerto quisiere fazer,   mal gelo vedaré yove,
"en todo myo reyno   non avrá buena sabore,"
Yas les va pesando   a ifantes de Carrione.

Los fideles y el rey   enseñaron los mojones,
librávanse del campo   todos a derredor.
Bien gelo demostraron   a todos seys commo son,
que por í serié vençido   qui saliesse del mojón.
Todos las yentes   esconbraron a derredor,
de seys astas de lanças   que non llegassen al mojón.

Sorteávanles el campo,   ya les partién el sol,
salién los fideles de medio,   ellos cara por cara son;
desí vinién los de mio Çid   a ifantes de Carrión,
e ifantes de Carrión   a los del Campeador;
cada uno dellos   mientes tiene al so.
Abraçan los escudos   delant los coraçones,
enclinavan las caras   sobre los arzones,
batién los cavallos   con los espolones,
tembrar querié la tierra   dond eran movedores.
Cada uno dellos   mientes tiénet al so;
todos tres por tres   ya juntados son:
cuédanse que essora cadrán muertos   los que están
    aderredor.

Per Vermudoz,   el que antes rebtó,
con Ferránt Gonçálvez   de cara se juntó
firiensse en los escudos   sin todo pavor.
Ferrán Gonçalvez a don Pero   el escudol passó,
prísol en vázio,   en carne nol tomó,
bien en dos logares   el astil le quebró.
Firme estido Per Vermudoz,   por esso nos encamó;
un colpe reçibiera,   mas otro firió:
crebantó la bloca del escudo,   apart gela echó,
passógelo todo,   que nada nol valió.
Metiól la lança por los pechos,   çerca del coraçon;
tres dobles de loriga teníe Fernando,   aquestol prestó.
Las dos le desmanchan   e la terçera fincó:
el belmez con la camisa   e con la guarnizón
de dentro en la carne   una mano gela metió;
por la boca afuera   la sángrel salió;

It passed Bermúdez on the side, his flesh it did not bite.
The wooden spear was snapped in twain, Bermúdez sat
upright,
He neither flinched nor swerved, like a true perfect
knight.
A good stroke he received, but a better he had given;
He struck the shield upon the boss, in sunder it is riven,
Then on and deep in Ferrán's breast the lance's point is
driven,
Far into his breast-plate it went, and nothing would avail;
Fernando wore two breast-plates, besides his
coat-of-mail;
The two are riven in sunder, the third stood him in stead,
The mail sunk in his breast, the mail and the spear-head,
The blood was spurting from his mouth in streams of gory
red.
The blow had snapped his girdle, also his saddle girth,
It knocked him from his charger's back, and cast him to
the earth.
The people think that he is dead as he lies on the sand;
Bermúdez put his land aside and took his sword in hand.
Ferrán González knew the blade which he had worn of
old,
Before the mighty blow came down, he yielded and cried,
"Hold!"

crebáronle las çinchas,   ninguna nol ovo pro,
por la copla del cavallo   en tierra lo echó.
Assí lo tenién las yentes   que mal ferido es de muort.
En elle dexó la lança   e mano al espada metió,
quando lo vido Ferrán Gonçalvez,   conuvo a Tizón;
antes que el colpe esperasse   dixo: "vençudo so".
Atorgaróngelo los fideles,   Per Vermudos le dexó.

Antolínez now fights Diego González of Carrión, and finally Muño Gustioz battles Assur
González.

Antolínez and Diego then charged and helmets flashed,
Their spears were shivered with the shock, so furiously
they clashed.
Antolínez drew forth the blade which Diego once had
worn,
Eagerly he aimed the blow for the vengeance he had
sworn,
Right through Diego's helm the blade's sharp edge has
borne,
The crest and helm are lopped away, the coif and hair are
shorne.
He stood astounded with the stroke, now trembling and
forlorn,
He waved his sword above his head, he made a piteous
cry,
"O save , save me from that blade, Almighty Lord on
high!"
Antolínez came fiercely on to give the fatal stroke,
Diego's courser reared upright, and through the barrier
broke;
Antolínez has won the bout, although his blow has
missed,
He drove Diego from the field, and stands within the list.
I tell you next of Muño Gustioz, two combats now are
done;
How he fought Assur González, you shall hear of this
anon.
Assur González was a bold, a fierce and hardy knight,

Don Martino e Díag Gonçalvez   firiéronse de las lanças,
tales foron los colpes   que les crebaron amas.
Martín Antolínez   mano metió al espada,
relumbra tod el campo,   tanto es linpia e clara;
diol un colpe,   de traviéssol tomava:
el casco de somo   apart gelo echava,
las moncluras del yelmo   todas gelas cortava,
allá levó el almófar,   fata la cofia llegava,
la cofia e el almófar   todo gelo levava,
ráxol los pelos de la cabeça,   bien a la carne llegava;
lo uno cayó en el campo   e lo al suso fincava.

Quando este colpe a ferido   Colada la preçiada,
vido Díag Gonçálvez   que no escaparié con el alma;
bolvió la rienda al cavallo   por tornase de cara,
espada tiene en mano   mas no la ensayava.
Essora Martín Antolínez   reçibiól con el espada,
un cólpel dió de llano   con lo agudo nol tomava.
Essora el ifante   tant grandes vozes dava:
"¡Valme, Dios glorioso,   señor, cúriam deste espada!"
El cavallo asorrienda,   e mesurándol del espada.
Sacól del mojón;   don Martino en el camp fincava.

Los dos han arrancado;   dirévos de Muño Gustioz,
con Anssuor Gonçálvez   cómmo se adobó.
Firiénsse en los escudos   unos tan grandes colpes.
Anssuor Gonçálvez,   forçudo e de valor,
firió en el escudo   a don Muño Gustioz,
tras el escudo   falssole la guarnizón;

He rode at Muño Gustioz, with all his force and might;
He struck the shield and pierced it through, but then the
    point came wide,
It passed around Muño Gustioz, betwixt his arm and side;
Sternly, like a practiced knight, brave Muño met him
    there,
His lance he levelled steadfastly, and through the shield
    hit bare;
He bore the point into his breast, but just outside the
    heart;
It took him through the body, but in no mortal part;
The shaft stood out behind his back a good cloth-yard and
    more;
The pennon and the point were dripping down with gore,
Muño still clenched his spear in hand, he passed and
    forced it round,
He wrenched him from the saddle, and cast him to the
    ground.
His horse sprang forward with the spur, he plucked the
    spear away,
He wheeled and came around again to pierce him where
    he lay.
Then Cried Gonzalo Asurez, "For God's sake spare my
    son!
The other two have yielded, the field is fought and won!"

JOHN HOOKHAM FRERE

en vázio fue la lança   ca en carne nol tomó.
Este colpe fecho,   otro dió Muño Gustioz:
por medio de la bloca,   el escúdol crebantó;
nol pudo guarir,   falssóle la guarnizón,
apart le priso,   que non cab al coraçón
metiól por la carne adentro   la lança con el pendón,
de la otra part   una braça gela echó.
con él dió una tuerta,   de la siella lo encamó,
al tirar de la lança   en tierra lo echó;
vermejo salió el astil,   e la lança y el pendón.
Todos se cuedan   que ferido es de muort.
La lança recombró   e sobrél se paró;
dixo Gonçalvo Anssuórez: "¡Nol firgades, por Dios!
"vençudo es el campo,   quando esto se acabó!"

Gonzalo de Berceo

Spain, *ca.* 1195–1264

Berceo, a monk, was the first person of known name to write in Spanish. He was educated in the monastery of San Millán de la Cogolla, a famous cultural center of its epoch. His poetry, written in the Castilian dialect, reflects a zealous piety calculated to bolster the faith of his readers. The poet's work shows very little originality; of his twenty-five *Miracles of Our Lady (Milagros de Nuestra Señora)*, twenty-four are from well-known Latin texts.

  Berceo's poetic tone is popular and fluid and has the ring of a true preacher-poet of the people, polished but simple. The verse is Alexandrine, in a form known as the *cuaderna vía*, having fourteen syllables to the line, with each strophe (quatrain) maintaining the same rhyme. In Spanish this kind of poetry is called the *mester de clerecía*, meaning "clerical verse," as opposed to the *mester de juglaría*, or folk poetry of the minstrels.

San Miguel de la Tumba

from *Miracles of Our Lady*

San Miguel de la Tumba is a convent vast and wide;
The sea encircles it around, and groans on every side;
It is a wild and dangerous place, and many woes betide
The monks who in that burial-place in penitence abide.

Within those dark monastic walls, amid the ocean flood,
Of pious, fasting monks there dwelt a holy brotherhood;
To the Madonna's glory there an altar high was placed,
And a rich and costly image the sacred altar graced.

Sant Migael de la Tunba

from *Milagros de Nuestra Señora*

  Sant Migael de la Tunba es un grand monesterio,
el mar lo cerca todo, elli iaze en medio:
El logar perigloso, do sufren grand lazerio
los monges que hi viven en essi cimiterio.

  En esti monesterio que avemos nomnado,
avie de buenos monges buen convento provado,
altar de la Gloriosa rico e mui onrrado,
en él rica imagen de precio mui granado,

Exalted high upon a throne, the Virgin Mother smiled,
And, as the custom is, she held within her arms the Child:
The kings and wise men of the East were kneeling by her
   side:
Attended was she like a queen whom God had sanctified.
. . . .

Descending low before her face a screen of feathers
   hung,—
A moscader, or fan for flies, 't is called in vulgar tongue;
From the feathers of the peacock's wing 't was fashioned
   bright and fair,
And glistened like the heaven above when all its stars are
   there.

It chanced that, for the people's sins, fell the lightning's
   blasting stroke:
Forth from all four the sacred walls the flames consuming
   broke:
The sacred robes were all consumed, missal and holy
   book;
And hardly with their lives the monks their crumbling
   walls forsook.
. . . .

But though the desolating flame raged fearfully and wild,
It did not reach the Virgin Queen, it did not reach the
   Child;
It did not reach the feathery screen before her face that
   shone,
Nor injure in a farthing's worth the image or the throne.

The image it did not consume, it did not burn the screen;
Even in the value of a hair they were not hurt, I ween:
Not even the smoke did reach them, nor injure more the
   shrine
Than the bishop hight Don Tello has been hurt by hand of
   mine.

"Continuens et contentum,"—all was in ruins laid;
A heap of smouldering embers that holy pile was made:
But where the sacred image sat, a fathom's length around,
The raging flame dared not approach the consecrated
   ground.

It was a wondrous miracle to those that thither came,
That the image of the Virgin was safe from smoke and
   flame,—
That brighter than the brightest star appeared the feathery
   screen,—
And seated there the Child still fair, and fair the Virgin
   Queen.
. . . .

The Virgin Queen, the sanctified, who from an earthly
   flame
Preserved the robes that pious hands had hung around
   her frame,
Thus from an ever-burning fire her servants shall deliver,
And lead them to that high abode where the good are
   blessed for ever.

HENRY WADSWORTH LONGFELLOW

estava la imagen en su trono posada,
so fijo en sus brazos, cosa es costumnada
los reis redor ella, sedie bien compannada,
como rica reina de Dios santificada.
. . . .

Colgava delant ella un buen aventadero,
en el seglar lenguage dízenli moscadero:
De alas de pavones lo fizo el obrero,
luzie como estrellas semejant de luzero.

Cadió rayo del çielo por los graves peccados,
ençendió la eglesia de todos quatro cabos,
quemó todos los libros e los pannos sagrados,
por pocco que los monges que non foron quemados.
. . . .

Maguer que fue el fuego tan fuert e tan quemant,
nin plegó a la duenna, nin plegó al ifant,
nin plegó al flabello que colgava delant,
nin li fizo de danno un dinero pesant.

Nin ardió la imagen, nin ardió el flabello,
nin prisieron de danno quanto val un cabello,
solamiente el fumo non se llegó a ello,
nin nuçió mas que nuzo io al obispo don Tello.

Continens e contentum, fue todo astragado,
tornó todo carbones, fo todo asolado:
Mas redor de la imagen quanto es un estado,
non fizo mal el fuego, ca non era osado.

Esto tovieron todos por fiera maravella,
que nin fumo nin fuego non se llegó a ella,
que sedie el flabello más claro que estrella,
el ninno mui fermoso, formosa la ponzella.
. . . .

La Virgo benedicta reina general,
como libró su toca de esti fuego tal,
asín libra sus siervos del fuego perennal,
Liévalos a la gloria do nunqua vean mal.

The Book of Alexander

thirteenth century

The following selection is a description of spring from the long poem entitled *El libro de Alexander*, which in its entirety is a glorified and legendary life of Alexander the Great. It is filled with anachronistic details and contains a few descriptive passages of outstanding beauty. The poem, over ten thousand lines long, was written by an unidentified cleric of the thirteenth century. It has been attributed to Gonzalo de Berceo, to Lorenzo de Astorga, and to other poets, but its authorship remains uncertain.

Song of Spring

In the tender month of May in the bright and shining
    spring,
When the nightingale and thrush on the budding
    branches sing,
When the meadows and the hillocks don their robes of
    velvet green,
There comes a beauteous maiden both graceful and serene.
The magic of the maytide calls to lovers with the song
Of zephyrs rustling through the flowers, for to their
    hearts belong
The season's fairest treasure. And in the fields of heather
Like daisies woven in a wreath, young maidens sing
    together.
A gentle rain begins to fall, the crystal droplets nourish
The tender herb, that rich with grain, at harvest time shall
    flourish.
Beneath the arching bowers there is a wedding celebration
The ladies crowned with garlands gay all dance in
    jubilation.
This gladsome time, o'er young and old, doth cast a
    wondrous spell,
And lovers pass the hours away within the flowering dell.
In sweet repose their hearts are filled with love's strange
    mysteries,
And thoughts of love, like petals blown, are borne upon
    the breeze.
The sun pours forth his splendor, on his languorous
    journey goes
To touch the nestlings' dewy wings, to kiss the christened
    rose.
As though enchanted angry hornets stay their venomed
    sting,
While shouts of boys at frolicksome play, the fields are
    echoing.
And touched by fragrant orchard breath and maytide's
    fair display,
The noble Alexander proclaimed a holiday.
The fairest ladies and their lords, adorned in raiment
    bright,
Unto his palace made resort, to share their king's delight.

KATHARINE E. STRATHDEE

El mes era de mayo

El mes era de mayo, un tiempo glorïoso,
quando fazen las aves un solaz deleitoso,
son vestidos los prados de vestido fremoso,
da suspiros la duenna, la que non ha esposo.

Tiempo dolce e sabroso por bastir casamientos,
ca lo tempran las flores e los sabrosos vientos,
cantan las donzelletas, son muchas a convientos,
fazen unas a otras buenos pronunciamentos.

Caen en el verano las bonas rociadas,
entran en flor las miesses ca son ya espigadas,
fazen las duenyas triscas en camisas delgadas:
¡Entón casan algunos que pues messan las barvas!

Andan moças y viejas cobiertas en amores,
van coger por la sieta a los prados las flores,
dizen unas a otras:—''¡Bonos son los amores!''
Y aquellos plus tiernos tiénense por mejores.

Los días son grandes, los campos reverdidos,
son los passariellos del mal pelo exidos,
los távanos que muerden non son aún venidos,
luchan los monagones en bragas sen vestidos.

Juan Ruiz, archpriest of Hita

Spain, *ca.* 1283–1350

Juan Ruiz was the powerful, kaleidoscopic poet of the joy of life in Spanish medieval times. His *Book of Good Love (Libro de Buen Amor)* embodies the entire panorama of medieval experience. In it, the poet tells many separate tales (like Chaucer), but with a flavor that reveals the exotic mingling of the three cultures of Spain during his epoch: Christian, Moorish, Jewish

The archpriest's episodes are multicolored. They are ribald, festive, humorous, satiric, anticlerical, and they contain moral digressions, prayers, animal allegories—all linked together by a series of amorous adventures told as if they were autobiographical, as many of them may well have been. The critics are still divided concerning the moral tone of the book: Does it or does it not moralize? Are the apparent moralizations put in merely to heighten the festive and comic attitude, or perhaps simply to help the archpriest get by the church authorities, who admittedly were not overly prudish in those rollicksome days?

The Story of Peter Pious

> A very edifying tale wherein is related all that
> which befell Sir Peter Pious, a Painter of Brittany

"I'll tell you what befell a man who would not watch his
   dame:
'Twill pay you well to give close heed lest you be served
   the same:
A famous Breton painter once, Sir Peter Pious, came
To wed a young and lusty girl whose passion was aflame.

"Yet hardly was he wed a month before the artist quoth,
'I must away to Flanders, love, but upon my oath
I swear, I'll bring you back some gift.' His wife replied,
   'I'm loath
To see you leave my bed and board; pray, sir, remember
   both.'

"Thereat Sir Peter Pious said, 'But first, my lady fair,
Do let me paint upon your skin a picture quaint and rare,
A picture that will keep you chaste when you behold it
   there.'
Said she, 'Go work your will on me, forsooth you see me
   bare.'

"Below her belly-button, then, her drew with famous skill
The image of the Lamb of God, and sketched it with a
   will,
But when he left he stayed two years his business to
   fulfill—
Now how could any girl be true with all that time to kill!

"Her loneliness was hardly equalled, nor was the longing
   feigned.
But paradise though lost was sequelled by paradise
   regained
Because she found a sprightly lad who rubbed her where
   she pained,
Yet rubbed the Lamb of God so hard that not a trace
   remained.

Enxienplo de lo que contesçió a Don Pitas Payas

  Del qu' olvyda la muger te diré la fazaña:
sy vieres que es burla, dyme otra tan maña.
Era don Pitas Pajas, un pyntor de Bretaña;
casó con muger moça, pagávas' de conpaña.

  Antes del mes cunplido dixo él: "Nostra dona,
"yo volo yr a Frandes, portaré muyta dona."
Ella diz': "Monssner, andés en ora bona;
"non olvidés casa vostra nin la mía presona."

  Dixol' don Pitas Payas: "Doña de fermosura,
"yo volo fer en vos una bona fygura.
"porque seades guardada de toda altra locura."
Ella diz': "Monssener, fazet vuestra mesura."

  Pyntol' so el onbligo un pequeño cordero.
Fuerse don Pytas Pajas a ser novo mercadero.
Tardó allá dos anos, muncho fue tardinero,
Façías' le a la dona un mes año entero.

  Como era la moça nuevamente casada,
avíe coṇ su marido fecha poca morada;
tomó un entendedor e pobló la posada,
desifízos' el cordero, que dél non fynca nada.

  Quando ella oyó que venía el pyntor,
muy de prisa enbió por el entendedor;
díxole que le pyntase, como podiesse mejor,
en aquel logar mesmo un cordero menor.

  Pyntóle con la gran priessa un eguado carnero
conplido de cabeça, con todo su apero;
luego en ese día vino el menssajero:
que ya don Pytas Pajas desta venía çertero.

  Quando fue el pyntor ya de Frandes venido,
ffue de la su muger con desdén resçebido;
desque en el palaçio ya con ella estido,
la señal que l' feziera non le echó en olvido.

"Then came the news her painter man was coming home
at last,
So straight the damsel called the lad who'd been her sole
repast
And ordered him to paint on her another lamb full fast
Right on that very self-same spot the Lamb of God was
cast.

"He wrought upon her mightily but drew a ram with
horns,
Great prongs they were that sprouted out like sharp and
piercing thorns
(One other detail, too, he made which every ram adorns);
'Twas scarcely done ere Pious entered, limping on his
corns.

"Now when this poor long-truant husband stepped
inside the house
A torrent of abusive words descended from his spouse,
But through this matrimonial welcome Pious smelt a
mouse
Whereat he charged his faithful wife to doff her skirt and
blouse.

" 'You wretch,' she cried, as she undressed, 'Perhaps
you think I'm tainted!
Well, look! Here stand I naked, pure as any woman
sainted.'
Alack-a-day he raised his eyes to see the lamb he's painted
But when he saw that monstrous ram—Sir Peter Pious
fainted.

"As he came to, that fearful view once more bemazed his
eyes,
No lamb, thought he, could thus assume a grown up
ram's disguise.
'Look here,' he said, 'my faithful wife, come tell, but
without lies,
How came my little Lamb of God to grow to such a size?'

"Since women in such situations never lose their wits
She said, 'My lord, this might ram your two years' stay
befits
For during all that time your lamb was grown by little bits;
Had you not stayed so long you'd find him still beneath
my teats.'

"The moral lesson to this tale you'll find is clear as day—
Don't be a Peter Pious for some understudy gay;
Go entertain the girl you've got in love's peculiar way
But watch out lest another man comes hankering for play.

"Sir Peter Pious flushed the game, but after was unwilling
To hold the chase; perhaps he thought the exercise too
grilling.
Another sportsman caught the scent and rode without a
spilling
Until he clipped his quarry's tail and made a pleasant
killing.

"The lady doubtless reasoned thus. 'This man I wed at first,
Beside my second gallant is a very babe, ill-nursed;

Dixo don Pytas Pajas: "Madona, sy vos plaz'
"mostratme la figura e ¡aiam' buen solaz!"
Diz' la muger: "Monseñer, vos mesmo la catat:
"fey y ardidamente todo lo que vollaz."

Cató don Pytas Pajas el sobredicho lugar,
e vydo grand carnero con armas de prestar.
"Cómo, madona, es esto o como pode estar,
"que yo pynté corder, e trobo este manjar?"

Como en este fecho es syenpre la muger
sotil e malsabyda, diz': "¿Cómo, monsseñer,
"en dos anos petid corder non se fer carner?
"Veniésedes tenplano: trobaríades corder."

Por ende te castiga, non dexea lo que pides:
non seas Pytas Pamjas, para otro non errides.
Con dezires fermosos a la mujer conbydes:
desque telo prometa, guarda non lo olvides.

Pedro levanta la lyebre e la mueve del covil,
non la sygue nin la toma, faz' como caçador vyl;
otro Pedro que la sygue e la corre más sotil,
tómala; esto contesçe a caçadores mill.

Dyz' la muger entre dientes: "Otro Pedro es aqueste.
"Más garçón e más ardit, que 'l primero que ameste:
"el primero apost déste non vale más que un feste,
"con aqueste a por éste faré yo, ¡sy Dios me preste!"

Otrosí quando vyeres a quien usa con ella,
quier sea suyo o non, fáblale por amor della;
sy podieres, dal' algo, non le ayas querella:
ca estas cosas pueden a la mujer traella.

Por byen poquilla cosa del tu aver, que l' dyeres,
servirt' la lealmente, fará lo que quisieres,
fará por los dineros todo quanto pidieres:
que poco o que much, dal' cadaque podieres.

Since first is worst, then first be cursed, I'll take the better
  versed,
And while I durst, I'll slake his thirst and live in love
  immersed.'

"Now should you ever see a man conversing with a
  beauty,
No matter if the girl is his or not, make it your duty
To scrape acquaintance with him, don't adopt a manner
  snooty
But do him favors for her sake—'twill help you win your
  booty.

"A little money often helps to make a wondrous spree
For ne'er was woman born who would not jiggle for a fee.
If every man has got his price, each girl has two or three,
So be it much or be it little, give with gesture free."

ELISHA K. KANE

How Males Seek Females

Herein is related how man and the other animals desire
to have intercourse with their females according to
nature

Man labors, Aristotle says, upon a dual mission,
His first and most important care concerns his own
  nutrition,
His second, and the pleasantest, is afterward coition
With any dame that proffers him the opportune position.

If on my own authority about a point so mooted
I made this bold assertion I would surely be disputed.
But what a wise philosopher has said cannot be hooted,
Above all, when his arguments can never be confuted.

And that this venerable sage has spoken truth 'tis clear
For men and birds and animals—all critters far and near—
According to the laws of nature find their females dear;
Particularly man to whom the act brings extra cheer.

The beasts have all a stated time wherein they join to
  breed,
But man, superior to the brutes, can couple without need;
Wherefore he consecrates this act and writes it in his
  creed,
And then, to show his sanctity, he oft repeats the deed.

An incandescent coal indeed is passion's fierce desire;
The more you try to blow it out the hotter burns its fire.
What boots it if the soul should see her body in the mire
When nature makes of man a hog and urges him no
  higher?

So I, because I am a man, the same as any sinner,
Have got of woman all she had whenever I could win her.
To learn and sample is no shame for this sincere beginner
Since thus I choose the good from bad and make my
  errors slimmer.

ELISHA K. KANE

Aqui dize de cómo los omes quieren aver conpañia con las fenbras

Como dice Aristótiles, cosa es verdadera:
el mundo por dos cosas trabaja: la primera,
por aver manteneçia; la otra cosa era
por aver juntamiento con fenbra plazentera.

Sy lo dexies' de mío, sería de culpar;
dízelo grand filósofo: non so yo de raptar;
de lo que dize el sabio non devedes dudar,
ca por obra se prueba el sabio e su fablar.

Que diz' verdat el sabio claramente se prueba:
omes, aves, animalias, toda bestia de cueva
quiere, segunt natura, conpaña sienpre nueva;
e muncho más el ome, que toda cosa que s' mueva.

Digo muy más el ome, que de toda criatura:
todas a tienpo çierto se juntan con natura;
el ome de mal sesso todo tienpo syn mesura,
cadaque puede e quier' facer esta locura.

El ffuego ssienpre quiere estar en las çeniza,
comoquier que más arde, quanto más se atiza:
el ome, quando peca, bien vee que desliza;
mas non se parte ende, ca natura lo enriza.

E yo, porque so ome, como otro, pecador,
ove de las mugeres a vezes grand amor:
provar ome las cosas non es por ende peor,
e saber bien el mal, e usar lo mejor.

Praise of Little Women

I wish to make my sermon brief,—to shorten my
  oration,—
For a never-ending sermon is my utter destestation:
I like short women,—suits at law without
  procrastination,—
And am always most delighted with things of short
  duration.

A babbler is a laughing-stock; he's a fool who's always
  grinning;
But little women love so much, one falls in love with
  sinning.
There are women who are very tall, and yet not worth the
  winning,
And in the change of short for long repentance finds
  beginning.

To praise the little women Love besought me in my
  musing;
To tell their noble qualities is quite beyond refusing:
So I'll praise the little women, and you'll find the thing
  amusing;
They are, I know, as cold as snow, whilst flames around
  diffusing.

They're cold without, whilst warm within the flame of
  Love is raging;
They're gay and pleasant in the street,—soft, cheerful,
  and engaging;
They're thrifty and discreet at home,—the cares of life
  assuaging;
All this and more;—try, and you'll find how true is my
  presaging.

In a little precious stone what splendor meets the eyes!
In a little lump of sugar how much of sweetness lies!
So in a little woman love grows and multiplies:
You recollect the proverb says,—*A Word unto the wise.*

A pepper-corn is very small, but seasons every dinner
More than all other condiments, although 'tis sprinkled
  thinner:
Just so a little woman is, if Love will let you win her,—
There's not a joy in all the world you will not find in her.

And as within the little rose you find the richest dyes,
And in a little grain of gold much price the value lies,
As from a little balsam much odor doth arise,
So in a little woman there's a taste of paradise.

Even as the little ruby its secret worth betrays,
Color, and price, and virtue, in the clearness of its rays,—
Just so a little woman much excellence displays,
Beauty, and grace, and love, and fidelity always.

The skylark and the nightingale, though small and light of
  wing,
Yet warble sweeter in the grove than all the birds that
  sing:
And so a little woman, though a very little thing,

De las propiedades que las dueñas chicas han

Quiero abreviarvos, señores, la mi predicación,
ca siempre me pagé de pequeño sermón
de de dueña pequeña e de breve rrasón:
ca lo poco e bien dicho finca en el coraçón.

Del que mucho fabla rríen, quien mucho rríe es loco,
tyene la dueña chica amor grand e non de poco:
dueñas dy grandes por chicas, por grandes chicas non
  troco;
mas las chicas por las grandes non se rrepiente del troco.

De las chicas, que bien diga, el amor me fiso rruego,
que diga de sus noblesas e quiérolas dezir luego:
direvos de dueñas chicas, que lo tenedes en juego.
Son frías como la nieve e arden más que 'l fuego:

son frías de füera; en el amor ardientes,
en cama solaz, trebejo, plasenteras e rrientes.
En casa cuerdas, donosas, sosegadas, bienfasyentes;
muncho ál fallaredes, ado byen paredes mientes.

En pequeña girgonça yase grand rresplandor,
en açúcar muy poco yase mucho dulçor:
en la dueña pequeña yase muy grand amor:
pocas palabras cunple al buen entendedor.

Es pequeño el grano de la buena pimienta;
pero más que la nués conorta e más calyenta:
así dueña pequeña, sy todo amor consienta,
non ha plaser del mundo qu' en ella non se sienta.

Como en chica rrosa está mucha color,
e en oro muy poco gran preçio e grand valor,
como en poco balsamo yase grand buen olor:
ansy en chica dueña yase muy grand amor.

Como rroby pequeño tyene muncha bondad,
color, vertud y precio, noblesa e claridad:
asy dueña pequeña tiene muncha beldad,
fermosura e donayre, amor e lealtad.

Chica es la calandria e chicho el rroyseñor;
pero más dulçe canta, que otra ave mayor:
la muger, por ser chica, por eso non es pior;
con doñeo es más dulce, que açucar nin flor.

Son aves pequeñuelas papagayo e orior;
pero cualquiera dellas es dulçe gritador,
adonada, fermosa, preçiada, cantador:
bien atal es la dueña pequeña con amor.

En la muger pequena non ha conparación:
terrenal parayso es e consolançión,
solás e alegría, plaser e bendiçión,
¡mijor es en la prueva qu' en la salutaçión!

Ssyempre quis' muger chica, mas que grand' nin
  mayor:
¡non es desaguisado de grand mal ser foydor!
Del mal, tomar lo menos: díselo el sabidor:
¡por end' de las mugeres la menor es mijor!

Is sweeter far than sugar, and flowers that bloom in
   spring.

The magpie and the golden thrush have many a thrilling
   note,
Each as a gay musician doth strain his little throat,—
A merry little songster in his green and yellow coat:
And such a little woman is, when Love doth make her
   dote.

There's naught can be compared to her, throughout the
   wide creation;
She is a paradise on earth,—our greatest consolation,—
So cheerful, gay, and happy, so free from all vexation;
In fine, she's better in the proof than in anticipation.

If as her size increases are woman's charms decreased,
Then surely it is good to be from all the great released.
Now of two evils choose the less, —said a wise man of the
   East:
By consequence, of woman-kind be sure to choose the
   least.

                 HENRY WADSWORTH LONGFELLOW

FIFTEENTH CENTURY

Alonso (or Alfonso) de Cartagena

Spain, 1384–1456

Alonso de Cartagena was one of the most cultured men of his time; he was a good Latinist and translator of Seneca, and his *Difensorium Fidei* was a widely circulated defense of the converted Jews. Cartagena, who succeeded his father as the bishop of Burgos, was the author of several beautiful love lyrics in which "we meet with a storm of passion." The literary historian J. C. L. Simonde de Sismondi, with Cartagena in mind, commented: "Perhaps no poets have equalled the Spanish in describing the power of love, when the heart is abandoned to its impetuosity."[13] Thomas Roscoe, who translated the following poem, translated Sismondi's *Literature of the South of Europe* and many poems from the Italian and the Spanish into English.

The Power of Love

Oh! fierce is this flame that seizes my breath,
My body, my soul, my life, and my death;
It burns in its fury, it kindles desire,
It consumes, but alas! it will never expire.

How wretched my lot! No respite I know,
My heart is indifferent to joy or to woe;
For this flame in its anger kills, burns, and destroys,
My grief and my pleasures, my sorrows and joys.

In the midst of such perils, all methods I try,
To escape from my fate—I weep, laugh, and sigh;
I would hope, I would wish for some respite from grief,
But have not a wish, to wish for relief.

If I vanquish this foe, or if vanquished I be,
Is alike in the midst of my torments to me;
I would please, and displease, but between me and you,
I know not, alas! what I say or I do.

THOMAS ROSCOE

El amor

La fuerza del fuego que alumbra que ciega
mi cuerpo, mi alma, mi muerte, mi vida,
do entra, do hiere, do toca, do llega,
mata y no muere su llama encendida.
Pues ¿qué haré triste, que todo me ofende?
Lo bueno y lo malo me causan congoja,
quemándome el fuego que mata, que enciende,
su fuerza que fuerza, que ata, que prende,
que prende, que suelta, que tira, que afloja.

A do iré triste, que alegre me halle,
pues tantos peligros me tienen en medio,
que llore, que ría, que grite, que calle,
ni tengo, ni quiero, ni espero remedio.
No quiero que quiere, ni quiero querer,
pues tanto me quiere tan rabiosa plaga,
ni ser yo vencido, ni quiero vencer,
ni quiero pesar, ni quiero placer,
ni sé que me diga, ni sé que me haga.

Pain in Pleasure

O, labor not, impatient will,
With anxious thought and busy care!
Whatever be thy doom,—whate'er
Thy power, or thy perverseness,—still
A germ of sorrow will be there.

If thou wilt think of moments gone,
Of joys as exquisite as brief,
Know, memory, when she lingers on
Past pleasure, turns it all to grief.
The struggling toil for bliss is vain,
The dreams of hope are vainer yet,

Canción

Voluntad, no trabajéys
por alcançar buena vida,
que la mejor escogida
que fue, ni será, ni es,
cuydado es para después.

Que acordaros del passado
dulce tiempo que gastastes,
ya sabes que este cuydado
os mata más que gozastes;
por ende no trabajés
por alcançar buena vida,

13. J. C. L. Simonde de Sismondi, *Literature of the South of Europe,* trans. Thomas Roscoe (2 vols.; New York: Harper and Brothers, 1871), II, 136.

The end of glory is regret,
And death is but the goal of pain,
And memory's eye with tears is wet.

SIR JOHN BOWRING

porque es cosa conoscida
que su gloria muerta es
con la memoria después.

SIR JOHN BOWRING

No, That Can Never Be!

Yes! I must leave,—O, yes!
But not the thoughts of thee;
For that can never be!

To absence, loneliness,
'Tis vain,—'tis vain to flee;
I see thee not the less,
When memory's shades I see;
And how can I repress
The rising thoughts of thee?
No, that can never be!

Yet must I leave;—the grave
Shall be a home for me,
Where fettered grief shall have
A portion with the free.
I other than a slave
To thy strange witchery
Can never, never be!

Partir quiero yo

Partir quiero yo
mas no del querer,
que no puede ser.

El triste que quiere
partir y se va,
adonde estuviere
sin sí vivirá:
mas no que pondrá
en otra el querer,
que no puede ser.

De aqueste partir
mi gloria procede:
partiendo morir
la vida bien puede,
mas no que no quede
con vos el querer,
que no puede ser.

SIR JOHN BOWRING

John II, king of Castile
Spain, reigned 1407–1454

John II made his court the center of belles-lettres in Spain and assembled the best poets of his time around his throne. He was not a dynamic monarch, but he fostered the arts, especially poetry. Juan de Mena was his chronicler, and the anthology of poetry assembled and edited by one of his courtiers, Baena, was the most representative collection of fifteenth-century poetic expression in Spain. His courtiers often vied with each other in poetic composition, and John himself frequently tried his hand at creative writing, occasionally with success. His reign has often been referred to as the "portico of the Spanish Renaissance." The poems produced during his time were largely courtly lyrics of a conventional nature.

I Never Knew It, Love, Till Now

I ne'er imaged, Love, that thou
Wert such a mighty one; at will,
Thou canst both faith and conscience bow,
And thy despotic law fulfill:
I never knew it, Love, till now.

I thought I knew thee,—I thought
That I thy mazes had explored;
But I within thy nets am caught,
And now I own thee sovereign lord.
I ne'er imagined, Love, that thou

Amor nunca pensé

Amor nunca pensé
que tan poderoso eras,
que podrías tener maneras
para trastornar le fe.
hasta agora que lo sé.

Pensaba que conocido
te debiera yo tener,
mas no pudiera creer
que fueras tan mal sabido,
ni jamás no lo pensé

Wert such a mighty one; at will,
Thou bidd'st both faith and conscience bow,
And thy despotic law fulfill:
I never knew it, Love, till now.

aunque poderoso eras,
que podrías tener maneras
para trastornar la fe,
hasta agora que lo sé.

SIR JOHN BOWRING

Íñigo López de Mendoza, marqués de Santillana

Spain, 1398–1458

The aristocrat Santillana was one of the leading courtiers and poets during the reign of John II of Castile. His *serranillas,* which tell of the encounters of knights with rustic mountain girls, have a delightful charm that suggests the folk poetry of Spain, perhaps with a little extra flourish and polish. During the final two decades of his life, Santillana also composed forty-two sonnets, which were the first written in a language other than Italian. The Petrarchian influence in them is notable. and the constant theme is that of love unrequited.

Mountain Song

Once making a journey
To Santa María
From Calataveño,
From weary desire
Of sleep, down a valley
I strayed, where young Rosa
I saw, the milk maiden
Of lone Finojosa.

In a pleasant green meadow,
Midst roses and grasses,
Her herd she was tending,
With other fair lasses;
So lovely her aspect,
I could not suppose her
A simple milk-maiden
Of rude Finojosa.

I think not primroses
Have half her smile's sweetness.
Or mild modest beauty;
(I speak with discreetness)
O had I before hand
But know of this Rosa, .
The handsome milk-maiden
Of far Finojosa.

Her very great beauty
Had not so subdued,
Because it had left me
To do as I would.
I have said more, oh fair one!
By learning 'twas Rosa,
The charming milk-maiden
Of sweet Finojosa.

Serranilla de la Finojosa

   Moça tan fermosa
non vi en la frontera,
como una vaquera
de la Finojosa.

   Faziendo la vía
del Calatreveño
a Sancta María,
vencido del sueño,
por tierra fragosa
perdí la carrera,
do vi la vaquera
de la Finojosa.

   En un verde prado
de rosas e flores,
guardando ganado
con otros pastores,
la vi tan graciosa
que apenas creyera
que fuesse vaquera
de la Finojosa.

   Non creo las rosas
de la primavera
sean tan fermosas
nin de tal manera
(fablando sin glosa),
si antes sopiera
de aquella vaquera
de la Finojosa.

   Non tanto mirara
su mucha beldad
porque me dexara
en mi libertad.

THOMAS ROSCOE

Mas dixe: "Donosa"
(por saber quién era),
"¿dónde es la vaquera
de la Finojosa?"

Bien como rindo,
dixo: "Bien vengades;
que ya bien entiendo
lo que demandades:
non es deseosa
de amar, nin lo espera
aquessa vaquera
de la Finojosa."

Jorge Manrique
Spain, 1440–1479

One poem made Jorge Manrique great: "Ode on the Death of His Father," which has been beautifully translated by Longfellow. Manrique was also the composer of fifty love poems, but these
are shallow and filled with clichés. His famous ode, on the other hand, expresses in solemn and
sententious majesty a man's grief when confronted by the death of someone he loves. The perfect balance maintained between the universal and the particular is the poet's noteworthy
achievement in these lines. The Latin phrase, *Ubi sunt?* (Where are they now?), which calls to
mind the equally famous, "Where are the snows of yesteryear?" of François Villon of France, is
the repeated theme of the poem, but in the end Christian faith is rewarded, death has only liberated the soul of the departed father, which has now passed on to a higher state. Jorge Manrique
himself was killed at the age of thirty-nine in the assault on the castle of the marqués de Villena,
who had risen in rebellion against the Catholic Sovereigns.

Ode on the Death of His Father

O, let the soul her slumbers break!
Let thought be quickened and awake,—
   Awake to see
How soon this life is past and gone,
And death comes softly stealing on,—
   How silently!

Swiftly our pleasures glide away:
Our hearts recall the distant day
   With many sighs;
The moments that are speeding fast
We heed not; but the past—the past—
   More highly prize.

Onward its course the present keeps,
Onward the constant current sweeps,
   Till life is done;
And did we judge of time aright,
The past and future of their flight
   Would be as one.

Let no one fondly dream again
That Hope and all her shadowy train
   Will not decay

Coplas por la muerte de su padre

Recuerde el alma dormida,
abive el seso y despierte,
contemplando
cómo se passa la vida,
cómo se viene la muerte
tan callando;
   cuán presto se va el plazer,
cómo después de acordado,
da dolor,
cómo, a nuestro parescer,
cualquiera tiempo passado
fue mejor.

Pues si vemos lo presente
cómo en un punto se es ido
y acabado,
si juzgamos sabiamente,
daremos lo no venido
por passado.
   No se engañe nadie, no,
pensando que ha de durar
lo que espera
más que duró lo que vio,

Fleeting as were the dreams of old,
Remembered like a tale that's told,
　　They pass away.

Our lives are rivers gliding free
To that unfathomed, boundless sea,
　　The silent grave:
Thither all earthly pomp and boast
Roll to be swallowed up and lost
　　In one dark wave.

Thither the mighty torrents stray,
Thither the brook pursues its way,
　　And tinkling rill.
There all are equal. Side by side,
The poor man and the son of pride
　　Lie calm and still.

I will not here invoke the throng
Of orators and sons of song,
　　The deathless few;
Fiction entices and deceives,
And sprinkling o'er her fragrant leaves
　　Lies poisonous dew.

To One alone my thoughts arise,—
The Eternal Truth,—the Good and Wise:
　　To Him I cry,
Who shared on earth our common lot,
But the world comprehended not
　　His deity.

This world is but the rugged road
Which leads us to the bright abode
　　Of peace above;
So let us choose the narrow way
Which leads no traveller's foot astray
　　From realms of love.

Our cradle is the starting place;
In life we run the onward race,
　　And reach the goal;
When, in the mansions of the blest,
Death leaves to its eternal rest
　　The weary soul.

Did we but use it as we ought,
This world would school each wandering thought
　　To its high state.
Faith wings the soul beyond the sky,
Up to the better world on high
　　For which we wait.

Yes,—the glad messenger of love,
To guide us to our home above,
　　The Saviour;
Born amid moral cares and fears,
He suffered in this vale of tears
　　A death of shame.

Behold of what delusive worth
The bubbles we pursue on earth,
　　The shapes we chase,

pues que todo ha de pasar
por tal manera.

　　Nuestras vidas son los ríos
que van a dar en la mar,
que es el morir:
allí van los señoríos
derechos a se acabar
y consumir;
　　allí los ríos caudales,
allí los otros medianos
ya más chicos,
allegados son iguales,
los que biven por sus manos
y los ricos.

　　Dexo las invocaciones
de los famosos poetas
y oradores;
no curo de sus ficciones,
que traen yervas secretas
sus sabores.
　　Aquel solo me encomiendo,
aquel solo invoco yo
de verdad,
que en este mundo biviendo,
el mundo no conosció
su diedad.

　　Este mundo es el camino
para el otro, que es morada
sin pesar;
mas cumple tener buen tino
para andar esta jornada
sin errar.
　　Partimos cuando nascemos,
andamos mientra bivimos,
y llegamos
al tiempo que fenescemos;
assí que cuando morimos
descansamos.

　　Este mundo bueno fue
si bien usássemos dél
como devemos,
porque, según nuestra fe,
es para ganar aquel
que atendemos.
　　Y aun aquel fijo de Dios,
para sobirnos al cielo,
descendió
a nascer acá entre nos,
y a bivir en este suelo
do murió.

　　Ved de cuán poco valor
son las cosas tras que andamos
y corremos,
que, en este mundo traidor,
aun primero que muramos
las perdemos:

Amid a world of treachery!
They vanish ere death shuts the eye,
    And leave no trace.

Time steals them from us,—chances strange,
Disastrous accidents, and change,
    That come to all:
Even in the most exalted state,
Relentless sweeps the stroke of fate;
    The strongest fall.

Tell me,—the charms that lovers seek
In the clear eye and blushing cheek,—
    The hues that play
O'er rosy lip and brow of snow,—
When hoary age approaches slow,
    Ah, where are they?

The noble blood of Gothic name.
Heroes emblazoned high to fame
    In long array,—
How, in the onward course of time,
The landmarks of that race sublime
    Were swept away!

Some, the degraded slaves of lust,
Prostrate and trampled in the dust,
    Shall rise no more;
Others by guilt and crime maintain
the scutcheon that without a stain
    Their fathers bore.

Wealth and the high estate of pride,
With what untimely speed they glide,
    How soon depart!
Bid not the shadowy phantoms stay,—
The vassals of a mistress they,
    Of fickle heart.

These gifts in Fortune's hands are found;
Her swift-revolving wheel turns round,
    And they are gone!
No rest the inconstant goddess knows,
But changing, and without respose,
    Still hurries on.

Even could the hand of avarice save
Its gilded baubles, till the grave
    Reclaimed its prey,
Let none on such poor hopes rely;
Life, like an empty dream flits by,
    And where are they?

Earthly desires and sensual lust
Are passions springing from the dust,—
    They fade and die;
But, in the life beyond the tomb,
They seal the immortal spirit's doom
    Eternally!

The pleasure and delights which mask
In treacherous smiles life's serious task,
    What are they all,

dellas desfaze la edad,
dellas casos desastrados
que acaescen,
dellas, por su calidad,
en los más altos estados
desfallescen.

    Dezidme, la fermosura,
la gentil frescura y tez
de la cara,
la color y la blancura,
cuando viene la vejez
¿cuál se para?
    Las mañas y ligereza
y la fuerça corporal
de joventud,
todo se torna graveza
cuando llega el arraval
de senectud.

    Pues la sangre de los godos,
y el linage y la nobleza
tan crescida,
¡por cuántas vías y modos
se sume su grand alteza
en esta vida!
    Unos, por poco valer,
¡por cuán baxos y abatidos
que los tienen!
Y otros, por no tener,
con oficios no devidos
se mantienen.

    Los estados y riqueza,
que nos dexan a desora,
¿quién lo duda?
No les pidamos firmeza
pues que son de una señora
que se muda;
    que bienes son de Fortuna
que rebuelve con su rueda
presurosa,
la cual no puede ser una
ni estar estable ni queda
en una cosa.

    Pero digo que acompañen
y lleguen hasta la huessa
con su dueño:
por esso no nos engañen,
pues se va la vida apriessa
como sueño.
    Y los deleites de acá
son, en que nos deleitamos,
temporales,
y los tormentos de allá,
que por ellos esperamos,
eternales.

    Los plazeres y dulçores
desta vida trabajada

But the fleet coursers of the chase,—
And death an ambush in the race,
    Wherein we fall?

No foe, no dangerous pass we heed,
Brook no delay,—but onward speed,
    With loosened rein;
And when the fatal snare is near,
We strive to check our mad career,
    But strive in vain.

Could we new charms to age impart.
And fashion with a cunning art
    The human face,
As we can clothe the soul with light,
And make the glorious spirit bright
    With heavenly grace,—

How busily, each passing hour,
Should we exert that magic power!
    What ardor show
To deck the sensual slave of sin,
Yet leave the freeborn soul within
    In weeds of woe!

Monarchs, the powerful and the strong,
Famous in history and in song
    Of olden time,
Saw, by the stern decrees of fate,
Their kingdom lost, and desolate
    Their race sublime.

Who is the champion? Who the strong?
Pontiff and priest, and sceptered throng?
    On these shall fall
As heavily the hand of Death,
As when it stays the shepherd's breath
    Beside his stall.

I speak not of the Trojan name,—
Neither its glory nor its shame
    Has met our eyes;
Nor of Rome's great and glorious dead,—
Though we have heard so oft, and read,
    Their histories.

Little avails it now to know
Of ages past so long ago,
    Nor how they rolled;
Our theme shall be of yesterday
Which to oblivion sweeps away,
    Like days of old.

Where is the king Don Juan? Where
Each royal prince and noble heir
    Of Aragón?
Where are the courtly gallantries?
The deeds of love and high emprise,
    In battle done?

Tourney and joust, that charmed the eye,
And scarf, and gorgeous panoply,
    And nodding plume,—

que tenemos,
¿qué son sino corredores,
y la muerte la celada
en que caemos?
    No mirando nuestro daño,
corremos a rienda suelta
sin parar;
desque vemos el engaño
y queremos dar la buelta,
no hay lugar.

    Si fuesse en nuestro poder
tornar la cara fermosa
corporal,
como podemos fazer
el ánima glorïosa,
angelical,
    ¡qué diligencia tan biva
toviéramos toda hora,
y tan presta,
en componer la cativa,
dexándonos la señora
descompuesta!

    Essos reyes poderosos
que vemos por escrituras
ya passadas,
con casos tristes, llorosos,
fueron sus buenas venturas
trastornadas:
    assí que no hay cosa fuerte,
que a papas y emperadores
y prelados,
assí los trata la Muerte
como a los pobres pastores
de ganados.

    Dexemos a los troyanos,
que sus males no los vimos,
ni sus glorias;
dexemos a los romanos,
aunque oímos y leímos
sus estorias,
    no curemos de saber
lo de aquel siglo passado
qué fue dello;
vengamos a lo de ayer,
que tan bien es olvidado
como aquello.

    ¿Qué se fizo el rey don Juan?
Los infantes de Aragón,
¿qué se fizieron?
¿Qué fue de tanto galán?
¿Qué fue de tanta invención
como truxieron?
    Las justas y los torneos,
paramentos, bordaduras,
y cimeras,

What were they but a pageant scene?
What but the garlands, gay and green
    That deck the tomb?
Where are the high-born dames, and where
Their gay attire and jewelled hair,
    And odors sweet?
Where are the gentle knights, that came
To kneel, and breathe love's ardent flame,
    Low at their feet?

Where is the song of Troubadour?
Where are the lute and gay tambour
    They loved of yore?
Where is the mazy dance of old,—
The flowing robes, inwrought with gold,
    The dancers wore?

And he who next the sceptre swayed,
Henry, whose royal court displayed
    Such power and pride,—
O, in what winning smiles arrayed,
The world its various pleasures laid
    His throne beside!

But, O, how false and full of guile
That world, which wore so soft a smile
    But to betray!
She, that had been his friend before,
Now from the fated monarch tore
    Her charms away.

The countless gifts,—the stately walls,
The royal palaces, and halls,
    All filled with gold;
Plate with armorial bearings wrought,
Chambers with ample treasures fraught
    Of wealth untold;

The noble steeds, and harness bright,
The gallant lord, and stalwart knight,
    In rich array;—
Where shall we seek them now? Alas!
Like the bright dew-drops on the grass,
    They passed away.

His brother, too, whose factious zeal
Usurped the sceptre of Castile,
    Unskilled to reign,—
What a gay, brilliant court had he,
When all the flower of chivalry
    Was in his train!

But he was mortal, and the breath
That flamed from the hot forge of Death
    Blasted his years;
Judgment of God! that flame by thee,
When raging fierce and fearfully,
    Was quenched in tears!

Spain's haughty Constable,—the true
And gallant Master,—whom we knew
    Most loved of all,—

¿fueron sino devaneos?
¿qué fueron sino verduras
de las eras?

    ¿Qué se fizieron las damas.
sus tocados, sus vestidos,
sus olores?
¿Qué se fizieron las llamas
de los fuegos encendidos
de amadores?
    ¿Qué se fizo aquel trobar,
las músicas acordadas
que tañían?
¿Qué se fizo aquel dançar,
aquellas ropas chapadas
que traían?

    Pues el otro su heredero,
don Enrique, ¡qué poderes
alcançava!
¡Cuán blando, cuán falaguero
el mundo con sus plazeres
se le dava!
    Mas veréis cuán enemigo,
cuán contrario, cuán cruel
se le mostró,
aviéndole sido amigo,
cuán poco duró con él
lo que le dio.

    Las dádivas desmedidas,
los edificios reales
llenos de oro,
las vaxillas tan febridas,
los enriques y reales
del tesoro,
    los jaezes, los cavallos
de su gente, y atavíos
tan sobrados,
¿dónde iremos a buscallos?
¿qué fueron sino rocíos
de los prados?

    Pues su hermano el inocente
que en su vida sucessor
se llamó,
¡qué corte tan excelente
tuvo, y cuánto grand señor
le siguió!
    Mas, como fuesse mortal,
metióle la Muerte luego
en su fragua.
¡O, juizio divinal!:
cuando más ardía el fuego,
echaste agua.

    Pues aquel grand condestable,
maestre que conoscimos
tan privado,
no cumple que dél se fable,

Breathe not a whisper of his pride;
He on the gloomy scaffold died,—
    Ignoble fall!

The countless treasures of his care,
His hamlets green and cities fair,
    His mighty power,—
What were they all but grief and shame,
Tears and a broken heart, when came
    The parting hour?

His other brothers, proud and high,—
Masters, who, in prosperity,
    Might rival kings,—
Who made the bravest and the best
The bondsmen of their high behest,
    Their underlings,—

What was their prosperous estate,
When high and exalted and elate
    With power and pride?
What, but a transient gleam of light,—
A flame, which, glaring at its height,
    Grew dim and died?

So many a duke of royal name,
Marquis and count of spotless fame,
    And baron brave,
That might the sword of empire wield,—
All these, O Death, hast thou concealed
    In the dark grave!

Their deeds of mercy and of arms,
In peaceful days, or war's alarms,
    When thou dost show,
O Death, thy stern and angry face,
One stroke of thy all-powerful mace
    Can overthrow!

Unnumbered hosts, that threaten nigh,—
Pennon and standard flaunting high,
    And flat displayed,—
High battlements intrenched around,
Bastion, and moated wall, and mound,
    And palisade,

And covered trench, secure and deep,—
All these cannot one victim keep,
    O Death, from thee,
When thou dost battle in thy wrath,
And thy strong shafts pursue their path
    Unerringly!

O world! so few the years we live,
Would that the life which thou dost give
    Were life indeed!
Alas! thy sorrow fall so fast,
Our happiest hour is when, at last,
    The soul is freed.

Our days are covered o'er with grief,
And sorrows neither few nor brief
    Veil all in gloom;

sino sólo que lo vimos
degollado.
    Sus infinitos tesoros,
sus villas y sus lugares,
su mandar,
¿qué le fueron sino lloros?
¿qué fueron sino pesares
al dexar?

    Pues los otros dos hermanos,
maestres tan prosperados
como reyes,
que a los grandes y medianos
truxieron tan sojuzgados
a sus leyes;
    aquella prosperidad
que tan alta fue sobida
y ensalçada,
¿qué fue sino claridad
que estando más encendida
fue amatada?

    Tantos duques excelentes,
tantos marqueses y condes
y varones
como vimos tan potentes,
di, Muerte, ¿dó los escondes
y traspones?
    Y las sus claras hazañas
que fizieron en las guerras
y en las pazes,
cuando tú, cruda, te ensañas,
con tu fuerça las atierras
y desfazes.

    Las huestes innumerables,
los pendones y estandartes
y vanderas,
los castillos impunables,
los muros y baluartes
y barreras,
    la cava honda, chapada,
o cualquier otro reparo,
¿qué aprovecha?
que si tú vienes airada,
todo lo passas de claro
con tu flecha.

    ¡Oh, mundo! Pues que nos matas,
fuera la vida que diste
toda vida;
mas según acá nos tratas,
lo mejor y menos triste
es la partida
    de tu vida, tan cubierta
de tristezas y dolores,
despoblada;
de los bienes tan desierta,
de placeres y dulzores
despojada.

Left desolate of real good,
Within this cheerless solitude
    No pleasures bloom.

Thy pilgrimage begins in tears,
And ends in bitter doubts and fears,
    Or dark despair;
Midway so many toils appear,
That he who lingers longest here
    Knows most of care.

Thy goods are bought with many a groan,
by the hot sweat of toil alone,
    And weary hearts;
Fleet-footed is the approach of woe,
But with a lingering step and slow
    Its form departs.

And he, the good man's shield and shade,
To whom all hearts their homage paid,
    As Virtue's son,—
Rodrick Manrique,—he whose name
Is written on the scroll of Fame,
    Spain's champion;

His signal deeds and prowess high
Demand no pompous eulogy,—
    Ye saw his deeds!
Why should their praise in verse be sung?
The name that dwells on every tongue
    No minstrel needs.

To friends a friend;—how kind to all
The vassals of this ancient hall
    And feudal fief!
To foes how stern a foe was he!
And to the valiant and the free
    How brave a chief!

What prudence with the old and wise!
What grace in youthful gayeties!
    In all how sage!
Benignant to the serf and slave,
He showed the base and falsely brave
    A lion's rage.

His was the Octavian's prosperous star,
The rush of Caesar's conquering car
    At battle's call;
His, Scipio's virtue; his, the skill
And the indomitable will
    Of Hannibal.

His was a Trojan's goodness; his
A Titus' noble charities
    And righteous laws;
The arm of Hector, and the might
Of Tully, to maintain the right
    In truth's just cause;
The clemency of Antonine;
Aurelius' countenance divine
    Firm, gentle, still;

Es tu comienzo lloroso,
tu salida siempre amarga
y nunca buena,
lo de enmedio trabajoso,
y a quien das vida más larga
das más pena.
    Así los bienes—muriendo
y con sudor—se procuran
y los das;
los males vienen corriendo;
después de venidos, duran
mucho más.

    Aquel de buenos abrigo,
amado por virtuoso
de la gente,
el maestre don Rodrigo
Manrique, tanto famoso
y tan valiente;
    sus grandes fechos y claros
no cumple que los alabe,
pues los vieron,
ni los quiero fazer caros,
pues el mundo todo sabe
cuáles fueron.

    ¡Qué amigo de sus amigos!
¡Qué señor para criados
y parientas!
¡Qué enemigo de enemigos!
¡Qué maestro de esforçados
y valientes!
    ¡Qué seso para discretos!
¡Qué gracia para donosos!
¡Qué razón!
¡Qué benigno a los subjetos!
y a los bravos y dañosos,
un león!

    En ventura Octavïano,
Julio César en vencer
y batallar;
en la virtud, Africano,
Aníbal en el saber
y trabajar;
    en la bondad, un Trajano,
Tito en liberalidad
con alegría;
en su braço, Aurelïano,
Marco Atilio en la verdad
que prometía.

    Antonio Pío en clemençia,
Marco Aurelio en igualdad
del semblante;
Adrïano en elocuencia,
Teodosio en umildad
y buen talante.

The eloquence of Adrian;
And Theodosius' love to man,
    And generous will;

In tented field and bloody fray,
An Alexander's virgorous sway
    And stern command;
The faith of Constantine; ay, more,—
The fervent love Camillus bore
    His native land.

He left no well filled treasury,
He heaped no pile of riches high,
    Nor massive plate;
He fought the Moors,—and, in their fall,
City and tower and castled wall
    Were his estate.

Upon the hard-fought battle-ground
Brave steeds and gallant riders found
    A common grave;
And there the warrior's hand did gain
The rents, and the long vassal train,
    That conquest gave.

And if, of old, his halls displayed
The honored and exalted grade
    His worth had gained,
So, in the dark, disastrous hour,
Brothers and bondsmen of his power
    His hand sustained.

After high deeds, not left untold,
In the stern warfare which of old
    'Twas his to share,
Such noble leagues he made, that more
And fairer regions than before
    His guerdon were.

These are the records, half-effaced,
Which with the hand of youth, he traced
    On history's page;
But with fresh victories he drew
Each fading character anew
    In his old age.

By his unrivalled skill, by great
And veteran service to the state,
    By worth adored,
He stood, in his high dignity,
The proudest knight of chivalry,—
    Knight of the Sword.

He found his cities and domains
Beneath a tyrant's galling chains
    And cruel power;
But, by fierce battle and blockade,
Soon his own banner was displayed
    From every tower.

By the tried valor of his hand
His monarch and his native land
    Were nobly served;—

Aurelio Alexandre fue,
en diciplina y rigor
    de la guerra;
un Constantino en la fe,
Camilo en el grand amor
    de su tierra.

No dexó grandes tesoros,
ni alcançó muchas riquezas
    ni vaxillas,
mas fizo guerra a los moros,
ganando sus fortelezas
    y sus villas;
y en las lides que venció,
muchos moros y cavallos
    se perdieron;
y en este oficio ganó
las rentas y los vassallos
    que le dieron.

Pues por su onra y estado,
en otros tiempos passados
    ¿cómo se huvo?
Quedando desamparado,
con hermanos y criados
    se sostuvo.
Después que fechos famosos
fizo en esta dicha guerra
    que fazía,
fizo tratos tan onrosos
que le dieron aun más tierra
    que tenía.

Estas sus viejas estorias
que con su braço pintó
    en joventud,
con otras nuevas victorias
agora las renovó
    en senectud.
Por su grand abilidad,
por méritos y ancianía
    bien gastada,
alcançó la dignidad
de la grand cavallería
    del Espada.

Y sus villas y sus tierras
ocupades de tiranos
    las falló,
mas por cercos y por guerras
y por fuerça de sus manos
    las cobró.
Pues nuestro rey natural,
si de las obras que obró
    fue servido,
sígalo el de Portugal
y en Castilla quien siguió
    su partido.

Después de puesta la vida
tantas vezes por su ley

Let Portugal repeat the story,
And proud Castile, who shared the glory
     His arms deserved.

And when so oft, for weal or woe,
His life upon the fatal throw
     Had been cast down,—
When he had served, with patriot zeal
Beneath the banner of Castile,
     His sovereign's crown,—

And done such deeds of valor strong,
That neither history nor song
     Can count them all;
Then, on Ocaña's castled rock,
Death at his portal came to knock,
     With sudden call,—

Saying, "Good Cavalier, prepare
To leave this world of toil and care
     With joyful mien;
Let thy strong heart of steel this day
Put on its armour for the fray,—
     The closing scene.

"Since thou hast been, in battle-strife,
So prodigal of health and life,
     For earthly fame,
Let virtue nerve thy heart again;
Loud on the last stern battle-plain
     They call thy name.

"Think not the struggle that draws near
Too terrible for man, nor fear
     To meet the foe;
Nor let thy noble spirit grieve,
Its life of glorious fame to leave
     On earth below.

"A life of honor and of worth
Has no eternity on earth,—
     'Tis but a name;
And yet its glory far exceeds
That base and sensual life which leads
     To want and shame.

"The eternal life, beyond the sky,
Wealth cannot purchase, nor the high
     And proud estate;
The soul in dalliance laid,—the spirit
Corrupt with sin,—shall not inherit
     A joy so great.

"But the good monk, in cloistered cell,
Shall gain it by his book and bell,
     His prayers and tears;
And the brave knight, whose arm endures
Fierce battle, and against the Moors
     His standard rears.

"And thou, brave knight, whose hand has poured
The life-blood of the pagan horde
     O'er all the land,

     al tablero,
después de tan bien servida
la corona de su rey
verdadero,
    después de tanta hazaña
a que non puede bastar
cuenta cierta,
en su villa de Ocaña
vino la Muerte a llamar
a su puerta,

    diziendo: "Buen cavallero,
dexad el mundo engañoso
y su halago;
vuestro coraçón de azero
muestre su esfuerço famoso
en este trago;
    y pues de vida y salud
fezistes tan poca cuenta
por la fama,
esfuércese la virtud
para sofrir esta afruenta
que vos llama.

    "No se os faga tan amarga
la batalla temerosa
que esperáis,
pues otra vida más larga
de la fama glorïosa
acá dexáis.
    Aunque esta vida de onor
tampoco no es eternal
ni verdadera,
mas, con todo, es muy mejor
que la otra temporal,
perescedera.

    "El bivir que es perdurable
no se gana con estados
mundanales,
ni con vida deleitable
en que moran los pecados
infernales;
    mas los buenos religiosos
gánanlo con oraciones
y con lloros;
los cavalleros famosos,
con trabajos y aflicciones
contra moros.

    "Y pues vos, claro varón,
tanta sangre derramastes
de paganos,
esperad el galardón
que en este mundo ganastes
por las manos;
    y con esta confïança,
y con la fe tan entera
que tenéis,

In heaven shalt thou receive, at length,
The guerdon of thy earthly strength
    And dauntless hand.

"Cheered onward by this promise sure,
Strong in the faith entire and pure
    Thou dost profess,
Depart,—thy hope is certainty;—
The third—the better life on high
    Thou shalt possess."

"O Death, no more, no more delay!
My spirit longs to flee away
    And be at rest,—
The will of Heaven my will shall be,—
I bow to the divine decree,
    To God's behest.

"My soul is ready to depart,—
No thought rebels,—the obedient heart
    Breathes forth no sigh;
The wish on earth to linger still
Were vain, when 'tis God's sovereign will
    That we shall die.

"O thou, that for our sins didst take
A human form, and humbly make
    Thy home on earth!
Thou, that to thy divinity
A human nature didst ally
    By mortal birth,—

"And in that form didst suffer here
Torment, and agony, and fear,
    So patiently!
By thy redeeming grace alone,
And not for merits of my own,
    O, pardon me!"

As thus the dying warrior prayed,
Without one gathering mist or shade
    Upon his mind,—
Encircled by his family,
Watched by affection's gentle eye,
    So soft and kind,—

His soul to Him who gave it rose;
God lead it to its long respose,
    Its glorious rest!
And, though the warrior's sun has set,
Its light shall linger round us yet,
    Bright, radiant, blest.

               HENRY WADSWORTH LONGFELLOW

partid con buena esperança
que estotra vida tercera
ganaréis."

  —"No gastemos tiempo ya
en esta vida mezquina
por tal modo,
que mi voluntad está
conforme con la divina
para todo;
  y consiento en mi morir
con voluntad plazentera,
clara y pura,
que querer ombre bivir
cuando Dios quiere que muera,
es locura.

  "Tú, que por nuestra maldad,
tomaste forma servil
y baxo nombre,
Tú, que a tu divinidad
juntaste cosa tan vil
como el ombre;
  Tú, que tan grandes tormentos
sofriste sin resistencia
en tu persona,
no por mis merescimientos,
mas por tu sola clemencia
me perdona."

  Assí con tal entender,
todos sentidos umanos
conservados,
cercado de su muger,
de sus fijos y hermanos
y criados,
  dio el alma a quien gela dio,
el cual la ponga en el cielo
en su gloria.
y aunque la vida murió,
nos dexó harto consuelo
su memoria.

Ancient Ballads
fifteenth and sixteenth centuries

The ballads of Spain, called *romances* in Spanish, are an essential key to understanding the country and its literature. Most authorities believe the ballads represent the breaking up of the epic tradition. But in such matters there is no reason to trust the authorities, who once believed mistakenly that the epic was the earliest form of Spanish literature and that the Moors never composed poetry in Spanish. It is quite possible that at least some of the *romances* grew out of the same tradition as the early *kharjas*, found additional inspiration in the various heroes and stories of the epics, often fused the two currents, and then took on a vigorous life of their own.

Certainly by the time of Ferdinand and Isabella, the *romances* were almost universally popular in Spain. Everybody was singing their words and dancing to their melodies. Isabella was so fond of music that she kept forty court musicians in constant attendance. By the end of the fifteenth century the ballads had begun to be collected, and in 1511 the first large collection, known as the *Cancionero general*, came out. Many other collections followed, and the various volumes of the *Romancero general*, published between 1600 and 1614, completed the picture.

Among the best known of the countless *romances* of Spain are "Count Arnaldos," "Rosa fresca," and "Fonte frida," (included herein), three brief, sharp lyrics about mystery and love. There were also ballads of many other kinds: Jewish, Moorish, historic, heroic.

Interest in the traditional *romances* of Spain faded after the Golden Age. Indeed, that great period of Spanish literature paralleled the popularity of the ballad tradition, and the two currents—one artistic and literary, the other traditional and anonymous—died off together. Interest was reawakened in the ballads a century and a half later during the period of Romanticism in the first half of the nineteenth century. Spanish and German folklorists dedicated serious studies to them, and new collections were assembled and published.

The English Romantic poets had a field day with the ancient Spanish ballads. Archbishop Thomas Percy, in his *Reliques of the Ancient English Poetry* (1765), which some critics point to as marking the beginnings of Romanticism in English literature, translated and published two of them. One of these is included among our selections. The archbishop later made translations of five additional *romances*. Sir Walter Scott's son-in-law, John Gibson Lockhart, editor of the famous *Quarterly Review*, published an entire book of them, the *Ancient Spanish Ballads*, in 1823. Thomas Rodd, Sir John Bowring, James Young Gibson, Robert Southey, Hookham Frere, M. G. Lewis, Lord Byron, and many other noted British writers also translated ballads from the Spanish. Sir John Bowring's *Ancient Poetry and Romances of Spain* (1824), is a landmark in the literature of translation and is by far the best of the lot.

These Spanish ballads capture and eternalize the concept of Spain as a "renowned, romantic land."[14] They incorporate the exotic intermingling of the three cultures and religions that made Spain what she is today; and they are a form of literature that is characteristic, nostalgic, voluminous, at times intensely stirring and beautiful, poetically unique.

The verse form of the *romances* was also distinctively Spanish. They had sixteen-syllable lines with a break in the middle and were assonant, so that the clear, open vowel sounds of the language produced a majestic cadence. When they are translated into English, it is impossible to preserve this assonantal, repeated, single-vowel sound that gives the *romances* in Spanish such a strong tone of unity. Britain is the only other European country where balladry achieved an importance comparable with that of the *romances* in Spain, but the British ballads with their marked rhyme scheme produced quite a different effect.

The Lamentation of Don Rodrigo

Alone upon the battle ground, beneath a dying star,
Rodrigo gazed in bleak despair, his hosts were scattered
  far;

Romance de Don Rodrigo

Las huestes de don Ridrigo   desmayaban y huían
cuando en la octava batalla   sus enemigos vencían.
Rodrigo deja sus tiendas   y del real se salía:

14. George Gordon Byron, *The Works of Lord Byron* (Boston: Phillips Sampson and Co., 1857), 22. (The quotation is from "Childe Harold's Pilgrimage," Canto I, stanza XXXV.)

Eight battles had they bravely fought against the Moorish
band,
No hope remained within their hearts to save their native
land.
Rodrigo sadly turned away, forespent with grief and pain,
And journeyed in the trackless night across the barren
plain.
The king descended from his steed, for now 'twas lame and
blind,
Alone he staggered faint and sick, no shelter could he
find.
His sword was stained with blood and dust, as though
from darkest hell
It had been plucked, its scarlet hue a tale of gore did tell;
His coat of mail, that set with jewels, had glistened in the
sun
Now seemed to him a mourning cloth that some dark fate
had spun.
At dawn he climbed a hill that towered above that harsh
terrain,
Beneath him lay his banners torn, his noble soldiers slain.
And as the king in sorrow stared upon the cheerless
morn,
He heard a cry of victory: the Arab shout of scorn!
He searched for the brave captains that led the hosts of
Spain,
But he beheld their lifeless forms upon the gory plain.
Rodrigo could no longer bear the burden of his woe,
These words he spoke as from his eyes the bitter tears did
flow:
"Last night I was the king of Spain, today no fief
command.
Last night fair castles held my train, today bereft I stand,
The sun shall set forever on my kingdom and my reign,
The dawn will find no trace of me throughout this vast
domain.
Oh hapless day when first I bore my scepter and my
sword!
Accursèd hour that I was named Hispania's ruling Lord!
Oh fate most cruel that I should see the sun go down this
night!
Oh death, thou art victorious! Why fearest now to smite?"

KATHARINE E. STRATHDEE

solo va el desventurado,   sin ninguna compañía.
El caballo de cansado   ya mudar no se podía:
camina por donde quiere,   que no le estorba la vía.
El rey va tan desmayado,   que sentido no tenía;
muerto de sed y hambre,   que de velle era gran mancilla;
iba tan tinto de sangre,   que una brasa parecía.
Las armas lleva abolladas,   que eran de gran pedrería;
la espada lleva hecha sierra   de los golpes que tenía;
el almete de abollado   en la cabeza se le hundía;
la cara lleva hinchada   del trabajo que sufría.

Subióse encima de un cerro   el más alto que veía;
desde allí mira su gente   cómo iba de vencida.
De allí mira sus banderas,   y estandartes que tenía,
cómo están todos pisados   que la tierra los cubría;
mira por los capitanes   que ninguno parescía;
mira el campo tinto en sangre,   la cual arroyos corría.
El triste de ver aquesto   gran mancilla en sí tenía;
llorando de los sus ojos   de esta manera decía:
—Ayer era rey de España,   hoy no lo soy de una villa;
ayer villas y castillos,   hoy ninguno poseía;
ayer tenía criados,   hoy ninguno me servía,
hoy no tengo ni una almena   que pueda decir que es mía.
¡Desdichada fue la hora,   desidchado fue equel día
en que nací y heredé   la tan grande señoría,
pues lo había de perder   todo junto y en un día!
¡Oh muerte! ¿por qué no vienes   y llevas esta alma mía
de aqueste cuerpo mezquino,   pues se te agradecería?

Count Arnaldos

Who has ever met such fortune
On the waters of the sea,
As the lucky Count Arnaldos
On that Saint John's day when he
Held on his arm a falcon
As he went to chase the game!
And he saw a splendid galley
That to shore advancing came,
All its fluttering sails were silken,
All its shrouds of flounces clear,

El Conde Arnaldos

¡Quién hubiese tal ventura
sobre las aguas del mar
como hubo el conde Arnaldos
la mañana de san Juan!
Con un falcón en la mano
la caza iba a cazar,
y venir vio una galera
que a tierra quiere llegar;
las velas traía de seda,
la ejarcia de un cendal.

And the sailor who was helmsman
Sang a song so sweet to hear
That the waves were calm and silent,
And the noisy storm-wind hushed,
And the fish that live the deepest
To the water's surface rushed;
While the restless birds were gathered
Listening on the masts, and still.
From his galley Count Arnaldos
This is how he pleaded then:
"In God's name I beg you sailor,
Sing that song for me again."
But the sailor thus responded
As he drifted on the sea:
"I sing my song only for those
Who come to sail with me."

JOHN A. CROW AND SIR JOHN BOWRING

Marinero que la manda,
diciendo viene un cantar
que la mar ponía en calma,
los vientos hace amainar,
los peces que andan al hondo,
arriba los hace andar;
las aves que andan volando,
las hace al mástil posar.
Allí habló el conde Arnaldos,
bien oiréis lo que dirá;
—Por Dios te ruego, marinero,
dígasme ora ese cantar.—
Respondióle el marinero,
tal respuesta lo fue a dar:
—Yo no digo mi canción
sino a quién conmigo va.

Fount of Freshness

Fount of freshness, fount of freshness,
Fount of freshness and of love,
Where the little birds seek comfort
In the waters up above,
All except the lonely sweetheart—
Widowed, grieving turtle-dove.
There the nightingale, the traitor!
Lingered on his giddy way;
And these words of hidden treachery
To the dove I heard him say:
"I will be thy servant, lady!
I will not thy love betray."
"Off! false-hearted, vile deciever!
Leave me, don't entice me now!
I've no heart to perch in meadows
On fresh lands or verdant bough!
Even these clear fountain waters
When I drink turn dark somehow.
Never will I think of marriage,
Never break the widow's vow,
For I want no children ever
To console or please me now.
Leave me, false one! faithless traitor!
Base one! vain one! sad one! go!
I will never be thy sweetheart,
I will never wed thee, no!"

SIR JOHN BOWRING

Romance de Fonte-Frida y con amor

Fonte-frida, Fonte-frida,
Fonte-frida y con amor,
de todas las avecicas
van tomar consolación,
si no es la Tortolica,
que está viuda y con dolor.
Por allí fuera a pasar
el traidor de Ruiseñor;
las palabras que le dice
llenas son de traición:
—Si tú quisieses, señora
yo sería tu servidor.
—Vete de ahí, enemigo,
malo, falso, engñador,
que ni poso en ramo verde
ni en prado que tenga flor;
que si el agua hallo clara
turbia la bebía yo;
que no quiero haber marido
porque hijos no haya, no;
no quiero placer con ellos.
ni menos consolación.
¡Déjame, triste enemigo,
malo, falso, ruin traidor,
que no quiero ser tu amiga
ni casar contigo, no!

Fresh Rose

"Rose of freshness, Rose of freshness,
Rose of beauty and of love,
When once I held you in my arms,
I did not serve you, no;
But now that you are gone from me,

Rosa fresca

"Rosa fresca, rosa fresca.
tan garrida y con amor,
cuando vos tuve en mis brazos,
no vos supe servir, no;
y agora que os serviría

I long to hold you so.''
"The blame for that was yours, my love,
Was yours, not mine, you know,
A letter came from you one day,
Your servant kept it though,
Instead he told a tale to me,
A tale he swore was so.
He said that you were married
Somewhere in old León,
Your children fair as flowers,
Your lady white as snow.''
"Who told you that, my sweetheart,
Told you a lie full blown,
For I was never in Castile
Nor neighbouring León
Except when I was very small
And was to love unknown.''

JOHN A. CROW

no vos puedo haber, no.''
—"Vuestra fue la culpa, amigo,
vuestra fue, que mía no;
enviástesme una carta
con un vuestro servidor,
y en lugar de recaudar
él dijera otra razón:
que érades casado, amigo,
allá en tierras de León:
que tenéis mujer hermosa
y hijos como una flor.''
—"Quien os lo dijo, señora,
no vos dijo verdad, no;
que yo nunca entré en Castilla
ni allá en tierras de León,
sino cuando era pequeño,
que no sabía de amor.''

Maytime

It happened in the month of May
In summer's warmest hour,
When shafts of wheat were ripening,
And fields were all in flower,
When the skylark sings his happy song,
And the nightingale responds,
When lovers cross their hearts and swear
To their truelove to belong;
All save for me who in my pain
Locked in this dingy cell,
Where night and day are both the same;
No difference could I tell
If there were not a tiny bird
Why at daybreak sang to me.
Alas, an archer killed that bird;
God, bring him misery!

JOHN A. CROW

Romance del prisionero

Que por mayo era, por mayo.
cuando hace la calor,
cuando los trigos encañan
y están los campos en flor.
cuando canta la calandria
y responde el ruiseñor,
cuando los enamorados
van a servir al amor;
sino yo, triste, cuitado,
que vivo en esta prisión;
que ni sé cuándo es de día
ni cuándo las noches son,
sino por una avecilla
que me cantaba al albor.
Matómela un ballestero;
déle Dios mal galardón.

Woe Is Me, Alhama!

The Moorish king rides up and down
Through Granada's royal town;
From Elvira's gates to those
Of Bivarambla on he goes.
     Woe is me, Alhama!

Letters to the monarch tell
How Alhama's city fell;
In the fire the scroll he threw,
And the messenger he slew.
     Woe is me, Alhama!

He quits his mule, and mounts his horse,
And through the street directs his course;
Through the street of Zacatín

Romance muy doloroso del sitio y toma de Alhama

Paseábase el Rey Moro
por la cuidad de Granada,
desde las puertas de Elvira
hasta las de Vivarrambla.
     ¡Ay de mi Alhama!

Cartas le fueron venidas
que Alhama era ganada,
las cartas echó al fuego,
y el mensagero mataba.
     ¡Ay de mi Alhama!

Descabalga de una mula,
y en un caballo cabalga.
Por el Zacatín arriba

To the Alhambra spurring in.
    Woe is me, Alhama!

When the Alhambra walls he gained,
On the moment he ordained
That the trumpet straight should sound
With the silver clarion round.
    Woe is me, Alhama!

And when the hollow drums of war
Beat the loud alarm afar,
That the Moors of town and plain
Might answer to the martial strain,—
    Woe is me, Alhama!

Then the Moors, by this aware
That bloody Mars recalled them there,
One by one, and two by two,
To a mighty squadron grew.
    Woe is me, Alhama!

Out then spake an aged Moor
In these words the king before:
"Wherefore call on us, O King?
What may mean this gathering?"
    Woe is me, Alhama!

"Friends! ye have, alas! to know
Of a most disastrous blow,—
That the Christians, stern and bold,
Have obtained Alhama's hold."
    Woe is me, Alhama!

Out then spake old Alfaqui,
With his beard so white to see:
"Good King, thou art justly served,—
Good King, this thou hast deserved.
    Woe is me, Alhama!

"By thee were slain, in evil hour,
The Abencerrage, Granada's flower;
And strangers were received by thee,
Of Cordova the Chivalry.
    Woe is me, Alhama!

"And for this, O King, is sent
On thee a double chastisement:
Thee and thine, thy crown and realm,
One last wreck shall overwhelm.
    Woe is me, Alhama!

"He who holds no laws in awe,
He must perish by the law;
And Granada must be won,
And thyself with her undone."
    Woe is me, Alhama!

Fire flashed from out the old Moor's eyes;
The monarch's wrath began to rise.
Because he answered, and because
He spake exceeding well of laws.
    Woe is me, Alhama!

subido se había el Alhambra,
    ¡Ay de mi Alhama!

Como en el Alhambra estuvo,
al mismo punto mandaba
que se toquen las trompetas
con añafiles de plata.
    ¡Ay de mi Alhama!

Y que atambores de guerra
apriesa toque al arma;
por lo que oigan sus moros,
los de la Vega y Granada.
    ¡Ay de mi Alhama!

Los moros que el son oyeron,
que al sangriento Marte llama,
uno a uno, y dos a dos,
un gran escuadrón formaba.
    ¡Ay de mi Alhama!

Allí habló un moro viejo;
desta manera hablaba:
¿Para qué nos llamas, Rey?
¿Para qué es esta llamada?
    ¡Ay de mi Alhama!

Habéis de saber, amigos,
una nueva desdichada:
que cristianos, con braveza,
ya nos han tomado Alhama.
    ¡Ay de mi Alhama!

Allí habló un viejo Alfaquí
de barba crecida y cana:
bien se te emplea, buen rey,
buen rey, bien se te empleaba.
    ¡Ay de mi Alhama!

Mataste los Abencerrages,
que eran la flor de Granada;
cogiste los tornadizos
de Córdoba la nombrada.
    ¡Ay de mi Alhama!

Por eso mereces, rey,
una pena bien doblada;
que te pierdas tú y el reino,
y que se pierda Granada.
    ¡Ay de mi Alhama!

Si no se respetan leyes,
es ley que todo se pierda;
y que se pierda Granada,
y que te pierdas en ella.
    ¡Ay de mi Alhama!

Fuego por los ojos vierte.
el rey que esto oyera.
Y como el otro de leyes
de leyes también hablaba.
    ¡Ay de mi Alhama!

"There is no law to say such things
As may disgust the ear of kings":—
Thus, snorting with his choler, said
The Moorish king. and doomed him dead.
     Woe is me, Alhama!

Moor Alfaqui! Moor Alfaqui!
Though thy beard so hoary be,
The king hath sent to have thee seized,
For Alhama's loss displeased;—
     Woe is me, Alhama!

And to fix thy head upon
High Alhambra's loftiest stone:
That this for thee should be the law,
And others tremble when they saw.
     Woe is me, Alhama!

"Cavalier! and man of worth!
Let these words of mine go forth;
Let the Moorish monarch know,
That to him I nothing owe.
     Woe is me, Alhama!

"But on my soul Alhama weighs,
And on my inmost spirit preys;
And if the king his land hath lost,
Yet others may hve lost the most.
     Woe is me, Alhama!

"Sires have lost their children,—wives,
Their lords,—and valiant men, their lives;
One what best his love might claim
Hath lost,—another, wealth or fame.
     Woe is me, Alhama!

"I lost a damsel in that hour,
Of all the land the loveliest flower;
Doubloons a hundred I would pay,
And think her ransom cheap that day."
     Woe is me, Alhama!

And as these things the old Moor said,
They severed from the trunk his head;
And to the Alhambra's wall with speed
'T was carried, as the king decreed.
     Woe is me, Alhama!

And men and infants therein weep
Their loss, so heavy and so deep;
Granada's ladies, all she rears
Within her walls, burst into tears.
     Woe is me, Alhama!

And from the windows o'er the walls
The sable web of mourning falls,
The king weeps as a woman o'er
His loss,—for it is much and sore.
     Woe is me, Alhama!

LORD BYRON

Sabe un rey que no hay leyes
de darle a reyes disgusto.
Eso dice el rey moro
relinchando de cólera.
     ¡Ay de mi Alhama!

Moro Alfaquí, moro Alfaquí,
el de la vellida barba,
el rey te manda prender,
por la pérdida de Alhama.
     ¡Ay de mi Alhama!

Y cortarte la cabeza,
y ponerla en el Alhambra,
por que a ti castigo sea,
y otros también en miralle.
     ¡Ay de mi Alhama!

Caballeros, hombres buenos,
decid de mi parte al rey,
al rey moro de Granada,
como no le debo nada.
     ¡Ay de mi Alhama!

De haberse Alhama perdido,
a mí me pesa en el alma.
Que si el rey perdió su tierra,
otros mucho más perdieron.
     ¡Ay de mi Alhama!

Perdieron hijos padres,
y casados las casadas:
Las cosas que más amaba
perdió el uno, y el otro fama.
     ¡Ay de mi Alhama!

Perdí una hija doncella
que era la flor desta tierra,
cien doblas daba por ella,
no me las estimo en nada.
     ¡Ay de mi Alhama!

Diciendo así el viejo Alfaquí,
le cortaron la cabeza,
y la elevan al Alhambra,
así como el rey lo manda.
     ¡Ay de mi Alhama!

Hombres, niños y mujeres,
lloran tan grande pérdida.
Lloraban todas las damas
cuantas en Granada había.
     ¡Ay de mi Alhama!

Por las calles y ventanas
mucho luto parecía:
Llora el rey como fembra,
que es mucho lo que perdía.
     ¡Ay de mi Alhama!

Fatima's Love

On the morn of John the Baptist, just at the break of day,
The Moors upon Granada's fields streamed out in bright
    array.
Their horses galloped o'er the sod, their lances flashed in
    air,
And the banners that their dames had wrought spread out
    their colors fair.
Their quivers bright flashed in the light with gold and silk
    brocade,
And the Moor who saw his love was there looked best in
    the parade,
And the Moor who had no lady love strove hard some
    love to gain.
'Mong those who from Alhambra's towers gazed on that
    warrior train.
There were two Moorish ladies there whom love had
    smitten sore;
Zarifa one, and Fatima the name the other bore.
Knit by warm friendship were their hearts till, filled with
    jealous pain,
Their glances met, as one fair knight came prancing o'er
    the plain.
Zarifa spoke to Fatima, "How has love marred thy face!
Once roses bloomed on either cheek, now lilies take their
    place;
And you, who once would talk of love, now still and silent
    stay.
Come, come unto the window and watch the pageant gay!
Abindarraez is riding by; his train is full in view;
In all Granada none can boast a choicer retinue."
Fatima then discreetly spoke, and without more ado:
"It is not love, Zarifa, that robs my cheek of rose;
No fond and anxious passion this mournful bosom
    knows;
My cheeks are pale and I am still and silent, it is true,—
For, ah! I miss my father's face, whom fierce Alabey slew.
And did I crave the boon of love, a thousand knights were
    fain
To fight for me in service true on yonder flowery plain.
And all the love I give to each to give me back again.
And for Abindarraez, whose heart and valiant might,
You praise and from the window watch, with rapturous
    delight—"
The lady stopped, for at their feet knelt down the
    well-loved knight.

                                        EPIPHANIUS WILSON

Romance de Fátima

La mañana de San Juan,
al punto que alboreaba,
grande fiesta hacen los moros
por la Vega de Granada.
Revolviendo sus caballos,
jugando van de las lanzas,
ricos pendones en ellas,
labrados por sus amadas.
Ricas aljabas vestidas
de oro y seda labradas:
El moro que amores tiene,
allí bien se señalaba.
Y el moro que no los tiene,
de tenerlos procuraba:
Mirando las damas moras
desde las torres de Alhambra,
entre las cuales había
dos de amor muy lastimadas,
la una se llama Jarifa,
la otra Fátima se llama.
Solían tratar amores,
aunque ahora no se hablan;
Jarifa, llena de celos,
a Fátima le hablaba:
—¡Ay Fátima, hermana mía,
cómo estás de amor tocada!
Solías tener colores,
veo que ahora te faltan.
Solías tratar amores,
ahora obras y callas;
pero si le quieres ver,
asómate a esa ventana,
y verás a Abindarráez
y su gentileza y gala.—
Fátima, como discreta,
de esta manera le habla:
—No estoy tocada de amores,
ni en mi vida los tratara;
si se perdió mi color,
tengo de ello justa causa.
Por la muerte de mi padre,
que aquel Alabez matara;
y si amores yo quisiera,
está, hermana, confiada.
Que allí veo caballeros
en aquella vega llana,
de quien pudiera servirme,
y dellos ser muy amada.
De tanto valor y esfuerzo,
cual de Abindarráez alabas.—
Con esto las damas moras
pusieron fin a su habla.

The Bridal of Andalla

"Rise up, rise up, Xarifa! lay the golden cushion down;
Rise up, come to the window, and gaze with all the town!
From gay guitar and violin the silver notes are flowing,
And the lovely lute doth speak between the trumpet's
　　lordly blowing;
And banners bright from lattice light are waving
　　everywhere,
And the tall, tall plume of our cousin's bridegroom floats
　　proudly in the air:
Rise up, rise up, Xarifa! lay the golden cushion down;
Rise up, come to the window, and gaze with all the town!

"Arise, arise, Xarifa! I see Andalla's face,—
He bends him to the people with a calm and princely
　　grace;
Through all the land of Xeres and banks of Guadalquivir
Rode forth bridegroom so brave as he, so brave and
　　lovely, never.
Yon tall plume waving o'er his brow, of purple mixed
　　with white,
I guess 'twas wreathed by Zara, whom he will wed
　　tonight.
Rise up, rise up, Xarifa! lay the golden cushion down;
Rise up, come to the window, and gaze with all the town!

"What aileth thee, Xarifa?—What makes thine eyes look
　　down?
Why stay ye from the window far, nor gaze with all the
　　town?
I've heard you say, on many a day,—and, sure, you said
　　the truth,—
Andalla rides without a peer among all Granada's youth.
Without a peer he rideth,—and yon milk-white horse
　　doth go,
Beneath his stately master, with a stately step and slow:
Then rise, O, rise, Xarifa, lay the golden cushion down;
Unseen here through the lattice, you may gaze with all the
　　town!"

The Zegri lady rose not, nor laid her cushion down,
Nor came she to the window to gaze with all the town;
But though her eyes dwelt on her knee, in vain her fingers
　　strove,—
And though her needle pressed the silk, no flower Xarifa
　　wove:
One bonny rose-bud she had traced, before the noise
　　drew nigh;
That bonny bud a tear effaced, slow dropping from her
　　eye.
"No, no!", she sighs,—"bid me not rise, nor lay my
　　cushion down,
To gaze upon Andalla with all the gazing town!"

"Why rise ye not, Xarifa, nor lay your cushion down?
Why gaze ye not, Xarifa, with all the gazing town?
Hear, hear the trumpet how it swells, and how the people
　　cry!
He stops at Zara's palace-gate—why sit ye still—oh, why!"

La hermosa Jarifa

Ponte a las rejas azules,　deja la manga que labras.
Melancólica Jarifa,　verás al galán Audalla.
que nuestra calle pasea　en una yegua alazana,
con un jaez verde oscuro,　color de muerta esperanza.
Si sales presto, Jarifa.　verás cómo corre y para,
que no lo iguala en Jerez　ningún ginete de fama.
Hoy ha sacado tres plumas,　una blanca y dos moradas,
que cuando corre lijero,　todas tres parecen blancas.
Si los hombres le bendicen,　¡peligro corren las damas!
Bien puedes salir a verle,　que hay muchas a las
　　ventanas.
¡Bien siente la yegua el día　que su amo viste galas,
que va tan briosa y loca　que revienta de lozana:
Y con la espuma del freno　tenidas lleva las bandas,
que entre las peinadas crines　el hermoso cuello enlazan!
Jarifa, que al moro adora,　y de sus celos se abrasa,
los ojos en la labor,　así le dice a su Aya:
—Días ha, Celinda amiga,　que sé cómo corre y para,
quien corre al primer deseo,　al segundo para el alma.
¡No me mandes que le vea,　pluguiera a fortuna varia,
que como sé lo que corre,　él supiera lo que alcanza!
¡Muy corrida me han tenido　sus carreras y mis ansias:
Las secretas por mi pena,　las públicas por mi fama!
Por más colores de plumas　no hayas miedo que allá
　　salga,
porque ellas son el fiador　de sus fingidas palabras:
Por otras puede correr　de las muchas que le alaban,
que basta que en mi salud　el tiempo toma venganza.

"At Zara's gate stops Zara's mate; in him shall I
          discover
The dark-eyed youth pledged me his truth with tears, and
          was my lover?
I will not rise, with weary eyes, nor lay my cushion down,
To gaze on false Andalla with all the gazing town!"

JOHN GIBSON LOCKHART

Girl with the Dark Hair

Girl with the dark hair
If you are asleep, be warned:
Half of your life is a dream
Which runs and slips by us,
As rapid in its flight
As a light sleep is wakened,
As brief while we are young
As when age is upon us,
For the sad disclosure
Of our fleet career
When it would wake us comes
Late and avails us nothing.
Your youth and beauty are
No more than a new merchant,
Rich to be left poor
By the lapse of time;
A glory of the world
And a veil for the eyes
And chains for the feet
And fetters for the fingers;
A ground for hazards,
A midden of envy,
A butcher of men,
A famous thief of time.
When death has shuffled
Ugly and fair together
In the narrow sepulcher
The bones do not know each other.
And though the cyprus is higher
And the cedar more lovely, neither
Burned into charcoal, is whiter
Than charcoal from the ash tree.
For in this woeful existence
Delight comes to us in dreams only
And distress and tribulation
When we are widest awake.
Dry autumn will consume
The flower of fresh April,
To unloved ivory
Turning your ebon hair.

W. S. MERWIN

Oh Pale Maiden

Oh pale maiden,
Sadness has faded

La morena

Si te durmieras, morena,
ten aviso que es el sueño
la mitad de nuestra vida,
que se nos pasa corriendo;
y que es tan veloz volando,
como ligera durmiendo;
tan breve en la juventud,
como cuando somos viejos,
porque el desengaño triste
de nuestro curso ligero,
cuando quiere despertarnos,
llega tarde y sin provecho.
Tu juventud y hermosura
no es más que un mercader nuevo,
que de rico queda pobre
con el discurso del tiempo:
Es una gloria del mundo,
y de los ojos un velo,
y un grillo para los pies,
y esposas para los dedos;
una ocasión de peligros,
y de la envidia un terrero;
un verdugo de los hombres,
famoso ladrón del tiempo.
Cuando la muerte baraja
a los hermosos y feos,
en la estrecha sepultura
no se conocen los huesos;
y aunque el ciprés sea más alto,
y más hermoso sea el cedro,
no por eso su carbón
es más blanco que el del fresno;
que en esta mísera vida
nos viene el placer a sueños,
y el disgusto y los pesares
cuando estamos más despiertos.
La flor de su nuevo abril
la quema el otoño seco,
que en marfil blanco y malquisto
convierte el ébano negro.

Descolorida zagala

Descolorida zagala,
a quien tristezas hicieron

The rose of your face
In the April of your days,
All the village wonders
At such melancholy;
Such suffering, they say,
Is of the soul, not the body.
If such is your condition,
If your bewitching eyes
Which once killed with joy
Are now dead with sadness,
If you never go out to the dancing,
And to you the tambourine
Sounds like a knell tolling
And a bell at a burying,
If when all the girls
Go out into the fields
For cresses and to plunder
The young almonds of their kernels
You remain in your little house
In a lightless room
So that even when the sun shines
You are clouded over,
Who will fail to say
That you suffer on your left side
And are little seen because
You merit no better acquaintance,
That I leave you and seek my pleasure
Where I have none
Often stealing away
In scorn of quiet nights,
That I ill-treat your soul
And that you are worse to your body
Since to purge it of love
You dose it with desire?
Come awake, my girl,
Wake out of your deep silence,
For the village speaks ill of me
And so do your father's eyes.
I have green slippers waiting for you
For the day when you set
Your fair foot on the floor,
And my mouth awaits you.
A little gown of light crimson
Will cover your body
Which more than four covet
As do I, who possess it.
You will have earrings of crystal
Which I pray you not to break
For words are of crystal, and those
Which I give I do not break.
And if still you will not recover
Your health, you for whom I lose mine,
Then give me the illness, my lady,
Or let us share it between us,
For if you must be ill I would rather
That I were the sufferer;
Not you, who are my soul,
But I, who am your body.

perder el color de rosa
en el abril de su tiempo:
Toda la aldea murmura
tan melancólico extremo,
y dicen que tanto mal
es del alma y no del cuerpo,
si ya vuestra condición
y vuestros ojos risueños,
que mataban de alegría,
están de tristeza muertos;
si ya no sales al baile,
y el repique del pandero
decís que tañe a difunto,
y que es campana de entierro;
si cuando todas las mozas
van al campo a coger berros,
y a despojar de su fruta
a los tempranos almendros,
os estáis en vuestra choza
en un oscuro aposento,
que aunque el sol está con vos
está de nubes cubierto,
¿Quién ha de haber que no diga
que os quejáis del lado izquierdo,
y que tan poco os conozco,
porque tan poco os merezco,
que os dejo, y busco mi gusto
en partes que no le tengo;
y que por ratos hurtados
seguras noches desprecio,
y que trato mal vuestra alma,
y vos peor vuestro cuerpo,
pues por purgarle de amor
le dais jarabes de celos?
Despertad, zagala mía,
de ese profundo silencio,
que la aldea me maldice,
y me mira mal mi suegro.
Para el día que pongáis
la bella planta en el suelo,
os tengo verdes servillas,
y mi propia boca os tengo;
sayuelo de grana blanca
ha de cubrir vuestro cuerpo,
que más de cuatro os le envidien,
y aun a mí, que le poseo.
Tendréis zarcillos de vidrio,
y no los quebréis os ruego,
que son palabras de vidrio
y las que doy no las quiebro;
y si no pensáis cobrar
salud, por quien yo la pierdo,
dadme el mal, señora mía,
o partámosle por medio;
que si enferma habéis de estar,
mejor es que esté yo enfermo;
vos no, que sois alma mía,
yo sí, que soy vuestro cuerpo.

W. S. MERWIN

Gentle River

Gentle river, gentle river,
Lo, thy streams are stain'd with gore,
Many a brave and noble captain
Floats along thy willow'd shore.

All beside thy limpid waters,
All beside thy sands so bright,
Moorish Chiefs and Christian Warriors
Join'd in fierce and mortal fight.

Lords, and dukes, and noble princes
On thy fatal banks were slain:
Fatal banks that gave to slaughter
All the pride and flower of Spain.

There the hero, the brave Alonzo
Full of wounds and glory died:
There the fearless Urdiales
Fell a victim by his side.

Lo! where yonder Don Saavedra
Thro' their squadrons slow retires;
Proud Seville, his native city,
Proud Seville his worth admires.

Close behind a renegado
Loudly shouts with taunting cry;
Yield thee, yield thee. Don Saavedra,
Dost thou from the battle fly?

Well I know thee, haughty Christian,
Long I liv'd beneath thy roof;
Oft I've in the lists of glory
Seen thee win the prize of proof.

Well I know thy aged parents,
Well thy blooming bride I know;
Seven years I was thy captive,
Seven years of pain and woe.

May our prophet grant my wishes,
Haughty chief, thou shalt be mine:
Thou shalt drink that cup of sorrow,
Which I drank when I was thine.

Like a lion turns the warrior,
Back he sends an angry glare:
Whizzing came the Moorish javelin,
Vainly whizzing through the air.

Back the hero full of fury
Sent a deep and mortal wound:
Instant sunk the Renegado,
Mute and lifeless on the ground.

With a thousand Moors surrounded,
Brave Saavedra stands at bay:
Wearied out but never daunted,
Cold at length the warrior lay.

Near him fighting great Alonzo
Stout resists the Paynim bands:

Río Verde

Río verde, río verde,
¡quánto cuerpo en ti se baña
de Christianos y de Moros
muertos por la dura espada!
Y tus ondas cristalinas
de roxa sangre se esmaltan:
entre Moros y Christianos
muy gran batalla se trava.
Murieron Duques y Condes,
grandes señores de salva:
murió gente de valia
de la nobleza de España.
En ti murió don Alonso,
que de Aguilar se llamaba;
el valeroso Urdiales,
con don Alonso acababa.
Por un ladera arriba
el buen Sayavedra marcha;
natural es de Sevilla,
de la gente mas granada.
Tras el iba un Renegado.
desta manera le habla;
date, date, Sayavedra,
no huyas de la Batalla.
Yo te conozco muy bien,
gran tiempo estuve en tu casa;
y en la Plaça de Sevilla
bien te vida jugar cañas.
Conozco a tu padre y madre,
y a tu muger doña Clara;
siete años fui tu cautivo,
malamente me tratabas.
Y aora lo serás mío,
si Mahoma me ayudara;
y también te trataré,
como a mí me tratabas.
Sayavedra que lo oyera,
al Moro bolbió la cara;
Tiróle el Moro una flecha,
pero nunca le acertaba.
Hirióle Sayavedra
de una herida muy mala:
muerto cayó el Renegado
sin poder hablar palabra.
Sayavedra fue cercado
de mucha Mora canalla,
y al cabo cayó allí muerto
de una muy mala lançada.
Don Alonso en este tiempo
bravamente peleava,
y el cavallo le avían muerto.
y le tiene por muralla.
Mas cargaron tantos Moros
que mal le hieren y tratan:
De la sangre, que perdía,
Don Alonso se desmaya.

From his slaughter'd steed dismounted
Firm intrench'd behind him stands.

Furious press the hostile squadron,
Furious he repels their rage:
Loss of blood at length enfeebles:
Who can war with thousands wage!

Where yon rock the plain o'ershadows
Close beneath its foot retir'd,
Fainting sunk the bleeding hero,
And without a groan expir'd.

THOMAS PERCY

Bernardo del Carpio's Fight

The peasant leaves his plough afield,
The reaper leaves his hook,
And from his hand the shepherd-boy
Lets fall the pastoral crook.

The young set up a shout of joy,
The old forget their years,
The feeble man grows stout of heart,
No more the craven fears.

All rush to Bernard's standard,
And on liberty they call;
They cannot brook to wear the yoke,
When threatened by the Gaul.

"Free were we born," 'tis thus they cry,
"And willingly we pay
The duty that we owe our king,
Whose rule we all obey.

"But God forbid that we submit
To laws of foreign knaves,
Tarnish the glory of our sires,
And make our children slaves.

"Our hearts have not so craven grown,
So bloodless all our veins,
So vigorless our brawny arms,
As to submit to chains.

"Has the audacious Frank subdued
These seas and these our lands?
Shall he a bloodless victory have?
No, not while we have hands!

"And he shall learn that Leonese
Can bravely fight and fall,
But that they know not how to yield;
They are Castilians all.

"Shall the bold lions that have bathed
Their paws in Libyan gore,
Crouch basely to a feebler foe,
And dare the strife no more?

Al fin, al fin cayó muerto
al pie de un peña alta.
—Muerto queda don Alonso.
eterna fama ganara.

Con tres mil y más leoneses

Los labradores arrojan
de las manos los arados,
las hoces, los azadones;
los pastores los cayados;
los jóvenes se alborozan,
aliéntanse los ancianos,
los inútiles se animan,
fíngense fuertes los flacos,
todos a Bernardo acuden,
libertad apedillando,
que al infame yugo temen
con que los amaga el galo.
—Libres, gritaban, nacimos,
y a nuestro rey soberano
pagamos lo que debemos
por el divino mandato.
No permita Dios, ni ordene
que a los decretos de extraños
obliguemos a nuestros hijos,
gloria de nuestros pasados:
No están tan flacos los pechos,
ni tan sin vigor los brazos,
ni tan sin sangre las venas,
que consientan tal agravio.
¿El francés ha por ventura
esta tierra conquistado?
¿Victoria sin sangre quiere?
No, mientras tengamos manos.
Podrá decir de leoneses,
que murieron peleando;
pero que no se rindieron,
que al fin son castellanos.
¿Por qué un reino, y de leones,
que en sangre libia bañaron
sus encarnizadas uñas,
escucha medios tan bajos?
Déles el rey sus haberes,
mas no les dé sus vasallos;
que en someter voluntades
no tienen los reyes mando.

"Let the false king give up his lands,
But not his vassals yield;
For to surrender free-born souls
No king this power can wield!"

HENRY WADSWORTH LONGFELLOW

Fatima and Raduan

"False diamonds set in flint! the caverns of the mine
Are warmer than the breast that holds that faithless heart
   of thine;
Thou art fickle as the sea, thou art wandering as the wind,
And the restless ever-mounting flame is not more hard to
   bind.
If the tears I shed were tongues, yet all too few would be,
To tell of all the treachery that thou hast shown to me.
Oh! I could chide thee sharply—but every maiden knows
That she who chides her lover, forgives him ere he goes.

"Thou hast called me oft the flower of all Granada's
   maids,
Thou has said that by the side of me the first and fairest
   fades;
And they thought thy heart was mine, and it seemed to
   every one
That what thou didst to win my love, from love of me was
   done.
Alas! if they but knew thee, as mine it is to know,
They well might see another mark to which thine arrows
   go;
But thou giv'st me little heed—for I speak to one who
   knows
That she who chides her lover, forgives him ere he goes.

"It wearies me, mine enemy, that I must weep and bear
What fills thy heart with triumph, and fills my own with
   care.
Thou art leagued with those that hate me, and ah! thou
   know'st I feel
That cruel words as surely kill as sharpest blades of steel.
'Twas the doubt that thou wert false that wrung my heart
   with pain;
But, now I know thy perfidy, I shall be well again.
I would proclaim thee as thou art—but every maiden
   knows
That she who chides her lover, forgives him ere he goes."

Thus Fatima complained to the valiant Raduan,
Where underneath the myrtles Alhambra's fountains ran:
The Moor was inly moved, and blamless as he was,
He took her white hand in his own, and pleaded thus his
   cause:
"Oh, lady, dry those star-like eyes—their dimness does
   me wrong;
If my heart be made of flint, at least 'twill keep thy image
   long:

Fátima y Raduán

"¡Diamante falso y fingido,
engastado en pedernal!
¡Alma fiera en duro pecho
que ninguna fiera es más!
¡Ligero como los vientos,
mudable como la mar!
¡Inquieto como el fuego
hasta hallar su natural!
¡Si las lágrimas que vierto
fueran lenguas para hablar,
injurias me faltarían
para culpar tu maldad!
¡Qué injurias podré decirte!
Mas no te quiero injuriar;
porque al fin quien dice injurias
cerca está de perdonar.
A todas dices que son
las que contento te dan,
para tu gusto mentira,
y que yo soy tu verdad;
y con esto piensan todos
que debo a tu voluntad
cuantos caminos emprendes
para que te deba más.
¡Si como yo conociesen
tu condición natural
a otro blanco mirarían,
adonde tus flechas van!
Yo sé, traidor, que estas quejas
muy poca pena te dan,
porque al fin quien dice injurias
cerca está de perdonar.
Cansado estoy, enemigo,
de sufrir y de llorar
causa ajena y propios daños,
tu placer y mi pesar,
mis enemigos acoges,
porque al fin conoces ya
que cuando no puedan obras.
palabras me matarán.
Sopechas dudosas fueron
causa de todo mi mal;
y celos averiguados
convaleciéndome van.
Al cielo quiero dar voces;
pero mejor es callar,
porque al fin quien dice injurias
cerca está de perdonar."

Thou hast uttered cruel words—but I grieve the less for those,
Since she who chides her lover, forgives him ere he goes."

WILLIAM CULLEN BRYANT

Así Fátima se queja
al valiente Reduán,
en el jardín del Alhambra
al pie de un verde arrayán.
El moro que está sin culpa,
aunque no sin pena está,
asióle la blanca mano,
y así la comienza a hablar:
—Cesad, hermosas estrellas,
que no es bien que lloréis mas,
que si a mi me llamáis piedra,
en piedras hacéis señal;
y no penséis que me agravio
de injurias que me digáis,
porque al fin quien dice injurias
cerca está de perdonar.

The Warden of Molina

The warden of Molina, ah! furious was his speed,
As he dashed his glittering rowels in the flank of his good steed,
And his reins left dangling from the bit, along the white highway,
For his mind was set to speed his horse, to speed and not to stay.
He rode upon a grizzled roan, and with the wind he raced,
And the breezes rustled round him like a tempest in the waste.
In the Plaza of Molina at last he made his stand,
And in a voice of thunder he uttered his command:
       To arms, to arms, my captains!
       Sound, clarions, trumpets, blow;
       And let the thundering kettle-drum
       Give challenge to the foe.

"Now leave your feasts and banquetings and gird you in your steel!
And leave the couches of delight, where slumber's charm you feel;
Your country calls for succor, all must the word obey,
For the freedom of your fathers is in your hands to-day.
Ah, sore may be the struggle, and vast may be the cost;
But yet no tie of love must keep you now, or all is lost.
In breasts where honor dwells there is no room in times like these
To dally at a lady's side, kneel at a lady's knees.
       To arms, to arms, my captains!
       Sound, clarions; trumpets, blow;
       And let the thundering kettle-drum
       Give challenge to the foe.

"Yes, in the hour of peril away with pleasure's thrall!
Let honor take the lance and steed to meet our country's call.
For those who craven in the fight refuse to meet the foe

El alcalde de Molina

Batiéndole las ijadas
con los duros acicates,
y las riendas algo flojas,
porque corra y no se pare,
en un caballo tordillo,
que tras de sí deja el aire,
por la plaza de Molina
viene diciendo el Alcalde:
"¡Al arma, capitanes,
suenen clarines, trompas y atabales!"
Dejad los dulces regalos,
y el blando lecho dejadle;
Socorred a vuestra patria,
y librad a vuestros padres,
no se os haga cuesta arriba,
dejad el amor suave,
porque en los honrados pechos
en tales tiempos no cabe.
"¡Al arma, capitanes,
suenen clarines, trompas y atabales!"
Anteponed el honor
al gusto, pues menos vale,
que aquel que no le tuviere,
hoy aquí podrá alcanzalle;
que en honradas ocasiones,
y peligros semejantes,
se suelen premiar las armas
conforme el brazo pujante.
"¡Al arma, capitanes,
suenen clarines, trompas y atabales!"
Dejad la seda y el brocado
vestid la malla y el ante,
embrazad la adarga al pecho,
tomad lanza y corvo alfange;
haced rostro a la fortuna;
tal ocasión no se escape;
mostrad el robusto pecho

Shall sink beneath the feet of all struck by a bitter blow;
In moments when fair honor's crown is offered to the
    brave
And dangers yawn around our State, deep as the deadly
    grave,
'Tis right strong arms and sturdy hearts should take the
    sword of might,
And eagerly for Fatherland descend into the fight.
        To arms, to arms, my captains!
        Sound, clarions; trumpets, blow;
        And let the thundering kettle-drum
        Give challenge to the foe.

"Then lay aside the silken robes, the glittering brocade;
Be all in vest of leather and twisted steel arrayed;
On each left arm be hung the shield, safe guardian of the
    breast,
And take the crooked scimitar and put the lance in rest,
And face the fortune of the day, for it is vain to fly,
And the coward and the braggart now alone are doomed
    to die.
And let each manly bosom show, in the impending fray,
A valor such as Mars himself in fury might display.
        To arms, to arms, my captains!
        Sound, clarions; trumpets, blow;
        And let the thundering kettle-drum
        Give challenge to the foe.

He spoke, and at his valiant words, that rang through all
    the square,
The veriest cowards of the town resolved to do and dare;
And stirred by honor's eager fire forth from the gate they
    stream,
And plumes are waving in the air, and spears and
    falchions gleam;
And turbaned heads and faces fierce, and smiles in anger
    quenched,
And sweating steeds and flashing spurs and hands in fury
    clenched,
Follow the fluttering banners that toward the vega swarm,
And many a voice re-echoes the words of wild alarm.
        To arms, to arms, my captains!
        Sound, clarions; trumpets, blow;
        And let the thundering kettle-drum
        Give the challenge to the foe.

And, like the timid lambs that crowd with bleatings in the
    fold,
When they advancing to their throats the furious wolf
    behold,
The lovely Moorish maidens, with wet but flashing eyes,
Are crowded in a public square and fill the air with cries;
And tho', like tender women, 'tis vain for them to arm,
Yet loudly they re-echo the words of the alarm.
To heaven they cry for succor, and, while to heaven they
    pray,
They call the nights they love so well to arm them for the
    fray.

al furor del fiero Marte.
"¡Al arma, capitanes,
suenen clarines, trompas y atabales!"
A la voz mal entonada,
los ánimos más cobardes,
del honor estimulados.
ardiendo en cólera salen
con mil penachos vistosos
adornados los turbantes,
y siguiendo las banderas
van diciendo sin pararse:
"¡Al arma, capitanes,
suenen clarines, trompas y atabales!"
Cual tímidas ovejuelas,
que ven el lobo delante,
las bellas y hermosas moras
llenan de quejas el aire;
y aunque con femenil pecho
la que más puede más hace;
pidiendo favor al cielo
van diciendo por las calles:
"¡Al arma, capitanes,
suenen clarines, trompas y atabales!"
Acudieron al asalto
los moros más principales.
formándose en escuadrón
del vulgo y particulares;
contra doce mil cristianos,
que están talando sus panes,
toman las armas furiosos,
repitiendo en su lenguaje:
"¡Al arma, capitanes,
suenen clarines, trompas y atabales!"

> To arms, to arms, my captains!
> Sound, clarions; trumpets, blow;
> And let the thundering kettle-drum
> Give challenge to the foe.

The foremost Moorish nobles, Molina's chosen band,
Rush forward from the city the invaders to withstand.
There marshalled in a squadron with shining arms they
    speed,
Like knights and noble gentlemen, to meet their country's
    need.
Twelve thousand Christians crowd the plain, twelve
    thousand warriors tried,
They fire the homes, they reap the corn, upon the vega
    wide;
And in the warriors of Molina their furious lances ply,
And in their own Arabian tongue they raise the rallying
    cry.
> To arms, to arms, my captains!
> Sound, clarions; trumpets, blow;
> And let the thundering kettle-drum
> Give challenge to the foe.

EPIPHANIUS WILSON

Face Like a Flower

—Open the door to me,
Open it, face like a flower;
You have been mine since you were a child,
How much more so now.—
She with the face like a flower
Went down and opened the door;
They went to the garden
Hand in hand together.
Under a green rose tree
They set their table.
Eating and drinking
They fell asleep together.
When it was midnight
He awoke lamenting:
—What pain I have in my side,
Here in my side!—
—I will bring a learned doctor
For your healing.
I will give you a bag of money
For your spending.
I will bring you fresh bread
For your eating.—
—When you have killed a man
You talk of healing![15]

Cara de flor

—Abridme, cara de flor,
abridme la puerta.
Desde chica érais mía;
en demás ahora.—
Bajó cara de flor
abrirle la puerta;
toman mano con mano,
junto se van a la huerta.
Bajó un rosal verde,
allí metieron la mesa.
En comiendo y bebiendo,
junto quedaron dormiendo.
Al fin de media noche,
se despertó quejando:
—Dolor tengo en el lado,
que me responde al costado.
—Os traeré médico valido
que os vaiga mirando.
Os daré dinero en bolsa
que os vaiga gastando.
Os daré fodolas frescas
que vaigas comiendo.
—Despúes que matáis al hombre
miráis de sanarlo.

W. S. MERWIN

---

15. This ballad is one of the most beautiful love poems of the ancient Spanish Jews. The Jews of Spain called themselves *Sephardim*, which meant "the inhabitants of *Sepharad* or Spain."

Lady Alda's Dream

In Paris Lady Alda dwelled,
Proud Roland's promised bride,
Three hundred maids of honor there
Sat with her side by side;
Of all the maidens in the land
None fairer could you choose,
They all had on their silken robes,
And their embroidered shoes.

Around a single board they sat,
A single meal to share,
But Lady Alda sat alone,
The fairest of the fair;
A hundred wove the satin fine,
A hundred spun the gold,
A hundred played the music sweet
That cheered her heart and soul.

And as they struck the tuneful chords,
Their lady sank to sleep,
And while she slept she dreamed a dream,
That almost made her weep;
With frightened eyes she wakened up,
Her limbs quaking in fear,
She gave a cry so loud and shrill
That the whole town could hear.

"O Lady Alda what is this?
What is that fearful cry?"
"O maidens what a dream I've had,
I thought that I would die!
I found myself upon a hill
In a deserted place,
And then I saw a wild hawk fly
And from my hillock race.

A fierce eagle was in pursuit,
And sought to strike him down,
The panting hawk a shelter sought
Beneath my silken gown;
The furious eagle drew him forth,
While the poor hawk did shriek,
And struck its claws into his plumes,
And tore him with its beak."

"O Lady!" said her waiting maid,
"This dream is plain to me;
The wild hawk is thy noble spouse
Who came across the sea;
The eagle is thy royal self
With whom he is to wed,
The high hill is the holy Church,
Where nuptials will be said."

"If this be true, dear friend of mine,
I shall reward thee well;"
But morning dawned and letters came
In blood their words did tell
A tale of woe, a dismal tale,

Romance de Doña Alda

En París está doña Alda,
la esposa de don Roldán,
trescientas damas con ella
para bien la acompañar:
todas visten un vestido,
todas calzan un calzar,
todas comen a una mesa,
todas comían de un pan,
si no era doña Alda
que era la mayoral.
Las ciento hilaban el oro
las ciento tejen cendal,
ciento tañen instrumentos
para a doña Alda alegrar.
Al son de los instrumentos
doña Alda adormido se ha;
ensoñado había un sueño,
un sueño de gran pesar.
Despertó despavorida
con un dolor sin igual,
los gritos daba tan grandes
se oían en la ciudad.
—¿Qué es aquesto, mi señora,
qué es lo que os hizo mal?
—Un sueño soñé, doncellas,
que me ha dado gran pesar:
que me veía en un monte,
en un desierto lugar,
y de so los montes altos.
un azor vide volar;
tras dél viene una aguililla
que lo ahincaba muy mal.
El azor con grande cuita
metióse so mi brial;
el águila con gran ira
de allí lo iba a sacar;
con las uñas lo despluma,
con el pico lo deshace.
Allí habló su camarera,
bien oiréis lo que dirá:
—Aquese sueño, señora,
bien os lo entiendo soltar:
el azor es vuestro esposo,
que de España viene ya;
el águila sodes vos,
con la cual ha de casar,
y aquel monte era la iglesia
donde os han de velar.
—Si es así, mi camarera,
bien te lo entiendo pagar.
Otro día de mañana
cartas de lejos le traen;
tintas venían de fuera,
de dentro escritas con sangre,
que su Roldán era muerto
en la caza de Roncesvalles.

That rang throughout the halls,
Her peerless Roland had been slain
By Moors at Roncesvalles.

JAMES YOUNG GIBSON

The Wandering Knight's Song

My ornaments are arms,
My pastime is in war,
My bed is cold upon the wold,
My lamp yon star.

My journeyings are long,
My slumbers short and broken;
From hill to hill I wander still,
Kissing thy token.

I ride from land to land,
I sail from sea to sea:
Some day more kind I fate may find,
Some night kiss thee!

JOHN GIBSON LOCKHART

La constancia

Mis arreos son las armas,
mi descanso es pelear,
mi cama las duras peñas,
mi dormir siempre velar.
Las manidas son escuras,
los caminos por usar,
el cielo con sus mudanzas
ha por bien de me dañar,
andando de sierra en sierra
por orillas de la mar,
por probar si en mi ventura
hay lugar donde avadar.
Pero por vos, mi señora,
todo se ha de comportar.

RENAISSANCE

Juan del Encina

Spain, 1469–1529

Juan del (or de la) Encina, one of the great figures of the Spanish Renaissance, has often been called the father of the Spanish theater. The many short religious plays (*autos* and eclogues) that he wrote gave the drama of Spain an auspicious start. They were presented on a small stage in the palace of the Duke of Alba.

Encina's principal contribution to theatrical development was to secularize the medieval religious drama of Spain. He was also a musician of note and an extraordinarily gifted poet. One of the leading figures in Spanish art music of the Renaissance, he was the most prolific composer in the famous *Cancionero del palacio (Palace Song Book) ca.* 1528, lost for almost four hundred years until it was discovered by the musicologist Francisco Asenjo Barbieri in 1870. Encina composed sixty-eight songs in this priceless collection of over five hundred pieces. His poetic work was collected in his own *Cancionero*, which was first published in 1496, by which date many of his lyrics had become so popular that it was widely thought they were the products of anonymous folk poets.

Let Us Eat and Drink

Come, let's enjoy the passing hour;
For mournful thought
Will come unsought.

Come, let's enjoy the fleeting day.
And banish toil, and laugh at care;
For who would grief and sorrow bear,
When he can throw his griefs away?
Away, away!—begone! I say;
For mournful thought
Will come unsought.

So let's come forth from misery's cell,
And bury all our whims and woes;
Wherever pleasure flits and goes,
O, there we'll be! O, there we'll dwell!
'Tis there we'll dwell! 'Tis wise and well;
For mournful thought
Will come unsought.

Yes, open all your heart; be glad,—
Glad as a linnet on the tree;
Laugh, laugh away,—and merrily
Drive every dream away that's sad.
Who sadness takes for joy is mad;
And mournful thought
Will come unsought.

Gasajémonos de hucia

Gasajémonos de hucia,
que el pesar
viénese sin le buscar.

Gasajemos esta vida
descruciemos del trabajo,
quien pudiere haber gasajo
del cordojo se despida:
déle, déle despedida,
que el pesar
viénese sin le buscar.

De los enojos huyamos
con todos nuestros poderes,
andemos tras los placeres,
los pesares aburramos:
tras los placeres corramos,
que el pesar
viénese sin le buscar.

Hagamos siempre por ser
alegres y gasajosos,
cuidados tristes penosos
huyamos de los tener:
busquemos siempre el placer,
que el pesar
viénese sin le buscar.

SIR JOHN BOWRING

Don't Shut Your Door

Don't shut your door.—don't shut your door:
If Love should come and call,
'T will be no use at all.

If Love command, you'd best obey,—
Resistance will but hurt you,—
And make, for that's the safest way,
Necessity a virtue.
So don't resist his gentle sway,
Nor shut your door if he should call,—
For that's no use at all.

I've seen him tame the wildest beast,
And strengthen, too, the weakest:
He loves him most who plagues him least;
His favorites are the meekest.
The privileged guests who grace his feast
Have ne're opposed his gentle call,—
For that's no use at all.

He loves to tumble upside down
All classes, all connections;
Of those who fear or wear a crown
He mingles the affections,
Till all by Love is overthrown;
And moated gate or castle-wall
Will be no use at all.

He is a strange and wayward thing,—
Young. blind, and full of malice;
He makes a shepherd of a king,
A cottage of a palace.
'T is vain to murmur; and to fling
Your thoughts away in grief and gall
Will be no use at all.

He makes the coward brave, he wakes
The sleepy with his thunders;
In mirth he revels, and mistakes,
And miracles, and wonders;
And many a man he prisoner makes,
And bolts the door:—you cry and call;
But 't is no use at all.

Ninguno cierre las puertas

Ninguno cierre las puertas
si amor viniere a llamar,
que no le ha de aprovechar.

Al amor obedezcamos
con muy presta voluntad,
y pues es necesidad
de fuerza virtud hagamos:
al amor no resistamos
nadie cierre a su llamar,
que no le ha de aprovechar.

Amor amansa al más fuerte
y al más flaco fortalece,
al que menos le obedece
más le aqueja con su muerte
a su buena o mala suerte:
nadie debe repugnar,
que no le ha de aprovechar.

Amor muda los estados
las vidas y condiciones,
conforme los corazones
de los bien enamorados:
resistir a sus cuidados
nadie debe procurar,
que no le ha de aprovechar.

Aquel soberano amor
que se pinta niño y ciego,
hace al pastor palaciego
y al palaciego pastor:
contra su pena y dolor
ninguno debe lidiar,
que no le ha de aprovechar.

El que es amor verdadero
despierta al enamorado,
hace el medroso esforzado
y muy pulido al grosero:
quien es de amor prisionero
no salga de du mandar,
que no le ha de aprovechar.

SIR JOHN BOWRING

Gil Vincente
Spain, *ca.* 1470–1539

Portuguese-born Gil Vicente, one of the better dramatists of his epoch, wrote many beautiful lyric poems in Spanish. Some of his religious *autos* are partly in Portuguese, partly in Spanish. He was not influenced by the Italian poets but followed the simple, spontaneous language of the popular poetry of Spain. Some of his lyrics in this vein are among the most beautiful in the Spanish language. Vicente was also known as one of the leading Erasmists of his day.

She Is Wild

She is wild! She is wild!
Who will speak to the child?
On the hills pass her hours,
As a shepherdess free;
She is fair as the flowers,
She is wild as the sea!
She is wild! She is wild!
Who will speak to the child?

GOERGE TICKNOR

I Will Have No Husband—No!

They say they'll to my wedding go;
But I will have no husband—no!

I'll rather live serene and still
Upon a solitary hill,
Then bend me to another's will,
And be a slave in weal or woe:
No! I will have no husband—no!

No! mother! I've no wish to prove
The doubtful joys of wedded love—
And from those flowery pathways rove
Where innocence and comfort grow—
No! I will have no husband—no!

And heaven, I'm sure, ne'er meant that he
Should thy young daughter's husband be:
We have no common sympathy—
So let youth's bud unbroken blow—
For I will have no husband—no!

SIR JOHN BOWRING

Fair Is the Maiden

Fair is the maiden, who can be
As fair and beautiful as she?

Sailor, tell me from your ship
That sails the boundless sea,
Is there ship, or sail, or star
As beautiful as she?

Knight in shining armor clad,
O, did you ever see
Palfrey, arms, or battlefield
As beautiful as she?

Shepherd, as you guard your flock,
Tell me, could there be
Meadow, flock, or mountain range
As beautiful as she?

JOHN A. CROW

¡Sañosa está la niña!

¡Sañosa está la niña!
¡Ay, Dios!, ¿quién le hablaría?
En la sierra anda la niña
su ganado a repastar,
hermosa como las flores,
sañosa como la mar.
Sañosa como la mar
está la niña.
¡Ay, Dios!, ¿quién le hablaría?

Dicen que me case yo

Dicen que me case yo:
no quiero marido, no.

Más quiero vivir segura
n'esta sierra a mi soltura
que no estar en ventura
si casaré bien o no.
Dicen que me case yo:
no quiero marido, no,

Madre, no seré casada
por no ver vida cansada,
y quizá mal empleada
la gracia que Dios me dio.
Dicen que me case yo:
no quiero marido, no.

No será ni es nacido
tal para ser mi marido;
y pues que tengo sabido
que la flor yo me la só,
dicen que me case yo:
no quiero marido, no.

Muy graciosa es la doncella

Muy graciosa es la doncella
¡cómo es bella y hermosa!

Digas tú, el marinero
que en las naves vivías,
si la nave o la vela o la estrella
es tan bella.

Digas tú, el caballero
que las armas vestías,
si el caballo o las armas o la guerra
es tan bella.

Digas tú, el pastorcico
que el ganadico guardas,
si el ganado o los valles o la sierra
es tan bella.

Cristóbal de Castillejo

Spain, *ca.* 1490–1550

Castillejo was attached to the court of Ferdinand of Bohemia, the brother of Charles V. He was a cleric who led an irregular life, somewhat like that of Juan Ruiz, the archpriest of Hita. His poems often wavered between religious sentiment and lewdness. He was a follower of the ancient Spanish verse forms, which he managed beautifully.

Some Day

Some day, some day,
O troubled breast,
Shalt thou find rest.
If Love in thee
To grief give birth,
Six feet of earth
Can more than he;
There calm and free,
And unoppressed,
Shalt thou find rest.
The unattained
In life at last,
When life is passed,
Shall all be gained;
And no more pained,
No more distressed,
Shalt thou find rest.

Alguna vez

Alguna vez,
O pensamiento,
serás contento.
Si amor cruel
me hace guerra,
seis pies de tierra
podrán más que él:
allí sin él
y sin tormento,
serás contento.
Lo no alcanzado
en esta vida,
ella perdida
será hallado,
y sin cuidado
del mal que siento,
serás contento.

HENRY WADSWORTH LONGFELLOW

Antonio de Villegas

Spain, *ca.* 1500–1551

Villegas was born in Medina del Campo and is known mainly for his collection of poetry called the *Inventario de obras en metro castellano*, published in his native city in 1565. His best poems indicate his inspiration in the *cancioneros* and anonymous poetry of Spain.

Sleep and Dreams

On a rock where the moonlight gleam'd,
The maiden slept, and the maiden dream'd.

The maiden dream'd, for love had crept
Within her thoughtless heart, and seem'd
To picture him of whom she dream'd.
She dream'd,—and did I say she slept?
O no! her brain with visions teem'd:
The maiden on the rocky ground
Sleeps not, if love's wild dreams flit round.

Her heart's perplex'd by mystery,
And passing shades, and misty gleams;
And if she see not what she dreams,
She dreams of what she fain would see;
And 'tis her woe estranged to be,

En la peña

En la peña y sobre la peña
duerme la niña y sueña.

La niña que amor había
de amores se trasportaba;
con su amigo se soñaba,
soñaba, mas no dormía;
que la dama enamorada,
y en la peña,
no se duerme si amores sueña.

El corazón se le altera
con el sueño en que se vio;
si no vio lo que soñó
soñó lo que ver quisiera;
hace representación

While on the rocky mountain laid,
From all that cheers a love-sick maid.

And what is love, but dreams which thought,
Wild thought carves out of passion? throwing
Its veil aside, while, wing'd and growing,
The embryo's to existence brought,
False joys, fierce cares, with mysteries fraught;
As who by day of hunger dies,
Dreaming of feasts at midnight lies.

en la peña
de todo el sueño que sueña.

Sueños son que, amor, envías
a los que traes desvelados,
pagas despiertos cuidados
con fingidas alegrías;
quien muere de hambre los días,
de noche manjares sueña,
suso la peña.

SIR JOHN BOWRING

Pedro de Padilla

Spain, sixteenth century

Padilla was born in Linares in the first half of the sixteenth century. He joined the Carmelite order and became a Latin scholar of note; he also knew several modern languages. His *Tesoro de varias poesías* was first published in Madrid in 1575, and his *Romancero*, a collection of ballads of legendary and historic themes, appeared in 1583. He also composed a series of *coplas* imitating those of Jorge Manrique, but among his many poems those of a lighter lyrical nature have the most appeal.

Love Does What'er He Likes

Love does whate'er he likes, 'tis true,
But never what he ought to do.

It is, I find, his royal will
That I, o'erpower'd by love, should die,
And so 'tis his delight to fill
My cup with varied misery:
He tries my heart with every ill
That mortal patience ever knew,
Which surely he ought not to do!

There is no grief, there is no pain,
Which he inflicts not: when I fall
Subdued, he rouses me again,
And but to visit me with all
That ever bid a heart complain:
His embers do his birth renew,
Which, surely, they need not to do!

It would become him well to give,
For sorrows deep, and sufferings long,
One gleam of joy, one short reprieve,
One thought of bliss 'midst misery's throng.
But no! he flies the alternative,
And throws again the bolts he threw:—
He does not what he ought to do.

And ne'er a more obedient slave
Follow'd his banners; never one
Had higher claim, or ought to have—
What service wrought, what duties done,
What toils on shore, and risks on wave!

Hace el amor lo que quiere

Hace el amor lo que quiere,
¡mas ay! que no lo que debe.

Ha dado amor en gustar
de verme amando morir,
y ansí me hace sufrir
cuantos males puede dar:
hace su gusto en buscar
con que mi paciencia pruebe:
¡mas ay! que no lo que debe.

Ni hay mal ni desasosiego
con que deje de ofenderme,
y en llegando a deshacerme
vuelve a repararme luego:
hace que con su fuego
como fénix me renueve,
¡mas ay! que no lo que debe.

Debiera al menos un día,
pues me quiere atormentar,
para aliviarme en penar
darme una hora de alegría:
mas no lo hace, y porfía:
en hacer mi vida breve,
¡mas ay! que no lo que debe.

Ninguno con más cuidado
sus banderas ha seguido,
y en premio de lo servido
dejándome bien pagado,
hace por su desenfado

He does whate'er he will, 'tis true,
But never what he ought to do!

que tan dura carga lleve:
¡mas ay! que no lo que debe.

SIR JOHN BOWRING

The Wandering Knight

The mountain towers with haughty brow,
Its paths deserted be;
The streamlets through their currents flow,
And wash the mallows-tree.

O mother mine! O mother mine!
That youth so tall and fair,
With lips that smile, and eyes that shine,
I saw him wandering there:
I saw him there when morning's glow
Was sparkling on the tree,—
With my five fingers, from below,
I beckoned, "Come to me!"
The streamlets through their currents flow,
And wash the mallows-tree.

SIR JOHN BOWRING

La sierra es alta

La sierra es alta
y áspera de subir;
los caños corren agua
y dan en el toronjil.

Madre, la mi madre
de cuerpo atán garrido,
por aquella sierra
de aquel lomo erguido
iba una mañana
el mi lindo amigo;
llaméle con mi toca
y con mis dedos cinco . . .
Los caños corren agua
y dan en el toronjil.

Poems from the *Cancioneros*

fifteenth and sixteenth centuries

Happy Vale of Tormes

Thou happy vale of Tormes,
  Grow rich with sunny showers;
For my little maiden cometh,
  She comes to gather flowers!

Let mirth be in thy forest,
  And wealth upon thy plain;
Let all thy fragrant meadows
  Burst forth to life again,
With the ruddy pink and iris,
  All fresh with summer showers;
For my little maiden cometh,
  She comes to gather flowers!

Let all the grasses glisten
  With pearly drops of dew;
Let all thy gardens sparkle
  With gems of every hue;
The sun drive forth his chariot,
  With all the rosy hours;
For my little maiden cometh,
  She comes to gather flowers!

Bend, bend your heads, ye bushes,
  Beneath the gentle gales;
Pipe forth from every thicket,
  Ye tuneful nightingales;

Dichoso Tormes

Fertiliza tu vega,
dichoso Tormes,
porque viene mi niña
cogiendo flores.

De la fértil vega
y el estéril bosque
los vecinos campos
maticen y broten
lirios y claveles
de varios colores
porque viene mi niña
cogiendo flores

Vierta el alba perlas
desde sus balcones
que prados amenos
maticen y borden;
y el sol envidioso
pare el rubio coche;
porque viene mi niña
cogiendo flores.

El céfiro blando
sus yerbas retoce
y en las frescas ramas
claros ruiseñores

To greet the day that dawneth,
  And gladden all the bowers;
For my little maiden cometh,
  She comes to gather flowers!

saludan el día
con sus dulces voces;
porque viene mi niña
cogiendo flores.

JAMES YOUNG GIBSON

Galleys of Spain

Ye galleys of our land
  Arrest your oars again,
That he, my love, may rest,
  Who drags your heavy chain.

Bright galleys! on the surge
  Ye bear with every stroke,
The surges of my thoughts,
  Which fear and love awoke.
Upon the ocean's breast
  Its fair winds move again;
So let my lover rest
  Who drags your heavy chain.

The waters of the sea
  Though cold, inflame my soul;
My love's pure light would glow
  E'en at the icy pole.
That love on whirlwind's breast
  Would fly across the main,
To let my lover rest
  Who drags your heavy chain.

O wait! bright galleys now,
  In some fair harbour wait,
Or guard the narrow pass
  Of some not-distant strait;
Or, at the maid's behest,
  In tranquil port remain,
That he, my love, may rest,
  Who drags your heavy chain.

The winter hours draw nigh;
  Come, galleys, then, and stay,
In cheerful solitude,
  Within a sheltered bay
There ye may anchor rest,
  For there no dangers reign—
So let my lover rest
  Who drags your heavy chain.

Galeritas de España

Galeritas de España
parad los remos,
para que descanse
mi amado preso.

Galeritas nuevas
que en el mar soberbio
levantáis las olas
de mi pensamiento;
pues el viento sopla
navegad sin remos
para que descanse
mi amado preso.

En el agua fría
encendéis mi fuego,
que un fuego amoroso
arde entre los hielos;
quebrantad las olas
y volad con viento
para que descanse
mi amado preso.

Plegue a Dios que deis
en peñascos recios,
defendiendo el paso
de un lugar estrecho;
y que estéis parados
sin temer encuentro
para que descanse
mi amado preso.

Plegue a Dios que os manden
pasar el invierno
ocupando el paso
de un lugar estrecho;
y que quebrantados
os volváis al puerto,
para que descanse
mi amado preso.

SIR JOHN BOWRING

'Tis Time to Rise!

Long sleep has veiled my spirit's eyes:
'Tis time to rise!—'tis time to rise!

O, 'tis a dull and heavy sleep!
As if death's robe had wrapped the soul;

Mucho ha que el alma duerme

Mucho ha que el alma duerme,
bien será que recuerde.

Duerme sueño tan pesado
que como muerta cayó

As if the poisons, vices steep
In life's deep-dregged and mingled bowl,
Had chilled the blood, and dimmed the eyes:
But, lo! the sun towers o'er the deep:
'Tis time to rise!—'tis time to rise!

But angels sang in vain,—above
Their voices blended: "Soul, awake!
Hark to yon babe!—what wondrous love
Bids God an infant's weakness take!—
Long hast thou slept,—that infant's cries
Shall the dark mist of night remove:
'Tis time to rise!—'tis time to rise!"

SIR JOHN BOWRING

fuego que la adormeció
el veneno del pecado:
y pues el sol deseado
en los ojos ya le hiere,
bien será que recuerde.

Si ángeles no han podido
despertarla con cantar,
despierte, oyendo llorar
a Dios por ella nacido:
muy larga noche ha dormido,
y pues tal día le viene,
bien será que recuerde.

Yield, Thou Castle!

Yield, thou castle! yield!—
I march me to the field.

Thy walls are proud and high,
My thoughts all dwell with thee;
Now yield thee! yield thee!—I
Am come for victory;
I march me to the field.

Thy halls are fair and gay,
And there resides my grief;
Thy bridge, thy covered way,
Prepare for my relief;
I march me to the field.

Thy towers sublimely rise
In beauty's brightest glow;
There, there, my comfort lies.—
O, give me welcome now!
I march me to the field.

SIR JOHN BOWRING

Castillo, dáteme

Castillo, dáteme, date,
sino dártehe yo combate.

Castillo de alto cimiento
adó está mi pensamiento,
procede de ti el contento
que el corazón arrebate:
sino dártehe yo combate.

Castillo hermoso y dorado
do aposenta mi cuidado,
muéstrame tu puente o vado
por dar a mis penas mate,
sino dártehe yo combate.

Castillo de gran altura
dechado de la hermosura,
pues en ti está mi ventura
sus tiros y armas abate,
sino dártehe yo combate.

While My Lady Sleepeth

While my lady sleepeth,
    Zephyr, gently blow:
Wake her not, I pray thee,
    Lest she wake to woe.

Gently blow, gay Zephyr!
    Noiseless be thy tread—
Glide on wings of silence
    O'er her slumbering head.
Breathe as though the pearl-drops
    Hung on twilight's bed,
Where thy touch would linger
    As thy breezes blow.
Wake her not, I pray thee,
    Lest she wake to woe.

Mientras duerme mi niña

Mientras duerme mi niña,
céfiro alegre,
sopla más quedito,
no la recuerdes.

Sopla manso viento
al sueño suave,
que enseña a ser grave
con su movimiento;
dale el dulce aliento
que entre perlas finas
a gozar caminas
y ufano vuelves;
sopla más quedito,
no la recuerdes.

Wake her not—she slumbers—
    Peace is on her breast.
O, would I deprive her
    Of one dream of rest?
No!—but how I envy,
    How I deem thee blest,
Who, my gentle lady,
    Softly cradles so.
Wake her not, I pray thee,
    Lest she wake to woe.

Mira no despierte
    del sueño en que duerme,
que temo que el verme
    causará mi muerte.
¡Dichosa tal suerte!
    ¡Venturosa estrella
si a niña tan bella
    alentar mereces!
Sopla más quedito,
    no la recuerdes.

SIR JOHN BOWRING

On My Lap He Slept

On my lap he slept, and my raven hair
Shelter'd him from the sunbeams there.
Love! shall I rouse him to tell him so?
            O no! O no!

I comb'd my raven locks with care,
For he oft on their tresses smil'd;
And they were scatter'd by breezes wild,
Breezes which stole the fairest too—
He was fann'd by those breezes; my raven hair
Shelter'd him from the sunbeams there;
Love! shall I wake him to tell him so?
            O no! O no!

He call'd me cruel—but if he knew
This heart of mine—I heard him say,
My raven locks, and my chestnut hue,
Were his life's charm, and his life's decay.
Siren!—he cried—and then he flew
To my lap, where he slept, and my raven hair
Shelter'd him from the sunbeams there.
Love! shall I rouse him and tell him so?
            O no! O no!

A la sombra de mis cabellos

A la sombra de mis cabellos
mi querido se adurmió:
¿si le recordaré o no?

Peinaba yo mis cabellos
con cuidado cada día,
y el viento los esparcía
revolviéndose con ellos,
y a su soplo y sombra de ellos
mi querido se adurmió:
¿si le recordaré o no?

Díceme que le da pena
el ser en extremo ingrata,
que le da vida y le mata
esta mi color morena,
y llamándome sirena
él junto a mí se adurmió:
¿si le recordaré o no?

SIR JOHN BOWRING

I Lifted Up My Eyes to See

I lifted up my eyes to see
One dearer than myself to me.

    To gaze, I lifted them on high,
And bent them down again to sigh;
For I'm unblest;—I know not why:
I may no smile of favour see
From one so very dear to me.

    Why should I gaze, O why! to feel
Love's flattering poison through me steal;
To be condemn'd without appeal,
Surprised, controll'd, subdued to be,
By one so very dear to me.

Alzé los ojos

Alzé los ojos y vi
a quien amo más que a mí.

Alzélos para mirar,
bajélos para penar,
pues que no puedo gozar
tan solamente de un sí,
de quien amo más que a mí.

Si no alzara la vista,
de amores no entrara en lista,
ni gustara tal conquista,
ni sintiera lo que sentí,
por quien amo más que a mí.

O! could I but expect to wear,
Love's flowery garlands bright and fair,
And drink the joys beyond compare,
Of love's enrapturing witchery
From one so very dear to me!

But thoughts like these are only meet,
As grief's ambassadors to greet;
O would they were of favours sweet,
And I were born a bliss to be
To one so very dear to me!

SIR JOHN BOWRING

Si han de ser galardonados,
yo los doy por bien alzados,
por los gozos sublimados
que con ellos comprendí,
de quien amo más que a mí.

Pues fueron embajadores
al corazón de dolores,
séanlo ya de favores
si para dicha nací,
de quien amo más que a mí.

The Prisoner's Romance

Sir gaoler! leave the spirit free,
The spirit is a wanderer still:
O gaoler! leave the spirit free,
And chain the body, if you will.

My eyes between the iron bars
Still throw their living glances round,
And they shall be as Northern Stars,
By which the friendly port is found;
And theirs shall be a tongue to be
Heard when the mortal voice is still.
O gaoler! leave the spirit free,
And chain the body, if you will.

You cannot, cannot chain the soul,
Although the body you confine:
The spirit bursts through all control,
And soon is free, and so is mine.
Love has unbounded mastery
In this your prison. You fulfill,
Sir gaoler, Love's supreme degree:
Love is the lord imperial still.
O gaoler! leave the spirit free,
And chain the body, if you will.

SIR JOHN BOWRING

Deje el alma

Deje el alma que es libre
señor alcaide,
deje el alma que es libre,
y el cuerpo guarde.

Deje que mis ojos
entre estas rejas
al cuerpo cautivo
sirvan de lenguas,
nadie los detenga
mirando hablen:
deje el alma que es libre,
señor alcaide,
deje el alma que es libre,
y el cuerpo guarde.

No prende las almas
quien prende el cuerpo,
que el alma se rinde
sólo al deseo,
y amor es el dueño
de aquesta cárcel:
deje el alma que es libre,
señor alcaide,
deje el alma que es libre,
y el cuerpo guarde.

Garlands of Spring Time

O thou gay spring time
  Cover'd with flowers,
Crown with thy garlands
  Passion like ours.

Crown with white lilies,
  Jasmines, and roses;
Every gay floweret
  That odour discloses—
Violets, vervains,
  Pinks and all flowers:
Crown with your garlands
  Passion like ours.

Verde primavera

Verde primavera
llena de flores,
coronad de guirnaldas
a mis amores.

De blanca azucena
de jazmín y rosa,
mosqueta olorosa,
violeta y verbena,
de claveles llena
y de otras mil flores:
coronad de guirnaldas
a mis amores.

The tresses of gold
 That imprison the soul,
The bright suns of heaven
 In glory that roll;
While I weep o'er my sorrows,
 And gather sweet flowers—
O crown with their garlands
 Passion like ours.

That forehead serene,
 Where love sits confest,
Adorn with the zephyrs
 And balm of the East.
Adorn that bright temple
 With incense of flowers—
And crown with thy garlands
 Passion like ours.

SIR JOHN BOWRING

Las madejas de oro
que matan y prenden,
los soles que encienden
y el bien que yo adoro,
mientras mi mal lloro
escogiendo flores:
coronad de guirnaldas
a mis amores.

La serena frente
donde amor se anida,
dejad guarnecida
de aljófar de oriente:
el templo luciente
ornad de colores:
coronad de guirnaldas
a mis amores.

I'll Never Be Married

No! no! I'll never married be,
But love, and love,   and yet be free.

I will not wear a captive's chain,
 Nor own a master: they who wed,
First go to jail, and then remain
 In everlasting fetters led.
I can't imagine what they gain.
No! no! I'll never married be,
But love, and love,   and yet be free.

A wife can't out of window look
 Without a husband's grumbling loud:
Each slip's recorded in a book:
 I won't submit! I own I'm proud,
Too proud such busy knaves to brook.
No! no! I'll never married be,
But love, and love,   and yet be free.

Unmarried, I command at will;
 And youths press forward to obey:
I find them glad and grateful still,
 And who so prompt to serve as they?
Will lords a bride's desire fulfil?
No! no! I'll never married be,
But love, and love,   and yet be free.

I often see a married pair,
 I know they curse their luckless fate:
I've seen a woman tear her hair,
 And of connubial blessings prate;
Yet daily sink beneath despair.
No! no! I'll never married be;
But love, and love,   and yet be free.

SIR JOHN BOWRING

No quiero ser casada

No quiero ser casada,
sino libre enamorada.

No me quiero cautivar
ni meterme en sujeción,
pues lo mismo es casar
que condenarse a prisión,
y por aquesta razón
cierto no seré casada,
sino libre enamorada.

Si os ponéis a la ventana
el marido está gruñendo,
dice que sois muger vana
que está recato mintiendo:
prometo, pues esto entiendo
que no seré yo casada,
sino libre enamorada.

Si rogáis algun amigo
que faga falta algo por vos,
queda bien agradecido
piensa se lo manda Dios:
pues esto miramos nos
¿no es locura ser casada?
sino libre enamorada.

Los buenos de los casados
sin parar están riñendo
renegando de sus hados:
cuando los vemos riendo
están contentos fingiendo
que nunca logra casada,
sino libre enamorada.

Amaryllis

She sleeps; Amaryllis
'Midst flowerets is laid;
And roses and lilies
Make the sweet shade.

The maiden is sleeping,
Where through the green hills,
Manzanares is creeping
Along with his rills.

Wake not Amaryllis,
Ye winds in the glade,
Where roses and lilies
Make the sweet shade!

The sun, while upsoaring,
Yet tarries awhile,
The bright rays adoring
Which stream from her smile.

The wood-music still is,
To rouse her afraid,
Where roses and lilies
Make the sweet shade.

La niña reposa

Mientras duerme la niña.
flores y rosas,
azucenas y lirios
le hacen sombra.

En el prado verde
la niña reposa
donde Manzanares
sus arroyos brota.
No se mueve el viento,
ramas ni hojas,
que azucenas y lirios
le hacen sombra.

El sol la obedece
y su paso acorta,
que son rayos bellos
sus ojos y boca.
Las aves no cantan
viendo tal gloria,
que azucenas y lirios
le hacen sombra.

SIR JOHN BOWRING

Garcilaso de la Vega
Spain, 1503–1536

The Golden Age in Spanish poetry began in 1543 with the publication of the poems of Garcilaso and Juan Boscán. The rhythm and musical quality so pronounced in this small volume have never been surpassed in Spanish. Garcilaso revolutionized the poetry of his country by writing in the verse forms of the Italian Renaissance. He made popular the eleven-syllable line, and he adopted the Italian lyrical concept, which through his genius became an integral part of the Spanish poetic tradition.

Garcilaso was the pastoral poet par excellence of Spain. His poems present an idealized, schematic world of idea, of perfect man living in a perfect state, the key to which was love. This world had little to do with observed reality. Such perfection of man and his world was contrary to the doctrine of original sin, and the Councils of Trent (1545–1563), which rigorously reformed the Catholic church when it was confronted by the Protestant Reformation, eventually put an end to such thinking. The pastoral tradition was also met head-on by the realism of Spanish picaresque novels, which overwhelmed it.

When I Sit Down to Contemplate My Case

When I sit down to contemplate my case,
And to review the stages of the way,
I find from where my steps went first astray,
They might have lost me in a darker maze:
But when these memories pass, around I gaze,
And wonder whence could come a doom so dark;
I know I die, and suffer more to mark
My care conclude with my concluding race.

Cuando me paro a contemplar mi estado

Cuando me paro a contemplar mi estado,
y a ver los pasos por do me ha traído,
hallo, según por do anduve perdido,
que a mayor mal pudiera haber llegado;

mas cuando del camino estó olvidado,
a tanto mal no sé por dó he venido;
sé que me acabo, y más he yo sentido
ver acabar conmigo mi cuidado.

Yes, die I will, and so my spirit free
From her who well will know to undo and slay me
If so she wishes, such her wish will be,
For since my own will does to death betray me,
Hers, which is less my friend, must compass too
My death—if not, what is it she will do?

J. H. WIFFEN

Yo acabaré, que me entregué sin arte
a quien sabrá perderme y acabarme
si ella quisiere, y aun sabrá querello;

que pues mi voluntad puede matarme,
la suya, que no es tanto de mi parte,
pudiendo, ¿qué hará sino hacello?

Lady, Thy Face Is Written in My Soul

Lady, thy face is written in my soul;
And whenso'er I wish to chant my praise,
On that illumined manuscript I gaze:
Thou the sweet scribe art, I but read the scroll.
In this dear study all my days shall roll;
And though this book can ne'er the half receive
Of what in thee is charming, I believe
In that I see not, and thus see the whole
With faith's clear eye. I but received my breath
To love thee, my ill genius shaped the rest;
'Tis now that soul's mechanic act to love thee:
I love thee, owe thee more than I confessed;
I gained life by thee, cruel though I prove thee;
In thee I live, through thee I bleed to death.

J. H. WIFFEN

Escrito está en mi alma vuestro gesto

Escrito está en mi alma vuestro gesto,
y cuanto yo escrebir de vos deseo;
vos sola lo escrebistes, yo lo leo
tan solo, que aun de vos me guardo en esto.

En esto estoy y estaré siempre puesto;
que aunque no cabe en mí cuanto en vos veo,
de tanto bien lo que no entiendo creo,
tomando ya la fe por presupuesto.

Yo no nací sino para quereros;
mi alma os ha cortado a su medida;
por hábito del alma misma os quiero.

Cuanto tengo confieso yo deberos;
por vos nací, por vos tengo la vida,
por vos he de morir, y por vos muero.

From That Illumined Face

From that illumined face, pure, mild, and sweet,
A living spirit in keen lightning flies;
And by perception of my eager eyes,
I feel it stays not till their orbs repeat
Its ardour; blandly on the track they meet,
Which my charmed spirit, winged with warmth, pursues,
Undone, and clamouring for the good it views:
When absent, Memory in her holy heat
Paints its passed beauty, till my soul will glow,
Thinking it real, and divinely stirred,
On tiptoe fly to its embrace, but meeting
Nought but repulse from its angelic foe,
Whose aspect guards the gate, it dies with beating
Its heart against it, like a captive bird.

J. H. WIFFEN

De aquella vista buena y excelente

De aquella vista buena y excelente
salen espíritus vivos y encendidos,
y siendo por mis ojos recibidos,
me pasan hasta donde el mal se siente.

Encuéntranse el camino fácilmente,
con los míos, que, de tal calor movidos,
salen fuera de mí como perdidos,
llamados de aquel bien que está presente.

Ausente en mí, memoria la imagino;
mis espíritus, pensando que la vían,
se mueven y se encienden sin medida;

mas no hallando fácil el camino,
que los suyos entrando detenían,
revientan por salir do no hay salida.

Thinking the Path I Journeyed

Thinking the path I journeyed led me right,
I have fallen on such mishap, that not the pleas
Of fancy, nor the wildest images
Can for an instant minister delight.
The green field seems a desert, starry night
Obscure—the sprightliest conversation dead—
Sweet music harsh, and my most favorite bed

Pensando que el camino iba derecho

Pensando que el camino iba derecho,
vine a parar en tanta desventura,
que imaginar no puedo, aun con locura,
algo de que esté un rato satisfecho.
El ancho campo me parece estrecho,
la noche clara para mí es oscura,
la dulce compañía amarga y dura,

Of odorous violets, the hard field of fight.
Of sleep—(if sleep I have) that part alone
Visits my weary soul, which surely is
The frightful synonym of death, and last,
I deem, whate'er may be my spirit's tone,
Ere half run out its sands of weariness,
Each passing hour still heavier than the past.

J. H. WIFFEN

y duro campo de batalla el lecho.

Del sueño, si hay alguno, aquella parte
sola que es ser imagen de la muerte
se aviene con el alma fatigada.

En fin, que como quiera estoy de arte,
que juzgo ya por hora menos fuerte,
aunque en ella me vi, la que es pasada.

The Soft Shades of the Lily and Red Rose

The soft shades of the lily and red rose
Show their sweet colors on thy chaste warm cheek,
Thy radiant looks, so tender and so meek
Arouse the heart yet hold it in repose.
And as thy hair like strands of gold now glows
Casting its sheen upon thy neck so white,
Touched by the breeze that stirs and gives them light
Thy tresses in wild disarray do blow.
Pluck off the ripe fruit of thy joyous spring
Before time with its swift and angry sting
Covers thy precious head with lasting snow.
The icy wind will chill the tender rose,
And fleeting years bring change to everything
That Nature's law might keep its ordered flow.

ANONYMOUS TRANSLATOR

En tanto que de rosa y azucena

En tanto que de rosa y azucena
se muestra la color en vuestro gesto,
y que vuestro mirar ardiente, honesto,
enciende al corazón y lo refrena;

y en tanto que el cabello, que en la vena
del oro se escogió, con vuelo presto,
por el hermoso cuello blanco, enhiesto,
el viento mueve, esparce y desordena:

coged de vuestra alegre primavera
el dulce fruto, antes que el tiempo airado
cubra de nieves la hermosa cumbre.

Marchitará la rosa el viento helado,
todo lo mudará la edad ligera
por no hacer mudanza en su costumbre.

If Lamentations and Complaints Could Rein

If lamentations and complaints could rein
The course of rivers as they rolled along,
And move on desert hills, attired in song,
The savage forests, if they could constrain
Fierce tigers and chill rocks to entertain
The sound, and with less urgency than mine,
Lead tyrant Pluto and stern Proserpine,
Sad and subdued with magic of their strain;
Why will not my vexatious being, spent
In misery and in tears, to softness soothe
A bosom steeled against me? with more ruth
An ear of rapt attention should be lent
The voice of him that mourns himself for lost,
Than that which sorrowed for a forfeit ghost!

J. H. WIFFEN

Si quejas y lamentos pueden tanto

Si quejas y lamentos pueden tanto
que enfrenaron el curso de los ríos
y en los desiertos montes y sombríos
los árboles movieron con su canto;

si conviertieron a escuchar su llanto
los fieros tigres, y peñascos fríos,
si en fin con menos casos que los míos
bajaron a los reinos del espanto:

¿por qué no ablandará mi trabajosa
vida, en miseria y lágrimas pasada,
un corazón conmigo endurecido?

Con más piedad debría ser escuchada
la voz del que se llora por perdido,
que la del que perdió y llora otra cosa.

As the Fond Mother, When Her Suffering Child

As the fond mother, when her suffering child
Asks some sweet object of desire with tears,
Grants it, although her fond affection fears
'T will double all its sufferings; reconciled
To more appalling evils by the mild

Como la tierna madre que el doliente

Como la tierna madre que el doliente
hijo le está con lágrimas pidiendo
alguna cosa, de la cual comiendo,
sabe que ha de doblarse el mal que siente,

y aquel piadoso amor no le consiente

Influence of present pity, shuts her ears
To prudence; for an hour's repose, prepares
Long sorrow, grievous pain: I, lost and wild,
Thus feed my foolish and infected thought
That asks for dangerous aliment; in vain
I would with hold it; clamorous, again
It comes, and weeps, and I'm subdued, and naught
Can o'er that childish will a victory gain:
So have despair and gloom their triumphs wrought!

SIR JOHN BOWRING

que considere el daño que haciendo
lo que la pide hace, va corriendo,
y dobla el mal, y aplaca el acidente:

así a mi enferno y loco pensamiento,
que en su daño os me pide, yo querría
quitar este mortal mantenimiento,

mas pídemelo, y llora cada día
tanto que cuanto quiere le consiento,
olvidando su muerte y aun la mía.

Lines from the First Elegy

And now, larger than ever lies the curse
On this our time; and all that went before
Keeps altering its face from bad to worse;
And each of us has felt the touch of war—
War after war, and exile, dangers, fear—
And each of us is weary to the core
Of seeing his own blood along a spear
And being alive because it missed its aim;
Some folks have lost their goods and all their gear.
And everything is gone, even the name
Of house and home and wife and memory;
And what's the use of it? A little fame?
The nation's thanks? A place in history?
One day they'll write a book, and then we'll see.

JAMES B. TREND

Y agora muy mayor la desventura

Y agora muy mayor la desventura
de aquesta nuestra edad, cuyo progreso
muda de un mal en otro su figura.
¿A quién ya de nosotros el exceso
de guerras, de peligros y destierro
no toca, y no ha cansado el gran proceso?
¿Quién no vio desparcir su sangre al hierro
del enemigo? ¿Quién no vio su vida
perder mil veces y escapar por yerro?
¿De cuántos queda y quedara perdida
la casa y la mujer y la memoria,
y de otros la hacienda despedida?
¿Qué se saca de aquesto? ¿Alguna gloria?
Algunos premios o agradecimientos?
Sabrálo quien leyere nuestra historia.

From the First Eclogue

(SALICIO'S PLAINT)

Through thee the silence of the shaded glen,
Through thee the horror of the lonely mountain,
Pleased me no less than the resort of men;
The breeze, the summer wood, and lucid fountain,
The purple rose, white lily of the lake,
Were sweet for thy sweet sake;
For thee the fragrant primrose, dropped with dew,
Was wished when first it blew!
O, how completely was I in all this
Myself deceiving! O, the different part
That thou wert acting, covering with a kiss
Of seeming love the traitor in thy heart!
This my severe misfortune, long ago,
Did the soothsaying raven, sailing by
On the black storm, with hoarse, sinister cry,
Clearly presage! In gentleness of woe,
Flow forth, my tears!—'tis meet that ye should flow!

How oft, when slumbering in the forest brown,
Deeming it Fancy's mystical deceit,
Have I beheld my fate in dreams fore shown!
One day, methought that from the noontide heat
I drove my flocks to drink of Tagus' flood,

Écloga I

Por ti el silencio de la selva umbrosa,
por ti la esquividad y apartamiento
del solitario monte me agradaba;
por ti la verde hierba, el fresco viento,
el blanco lirio y colorada rosa
y dulce primavera deseaba.
¡Ay, cuánto me engañaba!
¡Ay, cuán diferente era
y cuán de otra manera
lo que en tu falso pecho se escondía!
Bien claro con su voz me lo decía
la siniestra corneja repitiendo
la desventura mía.
Salid sin duelo, lágrimas, corriendo.

¡Cuántas veces, durmiendo en la floresta,
reputándolo yo por desvarío,
vi mi mal entre sueños desdichado!
Soñaba que en el tiempo del estío
llevaba, por pasar allí la siesta,
a beber en el Tajo mi ganado;
y después de llegado,
sin saber de cuál arte,

And, under curtain of its bordering wood,
Take my cool siesta; but, arrived, the stream,
I know not by what magic, changed its track,
And in new channels, by an unused way,
Rolled its warped waters back;
Whilst I, scorched, melting with the heat extreme,
Went ever following, in their flight astray,
The wizard waves! In gentleness of woe,
Flow forth, my tears!—'tis meet that ye should flow!

In the charmed ear of what beloved youth
Sounds thy sweet voice? on whom revolvest thou
Thy beautiful blue eyes? on whose proved truth
Anchors thy broken faith? who presses now
Thy laughing lip, and hopes thy heaven of charms,
Locked in the embraces of thy two white arms?

J. H. WIFFEN

por desusada parte
y por nuevo camino el agua se iba;
ardiendo ya con la calor estiva,
el curso, enajenado, iba siguiendo
del agua fugitiva.
Salid sin duelo, lágrimas, corriendo.

Tu dulce habla ¿en cúya oreja suena?
Tus claros ojos ¿a quién los volviste?
¿Por quién tan sin respeto me trocaste?
Tu quebrantada fe ¿dó la pusiste?
¿Cuál es el cuello que, como en cadena,
de tus hermosos brazos anudaste?

Jorge de Montemayor
Spain, 1520–1561

Montemayor, a Portuguese by birth, spent most of his life in Spain and became one of the masters of Spanish prose. He was the author of the first pastoral novel in Spanish, the famous *Diana* (*ca.* 1559), in which is presented an idealized world of shepherds and shepherdesses, far removed from objective reality. Several very good poems are sprinkled throughout the novel, and Montemayor also published a two-volume *Cancionero* of his poetry in 1558. However, it is the elegant prose of the *Diana* which established this work as a landmark in Spanish literature. For the readers of today, this novel, except for its poems, may seem rather soporific.

To a Lock of Diana's Hair

Ah me! thou Relic of that faithless fair!
Sad changes have I suffered since that day
When, in this valley, from her long loose hair,
I bore thee, Relic of my Love! away.
Well did I then believe Diana's truth,
For soon true Love each jealous care represses;
And fondly thought that never other youth
Should wanton with the Maiden's unbound tresses.

Here on the cold clear Ezla's breezy side
My hand amid her ringlets wont to rove,
She proferred now the lock, and now denied,
With all the baby playfulness of Love.
Here the false Maid, with many an artful tear,
Made me each rising thought of doubt discover,
And vowed and wept—till Hope had ceased to fear,
Ah me! beguiling like a child her lover.

Witness thou how that fondest falsest hair
Has sighed and wept on Ezla's sheltered shore,
And vowed eternal truth, and made me swear,
My heart no jealousy should harbor more.
Ah! tell me! could I but believe those eyes?
Those lovely eyes with tears my cheek bedewing,

Redondillas á unos cabellos prendidos con un cordón de seda verde

Cabellos, ¡cuánta mudanza
he visto después que os ví,
y cuán mal parece ahí
ese color de esperanza!

¡Ay! cabellos, cuantos días
yo mi Diana miraba.
Si os traía ó si os dejaba,
con otras mil niñerías!

Y, ¡cuántas veces llorando
(¡ay, lágrimas engañosas!)
pedía celos de cosas
de que yo estaba burlando!

Los ojos que me mataban,
decid, dorados cabellos,
¿Qué culpa tuve en creellos,
pues ellos me aseguraban?

¿No vistéis vos que algun día
mil lágrimas derramaba,
basta que yo le juraba
que sus palabras creía?

When the mute eloquence of tears and sighs
I felt, and trusted, and embraced by ruin.

So false and yet so fair! so fair a mien
Veiling so false a mind who ever knew?
So true and yet so wretched! who has seen
A man like me, so wretched and so true?
Fly from me on the wind, for you have seen
How kind she was, how loved by her you knew me;
Fly, fly vain Witness what I once have been,
Nor dare, all wretched as I am, to view me!

One evening on the river's pleasant strand,
The Maid too well beloved sat with me,
And with her finger traced upon the sand,
"Death for Diana—not Inconstancy!"
And Love beheld us from his secret strand,
And marked his triumph, laughing to behold me,
To see me trust a writing traced in sand,
To see me credit what a Woman told me!

ROBERT SOUTHEY

Sobre el arena sentada
de aquel río la ví yo,
do con el dedo escribió
antes muerta que mudada.

Miren amor lo que ordena,
que un hombre llegue á creer
cosas dichas por mujer
y escritas en el arena.

Gregorio Silvestre

Spain, 1520–1569

Silvestre was born in Lisbon and was the son of the physician of the king of Portugal, but most of his life was spent in Spain and his writings are in Spanish. He was a chaplain, organist, and composer of music, and he also composed love lyrics of great charm. His youthful life was full of scandals. In his poetry Silvestre made some use of the Italian meters, but mainly he followed the Spanish school. In addition to his lighter lyrics he also wrote poems of a religious nature, *décimas* (a form he made famous), and sonnets. His *Obras poéticas* were first published in Lisbon in 1592.

Thou Long Hast Dwelled Within My Heart

Thou long hast dwelt within my heart,
But I'll transfer thee to my soul,
For that is my immortal part.

The soul, unworthy too, looks down
On the decaying, mortal clay,
But yet would claim, and call its own,
A star of such celestial ray
As thine, my fair! and make its throne
That soul immortal, there to dwell
In dignity unchangeable.

It is a mighty temple reared
On reason's and affection's base;
There sits the immortal spirit, sphered
In its glory, and its grace—
A palace and a resting place,
Where thou, its ruling head, shall be
Throned in its immortality.

And on the walls, in lines of gold,
I'll write thy splendid name,—I'll write—
O no! for angels shall behold

Dende el corazón al alma

Dende el corazón al alma
he propuesto de mudaros,
para jamás olvidaros.

El alma tiene aunque indina
por raíz el corazón,
para ser habitación
de huéspeda tan divina,
y quiere por más vecina
en sí misma ya albergaros,
para jamás olvidaros.

En este aposento tal
tenéis por piezas estrañas
el corazón, las entrañas,
y el alma por principal,
que en esta casa real
quiero yo perpetuaros
para jamás olvidaros.

Este palacio sagrado
tendrá por mejor renombre,
en mil partes vuestro nombre

That name in sculptured words of light.
And love thy beauties shall unfold
In their eternal beams, to shine
In immortality divine.

And then my heart, my sense, my soul,
Shall wait thy bidding, pleased to be
The very slaves to thy control,
Through heaven's untold eternity;
So years shall fly, so ages roll,
And I shall serve, and thou shalt live,
Long as heaven's sun a beam can give.

no escrito, sino entallado;
y al vivo tendrá cuidado
el amor de retrataros
para jamás olvidaros.

Tendré en estos aposentos
a vuestro mando rendidos
todos mis cinco sentidos
y todos mis pensamientos,
firmes, alegres, contentos
en serviros y agradaros,
para jamás olvidaros.

SIR JOHN BOWRING

Santa Teresa de Jesús
Spain, 1515–1582

Of Jewish extraction, Santa Teresa became one of the great Catholic mystics and the outstanding woman of her epoch in Spain. As a young girl she was fascinated by the books of chivalry and by the love affairs of her several male cousins. Alarmed at this turn of events, her father sent her to a convent. At the age of nineteen she became a Carmelite nun, and after a period of lukewarm spiritual life, she began to hear things through "the ears of the soul" and to have visions. She never withdrew from reality, however. Her life was actively dedicated to good works; she reformed the Carmelite order, founded seventeen convents, cared for the sick, performed many menial tasks. When a violent factional dispute broke out among the Carmelites, she was brought before the Inquisition but was found innocent. Her seven brothers, probably fearing that their Jewish ancestry would always make them suspect in Catholic Spain, fled to Peru.

On many occasions, Santa Teresa suffered serious illnesses, and at one time she was pronounced dead, wax was placed in her eyes, and her grave was prepared. When the nuns came for her body, she sat up, asked for food and drink, and began to tell of what she had seen and felt during her trance. Her poetry is on religious themes, and much of it falls within the best tradition of Spanish mysticism. The poetic style has great simplicity and sobriety. Allegory; popular refrains; short, rapid meters; and a deep fervor and sincerity characterize her verse.

If, Lord, Thy Love for Me Is Strong

If, Lord, Thy love for me is strong
As this which binds me unto Thee,
What holds me from Thee, Lord, so long,
What holds Thee, Lord, so long from me?

O soul, what then desirest thou?
—Lord, I would see Thee, who thus choose Thee.
What fears can yet assail thee now?
—All that I fear is but to lose Thee.

Love's whole possession I entreat,
Lord, make my soul Thine own abode,
And I will build a nest so sweet
It may not be too poor for God.

A soul in God hidden from sin
What more desires for thee remain,
Save but to love, and love again,

Si el amor que me tenéis

Si el amor que me tenéis.
Dios mío, es como el que os tengo,
decidme, ¿en qué me detengo?
O Vos ¿en qué os detenéis?

—Alma, ¿qué quieres de mí?
—Dios mío, no más que verte.
—Y ¿qué temes más de ti?
—Lo que más temo es perderte.

Un amor que ocupe os pido,
Dios mío, mi alma os tenga,
para hacer un dulce nido
adonde más la convenga.

Un alma en Dios escondida.
¿qué tiene que desear
sino amar y más amar

And, all on flame with love within,
Love on, and turn to love again?

y en amor toda encendida
tornarte de nuevo a amar?

ARTHUR SYMONS

Saint Teresa's Bookmark

Nada te turbe

The following lines were written by Saint Teresa as an inscription or motto on the bookmark of her Breviary.

Let nothing disturb thee,
Nothing affright thee;
All things are passing;
God never changeth.
Patient endurance
Attaineth to all things;
Who God possesseth
In nothing is wanting;
Alone God sufficeth.

Nada te turbe;
nada te espante;
todo se pasa;
Dios no se muda,
la paciencia
todo lo alcanza,
quien a Dios tiene,
nada le falta.
Sólo Dios basta.

HENRY WADSWORTH LONGFELLOW

Francisco de la Torre
Spain, last half of sixteenth century

It is known that this fine poet was matriculated in the University of Alcala in the early 1550s, but the dates of his birth and death are unknown. He returned from the wars in Lombardy to find his ladylove married to a wealthy old man who had formerly been the poet's own patron. Francisco buried the unrequited passion in his heart, and, like Petrarch, made it the subject of his best poems. He also composed a number of eclogues, but these are very inferior to those of Garcilaso. His poems were not published until Quevedo collected them, in 1631.

Francisco was inspired by the Italian poets (Varchi, Tasso, Amalteo), and his poetry reflects the fluidity of the Italian style. It is simple in statement, full of love and tenderness, and always characterized by good taste and a certain classic restraint. His sonnets often recall both in subject and style those of Petrarch.

Fair Is My Love

Bella es mi ninfa

Fair is my love, when to the summer air
  She doth her locks of tangled gold unbind:
Fair, when, relenting to my heart's despair,
  She bids her stern eyes grant one glance more kind:
  Fair, when, to still the troubled waves and wind,
She bids that light break forth, which I adore:
  Fair, when her gentlest grace of heavenly mind
Hath turn'd to joy the pining grief I bore:
Fair in her mildness; fair, though harsh, before:
  Fair, cruel; fair, disdainful; fair, still fair,
E'en when my heaven seems gloom for evermore:
  But her fair smile of beauty debonaire
Can ne'er be known, till seen in its own light;
Nor, seen, can word or thought report it right.

EDWARD CHURTON

Bella es mi ninfa, si los laços de oro
al apacible viento desordena;
bella, si de sus ojos enagena
el altivo desdén que siempre lloro.

Bella, si con la luz que sola adoro
la tempestad del viento y mar serena;
bella, si a la dureza de mi pena
buelve las gracias del celeste coro.

Bella si mansa, bella si terrible;
bella si cruda, bella esquiva, y bella
si buelve grave aquella luz del cielo

cuya beldad humana y apacible
ni se puede saber lo que es sin vella,
ni vista entenderá lo que es el suelo.

Fray Luis de León
Spain, 1527–1591

Fray Luis wrote religious prose and poetry in a highly polished style. His poetry embodies the essence of lyrical concinnity and has a simplicity and lightness that suggests rising upward, soaring. He was a professor at the famous University of Salamanca from 1531 until his death, but for five of those years he languished in a prison of the Spanish Inquisition because his interpretation of the Vulgate was condemned as being unorthodox. Fray Luis knew both Greek and Hebrew and was of Jewish descent—a background that may have made him suspect. Finally, he was acquitted, and he returned to his university chair.

His favorite poet, apart from the Biblical writers, was Horace, with whom he shared a love of solitude and the country life and a scorn for overwrought ambition and worldly possessions. A feeling of equilibrium, serenity, and mystical inner peace suffuses his very limited poetic output (only twenty-three poems), and he is regarded by some critics as the greatest lyric poet of his country.

Country Life

How tranquil is the day
For him who flees the world's unseemly din,
To seek the hidden way,
Which has throughout the years drawn in
The wisest men who on this earth have been.

No tension in his breast
Shows envy of the grandees' proud charade;
His heart is not impressed
With guilded ceilings made
By cunning Moors on jasper columns laid.

He does not care if fame
Should with its voice of praise revere
The mention of his name,
Or if vain tongues hold dear
What truth condemns in words outspoken here.

What gain to my content
Should some wild finger point me out,
If it is my intent
To breathless race about
Fanning the winds of anxious cares and doubt?

Oh, mountain, river, spring,
Oh, haven, sweet and sure,
My failing ship will bring
Me to your bay secure,
Safe from the ocean's storms all ships endure.

Give me unbroken sleep,
A day pure, joyous, free of care,
I shall not feel or keep
The maddening despair
Of those on birth or gold's exalted stair.

Let birds awaken me
With their untaught delightful trill;
Let not my reveille
Stir anxious fears that fill
With care those subject to another's will.

Oda I: Vida retirada

¡Qué descansada vida
la del que huye el mundanal ruido,
y sigue la escondida
senda por donde han ido
los pocos sabios que en el mundo han sido!

Que no le enturbia el pecho
de los soberbios grandes el estado,
ni del dorado techo
se admira, fabricado
del sabio moro, en jaspes sustentado.

No cura si la fama
canta con vos su nombre pregonera;
no cura si encarama
la lengua lisonjera
lo que condena la verdad sincera.

¿Qué presta a mi contento
si soy del vano dedo señalado,
si en busca de este viento
ando desalentado
con ansias vivas, y mortal cuidado?

¡Oh, campo! ¡Oh, monte! ¡Oh, río!
¡Oh, secreto seguro, deleitoso!
Roto casi el navío,
a vuestro almo reposo
huyo de aqueste mar tempestuoso.

Un no rompido sueño,
un día puro, alegre, libre quiero;
no quiero ver el ceño
vanamente severo
del que la sangre sube o el dinero.

Despiértenme las aves
con su cantar süave no aprendido,
no los cuidados graves
de que es siempre seguido
quien al ajeno arbitrio está atenido.

I want to live alone,
Enjoying all I owe to my kind fate,
My life wholly my own,
Free of love, zeal, and hate,
Suspicions, hope, and doubts intemperate.

Upon the mountainside
There is a garden planted by my hand;
It was my dearest pride
To view those flowers and stand
There thinking of the later fruited land.

In swift and eager haste
To cool and irrigate my little place,
From summits proud and chaste
A gushing spring will race
Bringing its waters to that famished space.

And there in peace and quiet,
Winding its narrow way among the trees,
It passes in a riot,
Across green fields and leas,
Sowing bright flowers that sway kissed by the breeze.

My garden feels the wind,
And casts a thousand odors on the air;
The leaves dance softly thinned,
And as they rustle there
Let those who hold scepters or wealth take care.

And those their treasure keep
Who trust a ship that storms made insecure;
I see them wait and weep,
But tears will not ensure
Their faith or help them those fierce winds endure.

There is a heavy blast
When bright day turns to blind and darkest night;
It lashes at the mast,
The heavens roar with fright,
Enriching the sea waters as they smite.

Let this suffice for me:
A humble board of simple food and peace;
Plates of gold filigree
For those who find surcease
From the dark fears that angry waves release.

While miserably the rest
Are burning with a thirst that seems to long
For what power may attest;
Ephemeral but strong,
Here in the shade I lie and sing my song.

With mythic laurel spray
In this cool shadow I am duly crowned;
I hear the psalter play
Stretched out upon the ground,
As I rejoice to its sweet measured sound.

JOHN A. CROW

Vivir quiero conmigo;
gozar quiero del bien que debo al cielo,
a solas, sin testigo,
libre de amor, de celo,
de odio, de esperanzas, de recelo.

Del monte en la ladera
por mi mano plantado tengo un huerto,
que con la primavera,
de bella flor cubierto,
ya muestra en esperanza el fruto cierto.

Y como codiciosa
de ver y acrecentar su hermosura,
desde la cumbre airosa
una fontana pura
hasta llegar corriendo se apresura;

y luego, sosegada,
el paso entre los árboles torciendo,
el suelo de pasada
de verdura vistiendo,
y con diversas flores va esparciendo.

El aire el huerto orea,
y ofrece mil olores al sentido;
los árboles menea
con un manso ruïdo,
que del oro y del cetro pone olvido.

Ténganse su tesoro
los que de un flaco leño se confían;
no es mío ver el lloro
de los que desconfían
cuando el cierzo y el ábrego porfían.

La combatida antena
cruje, y en ciega noche el claro día
se torna; al cielo suena
confusa vocería,
y la mar enriquecen a porfía.

A mí una pobrecilla
mesa, de amable paz bien abastada,
me baste; y la vajilla,
de fino oro labrada,
sea de quien la mar no teme airada.

Y mientras miserable-
mente se están los otros abrasando
con sed insaciable
del no durable mando,
tendido yo a la sombra esté cantando,

a la sombra tendido,
de yedra y lauro eterno coronado,
puesto el atento oído
al son dulce, acordado,
del plectro sabiamente meneado.

Epigram on the Real Presence

I

A rustic not conceiving in his mind
Things plain and manifest to all mankind,
Enquired of Faith one day, why it was said
The Almighty God was in the holy bread;
How the uncreated, eternal, infinite God,
Lay in a wafer, seemed exceeding odd;
And if He is, then it must next be said,
That God is broken with the broken bread.
"Hast thou a broken mirror e'er espied?"
Thus bringing brief conviction, Faith replied:
"When it is whole thine image meets thine eyes;
In every fragrant will that image rise.
Thus when the holy Priest, as need demands,
Divides the blessed Host with hallowed hands,
In every atom still contained will be
The Omnipresent, Infinite Deity."

II

If this be bread, why does it never waste,
So constantly consumed, yet always here?
If this be God, then how can it appear
Like bread we eat and seem bread to the taste?
If bread, why is it worshipped by the baker?
If God, can such a space a God comprise?
If bread, how is it it confounds the wise?
If God, how is it that we eat our Maker?
If bread, what good can such a morsel do?
If God, how can we break our Lord in two?
If bread, such saving virtue could it give?
If God, how can I see and touch it thus?
If bread, how could it come from Heaven to us?
If God, how can I look at it and live?"

ROBERT SOUTHEY

The Life of the Blessed

Region of life and light!
Land of the good whose earthly toils are o'er!
Nor frost nor heat may blight
Thy vernal beauty, fertile shore,
Yielding thy blessed fruits for evermore!

There, without crook or sling,
Walks the Good Shepherd; blossoms white and red
Round his meek temples cling;
And, to sweet pastures led,
His own loved flock beneath his eye is fed.

He guides, and near him they
Follow delighted; for he makes them go
Where dwells eternal May,
And heavenly roses blow,
Deathless, and gathered but again to grow.

He leads them to the height
Named of the infinite and long-sought Good,

Al propio asunto

I

A la Fe preguntó un Villano rústico,
criado en el aldea, en trato bárbaro,
una dificultad casi insolubile
acá a nuestro entender común y párvulo:
y fue, que como el Cuerpo real y físico
del Sacrosanto Dios, divino farmaco,
está en el todo, y en la parte íntegro
después que se divide aquel Pan cándido?
Al cual la Fe responde en breve término,
que como en un espejo sin obstáculo,
hecho trozos, en todas las partículas
ve uno su rostro entero en cualquier átomo;
del propio modo Dios en cualquier mínima
parte del sacro Pan, tan grande, y máximo,
esta como antes de que algún Presbítero
le parta, o le reparta, como es árbitro.

II

Si pan es lo que vemos, ¿cómo dura
sin que comiendo de él se nos acabe?
Si Dios, ¿cómo en el gusto a pan nos sabe?
¿Cómo de sólo pan tiene figura?
Si pan, ¿cómo le adora la criatura?
Si Dios, ¿cómo en tan chico espacio cabe?
Si pan. ¿cómo por ciencia no se sabe?
Si Dios, ¿cómo le come su hechura?
Si pan, ¿cómo nos harta siendo poco?
Si Dios es, ¿cómo puede ser partido?
Si pan, ¿cómo en el alma hace tanto?
Si Dios, ¿cómo le miro yo y le toco?
Si pan, ¿cómo del Cielo ha descendido?
Si Dios. ¿cómo no muero yo de espanto?

Morada del cielo

Alma región luciente,
prado de bienandanza, que ni al hielo
ni con el rayo ardiente
falleces, fértil suelo
producidor eterno de consuelo:

De púrpura y de nieve
florida la cabeza coronado,
a dulces pastos mueve,
sin honda ni cayado,
el buen Pastor en ti su hato amado.

El va, y en pos dichosas
le siguen sus ovejas, do las pace
con immortales rosas,
con flor que siempre nace,
y cuanto más se goza más renace.

Ya dentro a la montaña
del alto bien las guía; ya en la vena

And fountains of delight;
And where his feet have stood,
Springs up, along the way, their tender food.

And when, in the mid skies,
The climbing sun has reached his highest bound,
Reposing as he lies,
With all his flock around,
He witches the still air with numerous sound.

From his sweet lute flow forth
Immortal harmonies, of power to still
All passions born of earth,
And draw the ardent will
Its destiny of goodness to fulfil.

Might but a little part,
A wandering breath, of that high melody
Descend into my heart,
and change it till it be
Transformed and swallowed up, O love! in thee.

Ah! then my soul should know,
Beloved! where thou liest at noon of day;
And from this place of woe
Released, should take its way
To mingle with thy flock, and never stray.

WILLIAM CULLEN BRYANT

Serene Night

When yonder glorious sky,
Lighted with million lamps, I contemplate;
And turn my dazzled eye
To this vain mortal state,
All dim and visionary, mean and desolate:

A mingled joy and grief
Fills all my soul with dark solicitude;—
I find a short relief
In tears, whose torrents rude
Roll down my cheeks; or thoughts which thus intrude;—

Thou so sublime abode!
Temple of light, and beauty's fairest shrine!
My soul, a spark of God,
Aspiring to thy seats divine,
Why, why is it condemned in this dull cell to pine?

Why should I ask in vain
For truth's pure lamp, and wander here alone,
Seeking, through toil and pain,
Light from the Eternal One,
Following a shadow still, that glimmers and is gone?

Dreams and delusions play
With man,—he thinks not of his mortal fate:
Death treads his silent way;
The earth turns round; and then, too late,
Man finds no beam is left of all his fancied state.

Rise from your sleep, vain men!
Look round,—and ask if spirits born of heaven,

del gozo fiel las baña,
y les da mesa llena,
pastor y pasto él solo, y suerte buena.

Y de su esfera cuando
la cumbre toca altísimo subido
el sol, él sesteando,
de su hato ceñido,
con dulce son deleita el santo oído.

Toca el rabel sonoro,
y el inmortal dulzor al alma pasa,
con que envilece el oro,
y ardiendo se traspasa
y lanza en aquel bien libre de tasa.

¡Oh son, oh voz, siquiera
pequeña parte alguna descendiese
en mi sentido, y fuera
de sí el alma pusiese
y toda en ti, oh amor, la convirtiese!

Conocería dónde
sesteas, dulce Esposo, y desatada
de esta prisión a donde
padece, a tu manada
junta, no ya andará perdida, errada.

Oda VIII: Noche serena

Cuando contemplo el cielo
de innumerables luces adornado,
y miro hacia el suelo,
de noche rodeado,
en sueño y en olvido sepultado,

el amor y la pena
despiertan en mi pecho un ansia ardiente;
despiden larga vena
los ojos hechos fuente;
la lengua dice al fin con voz doliente:

Morada de grandeza
templo de claridad y hermosura:
mi alma que a tu alteza
nació, ¿qué desventura
la tiene en esta cárcel baja, escura?

¡Qué mortal desatino
de la verdad aleja ansí el sentido,
que de tu bien divino
olvidado, perdido,
sigue la vana sombra, el bien fingido?

El hombre está entregado
al sueño, de su suerte no cuidando;
y con paso callado
el cielo, vueltas dando,
las horas del vivir le va hurtando.

¡Ay! despertad, mortales!
Mirad con atención en vuestro daño.

And bound to heaven again,
Were only lent or given
To be in this mean round of shades and follies driven.

Turn your unclouded eye
Up to yon bright, to yon eternal spheres;
And spurn the vanity
Of time's delusive years,
And all its flattering hopes, and all its frowning fears.

What is the ground ye tread,
But a mere point, compared with that vast space,
Around, above you spread,
Where, in the Almighty's face,
The present, future, past, hold an eternal place?

List to the concert pure
Of yon harmonious, countless worlds of light!
See, in his orbit sure,
Each takes his journey bright,
Led by an unseen hand through the vast maze of night!

See how the pale Moon rolls
Her silver wheel; and, scattering beams afar
On Earth's benighted souls,
See Wisdom's holy star;
Or, in his fiery course, the sanguine orb of War;

Or that benignant ray
Which Love hath called its own, and made so fair;
Or that serene display
Of power supernal there,
Where Jupiter conducts his chariot through the air!

And, circling all the rest,
See Saturn, father of the golden hours:
While round him, bright and blest,
The whole empyreum showers
Its glorious streams of light on this low world of ours!

But who to these can turn,
And weigh them 'gainst a weeping world like this,—
Nor feel his spirit burn
To grasp so sweet a bliss,
And mourn that exile hard which here his portion is?

For there, and there alone,
Are peace, and joy, and never-dying love,—
There, on a splendid throne,
'Midst all those fires above,
In glories and delights which never wane nor move.

O, wondrous blessedness,
Whose shadowy effluence hope o'er time can fling!
Day that shall never cease,—
No night there threatening,—
No winter there to chill joy's ever-during spring.

Ye fields of changeless green,
Covered with living streams and fadeless flowers!
Thou parading serene!
Eternal, joyful hours
My disembodied soul shall welcome in thy bowers!

SIR JOHN BOWRING

¿Las almas immortales,
hechas a bien tamaño,
podrán vivir de sombra y solo engaño?

¡Ay!, levantad los ojos
a aquesta celestial eterna esfera:
burlaréis los antojos
de aquesa lisonjera
vida, con cuanto teme y cuanto espera.

¿Es más que un breve punto
el bajo y torpe suelo, comparado
a aqueste gran trasunto,
do vive mejorado
lo que es, lo que será, lo que ha pasado?

Quien mira el gran concierto
de aquestos resplandores eternales,
su movimiento cierto,
sus pasos desiguales
y en proporción concorde tan iguales:

la luna cómo mueve
la plateada rueda, y va en pos de ella
la luz do el saber llueve,
y la graciosa estrella
de Amor la sigue reluciente y bella;

y cómo otro camino
prosigue el sanguinoso Marte airado,
y el Júpiter benino,
de bienes mil cercado,
serena el cielo con su rayo amado;

rodéase en la cumbre
Saturno, padre de los siglos de oro;
del reluciente coro
su luz va repartiendo y su tesoro:

¿quién es el que esto mira
y precia la bajeza de la tierra,
y no gime y suspira
por romper lo que encierra
el alma y de estos bienes la destierra?

Aquí vive el contento,
aquí reina la paz; aquí, asentado
en rico y alto asiento,
está el Amor sagrado,
de glorias y deleites rodeado.

Inmensa hermosura
aquí se muestra toda, y resplandece
clarísima luz pura,
que jamás anochece;
eterna primavera aquí florece.

¡Oh, campos verdaderos!
¡Oh, prados con verdad dulces y amenos!
¡Riquísimos mineros!
¡Oh, deleitosos senos!
¡Repuestos valles, de mil bienes llenos!

San Juan de la Cruz
Spain, 1542–1591

This famous mystic, one of the finest poets of Spain's Golden Age, attended the University of Salamanca where Fray Luis de León was a professor. Like Santa Teresa, whom he admired, San Juan was a member of the Carmelite order and was of Jewish descent. Because of a violent jurisdictional dispute within the religious order, he was imprisoned in a cell in Toledo, and it was here that he wrote his passionate religious lyrics. To him, "the dark night of the soul" was a final stage of soul-suffering that precedes the union of the human soul with God, called by the poet "the mystical marriage."

San Juan wrote an incandescent lyric poetry that joined the limpid simplicity of his country's ballads and folk songs, the polished and refined language of the Renaissance, and the religious exaltation of the Old Testament prophets, who carried on personal conversations with their God. Garcilaso and the Bible's Song of Songs furnish much of his rhythm and imagery. Saint John's poems invariably describe the allegorical search of the beloved (the soul) for the lover (God). The flowing lines rise on spirals of increasing tension and beauty, for San Juan de la Cruz has, above all, written love poems of the most passionate, tender, and perfect kind. An English critic remarked, "Such poetry has never been written in Spain to women."[16]

It Was the Darkest Night

Once in the dark of night,
When love's consuming flames enraptured me,
Oh, fate of sweet delight!
I slipped out silently,
And left my house at peace when none could see.

In darkness and secure,
I climbed my secret stairway to the skies,
Oh, fate joyous and pure!
Unseen and in disguise
I left my house at peace to softly rise.

That night my soul took wing,
When no one saw or knew my hidden flight,
I did not see a thing,
And had no guide or light,
Save that which in my heart was burning bright.

The light that guided me,
More surely than the scorching noonday sun,
Led where impatiently
Waited a loving one
In a small refuge where he stood alone.

Oh, night, most holy guide,
Oh, night, more tender than the dawn's embrace,
Oh, night, that unified
Two lovers face to face
Transforming Bride to Bridegroom in that place.

Within my flowering breast,
Which whole and safe for Him alone I kept,
He came with me to rest,

La noche oscura

En una noche oscura,
con ansias en amores inflamada,
¡oh dichosa ventura!,
salí sin ser notada,
estando ya mi casa sosegada:

a escuras y segura,
por la secreta escala disfrazada,
¡oh dichosa ventura!,
a escuras y en celada,
estando ya mi casa sosegada;

en la noche dichosa,
en secreto, que nadie me veía,
ni yo miraba cosa,
sin otra luz y guía
sino la que en el corazón ardía.

Aquésta me guiaba
más cierto que la luz del mediodía,
a donde me esperaba
quien yo bien me sabía,
en parte donde nadie parecía.

¡Oh noche que guiaste!,
¡oh noche amable más que el alborada!,
¡oh noche que juntaste
amado con amada,
amada en el amado transformada!

En mi pecho florido,
que entero para él solo se guardaba,
allí quedó dormido,

---

16. Brenan, *Literature of the Spanish People*, 160.

And while in quiet he slept
The cedars fanned him as I softly stepped.

The wind from the redoubt
Blew off the stones and scattering his hair
Its hand reached out
Serene and bare
To strike me down and leave me senseless there.

Forgetting all I strayed,
My face upon the Loved One was inclined;
The world stood still, I prayed,
All cares to Him consigned,
And in the field of lilies lost to mind.

JOHN A. CROW

y yo le regalaba;
y el ventalle de cedros aire daba.

El aire de la almena,
cuando yo sus cabellos esparcía,
con su mano serena
en mi cuello hería,
y todos mis sentidos suspendía.

Quedéme y olvidéme,
el rostro recliné sobre el amado,
cesó todo, y dejéme,
dejando mi cuidado
entre las azucenas olvidado.

O Flame of Living Love

O flame of living love,
That dost eternally
Pierce through my soul with so consuming heat,
Since there's no help above,
Make thou an end of me,
And break the bond of this encounter sweet.

O burn that burns to heal!
O more than pleasant wound!
And O soft hand, O touch most delicate,
That dost new life reveal,
That dost in grace abound,
And, slaying, dost from death to life translate!

O lamps of fire that shined
With so intense a light
That those deep caverns where the senses live,
Which were obscure and blind,
Now with strange glories bright,
Both heat and light to His beloved give!

With how benign intent
Rememberest thou my breast
Where thou alone abidest secretly;
And in thy sweet ascent,
With glory and good possessed,
How delicately thou teachest love to me!

ARTHUR SYMONS

Llama de amor viva

¡Oh llama de amor viva
que tiernamente hieres
de mi alma en el más profundo centro!,
pues ya no eres esquiva,
acaba ya si quieres,
rompe la tela de este dulce encuentro.

¡Oh cauterio suave!,
¡oh regalada llaga!,
¡oh mano blanda! ¡oh toque delicado
que a vida eterna sabe,
y toda deuda paga!
Matando, muerte en vida la has trocado

¡Oh lámparas de fuego,
en cuyos resplandores
las profundas cavernas del sentido,
que estaba oscuro y ciego,
con extraños primores
calor y luz dan junto a su querido!

¡Cuán manso y amoroso
recuerdas en mi seno,
donde secretamente solo moras;
y en tu aspirar sabroso,
de bien y gloria lleno,
cuán delicadamente me enamoras!

Song of the Soul That Is Glad to Know God by Faith

How well I know that fountain's rushing flow
Although by night

Its deathless spring is hidden. Even so
Full well I guess from whence its sources flow
Though it be night.

Its origin (since it has none) none knows:
But that all origin from it arose
Although by night.

Cantar del alma que se huelga de conoscer a dios por fe

Que bien sé yo la fonte que mana y corre,
aunque es de noche.

Aquella eterna fonte está escondida,
que bien sé yo do tiene su manida,
aunque es de noche.

Su origen no lo sé, pues no le tiene,
mas sé que todo origen de ella viene,
aunque es de noche.

I know there is no other thing so fair And earth and heaven drink refreshment there Although by night.	Sé que no puede ser cosa tan bella, y que cielos y tierra beben de ella, aunque es de noche.
Full well I know its depth no man can sound And that no ford to cross it can be found Though it be night.	Bien sé que suelo en ella no se halla, y que ninguno puede vadealla, aunque es de noche.
Its clarity unclouded still shall be: Out of it comes the light by which we see Though it be night.	Su claridad nunca es escurecida, y sé que toda luz de ella es venida, aunque es de noche.
Flush with its banks the stream so proudly swells; I know its waters, nations, heavens, and hells Though it be night.	Sé ser tan caudalosas sus corrientes, que infiernos, cielos riegan, y las gentes, aunque es de noche.
The current that is nourished by this source I know to be omnipotent in force Although by night.	El corriente que nace de esta fuente, bien sé que es tan capaz y omnipotente, aunque es de noche.
From source and current a new current swells Which neither of the other twain excels Though it be night.	El corriente que de estas dos procede sé que ninguna de ellas le precede, aunque es de noche.
The eternal source hides in the Living Bread That we with life eternal may be fed Though it be night.	Aquesta eterna fonte está escondida en este vivo pan por darnos vida, aunque es de noche.
Here to all creatures is crying, hark! That they should drink their fill though in the dark, For it is night.	Aquí se está llamando a las criaturas, y de esta agua se hartan, aunque a escuras, porque es de noche.
This living fount which is to me so dear Within the bread of life I see it clear Though it be night.	Aquesta viva fuente, que deseo, en este pan de vida yo la veo, aunque de noche.

ROY CAMPBELL

Not Without Hope Did I Ascend

Not without hope did I ascend
Upon an amorous quest to fly
And up I soared so high, so high,
I seized my quarry in the end.

As on this falcon quest I flew
To chase a quarry so divine,
I had to soar so high and fine
That soon I lost myself from view.
With loss of strength my plight was sorry
From straining on so steep a course.
But love sustained me with such force
That in the end I seized my quarry.

The more I rose into the height
More dazzled, blind, and lost I spun.
The greatest conquest ever won
I won in blindness, like the night.
Because love urged me on my way
I gave that mad, blind, reckless leap
That soared me up so high and steep
That in the end I seized my quarry.

The steeper upward that I flew
On so vertiginous a quest

Tras de un amoroso lance

Tras de un amoroso lance,
y no de esperanza falto,
volé tan alto, tan alto,
que le dí a la caza alcance.

Para que yo alcance diese
a aqueste lance divino,
tanto volar me convino,
que de vista me perdiese;
y con todo, en este trance
en el vuelo quedé falto;
mas el amor fue tan alto,
que le dí a la caza alcance.

Cuando más alto subía,
deslumbróseme la vista,
y la más fuerte conquista
en oscuro se hacía,
más por ser de amor el lance
dí un ciego y oscuro salto,
y fui tan alto, tan alto,
que le dí a la caza alcancé.

Cuanto más alto llegaba
de este lance tan subido,

The humbler and more lowly grew
My spirit, fainting in my breast.
I said 'None yet can find the way'
But as my spirit bowed more low,
Higher and higher did I go
Till in the end I seized my prey.

By such strange means did I sustain
A thousand starry flights in one,
Since hope of Heaven yet by none
Was ever truly hoped in vain.
Only by hope I won my way
Nor did my hope my aim belie,
Since I soared up so high, so high,
That in the end I seized my prey.

tanto más bajo y rendido
y abatido me hallaba.
dije: No habrá quien alcance;
y abatíme tanto, tanto,
que fui tan alto, tan alto.
que le dí a la caza alcance.

Por una extraña manera
mil vuelos pasé de un vuelo,
porque esperanza de cielo
tanto alcanza cuanto espera;
esperé sólo este lance,
y en esperar no fui falto,
pues fuí tan alto, tan alto,
que le dí a la caza alcance.

ROY CAMPBELL

Alonso de Ercilla
Spain, 1533–1594

Born in Madrid, Ercilla is known in literature as the author of the great Chilean epic, *La Araucana*. Ercilla was a page in the palace of Philip II, and he accompanied the king on his journey to England in 1554. In London he met the newly appointed Spanish diplomatic representative to Chile, and through him became interested in America. Two years later Ercilla sailed for Chile, where he served as a captain in the army of García Hurtado de Mendoza in the relentless war against the Araucanian Indians. Ercilla's poem about the war, *La Araucana*, was largely written in the midst of the campaign. It appeared in three parts in 1569, 1578, and 1589, respectively. The work is not only the great epic of the Spanish New World but also the first production of high literary merit in the colonies. *La Araucana* embodies the ethics and dynamic spirit of the Spanish Renaissance, but the poet attempts to present the Indian point of view. Ercilla makes heroes of the famous Indian leaders and of the Araucanians as a group in verses of stirring splendor. William Hayley's English translation of extensive passages of the poem appeared in his *Poems and Plays*, in 1785.

Verses from *La Araucana*

I sing not love of ladies, nor of fights
Devised for gentle dames by courteous knights;
Nor feasts, nor tourneys, nor that tender care
Which prompts the Gallant to regale the Fair;
But the bold deeds of Valor's favorite train,
Those undegenerate sons of warlike Spain,
Who made Arauco their stern laws embrace,
And bent beneath their yoke her untamed race.

Of tribes distinguished in the field I sing;
Of nations who disdain the name of King;
Courage, that danger only taught to grow,
And challenge honor from a generous foe;
And preserving toils of purest fame,
And feats that aggrandize the Spanish name;
For the brave actions of the vanquished spread
The brightest glory round the victor's head.

La Araucana

No las damas, amor, no gentilezas
de caballeros canto enamorados,
ni las muestras, regalos y ternezas
de amorosos afectos y cuidados;
mas el valor, los hechos, las proezas
de aquellos españoles esforzados,
que a la cerviz de Arauco no domada
pusieron duro yugo por la espada.

Cosas diré también harto notables
de gente que a ningún rey obedecen,
temerarias expresas memorables
que celebrarse con razón merecen,
raras industrias, términos loables
que más los españoles engrandecen:
pues no es el vencedor más estimado
de aquello en que el vencido es reputado

. . . .

Many there are who, in this mortal strife,
Have reached the slippery heights of splendid life:
For Fortune's ready hand its succour lent;
Smiling she raised them up the steep ascent,
To hurl them headlong from that lofty seat
To which she led their unsuspecting feet;
E'en at the moment when all fears disperse,
And their proud fancy sees no sad reverse.

Little they think, beguiled by fair success,
That Joy is but the herald of Distress:
The hasty wing of Time escapes their sight,
And those dark evils that attend his flight:
Vainly they dream, with gay presumption warm,
Fortune for them will take a steadier form;
She, unconcerned at what her victims feel,
Turns with her wonted haste her fatal wheel.

[The Poet describes the Araucanians]

They are of bearless cheek and robust face,
Of bodies well-proportioned, tall and strong;
A wide-shouldered and broad-chested race,
Muscled from head to foot, stout limbs and long,
Courageous, agile, of swift-footed grace,
Valiant and spirited in war and song,
Steadfast in work and able to withstand
The bite of cold, hunger or scorching sand.

On the brave dignity of this free folk,
No king has ever thrown the servile yoke,
Nor any foreign tribe is there to boast
Of having overrun their crags and coast;
No neighboring band could ever dare afford
To move against this race with lifted sword:
Free and indomitable, fearsome and proud,
To no law subject and with heads unbowed.

The Indians first, by novelty dismayed,
As Gods revered us, and as Gods obeyed;
But when they found we were of woman born,
Their homage turned to enmity and scorn:
Their childish error when our weakness showed,
They blushed at what their ignorance bestowed;
Fiercely they burnt with anger and with shame,
To see their masters but of mortal frame.

Oh cureless malady! Oh fatal pest!
Embraced with ardor and with pride caressed,
Thou common vice, thou most contagious ill,
Bane of the mind, and frenzy of the will!
Thou foe to private and to public health;
Thou dropsy of the soul, that thirsts for wealth,
Insatiate Avarice!—'tis from thee we trace
The various misery of our mortal race.

WILLIAM HAYLEY

Muchos hay en el mundo que han llegado
a la engañosa alteza desta vida,
que fortuna los ha siempre ayudado
y dádoles la mano a la subida,
para después de haberlos levantado,
derribarlos con mísera caída,
cuando es menor el golpe y sentimiento
y menos el pensar que hay mudamiento.

No entienden con la próspera bonanza
que el contento es principio de tristeza,
ni miran en la súbita mudanza
del consumidor tiempo y su presteza;
mas con altiva y vana confianza
quieren que en su fortuna haya firmeza;
la cual, de su aspereza no olvidada,
revuelve con la vuelta acostumbrada.

. . . .

Son de gestos robustos, desbarbados,
bien formados los cuerpos y crecidos,
espaldas grandes, pechos levantados,
recios miembros, de niervos bien fornidos;
agiles, desenvueltos, alentados,
animosos, valientes, atrevidos,
duros en el trabajo y sufridores
de fríos mortales, hambres y calores.

. . . .

No ha habido rey jamás que sujetase
esta soberbia gente libertada,
ni extranjera nación que se jatase
de haber dado en sus términos pisada,
ni comarcana tierra que se osase
mover en contra y levantar espada:
siempre fue exenta, indómita, temida,
de leyes libre y de cerviz erguida.

. . . .

Por dioses, como dije, eran tenidos
de los indios los nuestros; pero olieron
que de mujer y hombre eran nacidos,
y todas sus flaquezas entendieron;
viéndolos a miserias sometidos
el error inorante conocieron,
ardiendo en viva rabia avergonzados
por verse de mortales conquistados.

¡Oh incurable mal! ¡oh gran fatiga,
con tanta diligencia alimentada!
¡Vicio común y pegajosa liga,
voluntad sin razón desenfrenada,
del provecho y bien público enemiga,
sedienta bestia, hidrópica, hinchada,
principio y fin de todos nuestros males!
¡oh insaciable codicia de mortales!

Fernando de Herrera

Spain, 1534–1597

Born in Seville, the son of a humble candle maker, Herrera received little formal education, but he was bright and diligent and taught himself through avid reading. He became a member of the entourage around Don Álvaro Colón y Portugal, count of Gelves, an enthusiast of the arts. Herrera fell passionately in love with the count's wife, who was the main inspiration for his amorous lyrics and elegies. Herrera also composed much heroic and patriotic poetry, which, though highly regarded in its day, has a grandiloquent ring for the contemporary reader. Lope de Vega admired Herrera and on reading his heroic verse remarked, "Here no other language in the world exceeds our own." [17] Herrera is the great poet of the Sevillian school. He is also famous for his critical edition of the works of Garcilaso de la Vega, which was published in 1580; his annotations in this work are in the best tradition of literary criticism.

Ideal Beauty

O Light serene! present in one who breathes
That love divine, which kindles yet restrains
The high-born soul—that in its mortal chains
Heavenward aspires for love's immortal wreaths!
   Rich golden locks, within whose clustered curls
Celestial and eternal treasures lie!
A voice that breathes angelic harmony
Among bright coral and unspotted pearls!
   What marvelous beauty! Of the high estate
Of immortality, within this light
Transparent veil of flesh, a glimpse is given;
   And in the glorious form I contemplate
(Although its brightness blinds my feeble sight)
The immortal still I seek and follow on to Heaven!

HENRY WADSWORTH LONGFELLOW

Soneto I

Serena Luz, en quien presente espira
divino amor, qu'enciende i junto enfrena
el noble pecho, qu'en mortal cadena
al alto Olimpo levantar s' aspira;

ricos cercos dorados, do se mira
tesoro celestial d'eterna vena;
armonía d'angélica Sirena,
qu'entre las perlas i el coral respira,

¿cuál nueva maravilla, cuál exemplo
de la immortal grandeza nos descubre
aquessa sombra del hermoso velo?

Que yo en essa belleza que contemplo
(aunqu'a mi flaca vista ofende i cubre),
la immensa busco, i voi siguiendo al cielo.

The Disembodied Spirit

Pure Spirit! that within a form of clay
Once veiled the brightness of thy native sky;
In dreamless slumber sealed thy burning eye,
Nor heavenward sought to wing thy flight away!
   He that chastised thee did at length unclose
Thy prison doors, and give thee sweet release,
Unloosed the mortal coil, eternal peace
Received thee to its stillness and repose.
   Look down once more from thy celestial dwelling,
Help me to rise and be immortal there—
An earthly vapor melting into air;—
   For my whole soul with secret ardor swelling,
From earth's dark mansion struggles to be free,
And longs to soar away and be at rest with thee.

HENRY WADSWORTH LONGFELLOW

Soneto II

Alma bella, qu'en este oscuro velo
cubriste un tiempo tu vigor luziente
i, en hondo i ciego olvido, gravemente
fuiste escondida sin alçar el buelo,

Ya, despreciando este lugar, do el cielo
t'encerró i apuró con fuerça ardiente,
i, roto el mortal nudo, vas presente
a eterna paz, dexando en guerra el suelo.

Buelve tu luz a mi, i d'el centro tira
al ancho cerco d'immortal belleza,
como vapor terrestre levantado

Este espiritu opresso, que suspira
en vano por huir d'esta estrecheza,
qu'impide estar contigo descansado.

17. Lope de Vega, *Laurel de Apolo*, 218.

Juan López de Úbeda

Spain, sixteenth century

Born in Toledo, López de Úbeda founded a seminary in Alcalá de Henares, where, in 1582, his *Vergel de flores divinas (Garden of Divine Flowers)*, a collection of moralistic verse, appeared. It included his own poems and those of other authors, among them Fray Luis de León. Most of López de Úbeda's poems contain admonitions about how to lead a proper Christian life. The "vile worm," which had been used as a symbol of death in the *Cancionero de Baena* over a century earlier, again appears in his poetry. In the sonnet below, that symbol is given perhaps its greatest maturity of expression in the Spanish Renaissance.

Man's Fate

Vile composition, Earth inspired with breath,
Man, who at first wert made of dust and tears,
And then by law divine condemned to death;
When wilt thou check thy lusts in their careers?
Draw in that peacock's tail, forget thy pride,
Dust born of dust on which men's feet will tread,
Vomit the air that puffs thy hollow hide,
Thou wilt be dust entombed when thou art dead.
That pampered body with its lusty glow,
When most one cares for it, most goads one on,
And those two eyes that now deceive thee so,
Will be but sightless ash when thou art gone.
Thy pompous thoughts and empty ostentation
Will soon be rotting trash, and tears of desolation.

JOHN A. CROW

Ceniza espiritada

Ceniza espiritada, vil mistura,
hombre de polvo y lágrimas formado,
a la miseria misma subjetado,
¿de qué te ensoberbeces, vil criatura?

Deshaz la rueda, abaja tu locura,
vomita al aire de que estás hinchado,
que un poco de polvo eres, que hollado
serás mañana en la sepultura.

Y el cuerpo delicado que regalas,
cuanto le curas más, más él le atiza,
y esos tus ojos que te engañan tanto,

tus vanos pensamientos y tus galas,
tú y ello y cuanto tienes sois ceniza,
basura y podrición, lloro y quebranto.

Baltasar de Alcázar

Spain, 1530–1606

This Sevillian poet greatly admired Martial, whom he often imitated, and Horace, whom he translated. In some of his own poetry, he skillfully used the newly introduced Italian meters, but his best poems are in a light and festive vein. His style is melodious and flexible, and in a goodly number of his poems, his Andalusian humor and wit are displayed to advantage.

Woman's Jealousy

Talk not to me of all the frowns of fate,
Or adverse fortune; nor offend my ears
With tales of slavery's suffering in Algiers,
Nor galley's chains, heavy, disconsolate.
Speak not to me of fetter'd maniac's woes,
Nor proud one from his glory tumbled down:
Dimm'd honour,—friend-abandoned,—broken crown:
These may be heavy sorrows; but who knows
To bend his head beneath the storms of life
With holy patience,—he the shock will bear,
And see the thundering clouds disperse away.
But give to mortal man a jealous wife,—
Then misery,—galleys,—fetters,—frowns,—despair,—
Loss,—shame,—dishonour,—folly:—What are they?

SIR JOHN BOWRING

Ningún hombre se llame desdichado

Ningún; hombre se llame desdichado
aunque le siga el hado ejecutivo,
supuesto que en Argel viva cautivo,
o al remo en las galeras condenado.

Ni el propio loco, por furioso atado,
ni el que perdido llora estado altivo,
ni el que a deshonra trujo el tiempo esquivo,
o la necesidad a humilde estado.

Sufrir cualquiera pena es fácil cosa;
que ninguna atormenta tan de veras
que no la venza el sufrimiento tanto.

Mas el que tiene la mujer celosa,
ése tiene desdicha, Argel, galeras,
locura, perdición, deshonra y llanto.

Francisco de Aldana

Spain, 1537–1616

Francisco de Aldana was killed in the wars in Morocco along with King Don Sebastian of Portugal. His works were only recently collected and reprinted after many years of neglect. The Italian style of Ariosto strongly influenced his poetry, much of which would be considered too altisonant for today's taste. A few of his more simple lyrics, however, have stood the test of time.

The Native Land

Clear fount of light! my native land on high,
Bright with a glory that shall never fade!
Mansion of truth! without a veil or shade,
Thy holy quiet meets the spirit's eye.
There dwells the soul in its ethereal essence,
Gasping no longer for life's feeble breath;
But, sentinelled in heaven, its glorious presence
With pitying eye beholds, yet fears not, death.
Beloved country! banished from thy shore,
A stranger in this prison-house of clay,
The exiled spirit weeps and sighs for thee!
Heavenward the bright perfections I adore
Direct, and the sure promise cheers the way,
That, whither love aspires, there shall my dwelling be.

HENRY WADSWORTH LONGFELLOW

Al cielo

¡Clara fuente de luz nuevo y hermoso
rico de luminarias patrio cielo!
¡Casa de la verdad, sin nombre o velo,
de inteligencias ledo almo reposo!

¡Oh, cómo allá te estás, cuerpo glorioso,
tan lejos del mortal caduco anhelo,
casi un Argos divino alzado a vuelo,
de nuestro humano error libre y piadoso!

¡Oh patria amada! a ti suspira y llora
ésta, en su cárcel, Alma peregrina,
llevada errando de uno en otro instante.

Esa cierta beldad que me enamora,
suerte y sazón me otorgue tan benina,
que do sube el amor llegue el amante.

The Image of God

O Lord! who seest from yon starry height,
  Centered in one, the future and the past,
    Fashioned in thine own image, see how fast
The world obscures in me what once was bright
Eternal Sun! the warmth which thou hast given
  To cheer life's flowery April, fast decays;
    Yet, in the hoary winter of my days,
Forever green shall be my trust in heaven.

Celestial King! oh, let thy presence pass
  Before my spirit, and an image fair
    Shall meet that look of mercy from on high,
As the reflected image in a glass
  Doth meet the look of him who seeks it there,
    And owes its being to the gazer's eye.

HENRY WADSWORTH LONGFELLOW

O Rey Divino

Señor que allá en la estrellada cumbre,
todo lo ves en un presente eterno,
mira tu hechura en mí que al ciego infierno
la lleva su terrena pesadumbre:

eterno sol ya la encendida lumbre
do éste mi alegre abril florido y tierno
muere, y ver pienso al más nevado invierno,
más verde la raíz de su costumbre:

en mí tu imagen mira, O Rey Divino
con ojos de piedad, que al dulce encuentro
del rayo celestial verás volverla,

que a verse como en vidrio cristalino,
la imagen mira el que se espeja dentro,
y está en su vista dél, su mirar de ella.

Francisco de Figueroa

Spain, 1536–1617

This poet was born into a family of the lesser nobility in the city of Alcalá de Henares. At an early age he went to Italy, where he studied and later occupied himself with affairs of government for Charles V and Philip II. He was an enthusiast of the Italian meters, which he dominated completely, and he was so fluent in Italian that he composed many poems with alternate sentences in Italian and Spanish. He was also a great admirer of Horace, and some of his writings reflect the influence of that Latin poet. Among his contemporaries, Figueroa was known as "the divine," because of the refinement of his style. Shortly before his death he ordered that all of his poetry be burned, but several selections were saved by his friends and later published.

Sonnet on the Death of Garcilaso

A beauteous scion from the stateliest tree
That e'er in fertile mead or forest grew,
With freshest bloom adorned and vigor new,
Glorious in form, and first in dignity!
The same fell tempest, which by Heaven's decree
Around thy parent stock resistless blew,
And far from Tejo fair its trunk o'erthrew,
In foreign clime has stripped the leaves from thee:
And the same pitying hand has from the spot
Of cheerless ruin raised ye to rejoice,
Where fruit immortal decks the withered stem.
I will not, like the vulgar, mourn your lot;
But, with pure incense and exulting voice,
Praise your high worth, and consecrate your fame.

WILLIAM HERBERT

Soneto

O del árbol más alto y más hermoso
que produxo jamás fértil terreno,
tierno pimpollo ya de flores lleno,
y a par de otra cualquier planta glorioso.

El mismo viento airado y tempestuoso
que su tronco, tan lexos del ameno
patrio Tajo arrancó, por prado ajeno
te deshojó con soplo presuroso.

Y una misma también piadosa mano
os traspuso en el cielo, a do las flores
d'ambos han producido eterno fruto.

No os llore, como suele, el mundo en vano,
mas conságreos altar, ofrezca olores
con voz alegre y con semblante enxunto.

BAROQUE PERIOD

Miguel de Cervantes

Spain, 1547–1616

The famous author of *Don Quixote,* the first novel in European literature, also wrote a considerable amount of poetry, some of the best of it contained in that novel. In 1585 Cervantes first made himself known as a writer with the publication of the pastoral romance *Galatea,* a work that is not highly regarded today. Among his several plays, the tragedy *Numancia* does contain some very good verse. Cervantes' life was one of adventure and derring-do as well as dedication to writing. In 1571 he took part in the naval battle of Lepanto, in which the Turks were turned back by an allied fleet from western Europe. He was seriously wounded in that engagement, losing the use of his left hand. In 1575 he was captured and taken to Algiers as a slave, and it was five years before he was finally ransomed. Aside from *Don Quixote,* his masterpiece (Part I was published in 1605; Part II, in 1616), his fame today rests principally on his *Exemplary Novels* (1613), a book of excellent novellas.

Sonnet

In the dead silence of the peaceful night,
When others' cares are hushed in soft repose,
The sad account of my neglected woes
To conscious Heaven and Chloris I recite.
And when the sun, with his returning light,
Forth from the east his radiant journey goes,
With accents such as sorrow only knows,
My griefs to tell, is all my poor delight.
And when bright Phoebus, from his starry throne,
Sends rays direct upon the parched soil,
Still in the mournful tale I persevere.
Returning night renews my sorrow's toil.
And though from morn to night I weep and moan,
Nor Heaven nor Chloris my complainings hear.

CHARLES W. JARVIS

Soneto

En el silencio de la noche, cuando
ocupa el dulce sueño a los mortales,
la pobre cuenta de mis ricos males
estoy al cielo y a mi Clori dando.

Y al tiempo cuando el sol se va mostrando
por las rosadas puertas orientales,
con suspiros y acentos desiguales
voy la antigua querella renovando.

Y cuando el sol de su estrellado asiento
derechos rayos a la tierra envía,
el llanto crece y doblo los gemidos.

Vuelve la noche, y vuelvo al triste cuento,
y siempre hallo en mi mortal porfía
al cielo sordo, a Clori sin oídos.

Cardenio's Song

What causes all my grief and pain?
Cruel disdain.
What aggravates my misery?
Accursed jealousy.
How has my soul its patience lost?
By tedious absence crossed.
Alas! no balsam can be found
To heal the grief of such a wound,
When absence, jealousy, and scorn
Have left me hopeless and forlorn.

What in my breast this grief could move?
Neglected Love.

Canción de Cardenio

¿Quién menoscaba mis bienes?
¡Desdenes!
¿Y quién aumenta mis duelos?
¡Los celos!
¿Y quién prueba mi paciencia?
¡Ausencia!
De este modo en mi dolencia
ningún remedio se alcanza,
pues me matan la esperanza,
desdenes, celos y ausencia.

¿Quién me causa este dolor?
¡Amor!

What doth my fond desires withstand?
    Fate's cruel hand.
And what confirms my misery?
    Heaven's fixed decree.
Ah me! my boding fears portend
This strange disease my life will end;
For die I must, when three such foes,
Heaven, Fate, and Love, my bliss oppose.

My peace of mind what can restore?
    Death's welcome hour.
What gains Love's joys most readily?
    Fickle inconstancy.
Its pains what medicine can assuage?
    Wild Frenzy's rage.
'Tis, therefore, little widsom, sure,
For such a grief to seek a cure,
As knows no better remedy
Than frenzy, death, inconstancy.

¿Y quién mi gloria repuna?
    ¡Fortuna!
¿Y quién consiente mi duelo?
    ¡El cielo!
De este modo yo recelo
morir deste mal extraño,
pues se aunan en mi daño
amor, fortuna y el cielo.

¿Quién mejorará mi suerte?
    ¡La muerte!
Y el bien de amor ¿quién le alcanza?
    ¡Mudanza!
Y sus males ¿quién los cura?
    ¡Locura!
De ese modo no es cordura
querer curar la pasión
cuando los remedios son
muerte, mudanza y locura.

CHARLES W. JARVIS

Francisco de Velasco

Spain, *ca.* 1560–1630

Velasco was a poet who wrote many lyrics of great beauty about the fleeting quality of life. His *Coplas del nacimiento* was published in Burgos in 1604. Sir John Bowring made two of his poems famous among the English Romantics in his translations from the Spanish in *Ancient Poetry and Romances of Spain* (1824).

I Told Thee So!

I told thee, soul, that joy and woe
Were but a gust, a passing dew:
I told thee so,—I told thee so,—
And, O my soul, the tale was true!

This mortal life,—a fleeting thing,—
When most we love it, swiftest flies;
It passes like a shade and dies:
And while it flaps its busy wing,
It scatters every mist that lies
Round human hopes,—all air and dew.
I told thee so,—I told thee so,—
And, O my soul, the tale was true!

Like the dry leaf that autumn's breath
Sweeps from the tree, the mourning tree,—
So swiftly and so certainly
Our days are blown about by death:
For life is built on vanity;
Renewing days but death renew.
I told thee so,—I told thee so,—
And, O my soul, the tale was true!

O, let us seize on what is stable,
And not on what is shifting! All
Rushes down life's vast waterfall,

Bien te lo dige yo alma

Bien te lo dige yo alma
que esta vida toda es aire,
bien te lo dige yo
y a fe que no es donaire.

La vida de este suelo
cuando más la queremos,
más presto la perdemos,
porque se va de vuelo:
pásase con su consuelo
todo hecho aire:
bien te lo dige yo,
y a fe que no es donaire.

Vásele en un momento
la vida al que peca,
como la hoja seca
que se la lleva el viento:
porque su fundamento
va todo sobre aire:
bien te lo dige yo,
y a fe que no es donaire.

Echemos siempre mano
de lo que es perdurable,
y no de lo deleznable

On to that sea interminable
Which has no shore. Earth's pleasures pall;
But heaven is safe, and sacred too.
I told thee so,—I told thee so,—
And, O my soul, the tale was true!

porque se pasa en vano:
todo lo que es humano
vásenos como aire:
bien te lo dige yo,
y a fe que no es donaire.

SIR JOHN BOWRING

Alonso de Bonilla

Spain, early seventeenth century

Bonilla was one of the Spanish precursors of conceptism. His poetry is predominantly religious, and he was the author of numerous sonnets, ballads, and lyrics in praise of the Virgin Mary. Lope de Vega admired his "marvelous thoughts, expressed with such grace and perception that in this kind of poetry I have seen no one who can equal him." [18] A few of his shorter lyrics have survived the centuries and are still widely popular.

"Let's Hold Sweet Converse"

"Let's hold sweet converse, ere we part,
Beloved fair!" " 'Tis sweet to be
With thee, the husband of my heart!"
"I'll in the garden wait for thee."
"When?" "At the sacred vesper-bell."
"That is the hour in which I dwell
Within the souls I love, and there
Fill the pure shrine with praise and prayer."
"But if, when dawns the vesper hour,
I should be absent—" "Nay, my soul!
Lose not the holy, hallowing power
Of evening's serene control!"
"I'll come;—that hour shall not depart
Without thy smile who holdest my heart!"
"I'll in the garden wait for thee."
"When?" "At the sacred vesper-bell."
"Yes, come! O come!—my breast shall be
A garden of fair flowers for thee,
Where thou the fairest flowers shalt cull."
"And wilt thou give a flower to me?"
"Yes! flowers more bright, more beautiful,
Than ever in earth's gardens grew,
If thou wilt trust and love me too."
"Yes! I will trust and love thee well."
"I'll in the garden wait for thee."
"When?" "At the sacred vesper-bell."

¿Quieres hoy conversación?

"¿Quieres hoy conversación,
querida esposa?"—Sí quiero,
esposo del corazón—
"Pues en el jardín te espero."
—¿A qué hora?—"A la oración."
"A la oración no me niego,
que esta es la perfecta hora
en que a las almas me entrego."
—¿Y si a la oración no llego?
"Has por llegar a tal hora,
goza tan buena ocasión,
alma no quieres?"—Sí quiero,
esposo del corazón.—
"Pues en el jardín te espero."
—¿A qué hora?—"A la oración.
Si acaso te determinas
en mi pecho hallarás
jardín de flores divinas."
—¿Y alguna flor me darás?—
"Darte he flores peregrinas,
pero con tal condición
que me has de querer."—Sí quiero,
esposo del corazón.—
"Pues en el jardín te espero."
—¿A qué hora?—"A la oración."

SIR JOHN BOWRING

Lupercio Leonardo de Argensola

Spain, 1559–1613

The older of two brother poets, Lupercio L. de Argensola was the secretary of Empress Maria of Austria, wife of Maximilian II, for several years of her residence in Madrid. Argensola was also a

18. *Ibid.* 241.

chronicler of his native province of Aragón, and he became famous for his sonnets. He translated Horace into Spanish and unsuccessfully tried his hand at playwriting. He died in Naples in 1613.

Sonnet on Love

Thou, Love, by whom the naked soul is viewed,
Recount to us, with what disdains and heart
Of proof could Phyllis (with such form endued)
Resist so long thy sharpest golden dart.
And those close doubts, and struggling reasons show,
With which being vanquished she her wound concealed.
If it were Pride or Shame, which made her so
Deny with language, what dumb shows revealed.

What we without could see, was that her face
Like blushing Rose put on a crimson dye;
And her eyes hid themselves with bashful grace,
Like languishing Apollo, drawing nigh
His race's end; when his bright beams he shrouds,
And, with vermilion flakes, adorns the clouds.

SIR RICHARD FANSHAWE

Amor, tú que las almas ves desnudas

Amor, tú que las almas ves desnudas,
cuéntanos el desdén i la osadía
con que la hermosa Filis resistía
a tus doradas flechas más agudas.

I dinos las razones i las dudas
con que, después de herida, se encubría;
si sobervia o vergüenza detenía
lo que mostravan apariencias mudas.

Lo que nosotros vimos acá fuera
fue colorearse el rostro como rosa,
i huir de nuestros ojos sus dos soles;

cual suele Phebo al fin de su carrera,
robando su color a cada cosa,
las nubes adornar con arreboles.

Bartolomé Leonardo de Argensola
Spain, 1562–1631

The younger of the two Argensola brother poets, Bartolomé was ordained at the age of twenty-two and became the chaplain of Empress Maria of Austria when she was in Madrid. With his brother, Lupercio, he formed part of the Academia Poética Imitadora, which was frequently attended by Cervantes and Lope de Vega, both of whom praised his poems. These were published in 1634, after his death. Argensola wrote satires, sonnets, lyrics, epigrams. He also translated Horace and was well known as a scholar of the classics. In the words of Lope de Vega, Bartolomé "came from Aragón to reform the writing of the Castilian tongue in our poets."[19] The two Argensola brothers were often called "the Horaces of Spain."

I Must Confess, Don Juan

I must confess, Don Juan, on due inspection,
That dame Elvira's charming red and white,
Though fair they seem, are only hers by right,
In that her money purchased their perfection;
But thou must grant as well, on calm reflection,
That her sweet lie hath such a luster bright,
As fairly puts to shame the paler light,
And honest beauty of a true complexion!
And yet no wonder I distracted go
With such deceit, when 'tis within our ken
That nature blinds us with the self-same spell;
For that blue heaven above that charms us so,
Is neither heaven nor blue! Sad pity then
That so much beauty is not truth as well.

JAMES YOUNG GIBSON

Yo os quiero confesar, Don Juan

Yo os quiero confesar, don Juan, primero:
que aquel blanco y color de doña Elvira
no tiene de ella más, si bien se mira,
que el haberle costado su dinero.

Pero tras eso confesaros quiero
que es tanta la beldad de su mentira
que en vano a competir con ella aspira
belleza ygual de rostro verdadero.

Mas, ¿qué mucho que yo perdido ande
por un engaño tal, pues que sabemos
que nos engaña así Naturaleza?

Porque ese cielo azul que todos vemos
ni es cielo ni es azul: ¡Lástima grande
que no sea verdad tanta belleza!

19. *Ibid.*, 259.

Mary Magdalene

Blessed, yet sinful one, and broken-hearted!
The crowds are pointing at the thing forlorn,
In wonder and in scorn!
Thou weepest days of innocence departed;
Thou weepest, and thy tears have power to move
The Lord to pity and love.

The greatest of thy follies is forgiven,
Even for the least of all the tears that shine
On that pale cheek of thine.
Thou didst kneel down to Him who came from heaven,
Evil and ignorant, and thou shalt rise
Holy, and pure, and wise.

It is not much that to the fragrant blossom
The ragged brier should change; the bitter fir
Distill Arabian myrrh;
Nor that, upon the wintry desert's bosom,
The harvest should rise plenteous, and the swain
Bear home the abundant grain.

But come and see the bleak and barren mountains
Thick to their tops with roses; come and see
Leaves on the dry, dead tree:
The perished plant, set out by living fountains,
Grows fruitful, and its beauteous branches rise
For ever towards the skies.

WILLIAM CULLEN BRYANT

A Santa María Magdalena

¡O tú, siempre dichosa pecadora,
la que fuiste por tal con grande espanto
del vulgo con el dedo señalada!,
tus lágrimas con Christo pueden tanto,
que la menor lo enciende i enamora,
i a la culpa mayor dexa anegada.
Tú quedas en apóstol transformada,
i de ignorante i mala, santa i sabia.
No es mucho que la zarza en flor se mude
i que el álamo sude
en competencia de la mirra arabia,
i que cuando de yerba al campo priva,
la mies en abundancia se recoja.
Venid a ver de rosas i azucenas
las montañas estériles más llenas,
i un árbol seco revestido de hoja.
La planta antes inútil Dios cultiva;
regada en su jardín con agua viva,
es fructífera ya, i sus ramas bellas
tocan continuamente en las estrellas.

Soul and Sense

There are two principles in man that strive
For ever for the mastery: he is bound
Even to the vilest reptiles on the ground,
And to the meanest plant or flower alive;
Yet he has glory struggling in his breast—
Glory that has its fountain-source above:
He stands erect in majesty and love,
And power, and joy, and feels that he is blest.
Let him beware, then, that his earthly part
Bend not his heavenly to its narrow sphere,
Nor cloud with darkness this his mortal state;
And, if he faint a moment, let his heart
Find comfort in the thought—that even here
He may the stars sublimely contemplate!

SIR JOHN BOWRING

El hombre fue de dos principios hecho

El hombre fue de dos principios hecho,
tales, que, con jactancia verdadera,
a sus ojos le alega cualquier fiera
i cualquier planta parentesco estrecho.

Pero cuando él reconozió en su pecho
la gran porción del fuego de la esfera,
vio, con admiración de ver lo que era,
que a la divinidad tiene derecho.

Haz, pues, que, con trocado ministerio,
a la vaga altivez del albedrío
el sentido inferior la tienda redes.

I cuando él pretendiere, o Fabio mío,
hazerte siervo, acuérdate que puedes
mirar essas estrellas con imperio.

Tell Me, Thou Common Father

Tell me, Thou common Father,—tell me why,
(Since thou art just and good) dost thou permit
Successful fraud, securely throned, to sit,
While innocence, oppress'd, stands weeping by?

Why hast thou nerved that strong arm to oppose
Thy righteous mandates with impunity,

Dime, Padre Común

"Dime, Padre común, pues eres justo,
¿por qué ha de permitir tu providencia,
que, arrastrando prisiones la innocencia,
suba la fraude a tribunal augusto?

¿Quién de fuerzas al brazo, que robusto
haze a tus leyes firme resistencia,

While the meek man who served and reverenced Thee
Lies at the feet of Thine and virtue's foes?

Why (said I, in despair) should vice confound
All nature's harmony, and tower above
In all the pomp, and pride, and power of state?
Then I look'd upwards,—and I heard a sound
As from an angel, smiling through heaven's gate,
"Is earth a spot for heaven-born souls to love?"

SIR JOHN BOWRING

i que el zelo, que más las reverencia,
gima a los pies del venzedor injusto?

Vemos que vibran vitoriosas palmas
manos inicias, la virtud gimiendo
del triunfo en el injusto regocijo."

Esto dezía yo, cuando, riendo,
celestial nimfa aparezió, i me dijo:
"¡Ciego!, ¿es la tierra el centro de las almas?"

Nay Cleanse Thy Hair

Nay cleanse this filthy mixture from thy hair,
And give the untricked tresses to the gale!
The sun, as lightly on the breeze they sail,
Shall gild thy bright brown locks! thy cheek is fair,
Away then with this artificial hue,
This blush eternal! To the human face
Nature has given no imitable grace.
Why these black spots obtruding on the view
Of lily cheek? and these ear-jewels too
That ape the barbarous Indian's vanity?
Nor Lady! need that necklace there invite
The prying eye—we know thy neck is white:
Go to thy dressing-room again, and be
Artful enough to learn simplicity.

ROBERT SOUTHEY

Quita ese afeite, O Lais

Quita ese afeite, O Lais, que se azeda,
y el mismo en el olor su fraude acusa,
déjanos ver tu rostro, y si rehusa
el despegarse, quítalo con greda.

Que tirano la ley natural veda,
o que muertas el diestro acero atusa,
que alegren más que la beldad confusa
de bosque inculto, o bárbara arboleda.

Si lo blanco, y purpúreo, que reparte
Dios con sus rosas, puso en tus mejillas
con no imitable natural mixtura,

¿por qué con dedo ingrato las mancillas?
O Lais no más que en perfección tan pura
arte ha de ser el despreciar el arte.

Hope

To hope is good, but with such wild applause
Each promise Fabius thou dost entertain;
As if decreed thee by Fate certain laws,
Or in possession *now* it did remain.
Wisdom is armed 'gainst all that can succeed,
Time's changes and his stratagems: For such
His nature is, that when his wings we need
He will come creeping on his halting crutch.

Do not, if wise, then to thyself assure
The future, nor on present goods rely,
Or think there's any time from time secure:
For then when Patience sees her Harvest nigh,
That mocking Tyrant in an instant rears
A wall between the sickle and the ears.

SIR RICHARD FANSHAWE

Fabio, las esperanzas no son malas

Fabio, las esperanzas no son malas;
mas tú con tanto aplauso las acetas,
que a oráculos forzosos de profetas,
i aun a vivos efetos, las igualas.

Sabe que contra el Tiempo se arma Palas,
contra sus inconstancias i sus tretas;
que él es tal, que tropieza en sus muletas,
cuando le piden que use de sus alas.

I assí nunca en el término futuro,
ni en el presente (si eres sabio) digas
que hay tiempo que del tiempo esté seguro;

que cuando a fuerza de sufrir le obligas
a que acuda fiel, te pone un muro
de presto entre la hoz y las espigas.

Whether Thou Curl

Whether thou curl, or braid thy native gold,
And workst it pliant into every forme,
Or leavst it by thy maids to be unrolled,
Falling about thy neck like Danae's storme:
Or whether richly 'tis enamellèd

Ya el oro natural crespes

Ya el oro natural crespes o extiendas,
o a componerlo con industria aspires,
lucir sus lazos o sus ondas mires,
cuando libre a tus damas lo encomiendas;

With cheerful emeralds, and blue sapphire veins,
Or crowned with tossing plumes, which hide thy head,
Hunting the hart over the shining plains,

Venus mistakes thee for her rural Lover,
Whom late *Adonis* for his *Venus* tooke;
Whilst change of dresses doth by turns discover
A lovely swain, and goddess in thy looke.
But I, to whom they both united seeme,
In love with her, grow jealous straight of him.

SIR RICHARD FANSHAWE

o ya, por nueva ley de Amor, lo prendas
entre ricos diamantes y zafires,
o bajo hermosas plumas lo retires,
y el traje varonil fingir pretendas,

búscate Adonis por su Venus, antes
por su Adonis te tiene ya la diosa,
y a entrambos los engañan tus cabellos;

mas yo, en la misma duda milagrosa,
mientras se hallan en ti los dos amantes,
muero por ambos y de celos de ellos.

Anonymous Sonnet

seventeenth century

Had I a Thousand Souls

Had I a thousand souls with which to love thee,
  I'd throw them all, delighted, at thy feet;
Had I uncounted gold wherewith to move thee,
  'Twould seem unworthy all, and incomplete:
I fain would be an Argus but to view thee,
  And a Briareus round thy charms to cling;
Another Orpheus to play music to thee,
  A Homer thy perfections all to sing.
I would be May, to clothe thee with its splendour,
  And Love itself adoring to caress thee;
I'd call on fame, to speak my passion tender,
  I'd fain be the world's king, to serve and bless thee,
A sun to be thy light and thy defender,
  And heaven itself for ever to possess thee.

SIR JOHN BOWRING

Si mil almas tuviera

Si mil almas tuviera con que amaros,
dellas todas en vos hiciera empleo.
Si el otro fuera igual a mi deseo
pensara tener poco para daros.

Quisiera un Argos ser para miraros,
para conmigo uniros un Briarco,
para tañeros gustos, otro Orfeo,
y otro Homero mejor para cantaros.

Fuera el Mayo en belleza por vestiros,
en fuego el amor mismo por quereros,
la fama en lenguas por mi amor deciros.

Sol, para con sus rayos defenderos
del mundo, Rey para con el serviros,
y cielo para siempre poseeros.

Luis de Góngora

Spain, 1561–1627

Góngora was a priest, like so many other famous Spanish writers of his day. But his bishop pointed out in a complaint drawn up against him in 1589 that he was obnoxiously restive during religious ceremonies; he often attended the bullfights, which were prohibited to the clergy; and he lived a life of pleasure which was hardly that of a dedicated priest.

Góngora was far more successful as a poet, and his poetry embraced all aspects of that genre. He wrote many simple and beautiful lyrics and ballads in the popular style, he composed some very abstruse poems replete with mythological and historical allusions in a language of images which was unique, and he left a series of sonnets that are among the finest in Spanish. Vastly popular in the seventeenth century and during the first half of the eighteenth century, Góngora's poetry began to fall into neglect, and it even became difficult to make sense out of many of his compositions. The great Spanish critic, Menéndez y Pelayo, referred to his poetry as being "without ideas or subject matter, like mere splotches of color or mere successions of sounds."[20]

20. Marcelino Menéndez y Pelayo, *Antología de poetas líricos castellanos* (14 vols.; Madrid: Perlado, Páez, 1899–1919), XIV, 156.

The French symbolists and some perceptive Spanish writers "rediscovered" Góngora at the end of the nineteenth century, and the Generation of 1927 in Spain chose him as the poet-symbol of their group, which consisted of Lorca, Alberti, Guillén, Cernuda, Aleixandre, and others. Today Góngora is regarded as one of the greatest Spanish poets of all time.

A Rose

Blown in the morning, thou shalt fade ere noon,
What boots a life which in such haste forsakes thee?
Thou'rt wondrous frolic, being to die so soon,
And passing proud a little colour makes thee.
If thee thy brittle beauty so deceives,
Know then the thing that swells thee is thy bane;
For the same beauty doth, in bloody leaves,
The sentence of thy early death contain.
Some clown's coarse lungs will poison thy sweet flower,
If by the careless plough thou shalt be torn;
And many Herods lie in wait each hour
To murder thee as soon as thou art born—
Nay, force thy bud to blow—their tyrant breath
Anticipating life, to hasten death!

SIR RICHARD FANSHAWE

Vana rosa

Ayer naciste, y morirás mañana.
¿Para tan breve ser, quién te dio vida?
¿Para vivir tan poco estás lucida,
y para no ser nada estás lozana?

Si te engañó tu hermosura vana,
bien presto la verás desvanecida
porque en tu hermosura está escondida
la ocasión de morir muerte temprana.

Cuando te corte la robusta mano,
ley de la agricultura permitida,
grosero aliento acabará tu suerte.

No salgas, que te aguarda algún tirano;
dilata tu nacer para tu vida,
que anticipas tu ser para tu muerte.

A Rich Foole

Thee, senseless Stock, because th'art richly guilt,
The blinded people without cause admire,
And Superstition impiously hath built
Altars to that which should have beene the fire.
Nere shall my tongue consent to worship thee,
Since all's not Gold that glistens and is faire;
Carving but makes an Image of a Tree:
But Gods of Images are made by Prayer.

Sabean Incense in a fragrant Cloud
Illustriously suspended o'er thy Crowne
Like a King's Canopy, makes thee allowed
For more than man. But let them take thee downe,
And thy true value be once understood,
Thy dull Idolaters will finde th'art wood.[21]

SIR RICHARD FANSHAWE

Lugar te da sublime el vulgo ciego

Lugar te da sublime el vulgo ciego,
verde ya pompa de la selva obscura;
que no sin arte religión impura
aras te destinó, te hurtó al fuego.

Mudo mil veces yo la deidad niego,
no el esplendor a tu materia dura;
ídolos a los troncos la escultura,
dioses hace a los ídolos el ruego.

En lenguas mil de luz, por tantas de oro
fragrantes bocas el humor sabeo
te aclama, ilustremente suspendido.

En tus desnudos hoy muros ignoro
cuántas de grato señas te deseo,
leño al fin con lisonjas desmentido.

The Fall

The bloody trunk of him who did possess
Above the rest a hapless happy state,
This little stone doth seal, but not depress,
And scarce can stop the rowling of his fate.

En la muerte de Don Rodrigo Calderón

Sella el tronco sangriento, no le oprime,
de aquel dichosamente desdichado,
que de las inconstancias de su hado
esta pizarra apenas le redime;

---

21. The title that Fanshawe gives to this poem is deceiving. *Rich* is used here to mean richly embellished and *foole* means deceptive trifle or idol. The poem describes an idol of elaborately carved and embellished wood. This wood had formerly grown in a green forest but now adorns a temple after having been saved from the fire (wood's usual fate) by an impure religion. The poet refuses to worship the idol, but he admires and respects its artistic worth. Such idols, he says, only become gods if misled people worship them.

Brass tombs which justice hath denied his fault,
The common pity to his virtues pays,
Adorning an imaginary vault,
Which from our minds time strives in vain to raze.
Ten years the world upon him falsely smiled,
Sheathing in fawning looks the deadly knife
Long aimed at his head; that so beguiled
It more securely might bereave his life;
Then threw him to a scaffold from a throne,
Much doctrine lies beneath this little stone.

SIR RICHARD FANSHAWE

A Nightingale

With such variety and dainty skill
Yon nightingale divides her mournful song,
As if ten thousand of them through one bill
Did sing in parts the story of their wrong.
Nay, she accuses with such vehemence
Her ravisher, I think she would incline
The conscious grove thereof to have a sense
And print it on the leaves of that tall pine.
Yet happy she, who may her pain declare
In moving notes, and wandering through the woods
With uncut wings, but change divert her care!
But let Him melt away in silent floods,
Whom his Medusa turned into a stone,
That he might neither change, nor make his moan.

SIR RICHARD FANSHAWE

The Spring

Those whiter lilies which the early morn
Seems to have newly woven of sleaved silk,
To which (on banks of wealthy Tagus borne)
Gold was their cradle, liquid pearl their milk:
These blushing roses, with whose virgin leaves
The wanton wind to sport himself presumes,
Whilst from their rifled wardrobe he receives
For his wings purple, for his breath perfumes:

Both those, and these, my Celia's pretty foot
Trod up. But if she should her face display,
And fragrant breast, they'd dry down to the root,
(As with the blasting of the midday's ray)
And this soft wind which both perfumes and cools
Pass like the unregarded breath of Fools.

SIR RICHARD FANSHAWE

Soar High, My Love

Soar high, my Love, check not thy gallant flight
With thought of that ill-fated youth, to whom

piedad común en vez de la sublime
urna que el escarmiento le ha negado,
padrón le erige en bronce imaginado,
que en vano el tiempo las memorias lime.

Risueño con él, tanto como falso,
el tiempo, cuatro lustros en la risa,
el cuchillo quizá envainaba agudo.

Del sitial después al cadahalso
precipitado, ¡oh cuánto nos avisa!,
¡oh cuánta trompa es su ejemplo mudo!

Con diferencia tal, con gracia tanta

Con diferencia tal, con gracia tanta
aquel ruiseñor llora, que sospecho
que tiene otros cien mil dentro del pecho
que alternan su color por su garganta;

y aun creo que el espíritu levanta
—como en información de su derecho—
a escribir del cuñado el atroz hecho
en las hojas de aquella verde planta.

Ponga, pues, fin a las querellas que usa,
pues ni quejarse, ni mudar estanza
por pico ni por pluma se le veda;

y llore sólo aquel que su Medusa
en piedra convirtió, porque no pueda
ni publicar su mal, ni hacer mudanza.

Los blancos lilios que de ciento en ciento

Los blancos lilios que de ciento en ciento,
hijos del Sol, nos da la Primavera,
a quien del Tajo son en la ribera
oro su cuna, perlas su alimento;

las frescas rosas, que ambicioso el viento
con pluma solicita lisonjera,
como quien de una y otra hoja espera
purpúreas alas, si lascivo aliento,

a vuestro hermoso pie cada cual debe
su beldad toda. ¿Qué hará la mano,
si tanto puede el pie, que ostenta flores,

porque vuestro esplendor venza la nieve,
venza su rosicler, y porque en vano,
hablando vos, expiren sus olores?

No enfrene tu gallardo pensamiento

No enfrene tu gallardo pensamiento
del animoso joven mal logrado

(fallen like a star from his presumptuous height)
The grey sea was a diaphanous tomb.
Thy downy wings stretch to the gentle wind,
Avoiding the dead sea of cold despair,
And raised above the clouds, a passage find,
To the most flaming region of the air.

With active circles crown that golden sphere,
'Gainst which the Royal Bird refines his sight,
Showing what kind he is by looking there,
And melt thy wings yet at the noblest light.
Since to the Ocean and her pearly shore,
My glorious ruin now adds one title more.

SIR RICHARD FANSHAWE

el loco fin, de cuyo vuelo osado
fue ilustre tumba el húmido elemento.

Las dulces alas tiende al blando viento,
y sin que el torpe mar del miedo helado
tus plumas moje, toca levantado
la encendida región del ardimiento.

Corona en puntas la dorada esfera
do el pájaro real su vista afina,
y al noble ardor desátese la cera;

que al mar, do tu sepulcro se destina,
gran honra le será, y a su ribera,
que le hurte su nombre tu ruïna.

To Dr. Lewis Bavia, on His Ecclesiastical History

This offering to the world by Bavia brought
  Is poesy, by numbers unconfined;
  Such order guides the master's march of mind,
Such skill refines the rich-drawn ore of thought:
The style, the matter, gray Experience taught,
  Art's rules adorn'd what metre might not bind:
The tale hath baffled Time, that thief unkind,
And from Oblivion's bonds with toil hath bought
Three helmsmen of the sacred barque: the pen,
  That so these heavenly wardens doth enhance,—
No pen, but rather key of Fame's proud dome,
Opening her everduring doors to men,—
  Is no poor drudge recording things of chance,
Which paints her shadowy forms on tumbling foam.

EDWARD CHURTON

Para la cuarta parte de la Pontifical del doctor Babia

Este que Babia al mundo hoy ha ofrecido
poema, si no a números atado,
de la disposición antes limado,
y de la erudición después lamido,

historia es culta, cuyo encanecido
estilo, si no métrico, peinado,
tres ya pilotos del bajel sagrado
hurta al tiempo, y redime del olvido.

Pluma, pues, que claveros celestiales
eterniza en los bronces de su historia,
llave es ya de los tiempos, y no pluma.

Ella a sus nombres puertas immortales
abre, no de caduca, no, memoria,
que sombras sella en túmulos de espuma.

Life's Greatest Misery. Addressed to a Friend on His Marriage

To dine on meats high-spiced, and find your flask
  Has leak'd, and not a drop your thirst to tame;
To reach your posting-house dead-tired, and ask
  For mules, and find one trotting brute dead-lame;
  To try new boots, with luck not quite the same,
One with great pain you fit, and one you tear;
  To play Primero, and,—to win your game
Wanting the King,—to find the Knave is there;
To ply with gifts a thankless lady fair;
  To owe to bankers punctual as the day;
To ride uncloak'd, unfenced, through spungy air;
  To feed bad grooms who steal your corn and hay:
Count all the griefs you've known since life began;
The worst remains—to be a married man.

EDWARD CHURTON

Comer salchicas y hallar sin gota

Comer salchicas y hallar sin gota
el frasco, por haberse derramado;
llegar a tomar postas muy cansado
y daros una que tropieza y trota;

calzaros con gran premio la una bota
y romperse la otra en lo picado;
ir a primera, habiéndoos descartado
del rey de bastos, y acudir la sota;

servir a dama que no dando toma;
deber a genoveses puntüales;
pasear sin gualdrapa haciendo lodos;

tener familia que no sirva y coma...
añada quien quisiere otros mil males:
que el ser casado es el mayor de todos.

The Sirens

Young mariner, of hope so bold and gay,
  Venturing, with vessel trim and halyards strong,
  To courtly deeps, by Sirens' treacherous song
More haunted than the famed Campanian bay:
Forego thine oars, and either hand close lay
  To thine endanger'd ears:—thou sail'st along,
  Where, worse than hidden rocks and quicksands,
    throng
Bright forms, whose voices steal men's souls away.
That strain, whose glorious tones with sweetness
    swell,
  Breathing of youthful hope, or valour's praise,
O hear it not;—it is thine own death-knell.
  Fly from the witch, who, while her harp she plays,
Moves rocks, stays winds and waters by her spell:
  Gaze not; to hear is death,—'tis death to gaze.

EDWARD CHURTON

Love Sonnet

While to contend in brightness with thy hair
Sunlight on burnished gold may strive in vain,
While thy proud forehead's whiteness may disdain
The lilies of the field, which bloom less fair,
While each red lip at once more eyes will snare
Than the perfumed carnation bud new born,
And while thy graceful neck with queenly scorn
Outshines bright crystal on the morning air:

Enjoy thy hour, neck, ringlets, lips and brow,
Before the glories of this age of gold:
Earth's precious ore, sweet flowers, and crystal bright
Turn pale and dim; and Time with Fingers cold
Rifle the bud and bloom; and they, and thou
Become but ash, smoke, shadow, dust and night.[22]

EDWARD CHURTON

Pride of the Fourth and Liquid Element

Pride of the fourth and liquid element,
Sweet brook whose waters with soft music pass,
Stretching, pellucid and pre-eminent,
Their ribbon of bright silver through the grass,
Since Cupid on your smooth and quiet stream,
As she looks into it, portrays the snow
And scarlet of her face, for whom I seem
At times to freeze, at other times to glow,

Oh marinero, tú que, cortesano

Oh marinero, tú que, cortesano,
al Palacio le fías tus entenas,
al Palacio Real, que de Sirenas
es un segundo mar napolitano,

los reinos deja, y una y otra mano
de las orejas las desvía penas;
que escollo es, cuando no sirte de arenas,
la dulce voz de un serafín humano.

Cual su acento, tu muerte será clara,
si espira suavidad, si gloria espira
su armonía mortal, su beldad rara.

Huye de la que, armada de una lira,
si rocas mueve, si bajeles para,
cantando mata al que matando mira.

Mientras por competir con tu cabello

Mientras por competir con tu cabello
oro bruñido al sol relumbra en vano;
mientras con menosprecio en medio el llano
mira tu blanca frente el lilio bello;

mientras a cada labio, por cogello,
siguen más ojos que al clavel temprano,
y mientras triunfa con desdén lozano
del luciente cristal tu gentil cuello,

goza cuello, cabello, labio y frente,
antes que lo que fue en tu edad dorada
oro, lilio, clavel, cristal luciente,

no sólo en plata o víola troncada
se vuelva, mas tú y ello juntamente
en tierra, en humo, en polvo, en sombra, en nada.

¡Oh claro honor del líquido elemento!

¡Oh claro honor del líquido elemento,
dulce arroyuelo de luciente plata!
cuya agua entre la yerba se dilata
con regalado son, con paso lento.

Pues la por quien helar y arder me siento
mientras en ti se mira, Amor retrata
de su rostro la nieve y escarlata
en tu tranquilo y blando movimiento,

22. This sonnet is one of the best expressions in Spanish of the *carpe diem* ("enjoy this day") theme, which was made famous by the Roman poet Horace and was very popular among the Renaissance poets of Spain. Góngora's more direct antecedent is Garcilaso's "En tanto que de rosa y azucena" (translation herein). The final lines of Góngora's sonnet, however, with their anguished conclusion that life ends in total annihilation, are a far cry from the Renaissance point of view.

The English translation of the above sonnet mainly follows Edward Churton's version, made in the middle of the past century, but a few key words that were inaccurately translated have been altered by the editor.

Watch how you move; be careful to keep taut
The crystal bridle's wavy rein with which
You curb your current's striving to run faster.
It would be wrong if beauty should be caught,
Confused, in that deep breast, beauty so rich,
Caught by the watery trident's mighty master.

J. M. COHEN

The Song of Catharine of Aragon

O, take a lesson, flowers, from me,
How in a dawn all charms decay,—
Less than my shadow doomed to be,
Who was a wonder yesterday!

I, with the early twilight born,
Found, ere the evening shades, a bier;
And I should die in darkness lorn,
But that the moon is shining here:
So must ye die,—though ye appear
So fair,—and night your curtain be.
O, take a lesson, flowers, from me!

My fleeting being was consoled,
When the carnation met my view;
One hurrying day my doom has told,—
Heaven gave that lovely flower but two:
Ephemeral monarch of the wold,—
I clad in gloom, in scarlet he.
O, take a lesson, flowers, from me!

The jasmine, sweetest flower of flowers,
The soonest is its radiance fled;
It scarce perfumes as many hours
As there are star-beams round its head:
If living amber fragrance shed,
The jasmine, sure, its shrine must be.
O, take a lesson, flowers, from me!

The bloody-warrior fragrance gives;
It towers unblushing, proud, and gay;
More days than other flowers it lives,—
It blooms through all the days of May:
I'd rather like a shade decay,
Than such a gaudy being be.
O, take a lesson, flowers, from me.

SIR JOHN BOWRING

vete como te vas, no dejes floja
la undosa rienda al cristiano freno
con que gobiernas tu procaz corriente:

que no es bien que confusamente acoja
tanta belleza en su profundo seno
el gran señor del húmedo tridente.

Letrillas

Aprended, flores, de mí
lo que va de ayer a hoy,
que ayer maravilla fui,
y hoy sombra mía aun no soy.

La Aurora ayer me dio cuna,
la noche ataúd me dio;
sin luz muriera si no
me la prestara la luna:
pues de vosotras ninguna
deja de acabar así,

aprended, flores, de mí
lo que va de ayer a hoy,
que ayer maravilla fui,
y hoy sombra mía aun no soy.

Consuelo dulce el clavel
es a la breve edad mía,
pues quien me concedió un día,
dos apenas le dio a él:
efímeras del vergel
yo cárdena, él carmesí.

Aprended, flores, de mí
lo que va de ayer a hoy,
que ayer maravilla fui,
y hoy sombra mía aun no soy.

Flor es el jazmín, si bella,
no de las más vividoras,
pues dura pocas más horas
que rayos tiene de estrella;
si el ámbar florece, es ella
la flor que él retiene en sí.

Aprended, flores, de mí
lo que va de ayer a hoy,
que ayer maravilla fui,
y hoy sombra mía aun no soy.

El alhelí, aunque grosero
en fragancia y en color,
más días ve que otra flor,
pues ve los de un mayo entero:
morir maravilla quiero
y no vivir alhelí.

Aprended, flores de mí
lo que va de ayer a hoy,
que ayer maravilla fui,
y hoy sombra mía aun no soy.

A ninguna flor mayores
términos concede el Sol
que al sublime girasol,
Matusalén de las flores:
ojos son aduladores
cuantas en él hojas vi.

Aprended, flores, de mí
lo que va de ayer a hoy,
que ayer maravilla fui,
y hoy sombra mía aun no soy.

The Rosemary Spray

The flowers upon the rosemary spray,
  Young Maid, may school thy sorrow;
The blue-eyed flower, that blooms to-day,
  To honey turns to-morrow.

A tumult stirs thy tender breast,
  With jealous pain true-hearted,
That he, whom thy first love hath bless'd
  From thee hath coldly parted.

Ungracious boy, who slights thy love,
  And overbold, disdaining
To ask forgiveness, and remove
  The cause of thy complaining.

Hope, come and drive those tears away!
  For lovers' jealous sorrow,
Like dewy blue-eyed flower on spray,
  To honey turns to-morrow.

By thine own joy thou wast undone:
  A bliss thou coulds't not measure,
Like star at dawn too near the sun,
  Eclipsed thee by its pleasure.

Walk forth with eyes serene and fair;
  The pearls that deck the morning,
Are wasted in the day's fierce glare;
  With calmness tame his scorning.

Disperse those clouds that but dismay;
  Distrust that jealous sorrow:
The blue-eyed flower, that blooms to-day,
  To honey turns to-morrow.

EDWARD CHURTON

Give Me Warm Life and Spirits Free

Give me warm life and spirits free,
To mock the world that mocks at me.

  Let those, who climb on Glory's wings,
Rule the wide earth and all its kings:
For me, upon a lowlier throne,
I'll rule a kingdom all my own;
Each morn on simple table spread

Las flores del romero

Las flores del romero,
  niña Isabel,
  hoy son flores azules,
  mañana serán miel.

Celosa estás, la niña,
celosa estás de aquel
dichoso, pues le buscas,
ciego, pues no te ve,
ingrato, pues te enoja
y confiado, pues
no se disculpa hoy
de lo que hizo ayer.
Enjuguen esperanzas
lo que lloras por él;
que celos entre aquellos
que se han querido bien
  que son flores azules,
  mañana serán miel.

Aurora de ti misma,
que cuando a amanecer
a tu placer empiezas,
te eclipsan tu placer,
serénense tus ojos,
y más perlas no des,
porque al sol le está mal
lo que a la aurora bien.
Desata como nieblas
todo lo que no ve;
que sospechas de amantes
y querellas después
  hoy son flores azules,
  mañana serán miel.

Ande yo caliente

Ande yo caliente
y ríase la gente.

Traten otros del gobierno
del mundo y sus monarquías,
mientras gobiernan mis días
mantequillas y pan tierno,
y las mañanas de invierno

Fresh butter and sweet household bread;
And while, in Winter's driving storms
Mild lemon-punch my heart's blood warms,
Ensconced beneath a safe roof-tree
I'll mock the world that mocks at me.

Let lordlings feast in envied state
At boards that groan with gorgeous plate:
A sad physician, spectral Care,
Stands waiting on that golden fare,
Embittering all its lavish cost:
For me, whene'er I play the host,
The savoury sausage, neatly dress'd
By glowing fire, shall cheer my guest,
Poor as myself, but fancy-free
To mock the mocking world with me.

And when white-bearded January
With silvery snow hangs bush and berry,
And ice is on the mountain-snow,
In chafing-dish good store I'll throw
Of beech or chestnut fruits, nor fail
To win some neighbour's merry tale,—
Still merry, though the theme be sad,—
Of kings, who in old days went mad,
Who now are dead, and leave me free
To mock the world that mocks at me.

Far let the venturous merchant run,
To change the clime, and change the sun,
And seek in cold or torrid zone
For pearly shell or Indian stone:
The shells and shining stones for me
Are those beneath the poplar-tree,
That pave the fountain dark and clear,
Where oft the nightingale I hear:
Come, merchant, to the poplar-tree,
And mock the cheating world with me.

Let bold Leander wake to brave
In darksome night the foaming wave,
And seek his bride across the sea:
But quiet married men, like me,
Dry-shod on stepping-stones go down
To Madrigal from Yepes-Town,
O'er the calm ford, whose waters move
Soft as the idle hours of love,
And murmuring through the peaceful lea
Mock the mad world that mocks at me.

EDWARD CHURTON

naranjada y aguardiente,
    y ríase la gente.

Coma en dorada vajilla
el Príncipe mil cuidados,
como píldoras dorados;
que yo en mi pobre mesilla
quiero más una morcilla
que en el asador reviente,
    y ríase la gente.

Cuando cubra las montañas
de blanca nieve el enero,
tenga yo lleno el brasero
de bellotas y castañas,
y quien las dulces patrañas
del Rey que rabió me cuente,
    y ríase la gente.

Busque muy en hora buena
el mercader nuevos soles;
yo conchas y caracoles
entre la menuda arena,
escuchando a Filomena
sobre el chopo de la fuente,
    y ríase la gente.

Pase a media noche el mar,
y arda en amorosa llama,
Leandro por ver su dama;
que yo más quiero pasar
del golfo de mi lagar
la blanca o roja corriente,
    y ríase la gente.

Pues Amor es tan cruel
que de Píramo y su amada
hace tálamo una espada,
do se junten ella y él,
sea mi Tisbe un pastel
y la espada sea mi diente,
    y ríase la gente.

Lope de Vega
Spain, 1562–1635

Lope de Vega was one of Spain's greatest lyric poets as well as her most prolific dramatist. His style often followed that of the popular ballads and folk lyrics, but he also wrote some fine sonnets and a large amount of narrative poetry. He is perhaps the most modern, least dated, of the poets of the golden age. In his later years Lope became a priest, but that did not stop him from being in love with love. He lived life to the hilt and had "two wives, several mistresses, numerous children," as one of his biographers, Francis C. Hayes, points out.[23]

Lope's dramas ripple and sing with the lilt of the folk songs and ballads of his country. In this he shows some kinship with the twentieth-century poet and dramatist, García Lorca, who was his great admirer. But Lope also wrote much poetry that had a kind of baroque splendor about it, thus "showing the similarity of Lope's elaborate, complex embellishment to the euphuistic expressions of Shakespeare." The adjective *euphuistic* is here used to mean beautifully decorative and ornamental. The Spanish essayist Azorín wrote of Lope: "Lope's genius has fluttered around over everything on earth. Neither time nor space held secrets for him. His strength is pliant, light, smooth: an immense poet's strength, prodigious, titanic, yet appearing as simple as a child's."[24]

The Dream

To set my jealous soul at strife
    All things maliciously agree,
    Though sleep of Death the image be,
Dreams are the portraiture of life.
I saw, when last I closed my eyes,
    Celinda stoop to another's will;
    If specious apprehension kill,
What would the truth without disguise?
The joys which I should call mine own
    Me thought this rival did possess:
    Like dreams is all my happiness;
Yet dreams themselves allow me none.

THOMAS STANLEY

O burlas de amor ingrato

O burlas de amor ingrato,
que todas sois de una suerte,
sueño imagen de la muerte,
y de la vida retrato.

¿Qué importa que se desuelen,
los interiores sentidos,
si los de afuera dormidos,
sufrir sus engaños suelen?

Yo vi sin ojos mi dueño,
en ajena voluntad,
¡qué pudiera la verdad,
si pudo matarme el sueño?

River of Seville

River of Seville
How softly you flow,
Where white galleys sail
And green branches grow.

Ships loaded with silver
Break the water and roll,
They come from San Lucas
To the Tower of Gold.

Where is your homeland
My beautiful girl?
Though not from the Indies,
You are a pure pearl.

In one of those galleys
My sweetheart must be,
God, if only some sailor
Would now set him free!

Seguidillas

Río de Sevilla,
¡Cuán bien pareces
con galeras blancas
y ramos verdes!

Vienen de San Lúcar,
rompiendo el agua,
a la Torre del Oro,
barcos de plata.

¿Dónde te has criado,
la niña bella,
que, sin ir a las Indias,
toda eres perla?

En estas galeras
viene aquel ángel.
¡Quién remara a su lado
para librarle!

---

23. Francis C. Hayes, *Lope de Vega* (New York: Twayne Publishers, 1967), 22.
24. *Ibid.*, 83, ii.

Seville and Triana
With the river between!
Thus your ungrateful master
To my hope has been.

JOHN A. CROW

Sevilla y Triana
y el río en medio:
así es tan de mis gustos
tu ingrato dueño.

May Song

In the May mornings
Dawn kisses the ground,
The nightingales sing,
And the fields resound.

In the May mornings
There is a fresh breeze,
And nightingales cover
The green poplar trees.

The fountains all laugh
And shiny pearls throw
To the gay little flowers
That nearest them grow.

The plants put on silks
Of various hues,
No effort goes into
The colors they choose.

The flowering meadows
Bring joy to the ground,
The nightingales sing,
And the fields resound.

JOHN A. CROW

Maya

En las mañanicas
del mes de mayo
cantan los ruiseñores,
retumba el campo.

En las mañanicas,
como son frescas,
cubren ruiseñores
las alamedas.

Ríense las fuentes
tirando perlas
a las florecillas
que están más cerca.

Vístense las plantas
de varias sedas,
que sacar colores
poco las cuesta.

Los campos alegran
tapetes varios,
cantan los ruiseñores,
retumba el campo.

Tomorrow

Lord, what am I, that, with unceasing care,
Thou didst seek after me,—that thou didst wait,
Wet with unhealthy dews, before my gate,
And pass the gloomy nights of winter there?
O, strange delusion, that I did not greet
Thy blest approach! and, O, to heaven how lost,
If my ingratitude's unkindly frost
Has chilled the bleeding wounds upon thy feet!
How oft my guardian angel gently cried,
"Soul, from thy casement look, and thou shalt see
How he persists to knock and wait for thee!"
And, O, how often to that voice of sorrow,
"Tomorrow we will open," I replied!
And when the morrow came, I answered still,
  "Tomorrow."

HENRY WADSWORTH LONGFELLOW

Mañana

¿Qué tengo yo que mi amistad procuras?
¿Qué interés se te sigue, Jesús mío,
que a mi puerta, cubierto de rocío
pasas las noches del invierno escuras?

¡Oh, cuanto fueron mis entrañas duras
pues no te abrí! ¡Qué extraño desvarío
si de mi ingratitud el yelo frío
secó las llagas de tus plantas puras.

¡Cuántas veces el ángel me decía:
Alma, asómate agora a la ventana,
verás con cuanto amor llamar porfía!

¡Y cuántas, hermosura soberana,
"Mañana le abriremos" respondía,
para lo mismo responder mañana!

Song

Celinda, by what potent art
Or unresisted charm,

Doriano a los zarcillos de Lucinda

Si a las orejas te pones,
por zarcillos dos candados,

Dost thou thine ear and frozen heart
Against my passion arm?

Or by what hidden influence
Of powers in one combined,
Dost thou rob love of either sense,
Made deaf as well as blind?

Sure thou, as friends, united hast
Two distant deities,
And scorn within thy heart hast placed,
And love within thine eyes.

Of those soft fetters of thy hair,
A bondage that disdains
All liberty, do guard thine ear
Free from all other chains.

Then my complaint how canst thou hear,
Or I this passion fly,
Since thou imprisoned hast thine ear
And not confirmed thine eye?

THOMAS STANLEY

¿cómo sabrás mis cuidados,
ni escucharás mis razones?

Si así guardas los oídos,
¿por dónde entrarán mis penas,
temidas como Sirenas,
de tus cobardes sentidos?

Ya pretendo enmudecer,
que a quien no tiene lugar,
¿por dónde pueda escuchar,
cómo podrá responder?

Que para mis cuidados,
vivan de remedio inciertos,
traes los ojos abiertos,
y los oídos cerrados.

The Good Shepherd

    Shepherd! who with thine amorous, sylvan song
Hast broken the slumber that encompassed me,
Who mad'st Thy crook from the accursèd tree
On which Thy powerful arms were stretched so long!
    Lead me to mercy's ever-flowing fountains;
For Thou my shepherd, guard, and guide shalt be;
I will obey Thy voice, and wait to see
Thy feet all beautiful upon the mountains.
    Hear, Shepherd, Thou who for Thy flock art dying,
Oh, wash away these scarlet sins, for Thou
Rejoicest at the contrite sinner's vow!
    Oh. wait! to Thee my weary soul is crying,
Wait for me: Yet why ask it, when I see,
With feet nailed to the cross, Thou'rt waiting still for me!

HENRY WADSWORTH LONGFELLOW

Soneto

Pastor que con tus silbos amorosos
me despertaste del profundo sueño:
tú, que hiciste cayado de ese leño
en que tiendes los brazos poderosos,

vuelve los ojos a mi fe piadosos,
pues te confieso por mi amor y dueño
y la palabra de seguirte empeño
tus dulces silbos y tus pies hermosos.

Oye, pastor, pues por amores mueres,
no te espante el rigor de mis pecados
pues tan amigo de rendidos eres.

Espera, pues, y escucha mis cuidados...
Pero ¿cómo te digo que me esperes
si estás para esperar los pies clavados?

Ode

In the green season of my flowering years,
I loved, O Love! a captive in thy chains;
Sang of delusive hopes and idle fears.
And wept thy follies in my wisest strains;
Sad sport of time when under thy control,
So wild has grown my wit, so blind my soul.

But from the yoke which once my courage tamed,
I undeceived at length have slipped my head,
And in that sun whose rays my soul inflamed,
What scraps I rescued at my ease I spread.
So shall I altars to clear seeing raise,
And chant without alarm returning freedom's praise.

Oda

La verde primavera
de mis floridos años
pasé cautivo, amor, en tus prisiones,
y en la cadena fiera
cantando mis engaños,
lloré con mi razón tus sinrazones;
¡amargas confusiones
del tiempo, que ha tenido
ciega mi alma, y loco mi sentido!

Mas ya que el fiero yugo
que mi cerviz domaba,
desata el desengaño con tu afrenta,

So on their chains the ransomed captives dwell;
So carols one who cured relates his wound;
So slaves of masters, troops of battle tell,
As I my cheerful liberty resound.
Freed, sea and burning fire, from thy control,
Prison, wound, war, and tyrant of my soul.

Remain then, faithless friend, thy arts to try
On such as court alternate joy and pain;
For me, I dare her very eyes defy;
I scorn the amorous snare. the pleasing chain,
That held enthralled my cheated heart so long,
And charmed my erring soul unconscious of its wrong.

HENRY RICHARD FOX, LORD HOLLAND

y al mismo sol enjugo,
que un tiempo me abrasaba,
la ropa que saqué de la tormenta,
con voz libre y essenta
al desengaño santo
consagro altares, y alabanzas canto.

Cuanto contento encierra,
contar su herida el sano,
y en la patria su cárcel el cautivo,
entre la paz la guerra,
y el libre del tirano;
tanto en cantar mi libertad recibo,
¡O mar! ¡O fuego vivo!
Que fuiste al alma mía
herida, cárcel, guerra, y tiranía.

Quédate, falso amigo,
para engañar aquellos
que siempre están contentos y quejosos;
que desde aquí maldigo
los mismos ojos bellos,
y aquellos lazos dulces y amorosos
que un tiempo tan hermosos
tuvieron, aunque injusto,
asida el alma y engañado el gusto.

Sonnet on Old Age

Ye shadowy elms! when in this solitude
The rustic planted you, my infant mind
As yet unapt of reason, knew not good
From evil. Thirty winters has the wind
Stript from your trembling boughs the foliage sear,
And thirty times upon his radiant way
On you the Sun has poured his summer ray,
Gilding the foliage of the ripened year.
Your beauty has increased, and still it grows—
Alas! my youth is gone! and now all dark
And sad of mind. a man of many woes,
I in the mirror of your wrinkled bark
Know my own mournful image, and with tears
Reflect in anguish on my ill-spent years.

ROBERT SOUTHEY

Los olmos

Cuando por este margen solitario,
villano agricultor os transponía,
verdes olmos, apenas yo sabía
que fuese honesto bien, ni mal contrario;

treinta veces el Sol al Sagitario
saliendo de la casa húmeda y fría
del Escorpión, tocó desde aquel día
curso inmortal de su camino vario.

Crecistes, y creció vuestra belleza,
fue mi edad verde, como ya a mis daños
espejo vuestra rígida corteza;

los dos sin fruto, vemos sus engaños,
mas ¡ay! que no era en vos naturaleza,
perdí mi tiempo—lloraré mis daños.

Strange Shepherd

Strange shepherd, set my bellwether free,
You have a handsome ram to lead your sheep;
Give back the one that I so long to keep,
His loss is gain to you, but grief to me.
Give him this bell of tin shaped like a heart,
Do not deceive him with your yoke of gold;
Take this white bull as my ram's counterpart,
Who will at spring's first green be one year old.
Shall I describe my ram? His fleece is brown
And his soft eyes half close when he is led,

Suelta mi manso, mayoral extraño

Suelta mi manso, mayoral extraño,
pues otro tienes de tu igual decoro;
deja la prenda que en el alma adoro,
perdida por tu bien y por mi daño.

Ponle su esquila de labrado estaño
y no le engañen tus collares de oro;
toma en albricias este blanco toro
que a las primeras yerbas cumple un año.

Si pides señas, tiene el vellocino

As if in dreams no human understands.
If you believe he is not mine, go now
And set him free; see if he does not head
Straight for this hut to lick these salty hands.[25]

JOHN A. CROW

To My Solitude I Go

Lone I muse but feel not lonely,
Covert solitude's my lore;
For my company I only
Want my thoughts and nothing more.

I know not what this village has
Which is my home till death befall;
When I'm no longer what I was
I've made the longest trip of all.

With my lot I find no query,
But my understanding knows,
If a man's all soul he's very
Captive to his body's woes.

What I need I can see plainly,
But it seems entirely wrong
That an ignorant snob can vainly
Suffer with himself so long.

ANONYMOUS TRANSLATOR

Sonnet Right Off the Bat

She wants a sonnet from me, instantly!
Now here's a jam I wasn't in before!
A sonnet's fourteen lines, I hear—no more,
No less. (I really buffaloed those three!)
You'd think the rimes would have me up a tree,
But here I'm halfway through the second four.
If I can tally two and up the score
The octave's a dead duck. No stopping me!

Well look at Lope entering Line Nine!
I must have knocked it off in nothing flat
And breezed half through the sestet. Doing fine
Nearing the finish. As to where I'm at,
I rather think it's—hmm—the thirteenth line.
Here's fourteen. Care to count them? And that's that.

JOHN FREDERICK NIMS

pardo, encrespado, y los ojuelos tiene
como durmiendo en regalado sueño.

Si piensas que no soy su dueño, Alcino,
suelta y verásle si a mi choza viene,
que aún tienen sal las manos de su dueño.

A mis soledades voy

A mis soledades voy,
de mis soledades vengo,
porque para andar conmigo
me bastan mis pensamientos.

No sé qué tiene el aldea
donde vivo y donde muero,
que con venir de mí mismo
no puedo venir más lejos.

Ni estoy bien ni mal conmigo,
mas dice mi entendimiento
que un hombre que todo es alma
está cautivo en su cuerpo.

Entiendo lo que me basta
y solamente no entiendo
cómo se sufre a sí mismo
un ignorante soberbio.

Soneto de repente

Un soneto me manda hacer Violante,
que en mi vida me he visto en tanto aprieto;
catorce versos dicen que es soneto:
burla burlando van los tres delante.

Yo pensé que no hallara consonante
y estoy a la mitad de otro cuarteto,
mas si me veo en el primer terceto,
no hay cosa en los cuartetos que me espante.

Por el primer terceto voy entrando,
y parece que entré con pie derecho,
pues fin con este verso le voy dando.

Ya estoy en el segundo, y aun sospecho
que voy los trece versos acabando;
contad si son catorce, y está hecho.

---

25. This sonnet is about Lope's love for Elena Osorio. The poet was only seventeen when he fell passionately in love with this beautiful lady, who was the wife of Cristóbal Calderón, an itinerent actor, and the daughter of Lope's impresario. The marriage was never a good one, and as Calderón was often out of town on acting assignments, Lope had a clear field. The tempestuous affair lasted for five years, but the poet never forgot his Elena who was "the Etna of his love" and his ever idealized "Dorotea." Numerous poems attested this passion, proclaiming it without restraint. Possibly because of this, Elena broke with Lope and became the mistress of a wealthy gentleman, Francisco Perrenot de Granvela, who plied her generously with gold. Lope's fury knew no bounds and he fulminated against the two lovers in such coarse language that he was sued for libel and sent to jail.

In the above sonnet the bellwether (a tame ram who wears a bell in order to lead the flock) represents Elena, and the strange shepherd is Granvela. The poem was written just after the rupture with Elena, when Lope's passion was at its peak and he still had hopes of winning her back. He wrote several other sonnets using the same symbolism.

Juan Pérez de Montalbán

Spain, 1602–1638

This prolific poet, novelist, and playwright, the son of a bookseller of Jewish descent, was born in Madrid. He was the friend and confidante of Lope de Vega, of whom he was the first (and, unfortunately, unreliable) biographer. It was Montalbán who placed the number of Lope's plays at 1,800, and a figure no modern scholar accepts. Montalbán himself was the author of 58 plays, numerous novels, and a body of poetry that is frequently Gongoristic. A few of his simpler lyrics, such as those translated by Thomas Stanley in the seventeenth century, are minor but charming and very much like those of Stanley himself.

When Will Arrive the Day

When will arrive the Day,
Which must my life and sorrows terminate,
  That angry fortune may
(The tyrant goddess of all human state
  Her cruelty fulfilling)
By one kind death thus make an end of killing.
  When shall my troubled years
Be to a verdant grave of flowers restored?
  My injuries, my fears,
Too little merited, too much deplored?
  When shall my just complaint
From equal heaven receive a full restraint?
  Now I am thrown thus low,
What more can be desired by cruel Fate;
  No hope my sad thoughts know,
Of reinjoying their past happy state:
  Oh my afflicted mind!
Death woulds't thou come, a welcome thou shalt find.
    With patience forlorn,
I pass the Months, the years in solitude,
  The Evening and the Morn:
In vain my hopes thus striving to delude,
  My tears I constant keep,
And as I am Aurora, daily weep.
  When the Rebellious Sea,
Armed with Snow, strives to subdue this Rock,
  It seems my misery,
At once kindly to warn, and rudely mock:
  For so the Destinies
My life each minute offer to suprise.
  Soon as the morn appears,
And ushers in with dubious light the day.
  My real sorrow wears
So true a shade of death, that I betray
  My reason to that dream,
And (though awake) dead to my self do seem.
  All things within my view,
All things that grow and thrive by Nature's care,
  My sorrows do renew:
For by successive change they bettered are,
  But to me fortune still
Is therefore constant, because she first was ill.
  This Tree from January

Cuando ha de ser el día

¿Cuándo ha de ser el día
que tenga fin mi vida lastimosa
  y la fortuna mía
(del humano poder tirana dios)
  dexe de atormentarme
y de una vez acabe de matarme?
  ¿Cuándo en aquestas flores
tendrán verde sepulcro mis cuidados,
  mis miedos y rigores
mal merecidos, aunque bien llorados?
  ¿Y cuándo el cielo santo
impedirá la causa de mi llanto
  que quiere la fortuna
después de verme en tan humilde estado,
  sin esperanza alguna
de volver a gozar el bien pasado?
  ¡Ay, muerte, si llegaras,
que justos sentimientos me excusaras!
  Con alma cortesana
paso en la soledad el mes y el año,
  la tarde y la mañana,
y desta suerte mi esperanza engaño,
  llorando a cualquier hora,
que siempre lloro como soy Aurora.
  Ai el fiero mar se atreve
a conquistar esta robusta peña
  con injurias de nieve,
presumo que me avisa y que me enseña,
  que la muerte atrevida
llama a las puertas de mi triste vida.
  Cuando el alma despierta
con media luz introduciendo el día,
  suelo hallarme tan muerta,
que parece verdad la fantasía
  que engendro el sueño esquivo,
y no me puedo persuadir que vivo.
  Todo, en fin, me atormenta,
y más el ver que con igual cuidado
  todo crece y se aumenta
por mejorar de calidad y estado,
  y yo nunca he salido
de una fortuna, porque mala ha sido.
  El árbol que en enero

No livery but the hoary Frost receives,
    Yet May its dress doth vary,
Proudly adorning it with painted leaves:
    Unto the fruitfull plain,
What August stole, April restores again.
    This Sea sometimes enraged,
Swells up in Chrystal mountains to the skies,
    Yet often is assuaged,
But only I in constant miseries,
    Confined to endless grief,
Expect no liberty, nor hope relief.

THOMAS STANLEY

sólo se vio vestido de congojas,
    en el mayo primero
pintadas de colores ve las hojas,
    y el campo hermoso y verde
cobra en abril lo que en agosto pierde.
    Este mar, que enojado,
escalas de cristal pone a los cielos,
    suele estar sosegado,
y sola yo con ansias y desvelos,
    temiendo el hado injusto,
ni aguardo libertad, ni espero gusto.

Torment of Absence and Delay

Torment of absence and delay,
    That thus afflicts my memory,
Why do'st thou kill me every day,
    Yet will not give me leave to die?

Why dost thou suffer me to live?
    All hope of life in life denying?
Or to my patience tortures give,
    Never to die, yet ever dying?

To fair Narcissa's brighter eyes,
    I was by love's instruction guided,
A happiness I long did prize,
    But now am from their light divided.

Favours and gifts my suit obtained,
    But envious Fate would now destroy them;
Which if to lose I only gained,
    What greater pain than to enjoy them?

THOMAS STANLEY

Duro tormento de mi larga ausencia

Duro tormento de mi larga ausencia
que siempre aflijes la memoria mía,
¿de qué sirve matarme cada día
si no me das para morir licencia?

¿Qué me importa el vivir, si en la paciencia
hallo que muero con mayor porfía,
pues morir sin morir es tiranía
que sólo la ha sufrido mi paciencia?

De Narcisa gocé los ojos bellos,
gloria que merecí por largos plazos,
y ya me miro ausente della y dellos.

Confirmaron mi amor prendas y lazos,
mas si los merecí para perdellos,
¿qué mayor muerte que gozar sus brazos?

A Ladie Weeping

As when some brook flies from itself away,
The murmuring crystal loosely runs astray;
And as about the verdant plain it winds,
The meadows with a silver riband binds,
Printing a kiss on every flower she meets,
Losing herself to fill them with new sweets,
To scatter frost upon the lily's head,
And scarlet on the gilliflower to spread:
So melting sorrow, in the fair disguise
Of humid stars, flow'd from bright Cloris' eyes,
Which wat'ring every flower her cheek discloses,
Melt into jasmines here, there into roses.

THOMAS STANLEY

Corre con pies de sonorosa plata

Corre con pies de sonorosa plata
huyendo de sí mismo un arroyuelo,
y dando vueltas por el verde suelo,
con cinta de cristal las flores ata.

Cruza la selva, y cándido retrata
cuanto encuentra su líquido desvelo,
pisa un jazmín, y vistese su yelo,
axa una flor, y mirase escarlata.

Así de Clori en líquidas querellas
bajó, como pintada mariposa,
un diluvio de lágrimas, o Estrellas:

tocó las flores de su cara hermosa,
y como el agua se detuvo en ellas,
unas veces fue nieve, otras fue rosa.

Francisco de Quevedo

Spain, 1580–1645

Quevedo, like his contemporary rival Góngora, was a masterful sonneteer and an extremely successful composer of lighter popular pieces, ballads, and lyrics in the traditional style. He did not assay the kind of abstruse verse filled with encyclopedic allusions that Góngora wrote in his *Solitudes*, but he did develop his own obscure style known as conceptism. He and Góngora carried on a verbal battle for many years.

Quevedo was a prolific writer of prose as well as a prolific poet. He wrote one very popular picaresque novel, *El Buscón*; a large quantity of literary criticism; works of political and philosophical comment; satires; and festive pieces in which satire and moralization were almost always present.

Quevedo's poetry embraces all the subject matter of his prose works, but its main themes are the insecurity and anguish of man when he is confronted by the fleeting quality of life, his search for beauty, and his mortal weakness when he is overpowered by love. Quevedo was, in the words of Pedro Salinas, the "symbol of a tormented conscience in a world that was crumbling."[26]

Man's Day

The long day passes by, slow, unperceived;
So do the secret and the hidden hours
Approach in silence, then like wasted flowers
They snatch my youth away, I am bereaved,
The vital force has lost its magic glow.
My flowering years that died before they bloomed
Were in last winter's discontent entombed,
And lie between dark shadows and cold snow;
I did not feel the mute years slip away,
But now I weep their passing, and I see
Them mocking at my quickened tears today;
My penitence masks all desire in me,
For this deceit's my life as I conceive it,
While I await the end, and do not believe it.

JOHN A. CROW

Huye sin percibirse, lento, el día

Huye sin percibirse, lento, el día,
y la hora secreta y recatada
con silencio se acerca, y, despreciada,
lleva tras sí la edad lozana mía.

La vida nueva, que en niñez ardía,
la juventud robusta y engañada,
en el postrer invierno sepultada,
yace entre negra sombra y nieve fría.

No sentí resbalar mudos los años;
hoy los lloro pasados, y los veo
riendo de mis lágrimas y daños.

Mi penitencia deba a mi deseo,
pues me deben la vida mis engaños,
y espero el mal que paso, y no le creo.

Passing Time

Ahoy there, Life! Will no one answer me?
The silent years that I have lived unknowing,
Saw Fortune thwart my hope and stunt its growing;
The hours conceal my madness as they flee
With scarce a trace of how or where they went;
Both youth and health have gone and left me ailing,
Life passed me by, what has been lived is failing,
Blind fate has struck me low, I am forespent.
Yesterday's gone, I have not seen tomorrow,
Today is rushing by, how quickly fled!
All that I was, shall be, I am, this husk of sorrow;
Past, present, future merge within my head,
Infant and corpse they join in this grim horror
Whose brief succession binds me to the dead.

JOHN A. CROW

¡Ah de la vida!

¡Ah de la vida! ¿Nadie me responde?
Aquí de los antaños que he vivido;
la Fortuna mis tiempos ha mordido,
las Horas mi locura las esconde.

¡Que, sin poder saber cómo ni adónde,
la salud y la edad se hayan huído!
Falta la vida, asiste lo vivido,
y no hay calamidad que no me ronde.

Ayer se fue; Mañana no ha llegado;
Hoy se está yendo sin para un punto:
soy un Fue y un Será y un Es cansado.

En el hoy y mañana y ayer, junto
pañales y mortaja, y he quedado
presentes sucesiones de difunto.

26. Eleanor L. Turnbull (ed.), *Ten Centuries of Spanish Poetry* (Baltimore: The Johns Hopkins Press, 1955), 300.

Life Is a Dream

The past's a dream; it will be dust tomorrow,
First comes the void, and then a puff of smoke;
I plot ambitious plans, lay down my stroke
To hold a point against the encircling horror,
Brief battle of the war's impetuous course;
In my defense no peril will deter me,
For with these weapons I destroy my force
Held loosely by the flesh that will inter me.
The past is gone, the future is not here,
Today flits by with harrowing commotion
And thrusts me headlong toward my death and bier;
The hours are spades cast in a timeless ocean
Which when my cares and pain shed their last tear
Will carve upon my grave some foolish notion.

JOHN A. CROW

Death Warnings

    I saw the ramparts of my native land
One time so strong, now dropping in decay,
Their strength destroyed by this new age's way
That has worn out and rotted what was grand.
    I went into the fields; there I could see
The sun drink up the waters newly thawed;
And on the hills the moaning cattle pawed,
Their miseries robbed the day of light for me.
    I went into my house; I saw how spotted,
Decaying things made that old home their prize;
My withered walking-staff had come to bend.
    I felt the age had won; my sword was rotted;
And there was nothing on which I set my eyes
That was not a reminder of the end.

JOHN MASEFIELD

Rome in Her Ruins

    Amidst these scenes, O Pilgrim, seek'st thou Rome?
Vain is thy search—the pomp of Rome is fled;
Her silent Aventine is glory's tomb;
Her walls, her shrines, but relics of the dead.
    That hill, where Caesars dwelt in other days,
Forsaken mourns where once it towered sublime;
Each mouldering medal now far less displays
The triumphs won by Latium, than by Time.
    Tiber alone survives;—the passing wave
That bathed her towers now murmurs by her grave,
Wailing with plaintive sound her fallen fanes.
    Rome! of thine ancient grandeur all is past
That seemed for years eternal framed to last;—
Nought by the wave, a fugitive, remains.

FELICIA D. HEMANS

Fue sueño ayer; mañana será tierra

¡Fue sueño ayer; mañana será tierra!
¡Poco antes, nada; y poco después, humo!
¡Y destino ambiciones, y presumo
apenas punto al cerco que me cierra!

Breve combate de importuna guerra,
en mi defensa soy peligro sumo;
y mientras con mis armas me consumo,
menos me hospeda el cuerpo, que me entierra.

Ya no es ayer; mañana no ha llegado;
hoy pasa, y es, y fue, con movimiento
que a la muerte me lleva despeñado.

Azadas son la hora y el momento,
que, a jornal de mi pena y mi cuidado,
cavan en mi vivir mi monumento.

Miré los muros de la patria mía

Miré los muros de la patria mía,
si un tiempo fuertes, ya desmoronados,
de la carrera de la edad cansados,
por quien caduca ya su valentía.

Salíme al campo, vi que el Sol bebía
los arroyos del yelo desatados,
y del monte quejosos los ganados,
que con sombras hurtó su luz al día.

Entré en mi casa; vi que, amancillada,
de anciana habitación era despojos;
mi báculo, más corvo y menos fuerte.

Vencida de la edad sentí mi espada,
y no hallé cosa en que poner los ojos
que no fuese recuerdo de la muerte.

A Roma sepultada en sus ruinas

Buscas en Roma a Roma, ¡oh peregrino!,
y en Roma misma a Roma no la hallas:
cadáver son las que ostentó murallas,
y tumba de sí propio el Aventino.

Yace donde reinaba el Palatino;
y, limadas del tiempo las medallas,
más se muestran destrozo a las batallas
de las edades que blasón latino.

Sólo el Tibre quedó, cuya corriente,
si ciudad la regó, ya sepultura
la llora con funesto son doliente.

¡Oh Roma! En tu grandeza, en tu hermosura,
huyó lo que era firme, y solamente
lo fugitivo permanece y dura.

The Brief Year

The brief year sweeps all living things away,
It takes our mortal lives, rebuffs our zeal,
Mocks the cold marble and courageous steel
Which dare to challenge fate with time's delay.
Before the foot can walk its instinct follows
The road that ends this life where I now dream
My obscure fate: a poor and dismal stream
Which in great waves the angry black sea swallows.
Life's briefest moment means to stride along
This selfsame path despite myself each day,
For sleep or wakefulness do not restrict me;
The last cruel sigh and unsung bitter song
Is death itself, innate and here to stay;
But if it is God's law, why so afflict me?

JOHN A. CROW

On Death

Come death, fearsome to both strong men and wise,
My soul departs with an indignant groan
Under the shadows; remembrance leaves no bone
For these dry lips and cold unseeing eyes;
The noblest Romans went in such a way,
And so shall everything that has been born;
If you seek welcome from a man forlorn,
Bring to an end my worries, my decay!
These burning tears through which I scarcely see
The black circle that shuts away my sight
Are Nature's own, not sorrow on my part,
With my first breath this sigh began in me.
Today my fury wraps it all in night:
So shall my whole self die, mind, body, heart.

JOHN A. CROW

Sonnet on Love

The last shadow that takes the light of day
From me will close for good these loving eyes,
And will release this soul from mortal clay
Which has indulged its rapt and eager cries;
But no, upon that unknown farther shore
My flame will burst where frozen waters thaw,
Its memory will brightly burn once more
Without respect for man's most solemn law.

Soul that was prison to a god in chains,
Veins that have given fuel to so much fire,
Bones nobly burned to mock the heart's endeavor:
This body it will leave, but not its pains;
They will be ash, but quickened with desire;
They will be dust, but dust that loves forever.

JOHN A. CROW

Todo tras sí lo lleva el año breve

Todo tras sí lo lleva el año breve
de la vida mortal, burlando el brío
al acero valiente, al mármol frío,
que contra el Tiempo su dureza atreve.

Antes que sepa andar el pie, se mueve
camino de la muerte, donde envío
mi vida oscura: pobre y turbio río
que negro mar con altas ondas bebe.

Todo corto momento es paso largo
que doy, a mi pesar, en tal jornada,
pues, parado y durmiendo, siempre aguijo.

Breve suspiro, y último, y amargo,
es la muerte, forzosa y heredada:
mas si es ley, y no pena, ¿qué me aflijo?

La muerte

Ven ya, miedo de fuertes y de sabios:
irá la alma indignada con gemido
debajo de las sombras, y el olvido
beberán por demás mis secos labios.

Por tal manera Curios, Decios, Fabios
fueron; por tal ha de ir cuanto ha nacido;
si quieres ser a alguno bien venido,
trae con mi vida fin a mis agravios.

Esta lágrima ardiente con que miro
el negro cerco que rodea a mis ojos
naturaleza es, no sentimiento.

Con el aire primero este suspiro
empecé, y hoy le acaban mis enojos,
porque me deba todo al monumento.

Cerrar podrá mis ojos la postrera

Cerrar podrá mis ojos la postrera
sombra que me llevare el blanco día,
y podrá desatar esta alma mía
hora a su afán ansioso lisonjera;

mas no, de esotra parte, en la ribera,
dejará la memoria, en donde ardía;
nadar sabe mi llama la agua fría,
y perder el respeto a ley severa.

Alma a quien todo un dios prisión ha sido,
venas que humor a tanto fuego han dado,
médulas que han gloriosamente ardido:

su cuerpo dejará, no su cuidado;
serán ceniza, mas tendrá sentido;
polvo serán, mas polvo enamorado.

The Fly

Out of the Wine-Pot cry'd the Fly,
Whilst the Grave Frog sate croaking by,
Than live a Watry Life like thine,
I'd rather choose to dye in Wine.

I

I Never Water could endure,
Though ne're so Crystalline and Pure,
Water's a Murmurer, and they
Design more Mischief than they say;
Where Rivers smoothest are and clear,
Oh there's the Danger, there's the Fear;
But I'll not grieve to dye in Wine,
That Name is sweet, that Sound's Divine.
    Thus from the Wine-Pot, &c.

II

Dull Fish in Water live we know,
And such insipid Souls as thou;
While to the Wine do nimbly fly,
Many such pretty Birds as I:
With Wine refresh'd, as Flowers with Rain,
My Blood is clear'd, inspir'd my Brain;
That when the Tory Boys do sing,
I buz i'th' Chorus for the King.
    Thus from the Wine-Pot, &c.

III

I'm more belov'd than thou canst be,
Most Creatures shun thy Company;
I go unbid to every Feast
Nor wait for Grace, a famished beast:
There while I quaff in Choicest Wine,
Thou dost with Puddle-water dine,
Which makes thee such a Croaking thing.
Learn to drink Wine, thou Fool, and sing;
    Thus from the Wine-Pot, &c.

IV

In Gardens I delight to stray,
And round the Plants do sing and play:
Thy Tune no Mortal does avail,
Thou art the Dutchman's Nightingale:
Wouldst thou with Wine but wet thy Throat,
Sure thou would'st leave that Dismal Note;
Lewd Water spoils thy Organs quite,
And Wine alone can set them right.
    Thus from the Wine-Pot, &c.

V

Thy Comrades still are Newts and Frogs,
Thy Dwelling Saw-pits, Holes, and Bogs:
In Cities I, and Courts am free,
An Insect too of Quality.
What Pleasure, Ah! didst thou but know,
This Heav'nly Liquor can bestow:

Letrilla burlesca

Dijo a la rana el mosquito
desde una tinaja,
mejor es morir en el vino
que vivir en el agua.

Agua no me satisface,
sea clara, líquida y pura;
pues aun con cuanto murmura,
menos mal dice que hace:
nadie quiero que me cace,
morir quiero en mi garlito,
dijo a la rana el mosquito, etc.

En el agua hay solo peces,
y para que más te corras,
en vino hay lobos y zorras
y aves, como yo, a las veces:
en cueros hay pez, y peces,
todo cabe en mi distrito,
dijo a la rana el mosquito, etc.

No te he de perdonar cosa
pues que mi muerte disfamas;
y si borracho me llamas,
yo te llamará aguanosa.
Tú en los charcos enfadosa,
yo en las bodegas habito,
dijo a la rana el mosquito, etc.

Yo so ángel de la uva,
y en los sótanos más frescos,
ruiseñor de los tudescos,
sin acicate, ni tuba:
yo estoy siempre en una cuba,
y tú estás siempre en un grito,
dijo a la rana el mosquito, etc.

Que tienes tú que tratar,
grito de cienos y lodos,
pues tragándome a mí todos,
nadie te puede tragar.
Cantora de muladar,
yo soy luquete bendito,
dijo a la rana el mosquito, etc.

To drink, and drown thou'dst ne'er repine;
The Great Anacreon dy'd by Wine.
        Thus from the Wine-Pot, &c.

PHILIP AYRES

Madrigal

See Lisa where the Sculptor's art
Has formed thine image of this polished stone,
All perfect he performed his part,
Which Nature has not done.

Has Nature formed thy bosom white?
Look how the marble mocks the mountain snow!
Thy charms unrivalled meet the sight,
Thy matchless form I know.

On thy fair cheek that hue she spread,
The hue that flushes there so oft;
She made thy lips so roseate red,
Thy lips that seem so soft.

Ah Lisa, maid of marble heart,
Here justly are thou formed by him alone;
For here thou seemest what thou art,
So cold—so hard—in stone!

ROBERT SOUTHEY

Madrigal

¡Un famoso escultor, Lisi esquiva!
En una piedra te ha imitado viva,
y ha puesto más cuidado en retratarte
que la Naturaleza en figurarte:

pues si te dio blancura, y pecho helado,
él lo mismo te ha dado.
Bellísima en el mundo te hizo ella,
y él no te ha repetido menos bella;

mas ella, que te quiso hacer piadosa,
de materia tan blanda, y tan suave
te labró, que no sabe

del jazmín distinguirte, y de la rosa;
y él, que vuelta de advierte en piedra ingrata
de lo que tú te hiciste te retrata.

Diego de Saavedra Fajardo
Spain, 1584–1648

Saavedra Fajardo was one of the most noted essayists of his time. He served for many years as secretary of the Spanish embassy in Rome and was the author of a widely read book on what a prince should be like. He also wrote a work on Spanish poetry from the time of Juan de Mena to the end of the Golden Age. In this work, *República literaria,* he praises Góngora without reserve but downgrades Lope de Vega. Saavedra Fajardo was a secondary poet of his period, but a few of his compositions are still considered to be fine examples of seventeenth-century poetic art.

On a Death's Head, Covered with Cobwebs

[Ayres wrongly attributes this sonnet to Luis de Góngora.]

This mortal spoil, which so neglected lies,
    Death's sad Memento, now where spiders weave
    Their subtil webs, which innocence deceive,
Whose strength to break their toils cannot suffice:

Saw itself crown'd, itself triumphant saw,
    With mighty deeds proclaiming its renown;
    Its smiles were favours, terror was its frown,
The World of its displeasure stood in awe.

Where Pride ordaining laws did once preside,
Which land should peace enjoy, which wars abide,
    There boldly now these little insects nest;

Este mortal despojo, O caminante

Este mortal despojo, o caminante,
triste horror de la muerte, en quien la araña
hilos anuda, y la inocencia engaña,
que a romper lo sutil no fue bastante,

coronado se vio, se vio triunfante
con los trofeos de una y otra hazaña,
favor su risa fue, terror su saña,
atento el Orbe a su Real semblante.

Donde antes la soberbia, dando leyes
a la paz, y a la guerra, presidía,
se prenden hoy los viles animales.

Then raise not, Kings, your haughty plumes so high,
For in Death's cold embraces when you lie,
   Your bones with those of common subjects rest.

PHILIP AYRES

¿Que os arrogáis o príncipes, o reyes?
Si en los ultrajes de la muerte fría
comunes sois con los demás mortales.

Miguel de Guevara

Mexico, *ca.* 1585–1646

The following famous sonnet, called by many critics the most outstanding religious sonnet in the Spanish language, has been attributed to Santa Teresa, Fray Luis de León, San Juan de la Cruz, Saint Ignatius, and many others. It also appears in a great many anthologies as anonymous. Recent investigations indicate that it was probably written by the Mexican friar Miguel de Guevara, who was fluent in several Indian languages, which he used in preaching to the natives of central Mexico. This sonnet and several other poems in Guevara's handwriting appear at the end of a treatise entitled *Doctrinal Art and Method for Learning Matlalzingo in Order to Admininster the Holy Sacrament.* The treatise manuscript, dated 1634, is in the library of the Mexican Society of Geography and Statistics.

To Christ Crucified

I am not moved, my Lord, to love thee more
By promises of Heaven when I'm dead,
Nor does the risk of Hell fill me with dread
To keep me from offending thee whom I adore.
Thou movest me, Lord; I shudder to behold
Thee nailed upon that Cross, scoffed at, forlorn;
It torments me to see thy body torn
With agony until thy flesh is cold.
Thy love moves me more deeply than thy power,
For if there were no Heaven I'd revere thee.
And if there were no Hell I still would fear thee.
Thou needst give nothing for my love to flower;
Though every hope were lost, while thinking of thee,
Just as I love thee now, still would I love thee.

JOHN A. CROW

A Cristo crucificado

No me mueve, mi Dios, para quererte,
el cielo que me tienes prometido,
ni me mueve el infierno tan temido
para dejar por eso de ofenderte.

Tu me mueves, Señor; muéveme el verte
clavado en esa cruz, y escarnecido;
muéveme el ver tu cuerpo tan herido;
muévenme tus afrentas, y tu muerte.

Muévesme al tu amor en tal manera,
que aunque no hubiera cielo, yo te amara;
y aunque no hubiera infierno, te temiera.

No me tienes que dar, porque te quiera;
que aunque cuanto espero no esperara,
lo mismo que te quiero te quisiera.

Pedro de Castro y Anaya

Spain, first half of seventeenth century

This poet, very popular in his own day, but since then largely forgotten, belonged to one of the most famous families of Murcia. His *Auroras de Diana,* published in 1631, is the only work of his that has survived. Lope de Vega praised its "elegant verses and poetic prose." Montalbán and Calderón also favored the author with laudatory *décimas.* The *Auroras* went through six editions during a twenty-year period in the seventeenth century.

The Rivulet

Stay, rivulet, nor haste to leave
   The lovely vale that lies around thee!

Libre arroyuelo detente

Libre arroyuelo detente,
no te quieras despeñar

Why wouldst thou be a sea at eve,
   When but a fount the morning found thee?

Born when the skies began to glow,
   Humblest of all the rock's cold daughters,
No blossom bowed its stalk to show
   Where stole thy still and scanty waters.

Now on thy stream thy moonbeams look,
   Usurping, as thou downward driftest,
Its crystal from the clearest brook,
   Its rushing current from the swiftest.

Ah, what wild haste!—and all to be
   A river and expire in ocean!
Each fountain's tribute hurries thee
   To that vast grave with quicker motion.

Far better 'twere to linger still
   In this green vale, these flowers to cherish,
And die in peace, an aged rill,
   Than thus, a youthful Danube, perish.

WILLIAM CULLEN BRYANT

por ser a la tarde mar,
pues fuiste a la Aurora fuente.

Aborto, y no cristalino
te vio el Alba de una peña,
una flor de tu camino,
y en el Valle más vecino
quiere usurpar tu raudal
a todo arroyo el cristal,
la plata a toda corriente,
libre arroyuelo detente, etc.

¡Tanto correr por llegar
a río, y luego morir!
pues el crecer, y adquirir
te preciptan al mar.
Si corres para acabar
más vale sin tu desvelo
morir caduco arroyuelo,
que Danubio adolesciente,
libre arroyuelo detente, etc.

Pedro Calderón de la Barca
Spain, 1600–1681

Calderón brought the Spanish Golden Age to a glorious end. He was the Catholic baroque poet and dramatist par excellence. His famous play *Life Is a Dream (La Vida es Sueño)* aroused the admiration of the German Romantics, and in England Edward Fitzgerald, better known for his version of the *Rubaiyat,* translated eight of his plays.

   Calderón's poetry is harmonious and elevated. His dramas may lack immediacy by today's standards, but in their time his presentation of the dream-like quality of life and his moralization that man must boldly live out this dream by acting in the right way had tremendous appeal. The English poet Shelley found Calderón fascinating and translated portions of his poetry into English. A selection from Shelley's rendition is reproduced herein.

My Love's Confusion

When in my love's confusion and excess
I fancy many a fond unlikely chance,
Desire grows stronger, resolution less,
I linger more the more I would advance.
False to my nobler self, I madly seize
Up on a medicine alien to my ill;
And feeding still with that should cure disease,
At once my peace and reputation kill
By turns; as the conflicting passions fire,
And chase each other madly through my breast,
I worship and despise, blame and admire,
Weep and rejoice, and covet and detest.
Alas! a bitter bargain he must choose,
Who live with life, or life with love, must lose!

EDWARD FITZGERALD

Cuando mi confuso pensamiento

Cuando de mi confuso pensamiento,
necio amor, locos casos imagino,
menos me atrevo, y más me determino,
que sobra amor, y falta atrevimiento.

Desconocido a mi valor, intento
a un agravio remedio peregrino;
y animándole, apenas adivino,
verdugo de mi infamia el sentimiento.

Olvido ingrato, agradecido adoro,
aborrezco cobarde, amo atrevido,
llamo, y me huyo, quiero, y no deseo:

canto mis penas, y mis glorias lloro;
¡qué mucho viva, o muera arrepentido,
si he de perder la vida, o el deseo!

Sonnet on Life

These flowers of lordly pomp and joy's sweet breath
Which at the break of day unfold awaking,
In the cold arms of night will soon be making
A piteous wreath for vanity and death.
This hue that challenges the star-hung sky,
This iris stained with russet, gold, and snow,
Teaches what every human heart must know:
How much of life crowds each day passing by!
These roses flourish at the touch of dawn,
But bloom only to wither and grow old,
Each bud is birth and grave's symbolic pawn:
So has man felt his brevity foretold;
Born one day, dead the next, his years unfold,
And seem but hours when centuries have gone.

JOHN A. CROW

Justina's Temptation

The Daemon tempts Justina, who is a Christian

Daemon. Abyss of Hell! I call on thee,
          Thou wild misrule of thine own anarchy!
          From thy prison house set free
          Thy spirits of voluptuous death,
          That with their mighty breath
          They may destroy a world of virgin thoughts;
          Let her chaste mind with fancies thick as motes
          Be peopled from thy shadowy deep,
          Till her guiltless fantasy
          Full to overflowing be!
          And with sweetest harmony,
          Let birds, and flowers, and leaves, and all
            things move
          To love, only to love,
          Let nothing meet her eyes
          But signs of love's soft victories;
          Let nothing meet her ear
          But sounds of love's sweet sorrow,
          So that from faith no succor she may borrow,
          But, guided by my spirit blind
          And in a magic snare entwined,
          She may now seek Ciprian,
          Begin, while I in silence bind
          My voice, when thy sweet song thou hast
            begun.

One voice, singing within.
          What is the glory far above
          All else in human life?
    All. Love! love!

      *While these words are sung, the Daemon goes out at
        one door, and Justina enters at another.*

The voice. There is no form in which the fire
          Of love its traces has impressed not.

Soneto

Éstas, que fueron pompa y alegría,
despertando al albor de la mañana,
a la tarde serán lástima vana,
durmiendo en brazos de la noche fría.

Este matiz, que al cielo desafía,
iris listado de oro, nieve y grana,
será escarmiento de la vida humana:
¡tanto se emprende en término de un día!

A florecer las rosas madrugaron,
y para envejecerse florecieron:
cuna y sepulcro en un botón hallaron.

Tales los hombres sus fortunas vieron:
en un día nacieron y expiraron;
que pasados los siglos, horas fueron.

El Mágico Prodigioso

Demonio. Ea, infernal abismo,
          desesperado imperio de ti mismo,
          de tu prisión ingrata
          tus lascivos espíritus desata,
          amenazando ruina
          al virgen edificio de Justina.
          De mil torpes fantasmas que en el viento
          su casto pensamiento
          hoy se forme, su honesta fantasía
          se llene; y con dulcísima armonía
          todo provoque amores,
          los pájaros, las plantas y las flores.
          Nada miren sus ojos,
          que no sean de amor dulces despojos;
          nada oigan sus oídos,
          que no sean de amor tiernos gemidos;
          porque sin que defensa en su fe tenga,
          hoy a buscar a Cipriano venga,
          de su ciencia invocada,
          y de mi ciego espíritu guiada.
          Empezad, que yo en tanto
          callaré, porque empiece vuestro canto.   (*Vase.*)
Una voz. ¿Cuál es la gloria mayor
          desta vida?
Coro.   *Amor, amor.*
Una voz. No hay sujeto en que no imprima
          el fuego de amor su llama,
          pues vive más donde ama
          el hombre, que donde anima.
          Amor solamente estima
          cuanto tener vida sabe,
          el tronco, la flor y el ave:
          luego es la gloria mayor
          de esta vida....

Man lives far more in love's desire
Than by life's breath, soon possessed not.
If all that lives must love or die,
All shapes on earth, or sea, or sky,
With one consent to heaven cry
That the glory far above
All else in life is—

All.   Love! oh, love!

Justina.   Thou melancholy thought which art
So flattering and so sweet, to thee
When did I give the liberty
Thus to afflict my heart?
What is the cause of this new power
Which doth my fevered being move,
Momently raging more and more?
What subtle pain is kindled now
Which from my heart doth overflow
Into my senses?

All.   Love! oh, love!

Justina.   'Tis that enamored nightingale
Who gives me the reply;
He ever tells the same soft tale
Of passion and of constancy
To his mate, who rapt and fond,
Listening sits, a bough beyond.
Be silent, nightingale—no more
Make me think, in hearing thee
Thus tenderly thy love deplore,
If a bird can feel his so,
What a man would feel for me.
And, voluptuous vine, O thou
Who seekest most when least pursuing,
To the trunk thou interlacest
Art the verdure which embracest,
And the weight which is its ruin—
No more, with green embraces, vine,
Make me think on what thou lovest.
For whilst thus thy boughs entwine,
I fear lest thou shouldst teach me, sophist,
How arms might be entangled too.
Light-enchanted sunflower, thou
Who gazest ever true and tender
On the sun's revolving splendor!
Follow not his faithless glance
With thy faded countenance,
Nor teach my beating heart to fear,
If leaves can mourn without a tear,
How eyes must weep! O nightingale,
Cease from thy enamored tale—
Leafy vine, unwreathe thy bower,
Restless sunflower, cease to move,
Or tell me all, what poisonous power
Ye use against me—

All.   Love! Love! Love!

PERCY BYSSHE SHELLEY

Coro.   *Amor, amor.*

Justina (*asombrada y inquieta*).
Pesada imaginación,
al parecer lisonjera,
¿Cuándo te he dado ocasión
para que desta manera
aflijas mi corazón?
¿Cuál es la causa, en rigor,
deste fuego, deste ardor,
que en mí por instantes creces?
¿Qué dolor el que padece
mi sentido?

Coro (*dentro*).   *Amor, amor.*

Justina (*sosegándose*).
Aquel ruiseñor amante
es quien respuesta me da,
enamorando constante
a su consorte, que está
un ramo más adelante.
Calla, ruiseñor; no aquí
imaginar me hagas ya,
por las quejas que te oí,
cómo un hombre sentirá,
si siente un pájaro así.
Mas no: una vid fue lasciva,
que buscando fugitiva
va al tronco donde se enlace,
siendo el verdor con que abrace
el peso con que derriba.
No así con verdes abrazos
me hagas pensar en quien amas,
vid; que dudaré en tus lazos,
si así abrazan unas ramas,
cómo enraman unos brazos.
Y si no es la vid, será
aquel girasol, que está
viendo cara a cara al sol,
tras cuyo hermoso arrebol
siempre moviéndose va.
No sigas, no, tus enojos,
flor, con marchitos despojos,
que pensarán mis congojas,
si así lloran unas hojas,
cómo lloran unos ojos.
Cesa, amante ruiseñor;
desúnete, vid frondosa;
párate, inconstante flor,
o decid, ¿qué venenosa
fuerza usáis?

Coro (*dentro*).   *Amor, amor.*

Lines from *Life Is a Dream*

What is life but mad confusion?
What is life but mere illusion,
Shadow and falseness, that is all,
Where the greatest good is small;
Indeed all life is only dreams,
And dreams themselves no more than dreams.

MARY H. PARHAM

La Vida Es Sueño

¿Qué es la vida? Un frenesí.
¿Qué es la vida? Una ilusión,
una sombra, una ficción,
y el mayor bien es pequeño,
que toda la vida es sueño
y los sueños sueños son.

Sor Juana Inés de la Cruz

Mexico, 1648–1695

This Mexican nun of illegitimate birth, the finest poet of the colonial period in Spanish America, died at the age of forty-seven while caring for the ill during an epidemic in Mexico City. Precocious as a child, she soon acquired an impressive general knowledge that astonished even the professors at the University of Mexico. Before taking religious orders, she served for a time as a maid-in-waiting to the viceroy's wife; in this position she was famous for her beauty and her poetry. In the convent she continued writing, in addition to carrying out her many other chores. Much of her work is filled with the literary conceits so much in vogue in her day, but she also produced a body of sonnets and simple lyrics that are among the finest in Spanish. Some of these are poems with a strong feminist slant denouncing the double standard, and others speak intensely of love and loss. This has led some of her biographers to believe that she may have gone through a frustrated love affair. A passionate, even erotic, coloration, anomalous for a nun, permeates several of her best pieces. Her religious poetry reflects this same deep human feeling in sublimated terms.

To Her Portrait

This artifice of colors that you see
Which boasts the fairest vanities of art,
Ere its false logic and its gloss depart
Will dupe the senses and the memory.
Here flattery immune to time's outrage
Has cancelled out the horrors of the years,
And foiling their dread ravages appears
To vanquish both forgetfulness and age.

It is a shallow counterfeit of pride,
A fragile flower that opened in the wind,
A paltry refuge when fate closed the door,
It is a foolish caution put aside,
And outworn zeal that time has bent and thinned;
It is a corpse, dust, shadow, nothing more.

JOHN A. CROW

A su retrato

Éste, que ves, engaño colorido,
que del arte ostentando los primores,
con falsos silogismos de colores
es cauteloso engaño del sentido:

éste en quien la lisonja ha pretendido
excusar de los años los horrores,
y, venciendo del tiempo los rigores,
triunfar de la vejez y del olvido,

es un vano artificio del cuidado;
es una flor al viento delicada;
es un resguardo inútil para el hado;

es una necia diligencia errada;
es un afán caduco; y bien mirado,
es cadáver, es polvo, es sombra, es nada.

The Divine Narcissus

Seeking Narcissus in my weariness,
With never a rest to ease my vagrant feet,—
In longing and distress
From many days of journeying I greet

El Divino Narciso

De buscar a Narciso fatigada
sin permitir sosiego a mi pie errante,
ni a mi planta cansada,
que tantos ha va días que vagante

Alone the hedges green,
The only sign of where His step hath been.

Unto this bosky circle come, I yearn
Some tidings of my Well-Beloved to find,—
Though of the paths I learn
That this hath been His meadow twined
With flowery loveliness so rare
Naught but His kisses could have nursed them there.

How many, many days have I explored
The grove; and flower on flower, herb on herb,
Scented and tasted! Yea, without reward—
My heart a burden that my pains perturb,
My step a draggled vagabond,—to rove
Through Time turned centuries, and worlds a grove!

RODERICK GILL

examina las breñas,
sin poder encontrar más que las señas.

A este bosque he llegado donde espero
tener noticias de mi Bien perdido;
que si señas confiero,
diciendo está del prado lo florido,
que producir amenidades tantas
es por haber besado ya Sus plantas.

¡Oh, cuántos días ha que he examinado
la solva flor a flor, y planta a planta,
gastando congojado
mi triste corazón en pena tanta,
y mi pie fatigando vagabundo,
tiempo, que siglos son: selva, que es Mundo!

This Afternoon, My Love

This afternoon. my Love, as I pled weeping,
And in your eyes and countenance perceived
That words could not persuade you, sorely grieved
I offered you the rose my heart was keeping.
Love came to lend its succor in my plight;
What seemed impossible was then fulfilled,
For midst the tears that sorrow had distilled
My shattered heart grew precious in your sight.
No more of harshness, Love, not one word more;
Be not by jealous tyranny controlled,
Let not suspicion cloud the sky above,
For foolish shadows have no solid core;
Though it has turned to water you still hold
My bleeding heart within your hands, my Love.

JOHN A. CROW

Esta tarde, mi bien, cuando te hablaba

Esta tarde, mi bien, cuando te hablaba,
como en tu rostro y tus acciones vía
que con palabras no te persuadía,
que el corazón me vieses deseaba;

y Amor, que mis intentos ayudaba,
venció lo que imposible parecía:
pues entre el llanto, que el dolor vertía,
el corazón deshecho destilaba.

Baste ya de rigores, mi bien, baste;
no te atormenten más celos tiranos,
ni el vil recelo tu quietud contraste

con sombras necias, con indicios vanos,
pues ya en líquido humor viste y tocaste
mi corazón deshecho entre tus manos.

Stay, Fleeting Shadow

Stay, fleeting shadow of my love whose chain
Binds me to the sweet spell for which I sigh,
Illusion for whose sake I'd gladly die,
Sweet fiction's dream for whom I live in pain.
If to the lodestone of your charming grace
My heart delights to play obedient steel,
Why do you stir my churning blood to feel,
If but to flee and mock my eager chase?

But you cannot leave me and smugly boast
That you were tyrant to my valentine,
For though you slip the jealous net I've tossed
Whose coils so briefly round you did entwine,
It matters not you vanish like a ghost
If you are captive in these dreams of mine.

JOHN A. CROW

Detente, sombra de mi bien esquivo

Detente, sombra de mi bien esquivo,
imagen del hechizo que más quiero,
bella ilusión por quien alegre muero,
dulce ficción por quien penoso vivo.

Si al imán de tus gracias, atractivo,
sirve mi pecho de obediente acero,
¿para qué me enamoras lisonjero
si has de burlarme luego fugitivo?

Mas blasonar no puedas, satisfecho,
de que triunfa de mí tu tiranía;
que aunque dejas burlado el lazo estrecho

que tu forma fantástica ceñía,
poco importa burlar brazos y pecho
si te labra prisión mi fantasía.

Redondillas

Stupid men, forever prone
   To fix the blame on woman's reason,
   When 'tis merely your own treason
That creates her fault alone!

With an unrestrained desire
   For her downfall you are scheming;
   You are of her virtues dreaming
While to ill alone you fire.

Her resistance you oppose,
   Then, all serious, attaint her;
   Fickle, light and faithless paint her,
Though 'twas you the role that chose.

Stupidly you would procure
   Baser for a nobler treasure;
   Making Thaïs of your pleasure
A Lucretia chaste and pure.

Nothing could be funnier
   Than the tale of him befouling
   His own mirror, and then scowling
When the image was a blur.

'Twixt your favor and disdain
   You should keep position civil,
   Blaming her if she shows evil,
Mocking not her goodness vain.

Nothing suits your peevish mood;
   You keep changing your opinion,
   Blaming her for harsh dominion,
And blaming her for being kind.

Who commits the greater fault
   In matters of lawless passion,
   She, destroyed as you would fashion,
Or you who make the rash assault?

The greater evil who is in—
   When both in wayward paths are straying—
   The poor sinner for the paying,
Or he that pays her for the sin?

Come, from your flirting cease, and turn,
   (If maybe) to a cool reflection;
   Then blame the ardor of affection
In her you started first to burn!

                  GARRETT STRANGE

Redondillas

Hombres necios que acusáis
a la mujer sin razón,
sin ver que sois la ocasión
de lo mismo que culpáis:

si con ansia sin igual
solicitáis su desdén,
¿por qué queréis que obren bien
si las incitáis al mal?

Combatís su resistencia
y luego, con gravedad,
decís que fue liviandad
lo que hizo la diligencia.

Parecer quiere el denuedo
de vuestro parecer loco
al niño que pone el coco
y luego le tiene miedo.

Queréis, con presunción necia,
hallar a la que buscáis,
para pretendida, Thais,
y en la posesión, Lucrecia.

¿Qué humor puede ser más raro
que el que, falto de consejo,
él mismo empaña el espejo,
y siente que no esté claro?

Con el favor y el desdén
tenéis condición igual,
quejándoos, si os tratan mal,
burlándoos, si os quieren bien.

Opinión, ninguna gana;
pues la que más se recata,
si no os admite, es ingrata,
y si os admite, es liviana.

Siempre tan necios andáis
que, con desigual nivel,
a una culpáis por crüel
y a otra por fácil culpáis.

¿Pues cómo ha de estar tamplada
la que vuestro amor pretende,
si la que es ingrata, ofende,
y la que es fácil, enfada?

Mas, entre el enfado y pena
que vuestro gusto refiere,
bien haya la que no os quiere,
y quejaos en hora buena.

Dan vuestras amantes penas
a sus libertades alas,
y después de hacerlas malas
las queréis hallar muy buenas.

¿Cuál mayor culpa ha tenido
en una pasión errada:

la que cae de rogada,
o el que ruega de caído?

¿O cuál es más de culpar,
aunque cualquiera mal haga:
la que peca por la paga,
o el que paga por pecar?

Pues ¿para qué os espantáis
de la culpa que tenéis?
Queredlas cual las hacéis
o hacedlas cual las buscáis.

Dejad de solicitar,
y después, con más razón,
acusaréis la afición
de la que os fuere a rogar.

Bien con muchas armas fundo
que lidia vuestra arrogancia,
pues en promesa e instancia
juntáis diablo, carne y mundo.

NEOCLASSIC PERIOD

Tomás de Iriarte

Spain, 1750–1791

Iriarte was interested in the classics and translated Horace's *Art of Poetry* into Spanish. He composed Voltairian poems of his own and was hauled before the Inquisition for his heterodox statements. His claim to fame, however, rests almost entirely on his series of seventy-six fables in verse, some of them jibing at contemporary writers, others stating in facile rhyme choice bits of homespun philosophy that became popular all over the Spanish-speaking world. His "El burro flautista," translated by Robert Southey, is perhaps the best known of his poems in this vein. vein.

The Musical Ass

Judge, gentle Reader, as you will,
If this short tale be good or ill:
No hours in studying it were spent,
It just occurred by accident.

As strolling out, I sauntered o'er
The fields that lie around my door,
An ass across the meadow bent,
His heedless way by accident.

A carless shepherd boy had trod,
But just before that very road,
And on other thoughts intent,
Dropt his flute by accident.

The ass as he beheld it, goes
To smell it with enquiring nose;
And breathing hard, the strong breath went
Down the flute by accident.

The air in rushing to get free,
Awoke the voice of harmony;
And through the hollow channel sent
Sweet melodies by accident.

The shrill notes vibrate soft and clear,
Along his longitude of ear.
"Bravo!" exclaims the raptured brute,
"How masterly I play the flute!"

And hast thou, Reader, never known,
Some star-blest blockhead, like friend John,
Who following upon Folly's scent,
Stumbled on Truth by accident?

ROBERT SOUTHEY

El burro flautista

Esta fabulilla,
salga bien o mal,
me ha ocurrido ahora
por casualidad.

Cerca de unos prados
que hay en mi lugar,
pasaba un Borrico
por casualidad.

Una flauta en ellos
halló, que el zagal
se dejó olvidada
por casualidad.

Acercóse a olerla
el dicho animal,
y dio un resoplido
por casualidad.

En la flauta el aire
se hubo de colar,
y sonó la flauta
por casualidad.

"¡Oh—dijo el Borrico—,
qué bien sé tocar!
¡Y dirán que es mala
la música asnal!"

Sin reglas del arte
borriquitos hay,
que una vez aciertan
por casualidad.

The Dancing Bear

Some greater brute had caught a bear,
And made him dance from fair to fair,
  To please the gaping crowd;
The rabble mob, who like the sight,
Expressed by clamors their delight,
  And so the bear grew proud.

Conceited now as praise he sought,
He asked a monkey what he thought,
  And if he danced with taste.
"Most vilely," honest pug replied,
"Nay, nay, friend Monkey!" Bruin cried,
  "I'm sure you only jest.

"Come, come! all prejudice is wrong,
See with what ease I move along!"
  A Hog was by the place,
And cried, "According to my notions,
There's elegance in all your motions,
  I never saw such grace!"

Bruin, though out in his pretense,
Was yet a bear of common sense,
  "Enough!" he cries, grown sad.
"The Monkey's blaming I might doubt,
But approbation from that snout!
  I must dance very bad."

Thus he who gives his idle song
To all the motley-minded throng,
  Meets many a heavy curse;
Vexations on vexations rise,
Bad is the censure of the wise,
  The Blockhead's praise is worse.

ROBERT SOUTHEY

El oso, la mona y el cerdo

Un Oso, con que la vida
ganaba un Piamontés,
la no muy bien aprendida
danza ensayaba en dos pies.

Queriendo hacer de persona,
dijo a una Mona: "¿Qué tal?"
Era perita la Mona,
y respondióle: "Muy mal."

"Yo creo," replicó el Oso,
"que me haces poco favor.
¡Pues qué! ¿Mi aire no es garboso?
¿No hago el paso con primor?"

Estaba el Cerdo presente,
y dijo: "Bravo, ¡bien va!
bailarín más excelente
no se ha visto ni verá."

Echó el Oso, al oir esto,
sus cuentas allá entre sí,
y con ademán modesto
hubo de exclamar así:

"Cuando me desaprobaba
la Mona, llegué a dudar;
mas ya que el Cerdo me alaba,
muy mal debo de bailar."

Guarde para su regalo
esta sentencia un autor;
si el sabio no aprueba, ¡malo!
si el necio aplaude, ¡peor!

ROMANTICISM

José Zorrilla
Spain, 1817–1893

Zorrilla was born in Valladolid and educated in Madrid and Toledo, where he began the study of law. He abandoned law because of his preference for literature, in which field he made a dramatic entrance. At the funeral of Mariano José de Larra, the iconoclast who in 1837 had committed suicide at the age of twenty-eight, Zorrilla, a young, pale-faced man stepped forward and read some elegiac verses. Those present admired them, and he was immediately regarded as a gifted poet. In 1839 he married a widow who was sixteen years his senior. It was never a good marriage, for his wife's jealous rages became increasingly difficult to bear. In 1850, to escape from her, he fled first to France and then to Mexico, where Maximilian appointed him director of the National Theatre. He returned to Spain in 1866 and was received with tremendous acclaim. Zorrilla's lyric poems are among the finest fruits of Spanish Romanticism, and his drama in verse, *Don Juan Tenorio*, written in 1844, is still the most popular play on the Spanish stage.

The Dirge of Larra

On the breeze I hear the knell
Of the solemn funeral bell,
Marshalling another guest
To the grave's unbroken rest.

He has done his earthly toil,
And cast off his mortal coil,
As a maid, in beauty's bloom,
Seeks the cloister's living tomb.

When he saw the Future rise
To his disenchanted eyes.
Void of Love's celestial light,
It was worthless in his sight;
And he hurried, without warning,
To the night that knows no morning.

He has perished in his pride,
Like a fountain, summer-dried;
Like a flower of odorous breath,
Which the tempest scattereth;
But the rich aroma left us
Shows the sweets that have been reft us,
And the meadow, fresh and green,
What the fountain would have been.

Ah! the Poet's mystic measure
Is a rich but fatal treasure;
Bliss to others, to the master
Full of bitterest disaster.

Poet! sleep within the tomb,
Where no other voice shall come
O'er the silence to prevail,

A la memoria de Larra

Ese vago clamor que rasga el viento
es la voz funeral de una campana;
vano remedo del postrer lamento
de un cadáver sombrío y macilento
que en sucio polvo dormirá mañana.

Acabó su misión sobre la tierra,
y dejó su existencia carcomida,
como una virgen al placer perdida
cuelga el profano velo en el altar.
Miró en el tiempo el porvenir vacío,
vacío ya de ensueños y de gloria,
y se entregó a ese sueño sin memoria
que nos lleva a otro mundo a despertar.

Era una flor que marchitó el estío,
era una fuente que agotó el verano;
ya no se siente su murmullo vano,
ya está quemado el tallo de la flor,
todavía su aroma se percibe,
y ese verde color de la llanura,
ese manto de hierba y de frescura,
hijos son del arroyo creador.

Que el poeta en su misión,
sobre la tierra que habita
es una planta maldita
con frutos de bendición

Duerme en paz en la tumba solitaria,
donde no llegue a tu cegado oído
más que la triste y funeral plegaria
que otro poeta cantará por ti.

Save a brother-poet's wail;
That,—if parted spirits know
Aught that passes here below,—
Falling on thy pensive ear,
Softly as an infant's tear,
Shall relate a sweeter story
Than the pealing trump of glory.

If beyond our mortal sight,
In some glorious realm of light,
Poets pass their happy hours,
Far from this cold world of ours,
O, how sweet to cast away
This frail tenement of clay,
And in spirit soar above
To the home of endless love.

And if in that world of bliss
Thou rememberest aught of this,
If *not-Being*'s higher scene
Have a glimpse of what *has been*,
Poet! from the seats divine,
Let thy spirit answer mine.

A. H. EVERETT

Ésta será una ofrenda de cariño,
más grata, sí, que la oración de un hombre,
pura como la lágrima de un niño,
memoria del poeta que perdí.

Si existe un remoto cielo,
de los poetas mansión,
y sólo le queda al suelo
ese retrato de hielo,
fetidez y corrupción,
¡Digno presente, por cierto,
se deja a la amarga vida!
¡Abandonar un desierto
y darle a la despedida
la fea prenda de un muerto!

Poeta: si en el *no ser*
hay un recuerdo de ayer,
una vida como aquí
detrás de ese firmamento...
Conságrame un pensamiento
como el que tengo de ti.

Gustavo Adolfo Bécquer

Spain. 1836–1870

Bécquer is a belated romantic who lived and wrote a generation after romanticism was dead. He was a great poet who struck only a single note on his lyre, but that note became in his hands one of supreme beauty. He left only a small volume of poems and a few prose pieces. His poems are brief, intense, and compelling in their sincerity and anguish; his prose pieces are more fanciful and embrace an atmosphere of mystery.

Bécquer has often been called "the Spanish Heine," and this characterization describes him well. He represents the distillation of romanticism in Spain. He is unique. His poetry, which appears to be so simple, was not created in spontaneous outbursts of passion but was the result of much thought, polishing, agonizing, rewriting, condensation, and purification.

The Swallows

Dark swallows will return again with spring
To hang their nests upon your balcony someday,
And with a tapping of soft wings against your window,
Will call you as they play;

But those that lingered from their homeward flight
Your beauty and my happiness to learn,
The ones that came to know our names and faces,
Those ... never will return!

New honeysuckle may appear someday
And once more thread your garden walls as then;
At future dusks more beautiful than ever
Its flowers may bloom again;

Las golondrinas

Volverán las oscuras golondrinas
en tu balcón sus nidos a colgar,
y otra vez con el ala a sus cristales
jugando llamarán;

pero aquellas que el vuelo refrenaban
tu hermosura y mi dicha al contemplar,
aquellas que aprendieron nuestros nombres,
ésas... ¡no volverán!

Volverán las tupidas madreselvas
de tu jardín las tapias a escalar,
y otra vez a la tarde, aún más hermosas,
sus flores se abrirán;

But those that were our own, wet with their dew
Whose drops we used to see tremblingly turn
And fall like tears the weeping day had shed . . .
Those . . . never will return!

Someday your heart will hear new words of love
Breathe passionate against your ears again;
Perhaps your soul may awake from its deep slumber
And understand them then;

But silent and absorbed on bended knee
Before the altar where God's candles burn,
As I have worshipped you . . . Do not decieve yourself!
Such loves never return!

JOHN A. CROW

pero aquellas, cuajadas de rocío,
cuyas gotas mirábamos temblar
y caer, como lágrimas del día . . .
Ésas . . . ¡no volverán!

Volverán del amor en tus oídos
las palabras ardientes a sonar;
tu corazón de su profundo sueño
tal vez despertará;

Pero mudo y absorto y de rodillas,
come se adora a Dios ante su altar,
como yo te he querido . . . desengáñate,
¡así no te querrán!

To See the Hours of Fever

To see the hours of fever
And sleeplessness pass by,
Seated at my bedside,
Who will say good bye?

When my hand gropes trembling
With its dying grasp,
Seeking for a friendly hand,
Whose hand will it clasp?

When my eyes turn glassy
As my seeing dies,
Open still and staring
Who will close my eyes?

When the bell tolls for me,
(If there is a bell)
Who a prayer will murmur
As he hears its knell?

When my rigid body
In the earth lies dead,
Who at my forgotten grave
Tears will come to shed?

When again the sunlight
Floods some later day,
That I once was in the world
Who will think to say?

JOHN A. CROW

Al ver mis horas de fiebre

Al ver mis horas de fiebre
e insomnio lentas pasar,
a la orilla de mi lecho,
¿quién se sentará?

Cuando la trémula mano
tienda, próximo a expirar,
buscando una mano amiga,
¿quién la estrechará?

Cuando la muerte vidríe
de mis ojos el cristal,
mis párpados aún abiertos,
¿quién los cerrará?

Cuando la campana suene
(si suena en mi funeral),
una oración al oírla,
¿quién murmurará?

Cuando mis pálidos restos
oprima la tierra ya,
sobre la olvidada fosa,
¿quién vendrá a llorar?

¿Quién, en fin, al otro día,
cuando el sol vuelva a brillar,
de que pasé por el mundo,
¿quién se acordará?

The Harp

Half-hidden in a corner of the room,
Perhaps forgotten there for many a day,
Dusty and strangely stilled
The harp in shadows lay.

How many strains are resting on its strings
Like birds that sleep upon the branches of a tree,
Waiting the snow-white hand's familiar touch
To stir their melodies!

El arpa

Del salón en el ángulo oscuro,
de su sueño tal vez olvidada,
silenciosa y cubierta de polvo
veíase el arpa.

¡Cuánta nota dormía en sus cuerdas,
como el pájaro duerme en las ramas,
esperando la mano de nieve
que sabe arrancarlas!

Alas, how many times asleep, I thought,
Within one's soul the spark of genius lies,
Waiting, like Lazarus, that unknown voice to call:
"Wake up, arise!"

¡Ay!—pensé, ¡cuántas veces el genio
así duerme en el fondo del alma!,
y una voz, como Lázaro, espera
que le diga: "¡Levántate y anda!"

JOHN A. CROW

Rosalía de Castro

Spain, 1837–1885

Rosalía de Castro, from the province of Galicia, was one of the most deeply romantic poets of Spain. She was the daughter of a priest. Her unabashed bleeding heart is seldom mawkish because of her disciplined and intuitive control of poetic style. Her straightforward simplicity and sincerity have made her one of the best-loved poets of the nineteenth century, while the output of many of her altisonant contemporaries has largely been forgotten. She left an injunction that all of her unpublished manuscripts should be destroyed at her death.

Life Passes By

Hour after hour, day after day,
Between the ceaseless vigilance
Of earth and sky,
Like a torrent that hurls its spray
Life passes by.

Give back the flower its fragrant scent
When it is dry;
From the waves that kiss the seashore
And one by one caress it as they die,
Go gather all the murmurs that are spent
And on bronze plates their harmonies inscribe.

Years that have passed, laughter and tears,
Black torments of despair, sweet lies,
Alas! Where have they left their memories,
Alas, my soul, oh where?

El tiempo pasa

Hora tras hora, día tras día,
entre el cielo y la tierra que quedan
eternos vigías,
como torrente que se despeña
pasa la vida.

Devolvedle a la flor su perfume
después de marchita;
de las ondas que besan la playa
y unas tras otras besándola expiran,
recoged los rumores, las quejas,
y en las planchas de bronce grabar su armonía.

Tiempos que fueron, llantos y risas,
negros tormentos, dulces mentiras,
¡ay! ¿en dónde su rastro dejaron,
en dónde, alma mía?

JOHN A. CROW

Ramón de Campoamor

Spain, 1817–1901

One of the most popular Spanish poets, Campoamor is best known for his short rhymed statements with a proverbial twist. Like the maxims of Benjamin Franklin, these brief verses are still widely quoted. Campoamor also wrote some sentimental lyrics and a few longer narrative poems, one of which, *The Express Train*, a mixture of drama and romance, is still read with pleasure. In much that he composed, Campoamor tended toward the banal, but a few poems of his are very good, and the one that is translated below was included in Menéndez y Pelayo's anthology entitled *Las cien mejores poesías líricas de la lengua castellana (The One Hundred Best Lyrical Poems in the Spanish Language)*.

The English Hispanist James Fitzmaurice-Kelly points out that Campoamor began writing as a tumultuous, disheveled, Romantic poet. Campoamor soon realized that he had made a false start, and "being in many respects the incarnation of common sense, he recognized the absurdity (in him) of the romantic pose, perceived also that the days of Romanticism were numbered, left it in the lurch, and, after one or two bids for fame on the stage, reappeared as a poet with a subdued manner of his own . . . he did not aim at sublimity, but he was a most adroit versifier, an accomplished master of his art."[27]

What Time Does

With these couplets, Rose, I'm making,
There may fill your heart the dreary
    Songs I sing;
With my voice already quaking
And my eyes brimmed full of weary
    Tears that sting.

Now there are for you but glories,
Dances, joys, and pretty flowers,
    But someday
Nothing will remain but stories
Even of your footprint hours
    Washed away.

In life's festival of madness
Listen to your heart's own pleading
    Tragic breath,
That with hapless love and sadness
Tells us that all love is leading
    But to death.

How reluctantly hope reaches
And resists a creed so baneful
    In your youth!
The fact were not so sad it teaches,
If it were not, Rose, so painful
    In its truth!

As a friend I warn you fairly
It is true and should not grieve you
    Love dies fast;
I regret my words said barely,
But would you have me deceive you
    As those past?

A gust of wind sweeps violent, boldly,
Love comes, God molds one fortunate
    Of many a twain;
The draft of apathy blows so coldly,
And suddenly the one importunate
    Makes two again.

Love with ego is redundant,
And arranges as it rushes
    Good and bad;
In love pain is food abundant,
Pride and innocence it crushes
    All too glad.

Oh! How beautifully the lover
Till his continence is broken
    Will comply;

Lo que hace el tiempo
A Blanca Rosa de Osma

Con mis coplas, Blanca Rosa,
tal vez te cause cuidados
    por cantar
con la voz ya temblorosa,
y los ojos ya cansados
    de llorar.

Hoy para ti sólo hay glorias,
y danzas y flores bellas;
    mas después,
se alzarán tristes memorias,
hasta de las mismas huellas
    de tus pies.

En tus fiestas seductoras
¿no oyes del alma en lo interno
    un rumor,
que lúgubre a todas horas,
nos dice que no es eterno
    nuestro amor?

¡Cuánto a creer se resiste
una verdad tan odiosa
    tu bondad!
¡Y esto fuera menos triste
si no fuera, Blanca Rosa,
    tan verdad!

Te aseguro, como amigo,
que es muy raro, y no te extrañe,
    amar bien.
Siento decir lo que digo;
pero ¿quieres que te engañe
    yo también?

Pasa un viento arrebatado,
viene amor, y a dos en uno
    funde Dios;
sopla el desamor helado,
y vuelve a hacer, importuno,
    de uno, dos.

Que amor, de egoismo lleno,
a su gusto se acomoda
    bien y mal;
en él hasta herir es bueno,
se ama o no ama, aquí está toda
    su moral.

¡Oh! ¡qué bien cumple el amante,
cuando aun tiene la inocencia,
    su deber!

27. James Fitzmaurice-Kelly, *Some Masters of Spanish Verse* (Oxford: Oxford University Press, 1924), 160.

But to later under cover
Lustily his pleasure token
  Satisfy.

Is he blameable who craving
Seeks for newer loves thus scattering
  Love's power?
Yes, blameable as is the raving
Of the storm that passes shattering
  A flower.

Once we love with desperation,
Even love almost as madly
  Twice again.
How versatile life's dispensation!
And our dreams that ring so sadly,
  God, how vain!

Fate inconstant we discover
Like some usurer extends us
  Favor's glove:
First it gives us love sans lover,
Then the lover gives but sends us
  Little love!

Never is desire quite stable,
And I've never seen affection
  Twice the same.
Why deny my tale its fable:
Neither good nor bad direction
  Fixes blame.

Stealthily the old gleam settles
Always in us to mark faintly
  Some fresh bud,
Which will open all its petals
At the altar new love saintly
  Seems to flood!

Happiness is naught but folly;
May you never know its wavering
  As do I;
Trust in chance when melancholy,
If for destiny more favoring
  You sigh.

Who, then, is the one that makes us
Swallow all this gall so hateful,
  All this shame?
Life is the one! Life's pain awakes us!
Life is the faithless and ungrateful
  One to blame.

Life as it rushes by so breathless
Runs toward vertigo's infernal
  Fatuousness;
Seek in God for something deathless;
Life can lead but to eternal
  Nothingness . . .

JOHN A. CROW

Y ¡cómo, más adelante,
aviene con su consciencia
  su placer!

¿Y es culpable el que, sediento,
buscando va en nuevos lazos
  otro amor?
¡Sí! culpable como el viento
que, al pasar, hace pedazos
  una flor.

Se ama una vez sin medida,
y aun se vuelve a amar sin tino
  más de dos.
¡Cuán versátil es la vida!
¡Cuán vano es nuestro destino,
  Santo Dios!

Siempre el destino inconstante
nos da cual vil usurero
  su favor:
de amor primero y no amante;
después mucho amante, pero
  poco amor.

Nunca es estable el deseo,
ni he visto jamás terneza
  siempre igual.
Y ¿a qué negarlo? No creo
ni del bien en la fijeza,
  ni del mal.

¡Ay! un alma inteligente,
siempre en nuestra alma divisa
  una flor,
que se abre infaliblemente
al soplo de alguna brisa
  de otro amor.

Nunca sepas, Blanca Rosa,
que es la dicha una locura,
  cual yo sé;
si quieres ser venturosa,
ten mucha fe en la ventura,
  mucha fe.

¿Y quién es el responsable
de hacer tragar sin medida
  tanta hiel?
¡La vida! ¡ésa es la culpable!
La vida, sólo es la vida
  nuestra infiel.

La vida, que desalada,
de un vértigo del infierno
  corre en pos:
ella corre hacia la nada;
¿quieres ir hacia lo eterno?
  Ve hacia Dios.

MODERNISM

Manuel Gutiérrez Nájera

Mexico, 1859–1895

This Mexican modernist, with Carlos Díaz Dufóo, founded the famous review, *Revista Azul*, which carried throughout the hemisphere the prose and poetry of Mexican modernists. Gutiérrez Nájera was equally admired for his spritely prose sketches and his melodious, romantic poetry. His verse is a Mexican restatement of the French *mal du siècle*. It reflects a deep-rooted pessimism that emerged from both his own personal life and his extensive reading in French literature. Among his favorites were Musset, Gautier, Verlaine. Fusing these and other influences he created his own delicate, elegant, melancholy style.

For Then

I want to die young at the end of the day
On the high sea, with face to the sky,
When agony is but a dream far away
And the flight of my soul is a bird soaring by.

Let there be no sad tears as I draw my last breath,
At one and alone with the sky and the sea,
No sobbing, nor prayer, nor laments of death;
I only would hear the deep waves cover me.

To die when the bright glow of twilight is fading,
And catches the waves in its last net of light;
To be like that sun as its luminous shading
Expires and is lost in the arms of the night.

To die, and die young: before time has destroyed
The delicate fabric illusion has spun;
When life can still say: "I am yours," but the void
Of a final echo tells us death has won!

JOHN A. CROW

Para entonces

Quiero morir cuando decline el día
en alta mar y con la cara al cielo;
donde parezca un sueño la agonía,
y el alma, un ave que remonta el vuelo.

No escuchar en los últimos instantes,
ya con el cielo y con la mar a solas,
más voces ni plegarias sollozantes
que el majestuoso tumbo de las olas.

Morir cuando la luz triste retira
sus áureas redes de la onda verde,
y ser como ese sol que lento expira;
algo muy luminoso que se pierde.

Morir, y joven: antes que destruya
el tiempo aleve la gentil corona;
cuando la vida dice aún: "soy tuya",
¡aunque sepamos bien que nos traiciona!

José Asunción Silva

Colombia, 1865–1896

Silva was one of the most gifted Spanish American poets, but he cut short his promising life by suicide at the age of thirty-two. He was an avid reader of folk and fairy tales, and much of his verse is colored with recollections of childhood. There is also a profound strain of melancholy that emerges from his frustrated attempt to cling to a child's dream of the world. Silva's kinship with Heine, Poe, Baudelaire, Bécquer, and Campoamor make him one of the most fertile and most consummate initiators of the modernist movement. Silva was a great favorite of Unamuno, the famous Spanish leader of the Generation of 1898, who wrote a fine introduction to the first collection of the Colombian's poems, published in Spain in 1908. He pointed out that to comment on Silva was like commenting on Beethoven's music as the successive notes come forth, "whereas what each one of us feels is his own hurt, hopes, and dreams."[28]

Midnight Dreams

Last night when alone half-asleep I reclined
The dreams of my past were brought back to my mind.

The dreams of my hopes, of my glories and pleasures,
Of happiness missed—all to me were lost treasures.

Now closer they came in their solemn procession
Until the dark corners they took in possession;

A deep and grave silence reigned over the room,
And the clock's swinging pendulum stopped in the
   gloom.

A fragrance of faint and forgotten aroma
Appeared like a ghost of the past in my coma.

Old faces I saw that the tomb had long hidden;
Old voices forgotten were chatting unbidden.

The dreams approached nearer and found me asleep,
And then slipped away to a darker retreat.

Then treading the carpet they sneaked from my sight,
And mingling together were lost in the night.

JOHN A. CROW

Anoche, estando solo

Anoche, estando solo y ya medio dormido,
mis sueños de otras épocas se me han aparecido.

Los sueños de esperanzas, de glorias, de alegrías
y de felicidades, que nunca han sido mías,

se fueron acercando en lentas procesiones
y de la alcoba oscura poblaron los rincones.

Hubo un silencio grave en todo el aposento
y en el reloj la péndola detúvose un momento.

La fragancia indecisa de un olor olvidado
llegó como un fantasma y me habló del pasado.

Vi caras que la tumba desde hace tiempo esconde,
y oí voces oídas ya no recuerdo dónde.

¡Los sueños se acercaron y me vieron dormido;
se fueron alejando sin hacerme rüido

y sin pisar los hilos sedosos de la alfombra,
se fueron deshaciendo y hundiéndose en la sombra!

Laughter and Tears

Together one day we were laughing...
So much that it rang in our ears,
And the noise of hilarious laughter
Was suddenly changed into tears!

Then later, one night, still together,
We wept over meaningless fears,
So much that we found after weeping
A wonderful sweetness appears.

Sometimes in the midst of an orgy
Our sighs escape lost in the wine;
In the bitterest water of oceans
We search for the pearls most divine.

JOHN A. CROW

Risa y llanto

Juntos los dos reímos cierto día...
¡ay, y reímos tanto
que toda aquella risa bulliciosa
se tornó pronto en llanto!

¡Después, juntos los dos, alguna noche
lloramos mucho, tanto,
que quedó como huella de las lágrimas
un misterioso encanto!

Nacen hondos suspiros de la orgía
entre las copas cálidas;
y en el agua salobre de los mares
se forjan perlas pálidas.

Rubén Darío
Nicaragua, 1867–1916

Born in a small Central American country with a scant literary tradition, Rubén Darío became the leader of the modernist movement and the best known Spanish American poet of his day. He went to Chile when he was nineteen, and two years later, in 1888, his first famous work, *Azul*

---

28. Miguel de Unamuno (ed.), *Poesías. José Asunción Silva* (Barcelona: Ortega, 1908), vi.

(Blue), a group of prose sketches and poems, appeared. *Azul* was praised by the Spanish critic Juan Valera, who pointed out its strong French overtones and "art for art's sake" character. The main influences on this work were the French Parnassians (Leconte de Lisle, Catulle Mendès, etc.), Théophile Gautier, and Gustave Flaubert.

Darío's second famous work, *Prosas profanas (Secular Lyrics)*, appeared in 1896 and marked the high tide of the modernist movement. One of the translations that follows, "Sonatina," is from this work. By then, Darío's influences were the French symbolists, principally Verlaine, and some of the old Spanish poets, among them Berceo. Music is the mainstay of *Prosas profanas*. In 1905, Darío's finest work, *Cantos de vida y esperanza (Songs of Life and Hope)*, appeared. The poet's style had become much less elaborate, more direct, more intense, more personal, and more simple. He reflected influences from the poems of the old Spanish *cancioneros*. He fused that source of inspiration with his readings from the contemporary poets of Europe, and his modernism began to sing its lovely swan song.

Other poets will continue to follow the paths that Darío has opened. He was the first Spanish American poet to inspire a large following in Europe, and it was not until García Lorca came along a generation later that the current of inspiration was reversed. Darío is one of the most difficult, if not the most difficult, Hispanic poet to translate, because his particular music and personality are so dependent on the majestic and melodious language of Spain for their expression.

There Goes Your Sweetheart

When the poor fellow saw her pass by,
And heard them say: "There goes your sweetheart!..."
He heaved a sigh,
Asked for a cup of wine, threw back his cape.
—Let the poet improvise!
      And then he spoke
Of love, of pleasure, his destiny and mine.
And as the drunken troop applauded him,
A burning tear rolled down his cheek,
And fell at last into the cup of wine.
Later, he took the cup
And quaffed both drink and brine!

JOHN A. CROW

Cuando la vio pasar el pobre mozo

Cuando la vio pasar el pobre mozo,
y oyó que le dijeron:—¡Es tu amada!...
lanzó una carcajada,
pidió una copa y se bajó el embozo.
—¡Que improvise el poeta!
      Y habló luego
del amor, del placer, de su destino.
Y al aplaudirle la embriagada tropa,
se le rodó una lágrima de fuego,
que fue a caer al vaso cristalino.
Después, tomó su copa
y se bebió la lágrima y el vino.

My Own

My soul was pale,
A cocoon soft and frail,
And then a butterfly
Rosetinted in the sky.

A restless zephyr blowing,
My secret told unknowing.
"Oh, did you find your secret out one day?"

My love's own way!
Your secret is a song
Which to the moonbeam must belong.
"A melody you say?"

JOHN A. CROW

Dice mía

Mi pobre alma pálida
era una crisálida;
luego, mariposa
de color de rosa.

Un céfiro inquieto
dijo mi secreto.
—¿Has sabido tu secreto un día?

¡Oh Mía!
Tu secreto es una
melodía en un rayo de luna.
—¿Una melodía?

Sonatina

The princess is sad . . . and in languish reposes,
She signs for relief and her lips of blown roses
Have lost their gay laughter, have lost their fresh bloom.
The princess is pale on her throne and is waiting,
The keyboard is mute, a strange silence creating,
And the vase holds a flower that has lost its perfume.

The garden is filled with the peacocks' proud chatter,
The duenna is banal, jejune in her chatter,
And vested in red pirouettes the buffoon;
The princess not laughing, the princess not feeling,
Pursues in the sky where a star is concealing
An illusion as vague as the light of the moon.

Is she thinking perhaps of the prince of Galconda?
Or of him who has halted his carriage in wonder
To seek in her eyes for the beauty of night?
Or the king of the islands of fragrant rose bowers,
Or of him who is sovereign of diamonds and flowers,
Or of the proud lord of the pearls of Delight?

Alas, the poor princess with lips red as cherry,
Would now be a butterfly, swallow, or fairy,
Have wings that would carry her far in the sky.
She would soar to the sun on a shining stepladder,
Or the lilies of May with her verses make gladder,
Or be lost on the wind as it lifts the waves high.

She no longer wants the gold distaff or palace,
The magical falcon, the jester's red challis,
The swans' classic grace on the azure lagoon.
The flowers are all sad for the yearing king's daughter,
The lotus has withered with roots in the water,
To all the four corners dead roses are strewn.

Poor princess, her eyes have a look that distresses,
She's enmeshed in her jewels, her lavish lace dresses,
The palace of marble encages her soul.
The superb royal palace guard never relaxes,
A hundred giant negroes with giant battle-axes
With watchdogs and dragon would take a huge toll.

I wish that the cocoon would break its enclosure!
The princess grows sad in her pallid composure.
Oh, tower of ivory, oh, vision in white.
She would fly to a land where a dream prince would hail
  her.
(The princess is sadder, the princess grows paler)
A prince more resplendent than dawn after night.

Be silent, my child, says the fairy godmother,
On a swift wingèd steed never loved by another,
With a sword at his side and a falcon above,
Rides the knight who adores you, his whole body
  yearning,
He overcomes distance and Death and is burning
To impassion your lips with the kiss of his love!

JOHN A. CROW

Sonatina

La princesa está triste . . . ¿Qué tendrá la princesa?
Los suspiros se escapan de su boca de fresa,
que ha perdido la risa, que ha perdido el color.
La princesa está pálida en su silla de oro,
está mudo el teclado de su clave sonoro,
y en un vaso olvidada se desmaya una flor.

El jardín puebla el triunfo de los pavos reales . . .
Parlanchina, la dueña dice cosas banales,
y vestido de rojo piruetea el bufón.
La princesa no ríe, la princesa no siente;
la princesa persigue por el cielo de Oriente
la libélula vaga de una vaga ilusión.

¿Piena acaso en el príncipe de Golconda o de China,
o en el que ha detenido su carroza argentina
para ver de sus ojos la dulzura de luz,
o en el rey de las islas de las rosas fragantes,
o en el que es soberano de los claros diamantes,
o en el dueño orgulloso de los perlas de Ormuz?

¡Ay! la pobre princesa de la boca de rosa
quiere ser golondrina, quiere ser mariposa,
tener alas ligeras, bajo el cielo volar;
ir al sol por la escala luminosa de un rayo,
saludar a los lirios con los versos de Mayo,
o perderse en el viento sobre el trueno del mar.

Ya no quiere el palacio, ni la rueca de plata,
ni el halcón encantado, ni el bufón escarlata,
ni los cisnes unánimes en el lago de azur.
Y están tristes las flores por la flor de la corte;
los jazmines de Oriente, los nelumbos del Norte,
de Occidente las dalias y las rosas del Sur.

¡Pobrecita princesa de los ojos azules!
Está presa en sus oros, está presa en sus tules,
en la jaula de mármol del palacio real;
el palacio soberbio que vigilan los guardas,
que custodian cien negros con sus cien alabardas,
un lebrel que no duerme y un dragón colosal.

¡Oh, quién fuera hipsipila que dejó la crisálida!
(La princesa está triste. La princesa está pálida.)
¡Oh visión adorada de oro, rosa y marfil!
¡Quién volara a la tierra donde un príncipe existe
(La princesa está pálida. La princesa está triste.)
más brillante que el alba, más hermoso que Abril!

Calla, calla, princesa—dice el hada madrina—;
en caballo con alas hacia acá se encamina,
en el cinto la espada y en la mano el azor,
el feliz caballero que te adora sin verte,
y que llega de lejos, vencedor de la Muerte,
a encenderte los labios con su beso de amor.

Eheu

Here by this Latin sea
I speak the truth;
In stone, in oil, and wine I feel
My loss of youth.

Oh, Lord, how old I am,
Such age I show!
Where does my song come from,
And I... where will I go?

To know myself at heart
Will cost me yet again
Dark hours in the abyss
Of every How and When.

This shining Latin splendor,
Of what use was it,
When the "I" and the "not I"
Went down into the pit?

Among the clouds I walk,
Contented, strong, and free;
I know the secret winds
Of earth and sea.

A few vague confidences
Of Being and Not-being may
Stir fragments of consciences
Of Now and Yesterday.

Lost in a wilderness,
I began to shout;
I saw the sun go dead,
My tears gushed out![29]

JOHN A. CROW

¡Eheu!

Aquí, junto al mar latino,
digo la verdad:
Siento en roca, aceite y vino,
yo mi antigüedad.

¡Oh qué anciano soy, Dios santo;
oh, qué anciano soy!...
¿De dónde viene mi canto?
Y yo, ¿adónde voy?

El conocerme a mí mismo
ya me va costando
muchos momentos de abismos
y el cómo y el cuándo...

Y esta claridad latina,
¿de qué me sirvió
a la entrada de la mina
del yo y el no yo...?

Nefelibata contento,
creo interpretar
las confidencias del viento,
la tierra y el mar...

Unas vagas confidencias
del ser y el no ser,
y fragmentos de conciencias
de ahora y ayer.

Como en medio de un desierto
me puse a clamar;
y miré el sol como muerto
y me eché a llorar.

Alas for Him

Alas for him who probes into his heart, for he is lost;
Alas for him if he believes the ghost
Of grief or joy will ever come to stay:
Ignorance and oblivion are two gods at bay.
What the tree whispers to the passing wind,
What animals by instinct feel, our thoughts have thinned
And crystallized in words... this anguished cry.
Whatever else be written in a lie.

JOHN A. CROW

¡Ay, triste del que un día!

¡Ay, triste del que un día en su esfinge interior
pone los ojos e interroga! Está perdido.
¡Ay del que pide eurekas al placer o al dolor!
Dos dioses hay, y son: Ignorancia y Olvido.

Lo que el árbol desea decir y dice al viento,
y lo que el animal manifiesta en su instinto,
cristalizamos en palabra y pensamiento.
Nada más que maneras expresan lo distinto.

Melancholy

Brother, you have the light, share it with me.
My eyes are gone, I grope unseeing here
Lost in the storms and tempests that I fear,
Mad with sweet music, blind with my fantasy.

Melancolía

Hermano, tú que tienes la luz, dime la mía.
Soy como un ciego. Voy sin rumbo y ando a tientas.
Voy bajo tempestades y tormentas
ciego de ensueño y loco de armonía.

29. *Eheu* is the Latin word for *Alas*. This title was suggested to Darío by the famous line of Horace: "Eheu! fugaces labuntur anni" (Alas! the fleeting years glide by).

It is my fate to dream. The poet's role
Has been a coat-of-mail pressing its wall
Against my heart. And bloody thorns let fall
Red drops from my poor melancholy soul.
Sightless and mad I stumble as I go
Across this bitter world; the road is long,
But still not long enough to hold my song...
And in this staggering of breath and pain
I bear a cross that I can scarce sustain.
Don't you hear drops that fall—my lifeblood's flow?

JOHN A. CROW

Ése es mi mal. Soñar. La poesía
es la camisa férrea de mil puntas cruentas
que llevo sobre el alma. Las espinas sangrientas
dejan caer las gotas de mi melancolía.

Y así voy, ciego y loco, por este mundo amargo;
a veces me parece que el camino es muy largo,
y a veces que es muy corto...

Y en este titubeo de aliento y agonía,
cargo lleno de penas lo que apenas soporto.
¿No oyes caer las gotas de mi melancolía?

Julio Herrera y Reissig
Uruguay, 1875–1910

This gifted poet suffered throughout his life from severe cardiac disease, and he lived mostly in a world of books until his death at the age of thirty-five. He was the leader of a literary group that met at the Tower of the Panoramas, one of Latin America's best-known ivory towers, or refuges for poets. Herrera y Reissig read widely in contemporary French literature and was influenced particularly by Albert Samain and Jules LaForgue. He himself made frequent use of wild and abstruse poetic images and so represented modernism's most daring expression, which became a kind of ultramodernism, the forerunner of the movements in poetry soon to come.

Heraldic Decoration

*Oh, lady, who art the object of my
attentions, I shall always love you
though you rebuff me.*   Góngora

I dreamt you stood beside the icy wall
Where all existence ends, brilliant and tense,
Displaying as you walked your opulence
Of grieving velvet darkened like a pall.

Your foot, carved ivory, pure as a dove,
With pitiless Satanic vehemence
Wounded the patient souls of poor defence
Who gave themselves unto your perjured love.

My own sweet love, that followed as you spoke,
Like a blind lamb with sorrowful devotion,
The perfumed traces of your shadow's motion,

Sought out the torment of your regal yoke,
And then beneath your hangman's satin feet
I placed the carpet of my heart's defeat.

JOHN A. CROW

Decoración heráldica

*Señora de mis pobres homenajes
débote amor aunque me ultrajes.*
Góngora

Soñé que te encontrabas junto al muro
glacial donde termina la existencia,
paseando tu magnífica opulencia
de doloroso terciopelo oscuro.

Tu pie, decoro del marfil más puro,
hería, con satánica inclemencia,
las pobres almas, llenas de paciencia,
que aún se brindaban a tu amor perjuro.

Mi dulce amor, que sigue sin sosiego,
igual que un triste corderito ciego,
la huella perfumada de tu sombra,

buscó el suplicio de tu regio yugo,
y bajo el raso de tu pie verdugo
puse mi esclavo corazón de alfombra.

Delmira Agustini
Uruguay, 1886–1914

The daughter of an aristocratic Uruguayan family, Delmira Agustini was fascinated by the arts at a tender age, and she was writing poetry by the time she was ten. Her unique contribution to

Hispanic poetry is the intensity with which she extolled the erotic impulse and the all-consuming passion of love in a language of highly charged imagery. She married a man with whom she had absolutely nothing in common except physical attraction, and after a brief period, the marriage ended with the violent (suicidal-homicidal) death of both parties.

The Miraculous Ship

Prepare me a ship like a great thought recklessly given . . .
Some will call it "The Shadow," others "The Star."
By no caprice of hand or wind let it be driven;
I want it quickened, wild, lovely as roses are!

The rhythms of a God-sent heart will swell its sail
And power it, and I shall feel on this sweet ship
As safe and strong as in God's hands. In every gale
Through roughest seas its flashing prow will slip.

When I have laden it with all my pain and cast away,
I shall drive like the broken corolla of a lotus flower
Over the liquid horizon of the sea's vast heaving . . .

Ship, Oh sister soul. toward what distant and unseen bay
Of deepest revelations and unknown port's white tower
Shall be our course? . . . I die of life, of dreams, and of
  believing . . .

JOHN A. CROW

La barca milagrosa

Preparadme una barca como un gran pensamiento . . .
La llamarán "La Sombra" unos; otros, "La Estrella."
No ha de estar al capricho de una mano o de un viento;
¡yo la quiero consciente indomable y bella!

La moverá el gran ritmo de un corazón sangriento
de Vida sobrehumana; he de sentirme en ella
fuerte como en los brazos de Dios. En todo viento,
en todo mar templadme su prora de centella.

La cargaré de toda mi tristeza, y, sin rumbo,
iré como la rota corola de un nelumbo,
por sobre el horizonte líquido de la mar . . .

Barca, alma hermana: ¿hacia qué tierras nunca vistas,
de hondas revelaciones, de cosas imprevistas
iremos? . . . Yo ya muero de vivir y soñar . . .

Amado Nervo
Mexico, 1870–1919

Nervo abandoned his studies for the priesthood to become a journalist and poet. In 1900 he met Darío and several contemporary French writers in Paris. With Jesús Valenzuela he established the famous modernist Journal, *Revista Moderna*, in 1898; it continued until 1911. Nervo was subsidized by the Mexican government of Porfirio Díaz, which gave him diplomatic posts first in Madrid and then in South America. His poetry reflects his philosophical attitudes, which run the gamut from Christianity, to agnosticism, to a kind of Oriental pantheism. His best poems are simple, sincere statements of basic human emotions: love; the loss of love; the search for beauty, God, and, most of all, serenity.

Expectation

I feel something strange coming into my life.
Perhaps it is love? Perhaps it is death?
My face grows more pallid . . . my soul is in strife,
And my body is trembling with each solemn breath.

I feel some sublimity molding my clay,
Some fire in this miserable carcass of mine.
From the pebble celestial sparks seem to play,
And the proud royal purple these rags render fine.

I feel something solemn approaching in state.
With tremulous body and soul-fright I reel . . .
Let the scroll by fulfilled, and let God read my fate,

Expectación

Siento que algo solemne va a llegar en mi vida.
¿Es acaso la muerte? ¿por ventura el amor?
Palidece mi rostro . . . Mi alma está conmovida,
y sacude mis miembros un sagrado temblor.

Siento que algo sublime va a encarnar en mi barro,
en el mísero barro de mi pobre existir.
Una chispa celeste brotará del guijarro
y la púrpura augusta va el harapo a teñir.

Siento que algo solemne se aproxima, y me hallo
todo trémulo; mi alma de pavor llena está.
Que se cumpla el destino, que Dios dicte su fallo.

While kneeling I silently pray, hope and wait
To hear what pronouncement the ABYSS will reveal...

JOHN A. CROW

Mientras yo de rodillas, oro, espero y me callo,
para oir la palabra que el Abismo dirá...

I Shall Leave

I shall be ready, Father, gay or sad,
Resigned to leave when Thou hast spread the pall.
If to this world thy will brought me unclad,
Should I not part submissive at thy call?

One sole regret of conscience brings me anguish:
That in my younger years I should have asked
Of life its reasons... The leaf must languish
Questioning the course of winds that pass!

But now no doubt perturbs me as I pray:
I close my eyes, and as this journey's quest
Draws near the end of its long day,
My restlessness grows weary on the way,
And falls asleep resigned, in Thee to rest.

JOHN A. CROW

Me marcharé

Me marcharé, Señor, alegre o triste;
mas resignado, cuando al fin me hieras.
Si vine al mundo porque tú quisiste,
¿no he de partir sumiso cuando quieras?

... Un torcedor tan sólo me acongoja,
y es haber preguntado el pensamiento
sus porqués a la Vida... ¡Mas la hoja
quiere saber dónde la lleva el viento!

Hoy, empero, ya no pregunto nada;
cerré los ojos, y mientras el plazo
llega en que se termine la jornada,
mi inquietud se adormece en la almohada
de la resignación, ¡en tu regazo!

Leopoldo Lugones
Argentina, 1874–1938

Lugones was the outstanding modernist writer of Argentina, both in poetry and in prose. For many years he was director of the National Education Association of his country, and his published work contains several volumes on various aspects of Argentine history. He also wrote two books of short stories and a considerable amount of literary criticism. His voluminous poetry embraces every facet of that genre from the nineteenth century on, thus making him one of the most varicolored of all modernists. In his political ideology Lugones began as a socialist and ended as an apologist for extreme nationalism and military rule. This change in attitude alienated many of his friends. He committed suicide at the age of sixty-four.

White Solitude

Under the tranquility of sleep,
a lunar calm of shining silk,
the night
as if it were
the white body of silence,
gently reclines in that immensity.
And loosens
her hair,
in a prodigious foliage
of tree-lined streets.

Nothing is awake but the eye
of the clock ticking away in the gloomy tower,
burrowing uselessly into the infinite
like a hole opened in the sand.
The infinite,
rolled along on wheels

La blanca soledad

Bajo la calma del sueño,
calma lunar de luminosa seda,
la noche,
como si fuera
el blanco cuerpo del silencio,
dulcemente en la inmensidad se acuesta.
Y desata
su cabellera,
en prodigioso follaje
de alamedas.

Nada vive sino el ojo
del reloj en la torre tétrica,
profundizando inútilmente el infinito
como un agujero abierto en la arena.
El infinito,
rodado por las ruedas

of clocks, like a carriage that never arrives.	de los relojes, como un carro que nunca llega.
The moon digs out a white abyss of quietude, in whose opening things become dead bodies and shadows live like ideas. And one shudders at how near death is within that whiteness. And at the beauty of the world possessed by the ancience of the full moon. And the powerful need to be loved trembles in the wounded heart.	La luna cava un blanco abismo de quietud, en cuya cuenca las cosas son cadáveres y las sombras viven como ideas. Y uno se pasma de lo próxima que está la muerte en la blancura aquella. De lo bello que es el mundo poseído por la antigüedad de la luna llena. Y el ansia tristísima de ser amado, en el corazón doloroso tiembla.
There is a city in the air, an almost invisible city suspended, whose vague profile sketches on the luminous night, like watermarks on a sheet of paper, its multiple outlines. A city so far away, that it distresses with its absurd presence.	Hay una ciudad en el aire, una ciudad casi invisible suspensa, cuyos vagos perfiles sobre la clara noche transparentan, como las rayas de agua en un plïego, su cristalización poliédrica. Una ciudad tan lejana, que angustia con su absurda presencia.
Is it a city or a ship in which we were slowly abandoning the earth, silent and happy, and with such purity, that only our souls could live on in the whiteness of the full moon?...	¿Es una ciudad o un buque en el que fuésemos abandonando la tierra, callados y felices, y con tal pureza, que sólo nuestras almas en la blancura plenilunar vivieran?...
And suddenly a vague tremor passes through the serene light. The lines vanish, the immensity turns into white stone, and there only remains in the star-crossed night the certainty of your absence.	Y de pronto cruza un vago estremecimiento por la luz serena. Las líneas se desvanecen, la inmensidad cámbiase en blanca piedra, y sólo permanece en la noche aciaga la certidumbre de tu ausencia.

JOHN A. CROW

Enrique González Martínez
Mexico, 1871–1952

González Martínez was a medical doctor who practiced in the outlying rural areas of Mexico for seventeen years. In 1911 he came to Mexico City, where he formed part of the group of writers known as the Ateneo de México. He later became Mexican minister to Argentina and to Spain. His poetry, always very carefully wrought, is marked by a profound inner serenity despite the ever-present sense of nostalgia and loss. In his reaction against the ivory tower of modernism, he called upon the young poets to wring the neck of the deceptively plumaged swan and to heed instead the wisdom of the owl who sees in the darkness.

## Twist the Neck of the Swan	## Tuércele el cuello al cisne
Go twist the neck of the deceptive swan Whose white on the blue fountain seems unreal; The swan that moves in grace, but cannot feel The soul of things, or hear the earth's sweet song.	Tuércele el cuello al cisne de engañoso plumaje que da su nota blanca al azul de la fuente; él pasea su gracia no más, pero no siente el alma de las cosas ni la voz del paisaje.

Flee all conceits of language and of style,
Seek only rhythms that will beat at one
With life's own heart. Revere what life has done!
Let life accept your homage and your smile.

See how the sapient owl extends his wings
From Pallas' lap on his Olympian arc
Till on that tree he ends his noiseless flight.
Here is no graceful swan, no bird that sings,
But his disquieting eye pierces the dark
And plumbs the silent manuscript of night.

JOHN A. CROW

Huye de toda forma y de todo lenguaje
que no vayan acordes con el ritmo latente
de la vida profunda... y adora intensamente
la vida, y que la vida comprenda tu homenaje.

Mira al sapiente buho cómo tiende las alas
desde el Olimpo, deja el regazo de Palas
y posa en aquel árbol el vuelo taciturno...

El no tiene la gracia del cisne, mas su inquieta
pupila que se clava en la sombra, interpreta
el misterioso libro del silencio nocturno.

Tomorrow the Poets

Tomorrow the poets will write in divine
Verse that we bards of today cannot sing;
New constellations of brilliant design
To their restless soul search a new destiny bring.
The poets of tomorrow will write once again
Absorbed in an unknown and exotic song,
And on hearing our words will abruptly disdain
And reject every dream that has borne us along.

And all will be useless, and all be in vain,
There will be the same eagerness, mystery, pain,
And the same cruel hurt we have suffered so long;
Then before the same shadow that flits to and fro
They will pick up the dust-covered lyre in their woe,
And replay on its strings every note of our song.

JOHN A. CROW

Mañana los poetas

Mañana los poetas cantarán en divino
verso que no logramos entonar los de hoy;
nuevas constelaciones darán otro destino
a sus almas inquietas con un nuevo temblor.

Mañana los poetas seguirán su camino
absortos en ignota y extraña floración,
y al oir nuestro canto, con desdén repentino
echarán a los vientos nuestra vieja ilusión.

Y todo será inútil, y todo será en vano;
será el afán de siempre y el idéntico arcano
y la misma tiniebla dentro del corazón.

Y ante la eterna sombra que surge y se retira,
recogerán del polvo la abandonada lira
y cantarán con ella nuestra misma canción.

Ramón López Velarde
Mexico, 1888–1921

As a young man López Velarde studied for the priesthood, but he gave this up to study law, and finally he became a journalist and teacher. His early education left an indelible mark on his poetry, providing him with a symbolic frame in which to express the passion of his inner war—a conflict between Christianity and paganism. His poetry is finely crafted, extremely musical, filled with brilliant images. His frequent use of colloquial language gave his writing a unique flavor, yet he opened the way for a new baroque poetic expression. He felt a passionate love for his native Mexico and said that he could hardly wait to die so that he might be embraced by her forever.

His long poem "La Suave Patria" (*The Gentle Fatherland*) is known and loved by all Mexicans. To López Velarde the title of this poem really was "The Gentle Motherland," because he always regarded his country as a woman. He is characterized by two main feelings, "his obsession for death, and his love of flowers," according to Juan José Arreola. The oscillation between extinction and beauty has produced some of the finest poetry to come out of Mexico. Gutiérrez Nájera, Nervo, López Velarde, Gorostiza, Paz—all embody some portion of the equation.

Song of the Heart

An intimate music will never end
Transported here in a gold embrace
Love and Charity kiss and blend.

Don't you hear the tuning-fork of the heart?
Listen to the sound of the merry chase
Of those who were and of those who are.

My brothers of all the centuries and years
Have found in me their delayed accord,
Their harsh complaints. and their fury's tears.

I am the voice of the leaves that frisk,
The budding breast of the druid bard
With the forest as goddess and odalisque.

I am the pool where Scheherazade swims
In shining water with the ancient nudes
Like a pearl whose witness an eyeglass brims.

I am sighing Christianity sans schism
Leafing through the beatitudes
Of the Virgin who was my catechism.

And the new delight that now will ration
The hypnotic spells that its tango sings
To the mannequin and the price of fashion.

I shout that Genesis itself is round,
And court the ladies and material things
With a very Christian and a pagan sound.

Oh, Psyche, my soul, let your music start
Today's song of forests, of orgies and art,
A song of Mary, the sound of the heart.

JOHN A. CROW

El són del corazón

Una música íntima no cesa,
porque transida en un abrazo de oro
la Caridad con el Amor se besa.

¿Oyes el diapasón del corazon?
Oye en su nota múltiple el estrépito
de los que fueron y de los que son.

Mis hermanos de todas las centurias
reconocen en mí su pausa igual,
sus mismas quejas y sus propias furias.

Soy la fronda parlante en que se mece
el pecho germinal del bardo druida
con la selva por diosa y por querida.

Soy la alberca lumínica en que nada,
como perla debajo de una lente,
debajo de las linfas, Scherezada.

Y soy el suspirante cristanismo
al hojear las bienaventuranzas
de la virgen que fue mi catecismo.

Y la nueva delicia, que acomoda
sus hipnotismos de color de tango
al figurín y al precio de la moda.

La redondez de la Creación atrueno
cortejando a las hembras y a las cosas
con el clamor pagano y nazareno.

¡Oh Psiquis, oh mi alma: suena a són
moderno, a són de selva, a són de orgía
y a són mariano, el són del corazón!

GENERATION OF 1898

Miguel de Unamuno

Spain, 1864–1936

Unamuno was the spiritual leader of the Spanish Generation of 1898. His voluminous prose and poetry were a continuing clarion to his countrymen to reach back into their past and honor it. He was, one might say, a skeptical Catholic, one to whom doubt itself was an affirmation of faith. And he was Spanish to the core. Remembering that the German Goethe had died calling for more light (knowledge), Unamuno wrote, "Give us warmth, more warmth, O Lord, for we die of the cold not the darkness." In this he distinguished the Latin from the Nordic temperament. Speaking of the history of Spain he commented: "Other nations have left institutions, books. We have left souls!" [30]

Unamuno's poetry is the embodiment of his gut reaction to the universe about him. With intense feeling and love of country, he was often able to write lines of enduring beauty. Although he was a Basque and not a Castilian, he became one of the great voices of his adopted province.

Castile

In the rough palm of your hand
You lift me up, my own Castile,
To the sky that warms and refreshes your land,
To the sky, your master.

Parched, sinewy land of clear horizons,
Mother of hearts, stout arms, and ancient stories,
Your present self takes on the coloring
Of your past glories.

Your harsh, bare fields reach up to merge
With the meadow of the sky, immense, concave;
The sun finds its cradle in you, its sanctuary,
And then its grave.

Your vast expanse is all a mountain prairie,
In you I feel uplifted toward the sky,
It is a mountain air that is inhaled
Where your vast wastelands lie.

Altar of giants, land of Castile,
Into your air I shall send forth my songs,
If you are pleased they'll fall to earth again
Where poetry belongs.

Castilla

Tú me levantas, tierra de Castilla,
en la rugosa palma de tu mano,
al cielo que te enciende y te refresca,
　　　al cielo, tu amo.

Tierra nervuda, enjuta, despejada.
madre de corazones y de brazos,
toma el presente en ti viejos colores
　　　del noble antaño.

Con la pradera cóncava del cielo
lindan en torno tus desnudos campos,
tiene en ti cuna el sol y en ti sepulcro
　　　y en ti santuario.

Es todo cima tu extensión redonda
y en ti me siento al cielo levantado,
aire de cumbre es el que se respira
　　　aquí, en tus páramos.

¡Ara gigante, tierra castellana,
a ese tu aire soltaré mis cantos,
si te son dignos bajarán al mundo
　　　desde lo alto!

JOHN A. CROW

Manuel Machado

Spain, 1874–1947

Manuel Machado was the son of an eminent folklorist. He left his native Seville for Madrid when he was nine and was educated at the famous *Instituto Libre de Enseñanza,* headed by Francisco

---

30. Miguel de Unamuno, *Del sentimiento trágico de la vida* (Madrid: Renacimiento, 1913), 178.

Giner de los Ríos, where a whole generation of Spaniards received an inspiring humanistic education. His brother, Antonio Machado, one year younger than he, became in his mature years the great poet of Castile. Manuel, on the other hand, never ceased to poeticize nostalgically his native Andalusia. He knew French literature well, and the frequent French overtones in his work appear as bright impressionistic word paintings. His poetic style reflects the musicality of Rubén Darío and the Spanish American modernists, but his subject matter is less personal, more traditional than theirs. In his best moments Manuel Machado represents "one of the supreme forms of contemporary poetry," and among the poets of Spain he perhaps most completely epitomizes the modernist movement.[31]

Spring

> Youth, springtime of life . . .
> Carducci

Because spring is a woman . . . and possesses
Warm eyes, red lips, sweet breasts, and perfumed breath;
Because she comes like love with flowing tresses,
And full of life's gay thoughtlessness of death . . .

Because she gives us buds—white orange blooms—
Whose frail petals the golden fruits enclose . . .
Because she is illusion, and perfumes
Hope, beauty, song, and scents the generous rose . . .

You called her—master—Youth! . . . a facile word.
But not so fortunate although it may
Resound a thousand times when love is stirred.

Like Spring, Youth, too, is brief—a tender thing . . .
But gone, it never comes again our way
As do return—always!—the months of Spring.

JOHN A. CROW

La primavera

> *Gioventú, primavera della vità . . .*
> Carducci

. . . Porque es mujer la Primavera . . . Y tiene
cálidos ojos, labios rojos, dulces turgencias
y aliento perfumado. Y porque viene
llena de amor, de vida, de alegres inconsciencias . . .

Porque nos da flores—cándidos azahares—,
que luego son naranjas luminosas . . .
Porque es toda ilusión; porque toda es cantares,
belleza, sueños, rosas generosas . . .

La llamaste—maestro—¡Juventud! . . . Era fácil
el tropo, mas no tanto afortunado,
aunque en boca de todos resuene veces mil.

Como la Primavera, es tierna y grácil
la Juventud . . . Mas ella jamás ha retornado
como retornan ¡siempre! mayo gentil y abril.

Wild Rose

Savant lips, wild Rose,
Oh, can't you see
Your lips are so much wiser
Than mine could ever be?

Wild Rose,
So always right,
Your savant lips enclose
Heart-shaped delight . . .

Thus I to your rare art
And to your savant lips, wild Rose,
Surrender.

All Heaven is a part
Of the dear heart
Your sweet lips render.

Rosa

Labios sabios, Rosa loca,
¿sabes que
saben mucho más tus labios
de todo lo que yo sé?

Rosa loca,
tú siempre tienes razón
con tu boca
en forma de corazón . . .

Y a tu arte peregrina,
y a tus rojos labios sabios
yo me rindo.
            ¡Oh, la divina
golosina
de tus labios!

JOHN A. CROW

31. Federico de Onís, *Antología de la poesía española e hispanoamericana* (Madrid: Casa Editorial Hernando, 1934), 244.

Antonio Machado
Spain, 1875–1939

Born in Seville, Antonio and his brother Manuel moved with their parents to Madrid when Antonio was eight years old. Antonio slowly absorbed the high, dry, and melancholy austerity of his new homeland to such an extent that he became for many the great poet of Castile. He also studied at Giner's *Instituto Libre de Enseñanza*, and the moral elevation that characterizes his work is due in part to Giner's strong personal influence on him. Near the turn of the century, Antonio Machado lived in Paris for two years. He was then sent to Guatemala as a vice consul, and there he met Rubén Darío. He reacted against the external, showy style of Darío and turned his search ever more inward. In 1907 he accepted a post as professor of French in the Institute of Soria, a small provincial town in northern Castile, where he remained for seven years. In Soria he fell in love and married. His wife died, and in his grief, Antonio's spiritual essence slowly refined itself and took on the almost skeletal sobriety that was to characterize his finest poetry.

He was a member of the Generation of 1898 in Spain, along with Unamuno, Baroja, Azorín, and his brother Manuel; but Antonio never carried the banner for any literary movement or "ism" in vogue during the productive years of his life. He was steeped in the folk and artistic poetry of the Hispanic countries. But he was also a great admirer of Edgar Allan Poe, who, he said, "presents better than any other poet that I know, that conflict between the essential and the temporary, which is the beginning and perhaps the end, of all poetry." [32] Antonio's own poetry fused these same extremes in tenuous union and became a total commitment. Because of this, his poetry may very likely survive the vicissitudes of our epoch.

In the final weeks of the Spanish Civil War, Antonio Machado fled across the French frontier north of Barcelona, lived for a time in a railway boxcar on a siding, and died destitute in a tiny French village nearby.

Self-Portrait

My childhood has its memories of a courtyard in Seville,
A garden in the sunlight where I saw the lemons fall;
My youth, the twenty years of life spent here in old
 Castile,
My history, too many things I'd rather not recall.

I have not been a Don Juan, my style was drab and gray,
—You know with what sobriety I wear these awkward
 clothes—
But Cupid's arrow struck me, when it was I cannot say,
And then I loved as many girls as summer loving knows.

The fiery blood of Jacobins is coursing in my veins,
But what I write in poetry is from the magic spring,
And rather than be doctrinaire held fast by rigid chains,
I want to be man of good far more than anything.

I worship beauty and despite today's aesthetic creed,
I pluck the older roses from the garden of Ronsard,
I do not like the colors of this new cosmetic screed,
And I am not an artist of today's vanguardist art.

I cannot stand the warblings from a tenor's shallow nose,
Nor the chorus of the crickets as they chant to moon and
 sun,

Retrato

Mi infancia son recuerdos de un patio de Sevilla,
y un huerto claro donde madura el limonero;
mi juventud, veinte anos en tierra de Castilla;
mi historia, algunos casos que recordar no quiero.

Ni un seductor Mañara, ni un Bradomín he sido
—ya conocéis mi torpe aliño indumentario—,
mas recibí la flecha que me asignó Cupido,
y amé cuanto ellas pueden tener de hospitalario.

Hay en mis venas gotas de sangre jacobina,
pero mi verso brota de manantial sereno;
y, más que un hombre al uso que sabe su doctrina,
soy, en el buen sentido de la palabra, bueno.

Adoro la hermosura, y en la moderna estética
corté las viejas rosas del huerto de Ronsard;
mas no amo los afeites de la actual cosmética,
no soy un ave de esas del nuevo gay-trinar.

Desdeño las romanzas de los tenores huecos
y el coro de los grillos que cantan a la luna.
A distinguir me paro las voces de los ecos,
y escucho solamente, entre las voces, una.

32. Gerardo Diego (ed.), *Poesía española: Antología 1915–1931* (Madrid: Editorial Signo, 1932), 77.

I pause to separate the voices from the echoes,
And then among those voices hear but a single one.
Am I classic or romantic? I don't know what to say;
I prefer to form my verses as a captain's sword is made
Respected by the daring hand that wields and gives it
    sway,
Not by the cunning artifice of him who forged its blade.

I hold converse with the fellow who always walks with
    me,
The man who talks when all alone will someday speak
    with God;
My words become a warming chat about philanthropy
With this good friend who shares with me his secret
    promenade.

In the end I owe you nothing, you owe me all I've said,
I do my work and pay hard cash for everything I own,
The suit I wear, the place I live, even my daily bread,
And finally this narrow bed on which I lie alone.

When God's moment of truth arrives for that last
    rendezvous,
And my good ship is set to sail for all eternity,
I'll come aboard without delay to bid the world adieu,
Naked and empty-handed like the children of the sea.

JOHN A. CROW

The Land Is Barren

The land is barren and the soul howls
at the pale horizon like a starving wolf.
What do you seek, oh poet, in the setting sun?

The journey is cruel, for the road weighs upon the heart.
The icy wind, and approaching night,
and the agony of the distance!

Fallen trees stretch across the white road, rigid and black;
the distant hills are gold and blood. The sun has died . . .
What do you seek, oh poet, in the setting sun?

MARY H. PARHAM

Her Street Is Dark

Her street is dark. The tall housetops now shade
A dying sun; upon the balconies soft light is played.

Look! Can't you see inside that flowering window sill
The rose tint oval of a face remembered still?

Head pressed against the glass a blurred white stripe
Surges and vanishes like an old daguerreotype.

My steps the only sound on a deserted street . . .
A swollen sun that blots the west with slanting rays that
    meet.

O, love! My heart with agony now beats. Can it be she?
Move on . . . A star now lights the blue . . . It cannot be!

JOHN A. CROW

¿Soy clásico o romántico? No sé. Dejar quisiera
mi verso, como deja el capitán su espada:
famosa por la mano viril que la blandiera,
no por el docto oficio del forjador preciada.

Converso con el hombre que siempre va conmigo
—quien habla solo espera hablar a Dios un día—;
mi soliloquio es plática con este buen amigo
que me enseñó el secreto de la filantropía.

Y al cabo, nada os debo; debéisme cuanto he escrito.
A mi trabajo acudo, con mi dinero pago
el traje que me cubre y la mansión que habito;
el pan que me alimenta y el lecho en donde yago.

Y cuando llegue el día del último viaje,
y esté al partir la nave que nunca ha de tornar,
me encontraréis a bordo ligero de equipaje,
casi desnudo, como los hijos de la mar.

Desnuda está la tierra

Desnuda está la tierra,
y el alma aúlla al horizonte pálido
como loba famélica. ¿Qué buscas,
poeta, en el ocaso?

Amargo caminar, porque el camino
pesa en el corazón. ¡El viento helado,
y la noche que llega, y la amargura
de la distancia! . . . En el camino blanco

algunos yertos árboles negrean;
en los montes lejanos
hay oro y sangre . . . El sol murió . . . ¿Qué buscas,
poeta, en el ocaso?

La calle en sombra

La calle en sombra. Ocultan los altos caserones
el sol que muere; hay ecos de luz en los balcones.

¿No ves, en el encanto del mirador florido,
el óvalo rosado de un rostro conocido?

La imagen, tras el vidrio de equívoco reflejo,
surge o se apaga como daguerrotipo viejo.

Suena en la calle sólo el ruido de tu paso;
se extinguen lentamente los ecos del ocaso.

¡Oh angustia! Pesa y duele el corazón . . . ¿Es ella?
No puede ser . . . Camina . . . En el azul, la estrella.

Deep Song

The dusk sifted into my breathless room,
Wide open to a torrid summer night,
And wrapped its hands about my desolation
As I unwound its tattered shreds of light.

Then on the air a sudden blaze of sound:
Deep sobbing of a wistful, broken strain
That quivered with the sombre tremolos
Of tragic songs from my own southern Spain.

... And it was Love, a red and fiery flame...
Whose nervous hand upon the vibrant strings
A long and golden pause sustained
That soon flashed into stars with gilded wings—

... And it was Death, the scythe upon his shoulder,
Grim-faced and skeletal, with steps long-drawn and slow.
—Thus did I dream of him when but a child—

On the guitar, sonorous, tremulous below,
A brusque hand as it strummed would imitate
The lowering of a casket in the ground.
The breath of wind was but a solitary wail
That winnows ash and stirs the dust around.

JOHN A. CROW

From the Road

The clock struck twelve... twelve
Spade blows in the earth.
My hour is come—I cried... But silence
Answered me: Do not be frightened,
For you will never see the last drop fall
That trembles in the water-clock upon that wall.

On this familiar strand
You will respose for many long hours more,
Then one fine morning you will wake to see
Your ship is anchored to another shore.

Over the bitter earth
Sleep has its maze of paths and bars
Paths winding endlessly
And shaded parks, flowering in silence,
Deep crypts and ladders to the stars,
Carved altar screens of hopes and memories.
Little figures that pass and smile
—Gloomy playthings of the old—
Friendly images in file
At the flowering turn of the path today
And rose-tinted dreams
That mark a road... far away...

The flaming dusk is like a violet frieze
Smoking behind the tall black cypress trees,
In the shadowed street garden a fountain stands
With a naked Cupid of stone wings and eyes
Who dreams in silence. And in the marble basin
Dead water lies.

JOHN A. CROW

Cante hondo

Yo meditaba absorto, devanando
los hilos del hastío y la tristeza,
cuando llegó a mi oído,
por la ventana de mi estancia, abierta

a una caliente noche de verano,
el plañir de una copla soñolienta,
quebrada por los trémolos sombríos
de las músicas magas de mi tierra.

... Y era el Amor, como una rojo llama...
—Nerviosa mano en la vibrante cuerda
ponía un largo suspirar de oro,
que se trocaba en surtidor de estrellas—.

... Y era la Muerte, al hombro la cuchilla,
el paso largo, torva y esquelética.
—Tal cuando yo era niño la soñaba—.

Y en la guitarra, resonante y trémula,
la brusca mano, al golpear, fingía
el reposar de un ataúd en tierra.

Y era un plañido solitario el soplo
que el polvo barre y la ceniza avienta.

Del camino

Daba el reloj las doce... y eran doce
golpes de azada en tierra...
... ¡Mi hora!—grité—... El silencio
me respondió:—No temas;
tú no verás caer la última gota
que en la clepsidra tiembla.

Dormirás muchas horas todavía
sobre la orilla vieja,
y encontrarás una mañana pura
amarrada tu barca a otra ribera.

Sobre la tierra amarga,
caminos tiene el sueño
laberínticos, sendas tortuosas,
parques en flor y en sombra y en silencio;
    criptas hondas, escalas sobre estrellas;
retablos de esperanzas y recuerdos.
Figurillas que pasan y sonríen
—juguetes melancólicos de viejo—;
    imágenes amigas,
a la vuelta florida del sendero,
y quimeras rosadas
que hacen camino... lejos...

Las ascuas de un crepúsculo morado
detrás del negro cipresal humean...
En la glorieta en sombra está la fuente
con su alado y desnudo Amor de piedra,
que sueña mudo. En la marmórea taza
reposa el agua muerta.

When *the Being Who Is*

When *the Being Who is* the first great Void created,
And rested, he well deserved that right;
The day had its companionship in night,
And man for his absent beloved waited.
Let there be darkness! Then thinking man was born.
Cold, insubstantial, colorless and bland,
Filled with amorphous mist, weightless, forlorn,
The cosmic egg he lifted in his hand.

Take the almighty zero, the hollow sphere,
Face it courageously, erect and strong,
A wild and untamed heart sustains you here;
Such is the uncompleted miracle of breath;
Toast, poet, from your borderland a song
To silence, to oblivion and to death.

JOHN A. CROW

Rose of Fire

You are woven, lovers, of the thrust of spring,
In you earth, water, wind and sun combine,
Breathless in you the heaving mountains sing,
And in your eyes the flowering meadows
    shine.
Stroll through the spring whose fleeting days
    you share,
Drink unafraid the warm sweet milk of fate,
An offering from the shifty panther, but
    beware
If further on the wild beast lies in wait.

Go then to where the planet's axis bends
Toward the solstice of summer whose long
    days glow
Wilting the violet, yet green the almond tree
    will stand
Go where the afternoon of love's completion
    ends,
Thirsting and dry not far from springs that
    flow,
The rose of fire held proudly in your hand.

JOHN A. CROW

Perhaps

One day when I was heedless of my dream,
With eyes closed to the countryside around,
Spring came from nowhere, caught me in a stream
Of golden light that smiled on flowering ground.

I saw green leaves like tiny fingers springing
From swollen branch shoots on their foliaged dress,
And blossoms, yellow, red, and white danced bringing
Bright colors to that landscape's wilderness.

Cuando *el Ser que se es*

Cuando *el Ser que se es* hizo la nada
y reposó, que bien lo merecía,
ya tuvo el día noche y compañía
tuvo el hombre en la ausencia de la amada.

¡*Fiat umbra*! Brotó el pensar humano.
Y el huevo universal alzó, vacío,
ya sin color, desubstanciado y frío,
lleno de niebla ingrávida, en su mano.

Toma el cero integral, la hueca esfera,
que has de mirar, si lo has de ver, erguido.
Hoy que es espalda el lomo de tu fiera,

y es el milagro del no ser cumplido,
brinda, poeta, un canto de frontera
a la muerte, al silencio y al olvido.

Rosa de fuego

Tejidos sois de primavera, amantes,
de tierra y agua y viento y sol tejidos.
La sierra en vuestros pechos jadeantes,
en los ojos los campos florecidos,

pasead vuestra mutua primavera,
y aun bebed sin temor la dulce leche
que os brinda hoy la lúbrica pantera,
antes que, torva, en el camino aceche.

Caminad, cuando el eje del planeta
se vence hacia el solsticio de verano,
verde el almendro y mustia la violeta,

cerca la sed y el hontanar cercano,
hacia la tarde del amor, completa,
con la rosa de fuego en vuestra mano.

Acaso

Como atento no más a mi quimera
no reparaba en torno mío, un día
me sorprendió la fértil primavera
que en todo el ancho campo sonreía.

Brotaban verdes hojas
de las hinchadas yemas del remaje,
y flores amarillas, blancas, rojas,
alegraban la mancha del paisaje.

The sun in its dirunal course projected A shower of golden darts that swept below Where silver poplars saw themselves reflected Upon the stately river's soundful flow.	Y era una lluvia de saetas de oro el sol sobre las frondas juveniles; del amplio río en el caudal sonoro se miraban los álamos gentiles.
Through all my years of aimless wandering Until today I never saw the spring. Then bitterly I said in words bombastic:	"Tras de tanto camino es la primera vez que miro brotar la primavera", dije, y después, declamatoriamente:
"How late for happiness to come my way!" But after that, poised on the wide fantastic Wings of another dream, still do I say "Perhaps I shall attain my youth some day!"	"¡Cuán tarde ya para la dicha mía!" Y luego, al caminar, como quien siente alas de otra ilusión: "Y todavía ¡yo alcanzaré mi juventud un día!"

JOHN A. CROW

Juan Ramón Jiménez
Spain, 1881–1958

Juan Ramón Jiménez was awarded the Nobel Prize in 1956, and the award was widely applauded by lovers of Spanish poetry. Born in Andalusia, he was of a delicate and neurasthenic nature and was a man of excessive and tormented sensitivities. He read English, French, and German and was well versed in the literature of those languages. He especially admired Shakespeare, Shelley, Browning, Heine, Goethe, Góngora, Bécquer, the Machado brothers, and Darío. About 1905, he, Unamuno, and the Machados dreamed of a new burgeoning of poetry in Spain, and they all helped to bring this about.

In stating his "ideal synthesis" for poetic creativity, Jiménez listed the following items: (1) the influence of the *eternal* Spanish poetry found in the ancient ballads, Góngora, Bécquer. *Solitude.* (2) Modernism under the colossal genius of Darío of Nicaragua. *Solitude.* (3) Modern poetry of various countries, particularly Britain, France, Germany, the United States. *Solitude.* (4) Continued growth toward maturity and totality, with a profound hatred for all isms. *Solitude.* Note the repetition of the word *Solitude;* it is only in solitude, he believed, that a man can learn to know, focus, define, and express his true inner reality.[33]

Jiménez regarded poetry as "the eternal and fatal Contrary Beauty which tempts men of ardent spirit with its certain secret." He saw the poet himself as "the hidden creator of an unapplauded star."[34]

In 1916 Juan Ramón married a North American girl of Spanish family, Zenobia Camprubí, whose father was the owner and editor of the Spanish-language newspaper *La Prensa* in New York City. The poet remained in the United States for several years before returning to live in Spain. Zenobia was his beloved companion, helpmate, nurse, and inspiration throughout the remainder of his life. The Spanish Civil War sent him into permanent exile, and he passed his final years in the United States and Puerto Rico, where he died. In texture his poetry is light and soft as a floating feather, and often as difficult to grasp; in intensity it suggests unspeakable anguish; in essence it expresses the search for beauty and the love of beauty as a divine frenzy that drives men mad.

## Fleeting Return	## Retorno fugaz
What was she like, oh Lord, what changing thing? —Oh my deceiving heart and shifting brain!—	¿Cómo era, Dios mío, cómo era? —¡Oh corazón falaz, mente indecisa!—

33. *Ibid.*, 109.
34. *Ibid.*, 110.

Was she the passing of the wind and rain?
Was she the flight of the first thrust of spring?
As frail and fleeting as a thistledown
Blown off in summer... as nebulous and light
As a faint smile lost in a laugh outright...
Floating on air, a banner's gauzy gown!
Oh banner, smile, and thistledown, oh Spring
In perfect June, wind pure and innocent...
How wild your Mardi Gras, how saddened though!
All of your changes like a trembling wing
Ended in nothing—love's bitter mystery forespent!—
Say more, my love? That you once were is all I need to
   know!

JOHN A. CROW

¿Era como el pasaje de la brisa?
¿Como la huída de la primavera?

Tan leve, tan voluble. tan lijera
cual estival vilano... ¡Sí! Imprecisa
como sonrisa que se pierde en risa...
¡Vana en el aire, igual que una bandera!

¡Bandera, sonreír, vilano, alada
primavera de junio, brisa pura...
¡Qué loco fue tu carnaval, qué triste!

Todo tu cambiar trocóse en nada
—¡memoria, ciega abeja de amargura!—
¡No sé cómo eras, yo que sé que fuiste!

Song Sparrow

Song sparrow, sing a lay,
Softening the close of day!

A palace of enchanted halls
the pine grove touched with light.
In mournful lullaby it calls
to rivers in their flight.
Within the forest's closing night
There dwells a little sparrow.

Song sparrow, sing a lay,
Softening the close of day!

A gentle breeze now wrapped in dreams
is sighing in his sleep.
The sun casts iridescent beams
upon the pines that weep.
A silent vigil do we keep
In this strange hour, oh sparrow.

Within the calm of solitude
the soul forespent with care
now graced with sweet beatitude
is bowed in humble prayer.
And in the silent, trembling air
Is heard a lilting sparrow.

Song sparrow, sing a lay,
Softening the close of day!

His song the heart with rapture fills
The wind is silent now.
His chant is heard near rushing rills,
on leaf and bending bough
now sings the little sparrow.

Song sparrow, sing a lay,
Softening the close of day!

KATHARINE E. STRATHDEE

Verde verderol

Verde verderol,
¡endulza la puesta del sol!

Palacio de encanto,
el pinar tardío
arrulla con llanto
la huída del río.
Allí el nido umbrío
tiene el verderol.

Verde verderol,
¡endulza la puesta del sol!

La última brisa
es suspiradora;
el sol rojo irisa
al pino que llora.
¡Vaga y lenta hora
nuestra, verderol!

Verde verderol,
¡endulza la puesta del sol!

Soledad y calma;
silencio y grandeza.
La choza del alma
se recoje y reza.
De pronto, ¡oh belleza!,
canta el verderol.

Verde verderol,
¡endulza la puesta del sol!

Su canto enajena.
—¿Se ha parado el viento?—
El campo se llena
de su sentimiento.
Malva es el lamento,
verde el verderol.

Verde verderol,
¡endulza la puesta del sol!

She Came to Me in Purity

She came to me in purity,
clothed with innocence;
and I loved her as a little boy loves.

Then she began adorning herself
with gaudy finery;
and I hated her without knowing it.

She became a queen,
vainly displaying her treasure.
A galling wrath to the soul, and so senseless!

. . . But with time she shed her garments.
And I smiled upon her again.

She kept only the tunic
of her first innocence.
I believed in her once more.

And she cast off the tunic
and appeared before me in her nakedness . . .
Oh fire of my soul, poetry
unadorned and mine forever!

KATHARINE E. STRATHDEE

Dream Nocturne

The earth leads through the earth;
but you, sea,
lead through the sky.

With what sureness of silver and golden light
the stars mark for us
the course! One would say
that the earth is the road
of the body,
that the sea is the road of the soul—.

Yes, it seems
that the soul is the only traveler
on the sea; that the body, alone,
was left behind on the shore,
without her, taking leave of her,
heavy, cold, like one dead.

How similar
the sea voyage to that of death,
to that of eternal life.

DONALD F. FOGELQUIST

You Were Like the Jetting of a Fountain

You were like
The jetting of a fountain amid the shadows,
Little white rose!

Sad profanation
Came—and did not go away—

Vino, primero, pura

Vino, primero, pura,
vestida de inocencia;
y la amé como un niño.

Luego se fue vistiendo
de no sé qué ropajes;
y la fui odiando, sin saberlo.

Llegó a ser una reina,
fastuosa de tesoros . . .
¡Qué iracundia de yel y sin sentido!

. . . Mas se fue desnudando.
Y yo le sonreía.

Se quedó con la túnica
de su inocencia antigua.
Creí de nuevo en ella.

Y se quitó la túnica,
y apareció desnuda toda . . .
¡Oh pasión de mi vida, poesía
desnuda, mía para siempre!

Nocturno soñado

La tierra lleva por la tierra;
mas tú, mar
llevas por el cielo.

Con qué seguridad de luz de plata y oro,
nos marcan las estrellas
la ruta!—Se diría
que es la tierra el camino
del cuerpo,
que el mar es el camino
del alma—.

Sí, parece
que es el alma la sola viajera
del mar; que el cuerpo, solo,
se quedó allá en las playas,
sin ella, despidiéndola,
pesado, frío, igual que muerto.

¡Qué semejante
el viaje del mar al de la muerte,
al de la eterna vida!

Eras lo mismo

Eras lo mismo
que el chorro de una fuente entre las sombras,
¡rosita blanca!

El atropello triste
venía—y no se iba—,

Black, red, and violet
And you remained
Slender, fresh, pure...
Unblemished they became
And unblemished you remained.

Miracle of purity! You are like
The ray of moonlight through the forest
Little white lily.

DONALD F. FOGELQUIST

negro, rojo y violento;
y tú permanecías,
delgada, fresca, pura...
Ellos quedaban claros
y te quedabas clara tú...
¡Milagro de pureza! Eras lo mismo
que el rayo de la luna por los bosques,
¡lirito blanco!

Let Your Kiss Fall

Let your kiss fall
—Like a fountain—
Bright thread into the basin
Of my heart!

My heart, then, dreaming
Will give you back, doubly, the water of your kiss
Through the riverbed of sleep, down
Under life.

And the water of your kiss
—Oh new dawn of the fountain—
Will be eternal and eternal,
For its source will be my love.

DONALD F. FOGELQUIST

Deja chorrear tu beso

¡Deja chorrear tu beso
—lo mismo que una fuente—,
hilo fresco en la taza
de mi corazón!

Mi corazón, después, soñando,
te devolverá, doble, el agua de tu beso,
por el cauce del sueño, por debajo
de la vida.

Y el agua de tu beso
—¡oh nueva aurora de la fuente!—
será eterna y eterna,
porque su manantial será mi amor.

Hours, Gilded Ruins

Hours, gilded ruins
Of my yesterday!
            I come sweetly
To sit down among you,
Facing toward the sea, above the valley, beneath the sky
Of my memories.

The grass, so like
That other, made transparent by the sun,
Makes me weep. And the weeping
Floods my future
And drowns me in the grief that died.

And it is a gentle drowning
That draws me to itself with the tenderness
With which the things attract us
That we let go by without us,
Beneath the sky, in the valley, o'er the seas.

DONALD F. FOGELQUIST

Horas, ruinas doradas

¡Horas, ruinas doradas
de mi ayer!
            Vengo, dulce,
a sentarme en vosotras,
frente al mar, sobre el valle, bajo el cielo

La yerba, parecida
a la otra, porque el sol la trasparenta,
me hace llorar. Y el llanto
me inunda el porvenir
y me ahoga en las penas que murieron.

Y es un ahogarme suave,
que me atrae hacia sí, con la ternura
con que atraen las cosas
que dejamos pasar sin ir con ellas,
bajo el cielo, en el valle, por los mares...

March

Storm. The rainbow. The almond trees in bloom.
How the colored threads enlace
The murky cloud with the pink branch,
The thunder with the song of birds!

Marzo

Tormenta. El arco iris. Los almendros en flor.
¡Cómo los hilos de colores atan
la nube negra con la rama rosa,
el trueno con el canto de los pájaros!

Harmonious disorder
Of the sky and of the earth, which joins and fuses
Naked earth and heaven in one single
Womb of eagerness—of light and shadow—,of love,
Which spring will break.

DONALD F. FOGELQUIST

You Answered Me

You answered me
As if I myself were
Answering myself in you.
    —No, it was not you!
And the flower of your happiness
Had in its root
Black earth of sorrow.

—'Twas like a love
Given, without volition, amid dreams;
As in the soft and violent suggestion
Of a heliotrope by the sun.

Your lips, suffused
With blood, sighed "yes",
But your eyes, deep unto your soul,
Told me a sad and fearful *no*,
Withdrawing to the valley of the eternal.

DONALD F. FOGELQUIST

Ballad of the Morning of the Cross

God wears blue. The flute and the drum
now announce the cross of spring.
Long live the roses, the roses of love
amid the sunny verdure of the meadow!

Let us away, let us away to the country for rosemary,
Let us away, let us away
for rosemary and for love...

If I say to her: "Don't you want me to love you?,"
She will answer radiant with passion:
"When the cross of spring is in bloom
I shall love you with all my heart!

Let us away, let us away to the country for rosemary,
Let us away, let us away
for rosemary and for love...

The cross of spring will burst into bloom
and I shall tell her: "now the cross bloomed."
She will answer: "... do you want me to love you?"
And the morning will be filled with light!

Let us away, let us away to the country for rosemary,
Let us away, let us away
for rosemary and for love...

The flute and the drum will sob with love,

¡Armonioso desorden
del cielo y de la tierra, que une y funde
tierra y cielo desnudos en un solo
vientre de afán—de sombra y luz—,de amor
que romperá la primavera!

Me respondiste

Me respondiste como
si yo mismo estuviera
respondiéndome en ti.
    —¡No, no eras tú!—
Y la flor de tu dicha
tenía en su raíz
tierra negra de pena.

—Era igual que un amor
dado, sin voluntad, entre los sueños;
como en la sujestión suave y violenta
de un heliotropo por el sol...—

Tu boca suspiraba
que sí, a flor de sangre.
pero tus ojos, hondos hasta el alma
me decían un no medroso y triste,
apartándose al valle de lo eterno.

Balada de la mañana de la cruz

Dios está azul. La flauta y el tambor
anuncian ya la cruz de primavera.
¡Vivan las rosas, las rosas del amor
entre el verdor con sol de la pradera!

Vámonos, vámonos al campo por romero,
vámonos, vámonos
por romero y por amor...

Si yo le digo: ¿no quieres que te quiera?,
responderá radiante de pasión:
¡cuando florezca la cruz de primavera
yo te querré con todo el corazón!

Vámonos, vámonos al campo por romero,
vámonos, vámonos
por romero y por amor...

Florecerá la cruz de primavera,
y le diré: ya floreció la cruz.
Responderá:... ¿tú quieras que te quiera?
¡y la mañana se llenará de luz!

Vámonos, vámonos al campo por romero,
vámonos, vámonos
por romero y por amor...

Flauta y tambor sollozaron de amores,

the butterfly will come with its illusion . . .	la mariposa vendrá con su ilusión . . . ,
she will be the virgin of the flowers	¡ella será la virgen de las flores
and will love me with all her heart.	y me querrá con todo el corazón!

DONALD F. FOGELQUIST

Emilio Carrere

Spain, 1881–1947

Carrere was the poet par excellence of Bohemia in Spain. His sad, lilting verses have the flavor of the Parisian Left Bank and at their best suggest the lines of François Villon with a strong touch of Verlaine. Carrere was a great admirer of Verlaine and translated many of his poems into Spanish. In their day his own poems were tremendously popular among the young artists and students of Spain.

Federico de Onís states that Carrere represents the decadent aspects of postmodernism with a strong romantic tinge. He is an urban poet whose repeated theme is "the fallen woman, justified poetically by deep sensual love, piety, pain, fatality, mystery and death."[35]

The Gutter Muse

As down the street advancing
We trod the moonlit ground,
Sharp hunger madly dancing
Within us mocked its round.
Her lips were drawn in sorrow,
I kissed their wan repose.
"Why do you hate tomorrow,
And life, wild Rose?"
Weep not, Rose of the flesh,
For I shall rob with pleasure
The papal miter's mesh
For your curls' golden treasure.
And then a mocking sprite
Among the shadows hidden,
Heard me and laughed in spite,
    Unbidden, unbidden . . .

And on the rippling shimmer
Of an old fountain's spray
The moonbeams cast a glimmer
Of silver disks at play.
I saw her pale hand tremble,
Soft hand of marble hue;
"How fair snowflakes dissemble,
    How cruel too!
Don't tremble, I your lover
Will clothe your proud breasts in
The chaste but pompous cover
Of royal ermine skin."
And then a mocking sprite
Among the shadows hidden,
Heard me and laughed in spite,
    Unbidden, unbidden . . .

La Musa del arroyo

I

Cruzábamos tristemente
las calles llenas de luna,
y el hambre bailaba una
zarabanda en nuestra mente.

Al verla triste y dolida,
yo la besaba en la boda.
"¿Por qué aborreces la vida,
    risa loca?

No llores, rosa carnal,
que yo robaré el tesoro
de la tiara papal
para tus cabellos de oro."

Y un espíritu burlón
que entre las sombras había,
al escuchar mi canción
        se reía, se reía.

II

De la vieja fuente grata
en el sonor cristal,
la luna brillaba igual
que una moneda de plata.

Temblaba su mano breve
de blanca y sedeña piel.
"¡Qué bonita cae la nieve . . .
        y qué cruel!"

"No tiembles; yo haré un corpiño
para tus senos triunfales

35. Onís, *Antología*, 827.

Oh night of desolations,
Eternal did I stand
And vain my quaking hand
Knocked on closed habitations.
A violin was sighing
With distant melancholy
Which is our life of folly.
   "My love, O cease your crying!
Time is not to bereave,
This is my allegory
Of a fairy princess story
In a land of make-believe."
And then a mocking sprite
Among the shadows hidden,
Heard me and laughed in spite,
   Unbidden, unbidden...

   Tired will yielded to woes
Of poverty and madness!
My love's infinite sadness
In old and tattered clothes!
A tender word has covered
The wound that keeps on bleeding;
Dreams fill the undiscovered
Where this mad quest is leading.
   "The dawning breaks... Another
Day, and you shall see the magic
Which shields Chance from the tragic
And makes us call her mother."
Within the thick shade hidden
Lies Fate unpenetrated,
Laughs misery never sated,
   Unbidden, unbidden...

JOHN A. CROW

con la pompa del armiño
de los mantos imperiales."

Y un espíritu burlón
que entre las frondas había,
al escuchar mi canción
   se reía, se reía...

III

Noche de desolaciones,
eterna, que llamé en vano
con la temblorosa mano
en los cerrados mesones.

Lloraba un violín distante
con tanta melancolía
como nuestra vida errante.
   "¡Reina mía!

Da tu dolor al olvido;
yo te contaré la historia
de una princesa ilusoria
de un reino que no ha existido."

Y un espíritu burlón
y cruel que en la calle había,
al escuchar mi canción
   se reía, se reía...

IV

¡Triste voluntad rendida
al dolor de la pobreza!
¡Oh, la infinita tristeza
de la amada mal vestida!

Palabra de amor que esconde
la llaga que va sangrando
y andar, siempre andar. ¿Adónde?
   ¿Y hasta cuándo?

"Ya apunta la claridad...
Ya verás como se muestra
propicia y mágica nuestra
madre, la Casualidad."

Y en la encrucijada umbría
de la suerte impenetrable,
la Miseria, la implacable,
   se reía, se reía...

TWENTIETH CENTURY

Alfonsina Storni

Argentina, 1892–1938

Born in Switzerland but reared in provincial Argentina, Alfonsina Storni went to Buenos Aires at the age of twenty-one and briefly entered the business world before switching to journalism and literature, which she found immensely more satisfying. Her poetry expresses a strong feminism, sees women enchained in a male-dominated world, decries the double standard, and finally becomes a cry of agony when she concludes that men and women are living in a hostile universe.

Man

He has no notion how, but one day man appears,
A being fully made; born blind, within the dark he turns
His waxen eyes. An arm embraces him, he learns,
He sobs. A breast deceives him. He sucks, he perseveres.
Later, his sight will focus and dissolve the dark,
And he will see two eyes, a mouth, a brow and hair,
The muscles of his mobile face give back his stare.
He imitates, he smiles, his lamp has found its spark,
Dream, instinct, soul with coils of fire enfold it;
He frees them in the wind, he sings, he praises,
Miles overhead there is a light in space:
He sees a star; aroused, inspired, he reaches up to hold it,
And then another hand cuts off the hand he raises.

JOHN A. CROW

El hombre

No sabe cómo: un día se aparece en el orbe,
hecho ser; nace ciego; en la sombra revuelve
los acerados ojos. Una mano lo envuelve.
Llora. Lo engaña un pecho. Prende los labios. Sorbe.

Más tarde su pupila la tiniebla deslíe
y alcanza a ver dos ojos, una boca, una frente.
Mira jugar los músculos de la cara a su frente
y aunque quién es no sabe, copia, imita y sonríe.

Da una larga corrida sobre la tierra luego.
Instinto, sueño y alma trenza en lazos de fuego,
los suelta a sus espaldas, a los vientos. Y canta.

Kilómetros en alto la mirada le crece
y ve el astro; se turba, se exalta, lo apetece:
una Mano le corta la mano que levanta.

Vicente Huidobro

Chile, 1893–1948

Huidobro lived for an extended period in Europe, mainly in France, and his first two books of poems are in the tradition of French symbolism. He wrote a considerable number of poems in French. Then he moved into the area of cubism and created poems in "pictorial shapes" reminiscent of Guillaume Apollinaire. His principal contribution to Hispanic poetry is found in his rather vanguardist poems. He founded the movement known as creationism, which later merged into ultraism. Huidobro's essential idea in creationism was to create a poem as Nature creates a tree. Typical of his approach are these lines:

> Why do you sing the rose, O, Poets?
> Make it flower in the poem.
> Only for you live all things under the Sun.
> The poet is a small God.[36]

Sometimes he carries the point too far, and in writing some poems he reached into a shoe-box filled with adjectives on little cards, and pulled these out at random in order to construct strange images. When the young writers of Chile found this out, they lost faith in him.

36. Onís, *Antología*, 1129. (The quotation is from Huidobro's poem "Arte poética.")

Time of Waiting

Days go by
Eternity does not arrive or the miracle.

Days go by
The ship does not draw near
The sea does not become bud or belltower
The fall is not revealed.

Days go by
Stones weep with their blue bones
But the door is not opened
And nightfall is not revealed
Nor is knowledge in its crystal
Nor understanding nor appearance nor the dead
   leaf-storm of why . . .

Days go by
Adolescence does not emerge
Nor living atmosphere or mystery.

Days go by
The eye does not become a world
Sorrow does not become thought
The sea does not reach up to my feet as it dies.

Days go by
And she is the breathing of night breaking into sounds
And she is beautiful as a perfect smoothness
And is an abundance of willows and silences.

Days go by
She is a hurricane that unleashes its fury,
She is a huge tear that falls interminably
Like a star gone raving mad.

Days go by
The infinite peephole of tombs one by one
Does not break the onward flow of things,
A way is opened to the day and the hour
To age and its weeds.

Days go by
And the sound of the moon cannot be heard.

JOHN A. CROW

Nature Vive

He leaves the end of the world to the accordion
Pays for the last song with rain
Yonder where the voices unite an enormous cedar is born
More comfortable than the sky

A swallow says to me papa
An anemone says to me mama

Blue blue over yonder and in the mouth of the wolf
Mr. Blue Sky departing
What do you say Where will you go

Ah what beautiful blue blue arm

Tiempo de Espera

Pasan los días
La eternidad no llega ni el milagro

Pasan los días
El barco no se acerca
El mar no se hace flor ni campanario
No se descubre la caída

Pasan los días
Las piedras lloran con sus huesos azules
Pero no se abre la puerta
No se descubre la caída de la noche
Ni la ciencia en su cristal
Ni el comprender ni la apariencia ni la hojaresca del
   porqué

Pasan los días
No sale adolescencia
Ni atmósfera vivida ni misterio

Pasan los días
El ojo no se hace mundo
Las tristezas no se hacen pensamiento
El mar no llega hasta mis pies agonizando

Pasan los días
Y ella es pulmón de noches rompiéndose en sonidos
Y es hermosa como llanura comprendida
Es abundancia de sauces y silencios

Pasan los días
Ella es huracán que desata sus ruidos
Es una gran lágrima cayendo interminablemente
Como una estrella que se volviera loca

Pasan los días
El miraje infinito de las tumbas una a una
No detiene la marcha
Se abren paso hacia el día hacia las horas
Hacia la edad y sus malezas

Pasan los días
Y no se oye el ruido de la luna

Naturaleza viva

El deja al acordeón el fin del mundo
Paga con la lluvia la última canción
Allí donde las voces se juntan nace un enorme cedro
Más confortable que el cielo

Una golondrina me dice papá
Una anemona me dice mamá

Azul azul allí y en la boca del lobo
Azul Señor Cielo que se aleja
Qué dice usted é Hacia dónde irá

Ah el hermoso brazo azul azul

Give your arm to Mrs. Cloud	Dad el brazo a la Señora Nube
If you're afraid of the wolf	Si tenéis miedo del lobo
The wolf with the blue blue mouth	El lobo de la boca azul azul
With long long teeth	Del diente largo largo
To eat up grandmother nature	Para devorar a la abuela naturaleza
Mr. Sky scrape off your swallow	Señor Cielo rasque su golondrina
Mrs. Cloud put out your anemone	Señora Nube apague sus anemonas
The voices unite over the bird	Las voces se juntan sobre el pájaro
Larger than the tree of creation	Más grande que el árbol de la creación
Lovelier than a current of air between two stars	Más hermoso que una corriente de aire entre dos astros

H. R. HAYS

Federico García Lorca
Spain, 1898–1936

Lorca was steeped both in the folk tradition of his country and in the brilliant baroque poetry of Spain's Golden Age. In form and language he blended the two currents into a unique and harmonious whole. Most widely known for his dramatic gypsy ballads, Lorca also wrote some fine dramas, an excellent book of poetry on New York City, and many lovely lyrics that suggest the popular *coplas*. The American poet, Robert Bly, who translated many of Lorca's poems into English, wrote: "In Lorca you see desire still flying, hurtling through the air, like a tornado, putting new leaves on every tree it touches, writing as if he belonged to Cretan civilization . . . a desire for intensity as immense as Dickens' characters' desire for food." In some of his later poetry Lorca "adopted old Arab poetic forms to help entangle that union of desire and darkness, which ancient Arabs loved so much." [37]

In spite of all this, Lorca clung tenaciously to his erotic-dramatic child's dream of the world. In one of his early poems, some children ask why he is leaving the square in which they are playing, and he answers them in these characteristic lines, also translated by Robert Bly:

> My heart of silk
> is filled with lights,
> with lost bells,
> with lilies and bees.
> I will go very far,
> farther than those mountains,
> farther than the oceans,
> way up near the stars,
> to ask Christ the Lord
> to give back to me
> the soul I had as a child,
> matured by fairy tales,
> with its hat of feathers
> and its wooden sword.

Bly then adds: "There is no other poet like him in the history of poetry. Everyone who reads a poem of Lorca's falls in love with him and has a secret friend." [38]

At the outbreak of Spain's civil war, Lorca returned home from Madrid to his Granada, where he was a "small glory," as he said, but an impromptu firing squad rustled him out of the house in the middle of the night and killed him. The reasons for the action have never been made clear,

---

37. Robert Bly (ed.), *Selected Poems, Lorca and Jiménez* (Boston: Beacon Press, 1973), 102.
38. *Ibid.*, 104.

for Lorca was not a political activist by any stretch of the imagination. Thus martyred, he immediately became a beacon on both sides of the Atlantic, and his influence was strongly reflected in many of the poets who followed him. Rubén Darío had carried the influence of Spanish America over to Spain; Lorca now repaid the debt and brought Spain back to the New World.

My Child Went to the Sea

My child went to the sea
To count the waves and shells,
But at Seville's wide river,
She stopped and looked for me.

Five spotless ships were rocking
Between the flowers and bells,
Their oars were in the water,
Their keels riding in the swells.

Who sees inside the dazzling
Gold tower of Seville?
Five hidden voices answered,
Five rounded rings they fill.

The sky mounted the river
From shore to shining shore,
And in the russet twilight
Rocked five rings, not one more.

JOHN A. CROW

Mi niña se fue a la mar

Mi niña se fue a la mar,
a contar olas y chinas,
pero se encontró, de pronto,
con el río de Sevilla.

Entre adelfas y campanas
con los remos en el agua
cinco barcos se mecían,
y las velas en la brisa.

¿Quién mira dentro la torre
enjaezada, de Sevilla?
Cinco voces contestaban
redondas como sortijas.

El cielo monta gallardo
al río, de orilla a orilla,
en el aire sonrosado,
cinco anillos se mecían.

Consultation

Blue passion-flower!
Anvil of butterflies.
Do you thrive
On the slime of hours?

(Oh, childish poet,
Smash your time-piece!)

Clear blue star,
Navel of the dawn.
Do you thrive
On the shadow's foam?

(Oh, childish poet,
Smash your time-piece!)

Blue-tinted heart,
Lamp of my bedroom.
Do you beat well
Without my rhythmic blood?

(Oh, childish poet,
Smash your time-piece!)

I understand you and leave myself
Stored away in the wardrobe
Exposed to the insects of time.
Their metallic drops
Will not be heard in the calm
Of my bedroom.

Consulta

¡Pasionaria azul!
Yunque de mariposas.
¿Vives bien en el limo
de las horas?

(¡Oh, poeta infantil,
quiebra tu reloj!)

Clara estrella azul,
ombligo de la aurora.
¿Vives bien en la espuma
de la sombra?

(¡Oh, poeta infantil,
quiebra tu reloj!)

Corazón azulado,
lámpara de mi alcoba.
¿Lates bien sin mi sangre
filarmónica?

(¡Oh, poeta infantil,
quiebra tu reloj!)

Os comprendo y me dejo
arrumbado en la cómoda
al insecto del tiempo.
Sus metálicas gotas
no se oirán en la calma
de mi alcoba.

I shall sleep quietly
Just as you sleep,
Oh, stars and passion-flowers,
For at last, the butterfly,
Will flit on the hour
That flows
While from my body there springs
A rose.

JOHN A. CROW

Me dormiré tranquilo
como dormís vosotras
pasionarias y estrellas,
que al fin, la mariposa,
volará en la corriente
de las horas
mientras nace en mi tronco
la rosa.

JOHN A. CROW

Juan Ramón Jiménez

In the infinite white,
snow, spikenard and salt,
he lost his fantasy.

The color white, is walking,
over a silent carpet
of the feathers of a dove.

Eyeless, without gesture,
motionless it dreams,
but trembles inside.

In the infinite white,
what a pure, deep wound
was left by his dream!

In the infinite white.
Snow. Spikenard. Salt.

JOHN A. CROW

Juan Ramón Jiménez

En el blanco infinito,
nieve, nardo y salina,
perdió su fantasía.

El color blanco, anda,
sobre una muda alfombra
de plumas de paloma.

Sin ojos ni ademán
inmóvil sufre un sueño.
Pero tiembla por dentro.

En el blanco infinito,
¡qué pura y larga herida
dejó su fantasía!

En el blanco infinito.
Nieve. Nardo. Salina.

Ballad of a Sleepwalker

Green, how I love you, green!
Green wind, green branch and tree.
The horse that climbs the mountain,
And the ship that sails the sea.
As she dreams against the railing
The shadow upon her lies,
Green skin, and hair of green,
Cold silver are her eyes.
Under the gypsy moon,
Green, how I love you, green!
The world is watching her now,
The world that she has not seen.

Green, how I love you, green!
Great stars of frost soon gone,
And a fish-like shadow that hovers
Opened by the road of dawn.
The fig tree scrapes at the wind
With the sandpaper of its arms,
The mountain, an angry bobcat,
Bristles at those alarms!
But who will come? And from where?
Green flesh, hair green and free,
She leans on the grated railing
And dreams of the bitter sea.

Romance sonámbulo

Verde que te quiero verde.
Verde viento. Verdes ramas.
El barco sobre la mar
y el caballo en la montaña.
Con la sombra en la cintura
ella sueña en su baranda,
verde carne, pelo verde,
con ojos de fría plata.
Verde que te quiero verde.
Bajo la luna gitana,
las cosas la están mirando
y ella no puede mirarlas.

Verde que te quiero verde.
Grandes estrellas de escarcha
vienen con el pez de sombra
que abre el camino del alba.
La higuera frota su viento
con la lija de sus ramas,
y el monte, gato garduño,
eriza sus pitas agrias.
Pero ¡quién vendrá? ¿Y por dónde . . . ?
Ella sigue en su baranda,
verde carne, pelo verde,
soñando en la mar amarga.

"Old man, I want an exchange:
For your house my stallion,
For your mirror my saddle,
For your blanket my dagger.
Old man, I come spurting blood
From the mountain passes of Cabra."
"Young friend, believe me, if I could,
The deal would quickly be made,
But I hardly know who I am,
And my house is not mine to trade."
"Old man, I would like to die
With dignity in my own bed
Of cast iron, if that could be,
With white Holland sheets outspread.
What a wound they slashed in my chest!
Can't you see how much it has bled?"
"Three hundred scarlet roses
Stain your white shirt with blood,
It has the odor of salt,
Your sash cannot stanch its flood.
But I hardly know who I am,
In my own house I'm not understood."
"Well, let me at least climb up
To that lofty green balustrade,
Let me climb, let me climb up
To the refuge green shadows have made,
Where bannisters of scattered moonlight
On the tumbling water are played."

The two men kept climbing upward
Till near the green railing they stood.
Leaving a trail of their tears
Marked by a trail of blood.
Little tin lanterns are trembling,
On the tile rooftops they blow.
A thousand crystal tambourines
Wound the dawn with lights that glow.

Green, how I love you, green!
Green wind, Green tree and tall.
The two men keep climbing upward.
The long wind that lashes the wall
Leaves an acrid taste on the lips
Of basil, of mint, and of gall.
Old man, where is she, tell me?
Where has your bitter child gone?
How many times she has waited!
How main times waited alone!
Fresh face and jet black hair
On that green verandah till dawn!

The gypsy girl is rocking;
On the water's face she cries.
Green flesh and hair of green,
Cold silver are her eyes.
A frozen sliver of moon
Holds her over the pool once more,
The night becomes warm and friendly
As a small town plaza store.
Drunken Civil Guards are knocking,

—Compadre, quiero cambiar
mi caballo por su casa,
mi montura por su espejo,
mi cuchillo por su manta.
Compadre, vengo sangrando,
desde los puertos de Cabra.
—Si yo pudiera, mocito,
este trato se cerraba.
Pero yo ya no soy yo,
ni mi casa es ya mi casa.
—Compadre, quiero morir
decentemente en mi cama.
De acero, si puede ser,
con las sábanas de holanda.
¿No ves la herida que tengo
desde el pecho a la garganta?
—Trescientas rosas morenas
lleva tu pechera blanca.
Tu sangre rezuma y huele
alrededor de tu faja.
Pero yo ya no soy yo,
ni mi casa es ya mi casa.
—Dejadme subir al menos
hasta las altas barandas;
¡dejadme subir!, dejadme
hasta las verdes barandas.
Barandales de la luna
por donde retumba el agua.

Ya suben los dos compadres
hacia las altas barandas.
Dejando un rastro de sangre.
Dejando un rastro de lágrimas.
Temblaban en los tejados
farolillos de hojalata.
Mil panderos de cristal
herían la madrugada.

Verde que te quiero verde,
verde viento, verdes ramas.
Los dos compadres subieron.
El largo viento dejaba
en la boca un raro gusto
de hiel, de menta y de albahaca.
¡Compadre! ¿Dónde está, dime,
dónde está tu niña amarga?
¡Cuántas veces te esperó!
¡Cuántas veces te esperara,
cara fresca, negro pelo,
en esta verde baranda!

Sobre el rostro del aljibe
se mecía la gitana.
Verde carne, pelo verde,
con ojos de fría plata.
Un carámbano de luna
la sostiene sobre el agua.
La noche se puso íntima
como una pequeña plaza.
Guardias civiles borrachos

Knocking loudly against the door.
Green, how I love you, green!
Green wind. Green branch and tree.
The horse that climbs the mountain,
And the ship that sails the sea.[39]

en la puerta golpeaban.
Verde que te quiero verde.
Verde viento. Verdes ramas.
El barco sobre la mar.
Y el caballo en la montaña.

JOHN A. CROW

Amparo

Amparo,
how alone you are in your house
all dressed in white!
(Halfway between the jasmine
and the spikenard.)

You listen to the marvelous
gushing of water in your patio,
and the faint yellow trills
of the canary.
In the afternoon you see
the cypresses tremble with birds,
while you slowly embroider
letters on the canvas cloth.

Amparo,
how alone you are in your house,
all dressed in white!
Amparo,
how hard it is to say:
I love you!

JOHN A. CROW

Amparo

Amparo,
¡qué sola estás en tu casa
vestida de blanco!

(Ecuador entre el jazmín
y el nardo.)

Oyes los maravillosos
surtidores de tu patio,
y el débil trino amarillo
del canario.

Por la tarde ves temblar
los cipreses con los pájaros,
mientras bordas lentamente
letras sobre el cañamazo.

Amparo,
¡qué sola estás en tu casa,
vestida de blanco!
Amparo,
¡ y qué difícil decirte:
yo te amo!

The Gypsy and the Wind

Playing her parchment moon
Preciosa comes
along a watery path
of laurels and crystal lights.
The starless silence, fleeing
from her rhythmic tambourine,
falls where the sea whips and sings,
his night filled with silvery swarms.
High atop the mountain peaks
the sentinels are sleeping;
they guard the tall white towers
of the English consulate.
And gypsies of the water
for their pleasure erect
little castles of conch shells
and arbors of greening pine.

Playing her parchment moon

Preciosa y el aire

Su luna de pergamino
Preciosa tocando viene
por un anfibio sendero
de cristales y laureles.
El silencio sin estrellas,
huyendo del sonsonete,
cae donde el mar bate y canta
su noche llena de peces.
En los picos de la sierra
los carabineros duermen
guardando las blancas torres
donde viven los ingleses.
Y los gitanos del agua
levantan por distraerse,
glorietas de caracolas
y ramas de pino verde.

Su luna de pergamino

---

39. In this poem the young smuggler is fatally wounded by the Spanish Civil Guards, and as he staggers back to die of his wounds, the gypsy girl who loves him commits suicide by drowning herself in the cistern. Lorca's gypsies represent the primitive, spontaneous life urge, and the civil guards are the repressive force of civilization.

Preciosa comes.
The wind sees her and rises,
the wind that never slumbers.
Naked Saint Christopher swells,
watching the girl as he plays
with tongues of celestial bells
on an invisible bagpipe.

Gypsy, let me lift your skirt
and have a look at you.
Open in my ancient fingers
the blue rose of your womb.

Preciosa throws the tambourine
and runs away in terror.
But the virile wind pursues her
with his breath and burning sword.

The sea darkens and roars,
while the olive trees turn pale.
The flutes of darkness sound,
and a muted gong of the snow.

Preciosa, run, Preciosa!
Or the green wind will catch you!
Preciosa, run, Preciosa!
And look how fast he comes!
A satyr of low-born stars
with their long and glistening tongues.

Preciosa, filled with fear,
now makes her way to that house
beyond the tall green pines
where the English consul lives.

Alarmed by her anguished cries,
three riflemen come running,
their black capes tightly drawn,
and berets down over their brow.

The Englishman gives the gypsy
a glass of tepid milk
and a shot of Holland gin
which Preciosa does not drink.

And while she tells them, weeping,
of her strange adventure,
the wind furiously gnashes
against the slate roof tiles.

Preciosa tocando viene.
Al verla se ha levantado
el viento que nunca duerme.
San Cristobalón desnudo,
lleno de lenguas celestes,
mira a la niña tocando
una dulce gaita ausente.

—Niña, deja que levante
tu vestido para verte.
Abre en mis dedos antiguos
la rosa azul de tu vientre.

Preciosa tira el pandero
y corre sin detenerse.
El viento-hombrón la persigue
con una espada caliente.

Frunce su rumor el mar.
Los olivos palidecen.
Cantan las flautas de umbría
y el liso gong de la nieve.

¡Preciosa, corre, Preciosa,
que te coge el viento verde!
¡Preciosa, corre, Preciosa!
¡Míralo por donde viene!
Sátiro de estrellas bajas
con sus lenguas relucientes.

Preciosa, llena de miedo,
entra en la casa que tiene,
más arriba de los pinos,
el cónsul de los ingleses.

Asustados por los gritos
tres carbineros vienen,
sus negras capas ceñidas
y los gorros en las sienes.

El inglés da a la gitana
un vaso de tibia leche
y una copa de ginebra
que Preciosa no la bebe.

Y mientras cuenta, llorando,
su aventura a aquella gente,
en las tejas de pizarra
el viento, furioso, muerde.

KATHARINE E. STRATHDEE

The Guitar

The weeping of the guitar
begins.
The goblets of dawn
are shattered.
The weeping of the guitar
begins.
It is useless
to stop it.

La guitarra

Empieza el llanto
de la guitarra.
Se rompen las copas
de la madrugada.
Empieza el llanto
de la guitarra.
Es inútil
callarla.

It is impossible
to stop it.
It weeps monotonously
like the cry of water,
like the cry of the wind
on the fallen snow.
It is impossible
to stop it.
It weeps for things
that are far away.
Sands of the burning South
begging for white camelias.
It weeps arrow without target,
afternoon without morning,
and the first dead bird
on the branch.
Oh, guitar!
Heart pierced
by five sharp swords.

JOHN A. CROW

Nocturne of Emptiness

To see that all has gone,
To see the emptiness, the clothes,
Give me your gloove of moonlight, O my love!
Give me your other glove, lost in the grass.

Wind can root out snails
Dead in the elephant's hide
Inflate the frozen worms
From the tips of light or the apples.

Indifferent, faces drift
Under the lessened murmur of the grass
And in the corner, in the frog's little breast
Confusion of heart and mandolin.

In the great deserted square
The cow's head, newly severed, bawls,
And the forms that sought the trail of the snake
Were crystal, fixed and rigid.

To see that all has gone,
Give me your silent emptiness, my love!
Where the sky gathers in silence its abandoned cabins,
To see that all has gone.

Tomorrow's emptiness is singing here
with yesterday's upon my hands
Two toads of ashes, two rumors
Of my appearance, trickling, boiling over.

Within my love for your flesh,
What silence of trains, turned upside down!
What sprouting mummified limbs!
What heaven void of outlet!
O love, what heaven!

To see that all has gone,
To see the emptiness of cloud and river,

Es imposible
callarla.
Llora monótona
como llora el agua,
como llora el viento
sobre la nevada.
Es imposible
callarla.
Llora por cosas
lejanas.
Arena del Sur caliente
que pide camelias blancas.
Llora flecha sin blanco,
la tarde sin mañana,
y el primer pájaro muerto
sobre la rama.
¡Oh, guitarra!
Corazón malherido
por cinco espadas.

Nocturno del hueco

Para ver que todo se ha ido,
Para ver los huecos y los vestidos,
¡dame tu guante de luna,
tu otro guante perdido en la hierba,
amor mío!

Puede el aire arrancar los caracoles
muertos sobre la piel del elefante
y soplar los gusanos ateridos
de las yemas de luz o de las manzanas.

Los rostros bogan impasibles
bajo el diminuto griterío de las hierbas
y en el rincón o en el pechito de la rana
turbio de corazón y mandolina.

En la gran plaza desierta
mugía la bovina cabeza recién cortada
y eran duro cristal definitivo
las formas que buscaban el giro de la sierpe.

Para ver que todo se ha ido,
dame tu mudo hueco ¡amor mío!
Donde el cielo agrupa en silencio sus cabañas abandonadas,
Para ver que todo se ha ido.

Aquí cantan los huecos de mañana
con los huecos de ayer sobre mis manos
dos sapos de ceniza, dos rumores
de mi apariencia que mana y borbotea

(Dentro de ti amor por tu carne
¡qué silencio de trenes boca arriba!
¡cuánto brazo de momia florecido!
¡qué cielo sin salida! ¡amor! ¡qué cielo!)

Para ver que todo se ha ido,
para ver los huecos de nubes y ríos,

Give me your laurel branches, O my love, *To see that all has gone.*	*dame tus ramos de laurel, amor,* *para ver que todo se ha ido.*
Stone in the water, voice in the wind, Edges of love escaping the bloody trunk. Enough to touch the pulse-beat of our love For flowers to break in bloom for other children.	Es la piedra en el agua y es la voz en el aire bordes de amor que escapan de su tronco sangrante. Basta tocar el pulso de nuestro amor para que broten flores sobre otros niños
Pure emptiness for me revolving, for you in the dawn Keeping the trace of bloody branches Some plaster profile, calmly sketching The immediate surprise of the pointilliste moon Watching the solid forms that seek their void Mistaken dogs, half-eaten apples.	Ruedan los huecos puros por mí, por ti, en el alba conservando las huellas de las ramas de sangre y algún perfil de yeso, que tranquilo dibuja instantánea sorpresa de luna apuntillada. Mira formas concretas que buscan su vacío perros equivocados y manzanas mordidas.
When in my bed I count the murmurs of linen You have come, my love, to cover over my shelter. The hollow of an ant can fill the wind, But you go crying lost across my eyes.	Cuando cuento en la cama los rumores del hilo has venido, amor mío, a cubrir mi tejado. El hueco de una hormiga puede llenar el aire, pero tú vas gimiendo sin norte por mis ojos.
No, not across my eyes. Today you show Four ashen rivers in your arms, In the rough barracks where the captive moon Devours a sailor before the children's eyes.	No, por mis ojos no, que ahora me enseñas cuatro ríos ceñidos en tu brazo, En la dura barraca donde la luna prisionera devora a un marinero delante de los niños.
To see that all has gone. *O obstinate departed love!* *Yield not your emptiness.* *Let mine be lost on air!* *To see that all has gone.* [40]	*Para ver que todo se ha ido* *¡Amor inexpugnable, amor huido!* *No, no me des tu hueco.* *¡que ya va por el aire el mío!* *Para ver que todo se ha ido.*

ROLFE HUMPHRIES

César Vallejo
Peru, 1895–1938

Vallejo, well known for his Communist affiliation, was a poet of mixed blood who throughout his brief life was barely able to keep body and soul together with his journalistic writings; he died in poverty in Paris, at the age of forty-three. Vallejo's poetry explodes from his tortured inner consciousness in an almost total disregard for established literary elegance. His poems have been compared to German expressionism, but they also embody elements of Peruvian indigenism.

Vallejo traveled in Russia, a country he greatly admired; he chanted a paean to the Spanish Republicans destined to defeat in Spain's bitter civil war, and he was a defender of the humble masses and of leftist causes generally. His involvement with human suffering was obsessive and overwhelming. Vallejo was the outstanding initiator in his group in Peru, and after his death his reputation grew until he became known as one of the finest poets of his generation. His attitude may be aptly characterized by his famous statement: "The day I was born, God was sick."

Robert Bly, who has translated many of Vallejo's poems, characterizes his first book *Los heraldos negros (The Black Messengers)* as "a staggering book, sensual, prophetic, affectionate, wild. It has a kind of compassion for God, and compassion for death... and it moves with incredible leaps of imagination. I think it is the greatest single collection of poems I have ever read." [41]

40. This poem is from Lorca's *The Poet in New York,* written mainly in 1929–1930, during the poet's long stay in the city, but not published until 1940. Robert Bly calls it "the greatest book ever written about New York," but Roy Campbell, a contemporary poet of equal stature, characterizes it as "slightly mephitic." I lived at the same place as Lorca during most of his time in New York and frequently accompanied him on his jaunts about the city. My own impression is that in this book Lorca is out of his element and thus tends to overwrite in a kind of high-pitched frenzy. Even so, it contains flashes of fine poetry.
41. Robert Bly (ed.), *Neruda and Vallejo: Selected Poems* (Boston: Beacon Press, 1971), 170.

Dregs

This afternoon it is raining as never before,
And I do not want to go on living, my heart.

This afternoon is sweet, why shouldn't it be,
It is dressed in sorrow gracefully like a woman.

This afternoon in Lima it is pouring. And I remember
The cruel caverns of my ungratefulness,

My block of ice lying upon her poppy,
Stranger than her: "Don't be like that!"

My fierce black flowers, a savage
Hail of stones, and glacial distances,
And the silence of her dignity
Will paint its final period in flaming oils.

And that is why this afternoon, as never before,
I am going about with this owl, with this heart.
And other women pass; and seeing me depressed
They take a little of you
From the chasms of my pain.

This afternoon it is raining, it is pouring down,
And I do not want to go on living, my heart.

JOHN A. CROW

Heces

Esta tarde llueve, como nunca; y no
tengo ganas de vivir, corazón.

Esta tarde es dulce. ¿Por qué no ha de ser?
Viste gracia y pena; viste de mujer.

Esta tarde en Lima llueve. Yo yo recuerdo
las cavernas crueles de mi ingratitud;
mi bloque de hielo sobre su amapola,
más fuerte que su "No seas así!"

Mis violentas flores negras; y la bárbara
y enorme pedrada; y el trecho glacial.
Y pondrá el silencio de su dignidad
con óleos quemantes el punto final.

Por eso esta tarde, como nunca, voy
con este buho, con este corazón.

Y otras pasan; y viéndome tan triste.
toman un poquito de ti
en la abrupta arruga de mi hondo dolor.

Esta tarde llueve, llueve mucho. ¡Y no
tengo ganas de vivir, corazón!

The Black Messengers

There are blows in life, so brutal. "What can I say!"
Blows like God's hatred; as if feeling them,
The backwash of everything suffered
Were dammed up in the heart. "What can I say!"

They are not many; but they exist. They open dark lines
In the boldest faces and strongest back.
Perhaps they are the wild colts of savage Attilas;
Or the black messengers sent to us by Death.

They are the pitfalls of the Christs of the soul,
Of a beloved faith blasphemed by Fate.
These bloody blows are the cruching sounds
Of a piece of bread burned in the door of the oven.

And man, Poor mankind! He turns his eyes, as if
He were suddenly called from behind by a clap of the
     hands;
He turns his frenzied eyes, and everything that has been
     lived
Is dammed up, like a puddle of guilt, in the look on his
     face.

There are blows in life, so brutal, "What can I say!"

JOHN A. CROW

Los heraldos negros

Hay golpes en la vida, tan fuertes. ¡Yo no sé!
Golpes como del odio de Dios; como si ante ellos,
la resaca de todo lo sufrido
se empozara en el alma. ¡Yo no sé!

Son pocos; pero son. Abren zanjas obscuras
en el rostro más fiero y en el lomo más fuerte.
Serán tal vez los potros de bárbaros atilas;
o los heraldos negros que nos manda la Muerte.

Son las hondas caídas de los Cristos del alma,
de una fe adorable que el Destino blasfema.
Estos golpes sangrientos son las crepitaciones
de algún pan que en la puerta del horno se nos quema.

Y el hombre. Pobre. ¡Pobre! Vuelve los ojos, como
cuando por sobre el hombro nos llama una palmada;
vuelve los ojos locos, y todo lo vivido
se empoza, como charco de culpa, en la mirada.

Hay golpes en la vida, tan fuertes. ¡Yo no sé!

Leaf-Storm

Moon! Crown of a gigantic head
Dropping your leaves in yellow shadows,

Deshojación sagrada

¡Luna! ¡Corona de una testa inmensa,
que te vas deshojando en sombras gualdas!

Red Crown of a Jesus who is thinking
Sweet tragedies of emeralds.

Moon! Frenzied heart of the sky,
Why do you drift like that, inside the cup,
Filled with blue wine, toward the West,
Like the sad hull of a ship in distress?

Moon! And because you have flown in vain.
You are a holocaust of scattered opals,
Perhaps you are my gypsy heart
That wanders in the blue weeping poetic lines...

JOHN A. CROW

Footsteps Far Away

My father is sleeping. His majestic face
Tells me of a peaceful heart;
He is so sweet now...
If there is anything bitter in him, it may be me.

There is loneliness in the house; there are prayers;
And there is no news of the children today.
My father wakes up, he is listening
To the flight into Egypt, the blood-stopping good-bye.
He is so near now;
If there is anything far away in him, it may be me.

And my mother is walking out there in the orchard,
Tasting a taste that already has no taste.
She is now so gentle,
So much wing, so much going away, so much love.

There is loneliness in the house without a sound,
Without news, with greenness, without childhood.
And if there is something broken this afternoon,
And that falls and creaks,
It is two old white crooked roads.
Down them my heart is walking.

JOHN A. CROW

Anger

Anger that breaks a man into children
That breaks the child into equal birds
And the bird, then, into little eggs;
The anger of the poor
Has an oil against two vinegars.

Anger that breaks the tree into leaves,
The leaf, into unequal buds,
And the bud into telescopic grooves.
The anger of the poor
Has two rivers against many oceans.

Anger that breaks the good into doubts,
And doubt, into symmetrical arcs,
And the arc, then, into unexpected tombs.

¡Roja corona de un Jesús que piensa
trágicamente dulce de esmeraldas!

¡Luna! Alocado corazón celeste
¿por qué bogas así, dentro la copa
llena de vino azul, hacia el oeste,
cual derrotada y dolorida popa?

¡Luna! Y a fuerza de volar en vano,
te holocaustas en ópalos dispersos:
¡tú eres tal vez mi corazón gitano
que vaga en el azul llorando versos!...

Los pasos lejanos

Mi padre duerme. Su semblante augusto
figura un apacible corazón;
está ahora tan dulce...
si hay algo en él de amargo, seré yo.

Hay soledad en el hogar; se reza;
y no hay noticias de los hijos hoy.
Mi padre se despierta, ausculta
la huída a Egipto, el restañante adiós.
Está ahora tan cerca;
si hay algo en él de lejos, seré yo.

Y mi madre pasea allá en los huertos,
saboreando un sabor ya sin sabor.
Está ahora tan suave,
tan ala, tan salida, tan amor.

Hay soledad en el hogar sin bulla,
sin noticias, sin verde, sin niñez.
Y si hay algo quebrado en esta tarde,
y que baja y que cruje,
son dos viejos caminos blancos, curvos.
Por ellos va mi corazón a pie.

La cólera

La cólera que quiebra al hombre en niños,
que quiebra al niño en pájaros iguales,
y al pájaro, después, en huevecillos;
la cólera del pobre
tiene un aceite contra dos vinagres.

La cólera que al árbol quiebra en hojas,
a la hoja, en botones desiguales,
y al botón, en ranuras telescópicas;
la cólera del pobre
tiene dos ríos contra muchos mares.

La cólera que quiebra al bien en dudas,
a la duda, en tres arcos semejantes,
y al arco, luego, en tumbas imprevistas;

The anger of the poor
Has a sword against two daggers.

Anger that breaks the soul into bodies,
The body, into dissimilar organs,
And the organ, into octaves of thought.
The anger of the poor
Has a central fire against two craters.

JOHN A. CROW

The Day I Was Born

The day I was born
God was sick.

Everyone knows that I am alive,
That I am evil . . . and they do not know
of the December of that January.
Well, the day I was born
God was sick.

There is a void
in my metaphysical breath
that no man can probe:
the cloister of silence
that spoke out in open flame.

The day I was born
God was sick.

Brother, listen, listen . . .
Good. And don't leave me
without taking Decembers,
without leaving Januaries.

Well, the day I was born
God was sick.

Everyone knows that I am alive,
that I am still chewing . . . And they do not know
why in my poems creak,
like the obscure distaste of a coffin,
rasping winds
disentwined by the inquisitive
Sphinx of the Desert.
Everyone knows . . . And doesn't know
that Light is consumptive,
and Shadow full . . .
And they don't know that Mystery synthesizes . . .
that it is the sad, musical
hunchback that distantly heralds
the meridian passage from boundaries to Boundaries.

The day I was born
God was sick,
deathly.

KATHARINE E. STRATHDEE
AND MARY H. PARHAM

la cólera del pobre
tiene un acero contra dos puñales.

La cólera que quiebra al alma en cuerpos,
al cuerpo, en órganos desemejantes.
y al órgano, en octavos pensamientos;
la cólera del pobre
tiene un fuego central contra dos cráteres.

Yo nací un día

Yo nací un día
que Dios estuvo enfermo.

Todos saben que vivo,
que soy malo; y no saben
del diciembre de ese enero.
Pues yo nací un día
que Dios estuvo enfermo.

Hay un vacío
en mi aire metafísico
que nadie ha de palpar:
el claustro de un silencio
que habló a flor de fuego.

Yo nací un día
que Dios estuvo enfermo.

Hermano, escucha, escucha . . .
Bueno. Y que no me vaya
sin llevar diciembres,
sin dejar eneros.

Pues yo nací un día
que Dios estuvo enfermo.

Todos saben que vivo,
que mastico . . . Y no saben
por que en mi verso chirrían,
oscuro sinsabor de féretro.
luyidos vientos
desenrroscados de la Esfinge
preguntona del Desierto.
Todos saben . . . Y no saben
que la Luz es tísica,
y la Sombra gorda . . .
Y no saben que el Misterio sintetiza . . .
que él es la joroba
musical y triste que a distancia denuncia
el paso meridiano de las lindes a las Lindes.

Yo nací un día
que Dios estuvo enfermo,
grave.

Masses

At the end of the battle,
When the fighter was dead, a man came toward him
And said to him "Do not die, I love you so!"
But the corpse, alas, went on dying!

Then two approached him and repeated it,
"Do not leave us! Courage! Come back to life!"
But the corpse, alas, went on dying.

Then twenty came, a hundred, a thousand, five hundred
    thousand,
Clamoring, "So much love and nothing can be done about
    death!"
But the corpse, alas, went on dying.

Millions of individuals surrounded him,
With a common entreaty, "Stay with us, brother!"
But the corpse, alas, went on dying.

Then all the men of the earth
Surrounded him; the corpse looked at them sadly, full of
    emotions;
Sat up slowly,
Embraced the first man; and began to walk . . .

H. R. HAYS

Little Responsory for a Republican Hero

A book lay beside his dead belt,
A book was sprouting from his dead body.
They raised the hero
And, corporeal and sad, his mouth entered our breath.
We were all sweating, dog tired,
As we traveled the moons were following us;
And the dead man, too, was sweating with sadness.

And a book, in the battle of Toledo,
A book, a book behind, a book above, was sprouting from
    the corpse.

Poetry of the purple cheek, between reciting it
And keeping it silent,
Poetry in the moral letter that accompanied
His heart.
The book remained and nothing more, since there are
No insects in the tomb
And the air under the edge of his sleeve continued to
    grow moist
And to become gaseous, infinite.

We were all sweating, dog tired,
And the dead man, too, was sweating with sadness.
And a book, I saw it, feeling it,
A book behind, a book above,
Sprouted from the violent corpse.

H. R. HAYS

Masa

Al fin de la batalla,
y muerto el combatiente, vino hacia él un hombre
y le dijo: "¡No mueras; te amo tanto!"
Pero el cadàver ¡ay!, siguió muriendo.

Se le acercaron dos y repitiéronle:
"¡No nos dejes! ¡Valor! ¡Vuelve a la vida!"
Pero el cadáver ¡ay!, siguió muriendo.

Acudierion a él veinte, cien, mil, quinientos mil,
clamando: "¡Tanto amor, y no poder nada contra la
    muerte!"
Pero el cadáver ¡ay!, siguió muriendo.

Le roderaon millones de individuos,
con un ruego común: "¡Quédate hermano!"
Pero el cadáver ¡ay!, siguió muriendo.

Entonces, todos los hombres de la tierra
le rodearon; les vio el cadáver triste, emocionado;
incorporóse lentamente,
abrazó, al primer hombre; echóse a andar . . .

Pequeño responso a un héroe de la república

Un libro quedó al borde de su cintura muerta,
un libro retoñaba de su cadáver muerto.
Se llevaron al héroe,
y corpórea y aciaga entró su boca en nuestro aliento;
sudamos todos, el ombligo a cuestas;
caminantes las lunas nos seguían;
también sudaba de tristeza el muerto.

Y un libro, en la batalla de Toledo,
un libro, atrás un libro, arriba un libro, retoñaba del
    cadáver.

Poesía del pómulo morado, entre el decirlo
y el callarlo,
poesía en la carta moral que acompañara
a su corazón.
Quedóse el libro y nada más, que no hay
insectos en la tumba,
y quedó al borde de su manga el aire remojándose
y haciéndose gaseoso, infinito.

Todos sudamos, el ombligo a cuestas,
también sudaba de tristeza el muerto
y un libro, yo lo ví sentidamente,
un libro, atrás un libro, arriba un libro
retoñó del cadáver exabrupto.

Black Stone Lying on a White Stone

I will die in Paris, on a rainy day,
on some day I can already remember.
I will die in Paris—and I don't step aside—
perhaps on a Thursday, as today is Thursday, in autumn.

It will be a Thursday, because today, Thursday, setting
down
these lines, I have put my upper arm bones on
wrong, and never so much as today have I found myself
with all the road ahead of me, alone.

César Vallejo is dead. Everyone beat him,
although he never did anything to them;
they beat him hard with a stick and hard, also

with a rope. These are the witnesses:
the Thursdays, and the bones of my arms,
the solitude, and the rain, and the roads . . .

ROBERT BLY AND JOHN KNOEPFLE

Piedra negra sobre una piedra blanca

Me moriré en París con aguacero,
un día del cual tengo ya el recuerdo.
Me moriré en París—y no me corro—
tal vez un jueves, como es hoy, de otoño.

Jueves será, porque hoy, jueves, que proso
estos versos, los húmeros me he puesto
a la mala y, jamás como hoy, me he vuelto,
con todo mi camino, a verme solo.

César Vallejo ha muerto, le pegaban
todos sin que él les haga nada;
le daban duro con un palo y duro

también con una soga; son testigos
los días jueves y los huesos húmeros,
la soledad, la lluvia, los caminos . . .

Gabriela Mistral (pseudonym of Lucila Godoy Alcayaga)
Chile, 1889–1957

In Lucila Godoy's youth, her sweetheart, a railway clerk, committed suicide because of a misappropriation of funds. and as one of her biographers states, "The echo of that shot was the birth of the poet, Gabriela Mistral."[42] In 1914 she submitted three "Sonnets of Death" to a national poetry contest and was awarded first prize. Her symbolic pseudonym combined the names *Gabriel*, the archangel, and *mistral*, the wind that often sweeps across southern France.

Gabriela's profound maternal instinct was partially fulfilled a few years later when she adopted and reared the illegitimate son of her brother, who simply abandoned the child. But at age fifteen the boy (affectionately called "Yin-Yin") also committed suicide. Unable to accept this second "rejection" of her love, the poet insisted until her dying day that Yin-Yin had been murdered.

Gabriela wrote some of the most passionate poems of love, loss, and death in the Spanish language. Maternity and religion were also strong themes in her poetry. She became a mouthpiece for all of the frustrations and yearnings of the women of her culture. The body of her poetic output is very limited, but its quality is high. In 1945 she was awarded the Nobel Prize for literature, and was the first Latin American writer to be so honored.

In Latin America she was as much loved as a person and public figure as she was for being a poet. She was a teacher, college professor at Barnard College in New York, journalist, educational administrator, and consul. Whever she lived (Chile, Brazil, Mexico, Europe, United States), her home was a mecca for writers from many lands. Despite her international reputation she was always warm, approachable, encouraging, a friend to the great and humble folk equally. Undoubtedly she was the most deeply and widely loved woman in Latin America during this century.

The Prayer

Lord, often have my words in burning tone
Beseeched your mercy for another's need,

El ruego

Señor, tú sabes cómo, con encendido brío,
por los seres extraños mi palabra te invoca.

42. Sidonia C. Rosenbaum, *Modern Women Poets of Spanish America* (New York: Hispanic Institute, 1945), 174.

But now I pray for one who was my own,
My cup to drink, my honeycomb, my seed,

Marrow of my bones, sweet reason of my day,
Song to my ears, and binding of my dress;
Lord, since for those unknown I often pray,
Forgive the one I loved, your wrath suppress.

I swear that he was good, his soul contrite,
His gentle heart brought love to everything;
By nature he was pure as summer light,
The bearer of a miracle like the spring.

That he does not deserve my prayers, you say,
Whose fevered lips have never sought your grace,
Who without waiting for a sign from you one day
Smashed in his temples like a shattered vase.

But Lord, I say to you my hands caressed
Both the white lily of that silken brow
And the tormented heart in that dear breast;
It had the softness of an opening flower.

That he was cruel? Love was my shield and lever;
He knew my body's depths were his to shatter;
That he has stained my pool of joy forever?
Oh, Lord, I loved him so, it did not matter!

Here I stand now, with head and eyes bent low,
A suppliant this long evening as I speak;
Night after night I shall continue so
If you delay the answer that I seek.

The iron that drills, a cold pleasure renews
When it opens like sheaves that love encloses,
And the rough Cross (how well you know, King of the
     Jews),
Is softly borne like a garland of roses.

Forgive him, Lord, touch him with wind and light,
Your words a thousand fragrances enfold;
Each drop of water will be dazzling, bright,
The desert will bear flowers, stones turn to gold!

The dark eyes of wild beasts with tears will flow,
The peaks you forged of stone (Lord, save him!)
Will weep through the white eyelids of their snow,
And the whole earth will know that you forgave him.

JOHN A. CROW

Vengo ahora a pedirte por uno que era mío,
mi vaso de frescura, el panal de mi boca,

cal de mis huesos, dulce razón de la journada,
gorjeo de mi oído, ceñidor de mi veste.
Me cuido hasta de aquellos en que no puse nada.
¡No tengas ojo torvo si te pido por éste!

Te digo que era bueno, te digo que tenía
el corazón entero a flor de pecho, que era
suave de índole, franco como la luz del día,
henchido de milagro como la primavera.

Me replicas, severo, que es de plegaria indigno
el que no untó de preces sus dos labios febriles,
y se fue aquella tarde sin esperar tu signo,
trizándose las sienes como vasos sutiles.

Pero yo, mi Señor, te arguyo que he tocado,
de la misma manera que el nardo de su frente,
todo su corazón dulce y atormentado
¡y tenía la seda del capullo naciente!

¿Que fue cruel? Olvidas, Señor, que le quería,
y que él sabía suya la entraña que llagaba.
¿Que enturbió para siempre mis linfas de alegría?
¡No importa! Tú comprendes: ¡yo le amaba, le amaba!

Y amar (bien sabes de eso) es amargo ejercicio;
un mantener los párpados de lágrimas mojados,
un refrescar de besos las trenzas del cilicio
conservando, bajo ellas, los ojos extasiados.

El hierro que taladra tiene un gustoso frío,
cuando abre, cual gavillas, las carnes amorosas.
Y la cruz (Tú te acuerdas ¡oh Rey de los judíos!)
se lleva con blandura, como un gajo de rosas.

Aquí me estoy, Señor, con la cara caída
sobre el polvo, parlándote un crepúsculo entero,
o todos los crepúsculos a que alcance la vida,
si tardas en decirme la palabra que espero.

Fatigaré tu oído de preces y sollozos,
lamiendo, lebrel tímido, los bordes de tu manto,
y ni pueden huirme tus ojos amorosos
ni esquivar tu pie el riego caliente de mi llanto.

¡Di el perdón, dilo al fin! Va a esparcir en el viento
la palabra el perfume de cien pomos de olores
al vaciarse; todo agua será deslumbramiento;
el yermo echará flor y el guijarro esplendores.

Se mojarán los ojos oscuros de las fieras,
y, comprendiendo, el monte que de piedra forjaste
llorará por los párpados blancos de sus neveras:
¡Toda la tierra tuya sabrá que perdonaste!

Sonnet on Death

From the dark crypt where men put you away,
I'll lower you into the sun-drenched ground;
They did not know I'd share your grave some day,
That both of us would rest beneath this mound.

Soneto de la muerte I

Del nicho helado en que los hombres te pusieron,
te bajaré a la tierra humilde y soleada.
Que he de dormirme en ella los hombres no supieron,
y que hemos de soñar sobre la misma almohada.

I'll tuck you in the sunlit earth and leave
You sleeping like an infant sweet and mild;
The earth will form a cradle and receive
Your body gently as a wounded child.
Then I shall scatter dust and powdered roses,
And in that cloud of moonlike smoke perceive
Your face imprisoned underneath these stones;
Such is the resting place my heart imposes,
Because at this dark depth no hand will thieve
Or fight with me for your handful of bones!

JOHN A. CROW

Te acostaré en la tierra soleada, con una
dulcedumbre de madre para el hijo dormido,
y la tierra ha de hacerse suavidades de cuna
al recibir tu cuerpo de niño dolorido.

Luego iré espolvoreando tierra y polvo de rosas,
y en la azulada y leve polvareda de luna,
los despojos livianos irán quedando presos.

Me alejaré cantando mis venganzas hermosas,
¡porque a ese hondor recóndito la mano de ninguna
bajará a disputarme tu puñado de huesos!

The Thinker

The Thinker's chin rests on a furrowed hand,
His thought is that man's flesh belongs to the grave;
That mortal clay must bow to fate's demand.
But hates the end of all that beauty gave.
With love he trembled in his fiery spring,
When autumn came the cold truth drained his will:
That *we must die* has brought that brow its sting,
And grips the tortured bronze that night must fill.

His sinews writhe in a fixed agony,
And terror grips each fiber of his frame,
Rent like fall leaves by God's almighty breath
Which calls that bronze to life. There is no twisted tree
Seared by the plain's hot sun, no wounded lion in pain
Contorted like that man who ponders death.

JOHN A. CROW

El pensador de Rodin

Con el mentón caído sobre la mano ruda,
el Pensador se acuerda que es carne de la huesa,
carne fatal, delante del destino desnuda,
carne que odia la muerte, y tembló de belleza.

Y tembló de amor, toda su primavera ardiente,
y ahora, al otoño, anégase de verdad y tristeza.
El "de morir tenemos" pasa sobre su frente,
en todo agudo bronce, cuando la noche empieza.

Y en la angustia, sus músculos se hienden, sufridores.
Los surcos de su carne se llenan de terrores.
Se hiende, como la hoja de otoño, al Señor fuerte

que la llama en los bronces . . . Y no hay árbol torcido
de sol en la llanura, ni león de flanco herido,
crispados como este hombre que medita en la muerte.

The Helpers

While my baby sleeps,
the earth, unaware,
helps me to finish him.
The grass makes his hair,
the date-palm his fingers,
and the beeswax his nails.
The seashells give him hearing,
the red strawberry his tongue,
the rivulet brings him smiles,
and the mountain sends him patience.

(I left my baby unfinished
and I am confused and ashamed:
scarcely a brow, scarcely a voice,
scarcely a size you can see.)

They carry things, go and come,
enter and leave the door,
bringing tiny chipmunk ears,
teeth of mother-of-pearl.

In three Christmases he will be another,
changed from head to toe.
Tall as a reed he will stand,
straight as the pine tree on the slope.

Ayudadores

Mientras el niño se me duerme,
sin que lo sepa ni la tierra,
por ayudarme en acabarlo
sus cabellos hace la hierba,
sus deditos la palma-dátil
y las uñas la buena cera.
Los caracoles dan su oído
y la fresca roja su lengua,
y el arroyo le trae risas
y el monte le manda paciencias.
(Cosas dejé sin acabar
y estoy confusa y con vergüenza:
apenas sienes, apenas habla,
apenas bulto que le vean.)

Los que acarrean van y vienen,
entran y salen por la puerta
trayendo orejitas de *cuye*
y unos dientes de concha-perla.

Tres Navidades y será otro,
de los tobillos a la cabeza:
será talludo, será recto
como los pinos de la cuesta.

Then, like a crazy woman.
I will proclaim him through the town
with a shouting clearly heard
by the hills and meadows around.

DORIS DANA

Y yo iré entonces voceándolo
como una loca por los pueblos,
con un pregón que van a oirme
las praderías y los cerros.

One Word

I have in my throat one word
that I cannot speak, will not free
though its thrust of blood pounds me.
If I voiced it, it would scorch the living grass,
bleed the lamb, fell the bird.

I have to cut it from my tongue,
find a beaver's hole,
or bury it beneath lime and more quicklime
lest, soul-like, it break free.

I wish to give no sign of what I live
as this word courses through my blood, ebbs and flows,
rises, falls with each mad breath.
Though Job, my father, burning spoke it,
I will not give it utterance
lest it roll vagrant
and be found by river-women,
twist itself in their braids,
or mangle and blaze the poor thicket.

I wish to throw seeds so violent
they burst and smother it in one night
leaving not even a syllable's trace.
Or rip it from myself
with the serpent's severing tooth.

And return it to my house, enter and sleep,
torn from it, sliced from it;
wake after two thousand days
newly born out of sleep and oblivion.

Never again to remember the word between my lips,
that word of iodine and alum stone,
or ever again that one night,
the ambush in a foreign land,
the lightning bolt at the door
and my flesh abroad with no soul.

DORIS DANA

Una palabra

Yo tengo una palabra en la garganta
y no la suelto, y no me libro de ella
aunque me empuje su empellón de sangre.
Si la soltase, quema el pasto vivo,
sangra al cordero, hace caer al pájaro.

Tengo que desprenderla de mi lengua,
hallar un agujero de castores
o sepultarla con cales y cales
porque no guarde como el alma el vuelo.

No quiero dar señales de que vivo
mientras que por mi sangre vaya y venga
y suba y baje por mi loco aliento.
Aunque mi padre Job la dijo, ardiendo,
no quiero darle, no, mi pobre boca
porque no ruede y la hallen las mujeres
que van al río, y se enrede a sus trenzas
o al pobre matorral tuerza y abrase.

Yo quiero echarle violentas semillas
que en una noche la cubran y ahoguen
sin dejar de ella el cisco de una sílaba.
O rompérmela así, como a la víbora
que por mitad se parte con los dientes.

Y volver a mi casa, entrar, dormirme,
cortada de ella, rebanada de ella,
y despertar después de dos mil días
recién nacida de sueño y olvido.

¡Sin saber más que tuve una palabra
de yodo y piedra-alumbre entre los labios
ni saber acordarme de una noche,
de una morada en país extranjero,
de la celada y el rayo a la puerta
y de mi carne marchando sin su alma!

The Immigrant Jew

I go farther than the west wind,
farther than the stormy petrel I fly.
never sleep for walking.
A woman cut off from the earth,
they left me only the sea.

Home and habits and household gods
stayed behind in my village

Emigrada judía

Voy más lejos que el viento oeste
y el petrel de tempestad.
Paro, interrogo, camino
¡y no duermo por caminar!
Me rebanaron la Tierra,
sólo me han dejado el mar.

Se quedaron en la aldea

with linden trees and banks of reed grass
on the Rhine that taught me to speak.
I do not bring the mint
whose scent would make me weep.
I bring only my breath,
my blood, my anxiety.

I am two. One looks back,
the other turns to the sea.
The nape of my neck seethes with good-byes
and my breast with yearning.

The stream that flows through my village
no longer speaks my name;
I am erased from my own land and air
like a footprint on the sand.

With each stretch of road
all that was mine recedes,
a gush of resin, a tower,
a grove of oak trees.
My hands forget their ways
of making cider and bread.
With memory blown clean by the wind,
I arrive naked at the sea.

                    DORIS DANA

casa, costumbre, y dios lar.
Pasan tilos, carrizales
y el Rin que me enseñó a hablar.
No llevo al pecho las mentas
cuyo olor me haga llorar.
Tan sólo llevo mi aliento
y mi sangre y mi ansiedad.

Una soy a mis espaldas,
otra volteada al mar:
mi nuca hierve de adioses,
y mi pecho de ansiedad.

Ya el torrente de mi aldea
no da mi nombre al rodar
y en mi tierra y aire me borro
como huella en arenal.

A cada trecho de ruta
voy perdiendo mi caudal:
una oleada de resinas,
una torre, un robledal.
Suelta mi mano sus gestos
de hacer la sidra y el pan
¡y aventada mi memoria
llegará desnuda al mar!

A Pious One

I must see the lighthouse keeper,
go to his craggy rock,
feel the wave break in his mouth,
see the abyss in his eyes.
I want to find him, if he lives,
that old salt man of sea.

They say he looks only eastward,
walled-up alive at sea.
When I shatter his wave, I wish
he would turn his eyes from the abyss to me.

He knows all there is to know of night
which has become my bed and path;
he knows the octopus, sponge, and undertow,
and the senses slain by a scream.

His chastened breast
is spat upon by tides,
is shrilled by gulls,
is white as the maimed.
So still, so mute and unmindful
as though unborn.

But I go to the lighthouse tower
to climb the knife-edged path
and be with the man who will tell me
what is earthly and what divine.
In one arm I bring him a jug of milk,
in the other, a sip of wine.

Una piadosa

Quiero ver al hombre del faro,
quiero ir a la peña del risco,
probar en su boca la ola,
ver en sus ojos el abismo.
Yo quiero alcanzar, si vive,
al viejo salobre y salino.

Dicen que sólo mira al Este,
—emparedado que está vivo—
y quiero, cortando sus olas
que me mire en vez del abismo.

Todo se sabe de la noche
que ahora es mi lecho y camino:
sabe resacas, pulpos, esponjas,
sabe un grito que mata el sentido.

Está escupido de marea
su pecho fiel y con castigo,
está silbado de gaviotas
y tan albo como el herido
¡y de inmóvil, y mudo y ausente,
ya no parece ni nacido!

Pero voy a la torre del faro,
subiéndome ruta de filos
por el hombre que va a contarme
lo terrestre y lo divino,
y en brazo y brazo le llevo
jarro de leche, sorbo de vino . . .

On he goes listening to seas
in love with nothing but themselves.
Perhaps now he listens to nothing.
Fixed in forgetfulness and salt.

Y él sigue escuchando mares
que no aman sino a sí mismos.
Pero tal vez ya nada escuche,
de haber parado en sal y olvido.

DORIS DANA

Carlos Pellicer

Mexico, 1899–

Carls Pellicer, unlike most of the contemporary Spanish American poets, is profoundly optimistic. He clearly believes that man will prevail, that he can find harmony, peace, beauty, fulfillment. The Mexican critic, Alfonso Reyes, points out that Pellicer's eyes are sharp and clear in their perception of the visible world. His universe is vibrant, filled with color, movement, and rhythm. He is adept at capturing the perishable moment and scene imperishably. His poems are wholesome, strong and overflowing with the deep stir of life—an existential life that does not need to look beyond itself for substance or meaning.

My Will to Live That Has No Paradise

My will to live that has no paradise
Looks downward without seeing what goes on.
Is this the light of evening or of dawn?
My will to live that has no paradise...
Nor can the shadows of a noble grief
Exalt my fortune-favored flesh and breath.
A statue's life, unpopulated death
Without desire's bold cultivation or relief.

A dreamless sleep now quiets and brings shade
To the prodigious realm before my gaze
Reduced to the gray village man has made.
Without a kerchief's absence and reprise
Time passes with its cluster of drab days.
My will to live that has no paradise...

JOHN A. CROW

Soneto

Mi voluntad de ser no tiene cielo;
sólo mira hacia abajo y sin mirada.
¿Luz de la tarde o de la madrugada?
Mi voluntad de ser no tiene cielo.

Ni la penumbra de un hermoso duelo
ennoblece mi carne afortunada.
Vida de estatua, muerte inhabitada
sin la jardinería de un anhelo.

Un dormir sin soñar calla y sombrea
el prodigioso imperio de mis ojos
reducido a los grises de una aldea.

Sin la ausencia presente de un pañuelo
se van los días en pobres manojos.
Mi voluntad de ser no tiene cielo.

José Gorostiza

Mexico, 1901–1973

A professor of Mexican and Spanish American literature, Gorostiza, like Valéry and Rilke, was intensely subjective. He was inspired by the traditional reservoir of popular Spanish poetry, as were Lorca and Alberti in Spain, but he wrote in a deceptively simple style that often had deep philosophical overtones. His poems express a withdrawal from contemporary life and give voice to his country's characteristic cult of death. As his compatriot. Juan José Arreola, once said: "The Mexican is characterized by two things: his love for flowers and his obsession with death."[43] Gorostiza fuses this death-beauty syndrome in his poetry.

43. Juan José Arreola, in a lecture delivered at U.C.L.A., November 18, 1972.

Who Will Buy Me an Orange?

Who will buy me an orange
From the orange cart,
A ripe yellow orange
In the shape of a heart?

The salt of the sea on my lips,
That is all for me!
The ocean's salt in my veins,
As I tasted the sea.

No girl would give me her mouth
For a kiss to keep;
The white stalk of a kiss
Was not mine to reap.

No one asked for my blood
To drink and so
I don't know if it is flowing,
Or has stopped its flow.

As ships are often lost,
Such a fate for me!
As ships and clouds are lost,
I was lost on the sea.

Since nobody asks for it,
I have no heart.
Who will buy me an orange
From the orange cart?

¿Quién me compra una naranja?

¿Quién me compra una naranja
para mi consolación?
Una naranja madura
en forma de corazón.

La sal del mar en los labios
¡ay de mí!
la sal del mar en las venas
y en los labios recogí.

Nadie me diera los suyos
para besar.
La blanda espiga de un beso
yo no la puedo segar.

Nadie pidiera mi sangre
para beber.
Yo mismo no sé si corre
o si deja de correr.

Como se pierden las barcas
¡ay de mí!
como se pierden las nubes
y las barcas, me perdí.

Y pues nadie me lo pide,
ya no tengo corazón.
¿Quién me compra una naranja
para mi consolación?

JOHN A. CROW

Pauses II

The cricket does not sing. It ticks out
The music
Of a star.

It measures
the luminous pauses
With its hourglass.

It traces
The golden orbits
In ethereal desolation.

The good citizen thinks—
Notwithstanding—
A little music box is singing
Among the grass blades.

Pausas II

No canta el grillo. Ritma
la música
de una estrella.

Mide
las pausas luminosas
con su reloj de arena.

Traza
sus órbitas de oro
en la desolación etérea.

La buena gente piensa
—sin embargo—
que canta una cajita
de música en la hierba.

H. R. HAYS

The Bloom Hoists Its Banner

The bloom hoists its banner,
Water, in the pasture,
Oh, what a marketing
Of winged fragrance!

Iza la flor su enseña

Iza la flor su enseña,
agua, en el prado.
¡Oh, qué mercadería
de olor alado!

Oh, what a marketing Of delicate odor! How the breezes Are inflamed by its blushes!	¡Oh, qué mercadería de tenue olor! ¡cómo inflama los aires con su rubor!
What a flood of shouting Makes up the garden! "I, I the heliotrope!" "I, the jasmine."	¡Qué anegado de gritos está el jardín! "¡Yo, el heliotropo, yo!" "¿Yo? El jasmín."
Ah, but the water, What if it has no odor!	Ay, pero el agua, ay, si no huele a nada.
The night has a tree With fruits of amber; Ah, what a complexion The earth has, of emeralds!	Tiene la noche un árbol con frutos de ámbar; tiene una tez la tierra, ay, de esmeraldas.
The blood's pertinacity Goes in scarlet; Sleep goes in indigo; Joy goes golden.	El tesón de la sangre anda de rojo; anda de añil el sueño; la dicha, de oro.
Love has ferocious Hungry purples; But also its grain fields, Also its birds.	Tiene el amor feroces galgos morados; pero también sus mieses, también sus pájaros.
Ah, but the water, What if it shines not at all!	Ay, pero el agua, ay, si no luce a nada.
The taste of light, of cold light, Is the taste of the apple. What fruit of the daybreak Dawning so early!	Sabe a luz, a luz fría, sí, la manzana. ¡Qué amanecida fruta tan de mañana!
How you taste of nightfalls, You, anxiety! How your hummingbird Pecks at your bowels!	¡Qué anochecido sabes, tú, sinsabor! ¡cómo pica en la entraña tu picaflor!
Death tastes of earth, Anguish of bile, This dying in drops I taste like honey.	Sabe la muerte a tierra, la angustia a hiel. Este morir a gotas me sabe a miel.
Ah, but the water, What if the water is tasteless!	Ay, pero el agua, ay, si no sabe a nada.
(Dance)	(Baile)
Poor little thing of water, Alas, it has nothing, Alas for love drowning, Alas, in a glass of water.	Pobrecilla del agua, ay, que no tiene nada, ay, amor, que se ahoga, ay, en un vaso de agua.

H. R. HAYS

Pablo Neruda (pseudonym of Neftalí Ricardo Reyes Basualto)
Chile, 1904–1973

Neruda was the outstanding Spanish American poet of this century, and his being awarded the Nobel Prize for literature in 1971 was acclaimed by all who knew his work. He is not always an easy poet to understand, and some of his writing is outright propaganda, for Neruda was an enthusiastic Communist and occasionally allowed his political bias to overwhelm his aesthetic judgment. On the other hand, in his best poetry Neruda is incomparable, a Latin Walt Whitman.

The critic Amado Alonso stated the key to Neruda's poetic universe in these words: "Instead of the traditional poetic procedure, which describes a reality and suggests its poetic sense between the lines, poets like Neruda describe the poetic sense and nebulously suggest to what reality it refers."[44] Neruda is the prophet of disintegration; he sees things, institutions, people, the whole universe, as already disintegrated. He places the traditionally poetic alongside the obviously nonpoetic in his verses. His adjectives destroy their nouns; he uses oxymorons frequently.

In the beginning and at the end of his life, his poetry is more simple. Only a few months before his death he said, "It took a great effort for me to abandon obscurity for clarity, because obscurity in language had become among us the privilege of the literary class, and class prejudice had condemned popular expression . . . but I have decided that each day I shall be more simple in my new poems."

In much of his poetry Neruda appears to reject the world of objective reality, and his jumble of objects is as confusing as a surrealist painting. But what he is trying to do is to find and to sing about that point at which interior reality and exterior reality converge, and fantasy and imagination merge with the objective visible world. He repeatedly uses certain symbolic words. For example, he has stated that for him "the dove is the most complete expression of life, because of its formal perfection."[45] By extension, *dove* may also mean *love*. Therefore, if the word *dove* is modified by an adjective—black or yellow, for example—the poet will mean a black or a yellow life or love, that is, depressed, frayed, wasted, lamented, mourned.

The splendid qualities of life are indicated by such words as *roses, rosebushes, butterflies, bees, fish, salt, wine, swords*. The elemental aspect of the world is suggested by such words as *stone, earth, wool, fire, leather*. The artificial, opposing aspect of the world is suggested by *tailor, clothes, notaries, establishments*. The word *salt* often indicates the essence of things, but it may suggest the acid that eats things away. Neruda will also frequently use images like "wet flames," or "drenched stars." He explains that his home, Temuco, in the southern region of Chile, is a place where the rain envelops a person day after day implacably, so he became habituated to seeing everything, even fire, as enveloped by water.

Ars Poetica

Somewhere between shadow and space, between
  garrisons and virgins,
with a strangeness of soul and funeral dreams,
suddenly pale, the brow enshrouded
with a widower's fury at each new day of life,
ah, for all the unseen waters that fall upon my slumber
and for every fleeting sound that I capture, trembling,
I have the same absent thirst, the same feverish chill.
Hearing is born, a nameless dread
like a ghost advancing to the rhythm of the heart,
And in a deep dry hull of fixed proportion
like an humiliated lackey, like a tarnished mirror,
like an old brooch with sockets where the gems are
  missing,
or the smell of a silent house where the tenants stumble in

Arte poética

Entre sombra y espacio, entre guarniciones y doncellas,
dotado de corazón singular y sueños funestos,
precipitadamente pálido, marchito en la frente,
y con luto de viudo furioso por cada día de vida,
ay para cada agua invisible que bebo soñolientamente,
y de todo sonido que acojo temblando,
tengo la misma sed ausente y la misma fiebre fría,
un oído que nace, una angustia indirecta,
como si llegaran ladrones o fantasmas,
y en una cáscara de extensión fija y profunda,
como un camarero humillado, como una campana un
  poco ronca,
como un espejo viejo, como un olor de casa sola
en la que los huéspedes entran de noche perdidamente
  ebrios,

---

44. Amado Alonso, *Poesía y estilo de Pablo Neruda* (Buenos Aires: Sudaméricana, 1951), 72.
45. *Ibid.*, 127.

at night hopelessly drunk,
and the odor of old clothes strewn around, and an
  absence of flowers,
or perhaps differently put, even less melancholy—,
but suddenly truth, the wind that rhythmically lashes my
  chest,
nights of infinite substance that cave in on me where I lie,
the clamor of a day ablaze with sacrifice,
they look for the prophetic in me with haunted eyes
and a torrent of objects that seek incarnate echoes,
and a relentless pounding, and a muddled name.

KATHARINE E. STRATHDEE

y hay un olor de ropa tirada al suelo, y una ausencia de
  flores,
posiblemente de otro modo aun menos melancólico,
pero, la verdad, de pronto, el viento que azota mi pecho,
las noches de substancia infinita caídas en mi dormitorio,
el ruido de un día que arde con sacrificio,
me piden lo profético que hay en mí, con melancolía,
y un golpe de objetos que llaman sin ser respondidos
hay, y un movimiento sin tregua, y un nombre confuso.

Every Day You Play

Every day you play with the light of the universe.
Subtle visitor, you arrive in the flower and the water.
You are more than this white head that I hold tightly
as a cluster of fruit, every day, between my hands.

You are like nobody since I love you.
Let me spread you out among the yellow garlands.
Who writes your name in letters of smoke among the stars
  of the south?
Oh let me remember you as you were before you existed.

Suddenly the wind howls and bangs at my shut window.
The sky is a net crammed with shadowy fish.
Here all the winds let go sooner or later, all of them.
The rain takes off her clothes.

The birds go by, fleeing.
The wind. The wind.
I can contend only against the power of men.
The storm whirls dark leaves
and turns loose all the boats that were moored last night
  to the sky.

You are here. Oh, you do not run away.
You will answer me to the last cry.
Cling to me as though you were frightened.
Even so, at one time a strange shadow ran through your
  eyes.

Now, now too, little one, you bring me honeysuckle,
and even your breasts smell of it.
While the sad wind goes slaughtering butterflies
I love you, and my happiness bites the plum of your
  mouth.

How you must have suffered getting accustomed to me,
my savage, solitary soul, my name that sends them all
  running.
So many times we have seen the morning star burn,
  kissing our eyes,
and over our heads the grey light unwind in turning fans.

My words rained over you, stroking you.
A long time I have loved the sunned mother-of-pearl of
  your body.

Juegas todos los días

Juegas todos los días con la luz del universo.
Sutil visitadora, llegas en la flor y en el agua.
Eres más que esta blanca cabecita que aprieto
como un racimo entre mis manos cada día.

A nadie te pareces desde que yo te amo.
Déjame tenderte entre guirnaldas amarillas.
¿Quién escribe tu nombre con letras de humo entre
  las estrellas del sur?
Ah déjame recordarte cómo eras entonces, cuando
  aún no existías.

De pronto el viento aúlla y golpea mi ventana
  cerrada.
El cielo es una red cuajada de peces sombríos.
Aquí vienen a dar godos los vientos, todos.
Se desviste la lluvia.

Pasan huyendo los pájaros.
El viento. El viento.
Yo sólo puedo luchar contra la fuerza de los hombres.
El temporal arremolina hojas oscuras
y suelta toda las barcas que anoche amarraron al
  cielo.

Tú estás aquí. Ah tú no huyes.
Tú me responderás hasta el último grito.
Ovíllate a mi lado como si tuvieras miedo.
Sin embargo alguna vez corrió una sombra extraña
  por tus ojos.

Ahora, ahora también, pequeña, me traes madreselvas,
y tienes hasta los senos perfumados,
meintras el viento triste galopa matando mariposas
yo te amo, y mi alegría muerde tu boca de ciruela.

Cuánto te habrá dolido acostumbrarte a mí,
a mi alma sola y salvaje, a mi nombre que todos
  ahuyentan.
Hemos visto arder tantas veces el lucero besándonos los
  ojos
y sobre nuestras cabezas destorcerse los crepúsculos en
  abanicos girantes.

Mis palabras llovieron sobre ti acariciándote.

I go so far as to think that you own the universe.
I will bring you happy flowers from the mountains,
   bluebells,
dark hazels, and rustic baskets of kisses.
I want
to do with you what the spring does with the cherry trees.

W. S. MERWIN

Amé desde hace tiempo tu cuerpo de nácar soleado.
Hasta te creo dueña del universo.
Te traeré de las montañas flores alegres, copihues,
avellanas oscuras, y cestas silvestres de besos.
Quiero hacer contigo
lo que la primavera hace con los cerezos.

Your Breast Is Enough

Your breast is enough for my heart,
and my wings for your freedom.
What was sleeping above your soul will rise
out of my mouth to heaven.

In you is the illusion of each day.
You arrive like the dew to the cupped flowers.
You undermine the horizon with your absence.
Eternally in flight like the wave.

I have said that you sang in the wind
like the pines and like the masts.
Like them you are tall and taciturn,
and you are sad, all at once, like a voyage.

You gather things to you like an old road.
You are peopled with echoes and nostalgic voices.
I awoke and at times birds fled and migrated
that had been sleeping in your soul.

W. S. MERWIN

Para mi corazón

Para mi corazón basta tu pecho,
para tu libertad bastan mis alas.
Desde mi boca llegará hasta el cielo
lo que estaba dormido sobre tu alma.

Es en ti la ilusión de cada día.
Llegas como el rocío a las corolas.
Socavas el horizonte con tu ausencia.
Eternamente en fuga como la ola.

He dicho que cantabas en el viento
como los pinos y como los mástiles.
Como ellos eres alta y taciturna.
Y entristeces de pronto, como un viaje.

Acogedora como un viejo camino.
Te pueblan ecos y voces nostálgicas.
Yo desperté y a veces emigran y huyen
pájaros que dormían en tu alma.

Ode with a Lament

Oh, girl among the roses, oh pressure of doves,
Oh garrison of fishes and rosebuds,
Your soul is a bottle of thirsting salt,
And a bell filled with grapes is your skin.

Unfortunately, I have only fingernails to give you,
Or eyelashes, or melted pianos,
Or dreams that gush bubbling from my heart,
Dust-covered dreams that race like black horsemen,
Dreams filled with high speeds and great misfortunes.

I can only love you with kisses and poppies,
And with garlands drenched in the rain,
While staring at ashen horses and stray yellow dogs.

I can only love you with the waves at my back,
Between clouds of sulphur and preoccupied waters
Swimming against the cemeteries that flow in certain
   rivers,
With wet waves growing over sad graves of plaster,
Swimming over submerged hearts
And pale catalogues of unburied children.

There is much death, many funereal happenings,
In my unsheltered passions and desolate kisses

Oda con un lamento

Oh niña entre las rosas, oh presión de palomas,
oh presidio de peces y rosales,
tu alma es una botella llena de sal sedienta
y una campana llena de uvas es tu piel.

Por desgracia no tengo para darte sino uñas
o pestañas, o pianos derretidos,
o sueños que salen de mi corazón a borbotones,
polvorientos sueños que corren como jinetes negros,
sueños llenos de velocidades y desgracias.

Sólo puedo quererte con besos y amapolas,
con guirnaldas mojadas por la lluvia,
mirando cenicientos caballos y perros amarillos.

Sólo puedo quererte con olas a la espalda,
entre vagos golpes de azufre y aguas ensimismadas,
nadando en contra de los cementerios que corren en
   ciertos ríos
con pasto mojado creciendo sobre las tristes tumbas de
   yeso,
nadando a través de corazones sumergidos
y pálidas planillas de niños insepultos.

Hay mucha muerte, muchos acontecimientos funerarios

There is a water that falls on my head
While my hair is growing,
A water like time, a black unleashed spurt of water
With the voice of night, with a bird-cry,
In the rain, with an endless shadow
Of wet wings that protect my bones as I dress,
While interminably I examine myself in mirrors and in
  windows,
I hear someone behind me, sobbing my name,
In a sad voice eroded by time.

You are standing on the earth, filled
With sharp teeth and lightning flashes,
You generate kisses and kill the ants,
You sob with well-being, with onions, with bees,
With your first primer burning.
You are like a blue and green sword
And at each touch you ripple like a river.

Come to my soul, dressed in white, like a handful
Of blood-red roses and cups of ashes,
Come with an apple and a horse,
Becuase a dark room and a broken candelabra are there
And twisted chairs waiting for the winter,
And a dead dove, with a number.

JOHN A. CROW

There Is No Oblivion (Sonata)

If you ask me where I have been
I must say "It so happens."
I must speak of the ground darkened by stones,
of the river that destroys itself as it endures:
I know only the things that birds lose,
the sea left behind, or my sister crying.
Why so many places, why does one day
join with another? Why does a black night
gather in the mouth? Why dead people?

If you ask me where I come from, I must talk with broken
  things,
with utensils that are overly bitter,
with great beasts often rotted
and with my agonizing heart.

Those which have crossed are not memories
nor is the yellow dove that sleeps in oblivion,
but tear-drenched faces,
fingers at the throat,
and what is falling from the leaves:
the darkness of a day gone by,
of a day that has fed our sad blood.
Here are violets, swallows.
everything that we like and that appears
in sweet long cards
where time and sweetness stroll.

But let us not penetrate beyond those teeth,
let us not bite the shells gathered by silence,

en mis desamparadas pasiones y desolados besos,
hay el agua que cae en mi cabeza,
mientras crece mi pelo,
un agua como el tiempo, un agua negra desencadenada,
con una voz nocturna, con un grito
de pájaro en la lluvia, como una interminable
sombra de ala mojada que protege mis huesos,
mientras me visto, mientras
interminablemente me miro en los espejos y en los
  vidrios,
oigo que alguien me sigue llamándome a sollozos
con una triste voz podrida por el tiempo.

Tú estás de pie sobre la tierra, llena
de dientes y relámpagos.
Tú propagas los besos y matas las hormigas.
Tú lloras de salud, de cebolla, de abeja,
de abecedario ardiendo.
Tú eres como una espada azul y verde
y ondulas al tocarte, como un río.

Ven a mi alma vestida de blanco, como un ramo
de ensangrentadas rosas y copas de cenizas,
ven con una manzana y un caballo,
porque allí hay una sala oscura y un candelabro roto,
unas sillas torcidas que esperan el invierno,
y una paloma muerta, con un número.

No hay olvido

Si me preguntáis en dónde he estado
debo decir "Sucede."
Debo de hablar del suelo que oscurecen las piedras,
del río que durando se destruye:
no sé sino las cosas que los pájaros pierden,
el mar dejado atrás, o mi hermana llorando.
¿Por qué tantas regiones, por qué un día
se junta con un día? ¿Por qué una negra noche
se acumula en la boca? ¿Por qué muertos?

Si me preguntáis de dónde vengo, tengo que conversar
  con cosas rotas,
con utensilios demasiado amargos,
con grandes bestias a menudo podridas
y con mi acongojado corazón.

No son recuerdos los que se han cruzado
ni es la paloma amarillenta que duerme en el olvido,
sino caras con lágrimas,
dedos en la garganta,
y lo que se desploma de las hojas:
la oscuridad de un día transcurrido,
de un día alimentado con nuestra triste sangre.

He aquí violetas, golondrinas,
todo cuanto nos gusta y aparece
en las dulces tarjetas de larga cola
por donde se pasean el tiempo y la dulzura.

Pero no penetremos más allá de esos dientes,
no mordamos las cáscaras que el silencio acumula,

because I do not know what to answer:
there are so many dead people,
and so many sea walls that the red sun split
and so many heads that beat against ships,
and so many hands that have cupped kisses,
and so many things that I want to forget.

JOHN A. CROW

porque no sé qué contestar:
hay tantos muertos,
y tantos malecones que el sol rojo partía
y tantas cabezas que golpean los buques,
y tantas manos que han encerrado besos,
y tantas cosas que quiero olvidar.

Born in the Woods

When rice withdraws from earth
the grains of its flour,
when wheat hardens its little flanks and lifts up
    its thousand-handed face,
I hasten to the arbor where man and woman are linked
to touch the innumerable sea
of what endures.

I am not brother of the tool carried on the tide
as if in a cradle of aggressive pearl:
I do not tremble in the region of dying despoliation,
I do not wake to the thump of the darkness frightened
by the raucous clapper of the sudden bell,
I can not be, I am not the passenger
beneath whose shoes throb the last redoubts of the wind
and the rigid waves of time return to die.

I bear in my hand the dove that sleeps reclining on the
    seed
and in its thick ferment of lime and blood
lives August,
lives the month extracted from its deep goblet:
with my hand I surround the new shadow of the growing
    wing:
the root and the feather that tomorrow will form the
    thicket.

It never abates, neither next to the iron-handed balcony,
nor in the sea winter of the abandoned ones, nor in
    my slow step,
the immense swelling of the drop, or the eyelid that wants
    to be opened:
because I was born to be born, to cut off the passage
of everything that approaches, of everything that beats
    on my breast like a new
trembling heart.

Lives lying next to my costume like parallel doves,
or contained in my own existence and in my disordered
    sound
to be again, to seize the naked air of the leaf
and the moist birth of the earth in the garland:
    how long
must I return and be, how long does the fragrance
of the most buried flowers, of the waves most pounded
on the high rocks, keep in me its homeland
to be again fury and perfume?

How long does the hand of the woods in the rain

Naciendo en los bosques

Cuando el arroz retira de la tierra
los granos de su harina,
cuando el trigo endurece sus pequeñas caderas y levanta
    su rostro de mil manos,
a la enramada donde la mujer y el hombre se enlazan
    acudo,
para tocar el mar innumerable
de lo que continúa.

Yo no soy hermano del utensilio llevado en la marea
como en una cuna de nácar combatido:
no tiemblo en la comarca de los agonizantes despojos,
no despierto en el golpe de las tinieblas asustadas
por el ronco pecíolo de la campana repentina,
no puedo ser, no soy el pasajero
bajo cuyos zapatos los últimos reductos del viento
    palpitan
y rígidas retornan las olas del tiempo a morir.

Llevo en mi mano la paloma que duerme reclinada en la
    semilla
y en su fermento espeso de cal y sangre
vive Agosto,
vive el mes extraído de su copa profunda:
con mi mano rodeo la nueva sombra del ala que crece:
la raíz y la pluma que mañana formarán la espesura.

Nunca declina, ni junto al balcón de manos de hierro,
ni en el invierno marítimo de los abandonados, ni en mi
    paso tardío,
el crecimiento inmenso de la gota, ni el párpado que
    quiere ser abierto:
porque para nacer he nacido, para encerrar el paso
de cuanto se aproxima, de cuanto a mi pecho golpea
    como un nuevo
corazón tembloroso.

Vidas recostadas junto a mi traje como palomas paralelas,
o contenidas en mi propia existencia y en mi desordenado
    sonido
para volver a ser, para incautar el aire desnudo de la hoja
y el nacimiento húmedo de la tierra en la guirnalda: hasta
    cuándo
debo volver y ser, hasta cuándo el olor
de las más enterradas flores, de las olas más trituradas.
sobre las altas piedras, guarda en mí su patria
para volver a ser furia y perfume?

Hasta cuándo la mano del bosque en la lluvia

bring me close with all its needles
to weave the lofty kisses of the foliage?
Again
I hear approach like fire in smoke,
spring up from earthly ash,
light filled with petals, and pushing earth away
in a river of flowerheads the sun reaches my mouth
like an old buried tear that becomes seed again.

DONALD D. WALSH

Barcarole

If only you would touch my heart,
if only you would put your mouth on my heart,
your delicate mouth, your teeth,
if you would put your tongue like a red arrow
there where my dusty heart beats,
if you would blow on my heart, near the sea, weeping,
it would sound with a dark noise, with the sound of
    sleepy train wheels,
like wavering waters,
like a leafy autumn,
like blood,
with a noise of moist flames burning the sky,
dreaming like dreams or branches or rains,
or foghorns in a dreary port,
if you would blow on my heart, near the sea,
like a white ghost,
at the edge of the foam,
in the midst of the wind,
like an unchained ghost, at the edge of the sea, weeping.

Like an extended absence, like a sudden bell,
the sea spreads the sound of the heart,
raining, at nightfall, on a lonely coast:
night doubtless falls,
and its mournful shipwrecked-banner blue
peoples itself with planets of hoarse silver.

And the heart sounds like a sour snail,
call, oh sea, oh lament, oh melted fright
scattered in misfortunes and rickety waves:
from resonance the sea reveals
its recumbent shadows, its green poppies.

If you suddenly existed, on a gloomy coast,
surrounded by the dead day,
facing a new night,
filled with waves,
and if you blew on my heart cold with fear,
if you blew on its flaming dove movement,
its black bloody syllables would sound,
its incessant red waters would swell,
and it would sound, sound of shadows,
sound like death,
it would call like a tube filled with wind or weeping,
or a bottle squirting fright in spurts.

Barcarola

Si solamente me tocaras el corazón,
si solamente pusieras tu boca en mi corazón,
tu fina boca, tus dientes,
si pusieras tu lengua como una flecha roja
allí donde mi corazón polvoriento golpea,
si soplaras en mi corazón, cerca del mar, llorando,
sonaría con un ruido oscuro, con sonido de ruedas de tren
    con sueño,
como aguas vacilantes,
como el otoño en hojas,
como sangre,
con un ruido de llamas húmedas quemando el cielo,
soñando como sueños o ramas o lluvias,
o bocinas de puerto triste,
si tú soplaras en mi corazón, cerca del mar,
como un fantasma blanco,
al borde de la espuma,
en mitad del viento,
como un fantasma desencadenado, a la orilla del mar,
    llorando.

Como ausencia extendida, como campana súbita,
el mar reparte el sonido del corazón,
lloviendo, atardeciendo, en una costa sola:
la noche cae sin duda,
y su lúgubre azul de estandarte en naufragio
se puebla de planetas de plata enronquecida.

Y suena el corazón como un caracol agrio,
llama, oh mar, oh lamento, oh derretido espanto
esparcido en desgracias y olas desvencijadas:
de lo sonoro el mar acusa
sus sombras recostadas, sus amapolas verdes.

Si existieras de pronto, en una costa lúgubre,
rodeada por el día muerto,
frente a una nueva noche,
llena de olas,
y soplaras en mi corazón de miedo frío,
soplaras en la sangre sola de mi corazón,
soplaras en su movimiento de paloma con llamas,
sonarían sus negras sílabas de sangre,
crecerían sus incesantes aguas rojas,
y sonaría, sonaría a sombras,
sonaría como la muerte,

So it is, and the lightning would cover your tresses
and the rain would enter through your open eyes
to prepare the weeping that you silently enclose,
and the black wings of the sea would wheel around
you, with great claws, and croakings, and flights.

Do you want to be the solitary ghost that near the sea
plays upon its sad and sterile instrument?
If only you would call,
its prolonged sound, its malevolent whistle,
its arrangement of wounded waves,
someone would perhaps come,
someone would come.
from the peaks of the islands, from the red depths of the
   sea,
someone would come, someone would come.

Somebody would come; play furiously,
let it sound like the siren of a broken boat,
like a lament,
like a whinny in the midst of the foam and the blood,
like a ferocious water gnashing and echoing.

In the sea season
its snail of shadow circles like a shout,
the sea birds belittle it and fly away,
its roll call of sounds, its mournful crosspieces,
rise on the shore of the solitary sea.

DONALD D. WALSH

Autumn Returns

A day in mourning falls from the bells
like a trembling vague-widow cloth,
it is a color, a dream
of cherries buried in the earth,
it is a tail of smoke that restlessly arrives
to change the color of the water and the kisses.

I do not know if I make myself clear: when from on high
night approaches, when the solitary poet
at the window hears autumn's steed running
and the leaves of trampled fear rustle in his arteries,
there is something over the sky, like the tongue of a thick
ox, something in the doubt of the sky and the
   atmosphere.

Things return to their places,
the indispensable lawyer, the hands, the olive oil,
the bottles,
all the traces of life: the beds, above all,
are filled with a bloody liquid,
people deposit their confidences in sordid ears,
assassins go down stairs,
it is not this, however, but the old gallop,
the horse of the old autumn that trembles and endures.
The horse of the old autum has a red beard
and the foam of fear covers its cheeks

llamaría como un tubo lleno de viento o llanto,
o una botella echando espanto a borbotones.

Así es, y los relámpagos cubrirían tus trenzas
y la lluvia entraría por tus ojos abiertos
a preparar el llanto que sordamente encierras,
y las alas negras del mar girarían en torno
de tí, con grandes garras, y graznidos, y vuelos.

Quieres ser el fantasma que sople, solitario,
cerca del mar su estéril, triste instrumento?
Si solamente llamaras,
su prolongado son, su maléfico pito,
su orden de olas heridas,
alguien vendría acaso,
alguien vendría,
desde las cimas de las islas, desde el fondo rojo del mar,
alguien vendría, alguien vendría.

Alguien vendría, sopla con furia,
que suene como sirena de barco roto,
como lamento,
como un relincho en medio de la espuma y la sangre,
como un agua feroz mordiéndose y sonando.

En la estación marina
su caracol de sombra circula como un grito,
los pájaros del mar lo desestiman y huyen,
sus listas de sonido, sus lúgubres barrotes
se levantan a orillas del océano solo.

Vuelve el otoño

Un enlutado día cae de las campanas
como una temblorosa tela de vaga viuda,
es un color, un sueño
de cerezas hundidas en la tierra,
es una cola de humo que llega sin descanso
a cambiar el color del agua y de los besos.

No sé si se me entiende: cuando desde lo alto
se avecina la noche, cuando el solitario poeta
a la ventana oye correr el corcel del otoño
y las hojas del miedo pisoteado crujen en sus arterias,
hay algo sobre el cielo, como lengua de buey
espeso, algo en la duda del cielo y de la atmósfera.

Vuelven las cosas a su sitio,
el abogado indispensable, las manos, el aceite,
las botellas,
todos los indicios de la vida: las camas, sobre todo,
están llenas de un líquido sangriento,
la gente deposita sus confianzas en sórdidas orejas,
los asesinos bajan escaleras,
pero no es esto, sino el viejo galope,
el caballo del viejo otoño que tiembla y dura.

El caballo del viejo otoño tiene la barba roja
y la espuma del miedo le cubre las mejillas

and the air that follows it is shaped like an ocean
and a perfume of vague buried putrefaction.

Every day down from the sky comes an ashen color
that doves must spread over the earth:
the cord that forgetfulness and weeping weave,
time that has slept long years within the bells,
everything,
the old tattered suits, the women who see snow coming,
the black poppies that no one can look at without dying,
everything falls into the hands that I lift
in the midst of the rain.

DONALD D. WALSH

y el aire que le sigue tiene forma de océano
y perfume de vaga podredumbre enterrada.

Todos los días baja del cielo un color ceniciento
que las palomas deben repartir por la tierra:
la cuerda que el olvido y las lágrimas tejen,
el tiempo que ha dormido largos años dentro de las
    campanas,
todo,
los viejos trajes mordidos, las mujeres que ven venir la
    nieve,
las amapolas negras que nadie puede contemplar sin
    morir,
todo cae a las manos que levanto
en medio de la lluvia.

Jorge Guillén
Spain, 1893–

Born in Valladolid in the heartland of Castile, Guillén has lived successively in Switzerland, Germany, France, England, the United States. He has been a professor at Oxford University and in several universities in the United States. His residence in France extended over five years (1917–1923); he married a French woman, became fascinated with French poetry, translated Valéry, Claudel, and Supervielle into Spanish.

Gullién's poetry has an intangible and elusive quality that often makes it difficult to analyze but never difficult to feel. It is this spontaneous and intuitive response that Guillén wished to evoke. "Pure poetry," he once wrote, "is all that is left in the poem after the elimination of everything that is not poetry. *Pure* is equal to *simple*, chemically speaking."[46] Guillén is the preeminent "pure poet." He stands apart from his creations and has been regarded by some as cold. He polishes and repolishes his poem as a lapidary does his stones. His imagery is often abstract, but he catches the beauty of the visible world and the precious quality of life. His poems are songs of affirmation "in praise of the oneness of all being," as he has stated. "Man affirms himself in affirming Creation; he shares in a universal value, though his part will always be the lesser." Every object is dense with its own being, and reality's essence exists "even in the humblest particle of our planet."[47]

Poplars with River

Facing the gray white hill
At river level, the road
Anxiously perceives poplars
The profile of rain.

Beside the trembling leaves
Someone, never by himself,
Speaks alone to the river.
Poplars of wind and poetry?

Gently the river strings out
Its playfulness curve after curve
While in a slight tremor the poplars
Are sketched on the water.

Álamos con río

Frente al blanco gris del cerro,
a par del río, la ruta
divisa con ansiedad
álamos, perfil de lluvia.

Junto a las trémulas hojas
alguien, solitario nunca,
habla a solas con el río.
¿Álamos de brisa y musa?

Mansamente el río traza
su recreo curva a curva
mientras en leve temblor
los álamos se dibujas,

---

46. Diego (ed.), *Poesía española*, 195.
47. Norman Thomas di Giovanni (ed.), *Jorge Guillén, Cántico: A Selection* (Boston: Little, Brown, 1965), 8.

And as green as the river
Body after body of leaves they lull
The one who is lucky enough to hear
Poplars that are almost music.

Lucky upon the bank
Is the man who follows the river
That sharpens the water's company
And the poplars' flight.

JOHN A. CROW

y tan verdes como el río
follaje a follaje arrullan
al dichoso de escuchar
álamos de casi música.

¡Dichoso por la ribera
quien sigue el río que aguza
la compañía en el agua,
en los álamos la fuga!

Advent

Oh, moon! So many Aprils!
How wide and sweet the air!
All that I have lost
Returns with the winging birds.

Yes, with the little birds
That make at dawn a chorus
Of endless twittering,
Their unpremeditated art.

The moon is very near,
Silent and still the air.
The man I used to be waits for me
Beneath these thoughts.

At the crest of my pain
The nightingale will sing;
There are red embers
Between the sky and its gold.

The time I have lost,
Is it all gone? The hand
Disposes, like a fickle god,
Of this ageless moon.

JOHN A. CROW

Advenimiento

¡Oh luna! ¡Cuánto abril!
¡Qué vasto y dulce el aire!
Todo lo que perdí
volverá con las aves.

Sí, con las avecillas
que en coro de alborada
pían y pían, pían
sin designio de gracia.

La luna está muy cerca,
quieta en el aire nuestro.
El que yo fui me espera
bajo mis pensamientos.

Cantará el ruiseñor
en la cima del ansia.
¡Arrebol, arrebol
entre el cielo y las auras!

¿Y se perdió aquel tiempo
que yo perdí? La mano
dispone, dios ligero,
de esta luna sin año.

Nude

Whites, red roses. Barely a vein of blue.
  Remote, in the mind's eyes.
Points of growing light suggest
  Something hidden in the shadow.

Then color, struggling against the dark
  Falls into a pattern.
In the summer of the house
  A recumbent form emerges.

The outline becomes clearer
  In its pure stillness.
As sharp edges overcome and cut
  Through all uncertainty.

The flesh is naked. Its substance
  Resolves itself in repose.
One thing stands out: the marvelous
  Unfolding of a presence.

Desnudo

Blancos, rosas. Azules casi en veta,
  retraídos, mentales.
Puntos de luz latente dan señales
  de una sombra secreta.

Pero el color, infiel a la penumbra,
  se consolida en masa.
Yacente en el verano de la casa,
  una forma se alumbra.

Claridad aguzada entre perfiles,
  de tan puros tranquilos,
que cortan y aniquilan con sus filos
  las confusiones viles.

Desnuda está la carne. Su evidencia
  se resuelve en reposo.
Monotonía justa, prodigioso
  colmo de la presencia.

The sudden overpowering fullness
    Of a woman's body!
No trace of voice or flower. To what end?
    Oh absolute Present!

JOHN A. CROW

¡Plenitud inmediata, sin ambiente,
    del cuerpo femenino!
Ningún primor: ni voz ni flor. ¿Destino?
    ¡Oh absoluto Presente!

Child

Clear as running water,
Swirls of the blooming rose
Mysteries of snow:
Dawn and beach in a seashell.

Ever-going machine
Joyfulness of the moon
With the strength of patience:
Salt of the brutal wave.

Moment without history,
Stubbornly overfilled
With myths among other things:
The lone sea and its birds.

Grace that is priceless,
Grace unadorned, forever
Total in that look of a child:
The sea, the moment's unity.

Poet of purest games
Without break or interval,
Divine, without wisdom:
The sea, the untouched sea!

JOHN A. CROW

Niño

Claridad de corriente,
círculos de la rosa,
enigmas de la nieve:
aurora y playa en conchas.

Máquina turbulenta.
alegría de luna
con vigor de paciencia:
sal de la onda bruta.

Instante sin historia,
tercamente colmado
de mitos entre cosas:
mar sólo con sus pájaros.

Si rica tanta gracia,
tan sólo gracia, siempre
total en la mirada:
mar, unidad presente.

Poeta de los juegos
puros sin intervalos,
divino, sin ingenio:
¡el mar, el mar intacto!

Invocation

Be silent, Smile at me,
Love, with your naked mouth.

Waiting—as a soul
Unfolding its own shape—
Hovers over the lips,
Decides, and falls away.
    I desire to fathom,
    Fathom again—a proud,
    Inflaming tenderness—
    There in your coolness, in your spiraling
      ways.

With a kiss, below the kiss,
You I seek, and I beg all of you,
Basic, perfect, naked,
Radiant, comforting.
    O joy, even to the utmost hidden
    Abandonment of the spirit,
    Joy through a fullness
    That looks eternity in the face.

Be silent. Smile at me,
Love, with your naked mouth.

BARBARA HOWES

Invocación

Sabes callar. Me sonríe,
amor, desnuda tu boca.

Una espera—como un alma
que desenvuelve su forma—
sobre los labios ondula,
se determina, se aploma.
    Yo quiero profundizar,
    profundizar—imperiosa,
    encarnizada ternura—
    en tu frescor, en tus conchas.

Con el beso, bajo el beso
te busco, te imploro toda,
esencial, feliz, desnuda,
radiante, consoladora.
    Consuelo hasta el más recóndito
    desampara de la sombra,
    consuelo por plenitud
    que a la eternidad afronta.

Sabes callar. Me sonríe,
amor, desnuda tu boca.

Waking

Nothingness... Tenuous shadow...
And all at once... What is it? Who?

Poise after vertigo,
Poise suddenly there in the shambles
That sought to disclaim itself so,
Peacefully sleeping.

Self-denying. Denied, rather?
There breaks forth, in a sunburst of memory,
Upright on that instant
A fissure that opens on vacancy.
A cavern, perhaps?
A cavern... But where?
A chaos is coming to be, not yet here.
It plunges, almost to drowning it plunges. But
    when—?

And an agony, that bolt of the morning, lights
Oblivion's wilderness way.
While the astonished one plunges downward—and
    ceases to plunge—

And as I. Myself at this moment. Myself in this place.
I awaken. I am. I exist.
Once again, O divine adaptation!

BEN BELITT

Despertar

Nada. Tinieblas muelles.
Y de un golpe... ¿Qué, quién?

Restauración por vértigo,
brusca restauración en aquel bulto
que estaba así negándose,
dulcemente dormido.

Negándose. ¿Negado?
Por la memoria alboreada irrumpe,
vertical y de súbito,
una abertura hacia el vacío.
¿Es una sima?
Sima... ¿De dónde?
Aquel bulto se siente ser, no está.
Casi ahogándose cae, cae. ¿Cuándo?

Y una angustia, relámpago en albor,
ilumina el olvido y su desierto.
El atónito cae, se detiene.

Yo. Yo ahora. Yo aquí.
Despertar, ser, estar:
otra vez el ajuste prodigioso.

Dámaso Alonso

Spain, 1898–

Dámaso Alonso is one of the most respected scholars in Spain in this century. His work on Góngora was a revelation in the understanding of that difficult poet, and his book on San Juan de la Cruz sheds similar light on the work of that lyrical mystic. Dámaso was also the editor of an excellent anthology of medieval Spanish poetry and of another anthology of the popular poetry of Spain. He was a noted professor and for many years was closely associated with the Center of Historic Studies, while at the same time serving as head of the Residence for Students (*Residencia de Estudiantes*), where so many hundreds of foreign students went to take classes under the finest professors of Spain. He also taught Spanish literature in several foreign universities: Cambridge, Oxford, Columbia, Stanford, Berlin, Harvard. The weight of his scholarship has too often caused his own poetry to be overlooked, but many of Dámaso's poems are polished gems of the highest quality. Dámaso was not greatly interested in becoming identified with the new vanguarist currents but developed his own pungent, sharply honed style.

When asked by Gerardo Diego to give his definition of poetry, Dámaso responded: "Poetry is a fervor and a clarity. A fervor, a firm and intimate desire for union with the great heart of the world and the first cause. And a clarity through which the world itself is understood in an intense and unusual way."[48]

48. Diego (ed.), *Poesía española*, 218.

What Was She Like?

What was she like. O Lord, what
was she like?   Juan R. Jiménez

The door was open.
                    She came softly to me
Neither matter nor spirit. She brought the gentle sway
Of a ship that sails the ocean gracefully,
And the early light of a clear and sunlit day.
She was not rhythm, nor harmony, nor the play
Of color. The heart knows but cannot enfold her,
And what she then was like it could not say,
Because she is not form; there is no form to hold her.

Tongue, mortal clay, an artist's brush inept,
Intact, elusive flower, ineffable concept
In the clear starlit hours of my wedding night.
Singing in muted tones, with soft accent,
Feeling, shadow, and fortuitous accident,
She fills my waiting heart with magic light.

JOHN A. CROW

¿Cómo era?

¿Cómo era, Dios mío, cómo era?
                    Juan R. Jiménez

La puerta, franca.

                    Vino queda y suave.
Ni materia ni espíritu. Traía
una ligera inclinación de nave
y una luz matinal de claro día.

No era de ritmo, no era de armonía
ni de color. El corazón la sabe,
pero decir cómo era no podría
porque no es forma ni en la forma cabe.

Lengua, barro mortal, cincel inepto,
deja la flor intacta del concepto
en esta clara noche de mi boda,

y canta mansamente, humildemente,
la sensación, la sombra, el accidente,
mientras Ella me llena el alma toda!

Examples

The weathervane, and the locust.
But also the mill and the ant.

Grind your bread, mill, grind.
Spin out, weathervane, poetry.

What Martha made with her hands
Mary was dreaming.

God, is not truth. God did not know
Which one his favorite would be.

Because He was only the wind
That passes by and does not see.

JOHN A. CROW

Ejemplos

La veleta, la cigarra.
Pero el molino, la hormiga.

Muele pan, molino, muele.
Trenza, veleta, poesía.

Lo que Marta laboraba,
se lo soñaba María.

Dios, no es verdad, Dios no supo
cuál de las dos prefería.

Porque El era sólo el viento
que mueve y pasa y no mira.

Gerardo Diego

Spain, 1896–

Gerardo Diego, like Alberti, was educated by the Jesuits, but whereas Alberti became an ardent Communist as a result of the Spanish Civil War (1936–1939), Diego went to the other extreme and became a dedicated rightist. He was one of the first Spanish poets to embrace the new poetic creeds, many of which are reflected in his work. Diego himself stated that he felt a deep love for Lope de Vega, whom he worshiped, and for the twentieth-century Chilean poet, Vicente Huidobro, who headed the poetic school of creationism. Music is also a very strong influence in Diego's poetry, and he himself is an accomplished musician.

Diego's best-known work is an anthology of Spanish verse covering the years 1915–1931, in which seventeen poets (including Diego himself) are represented, each with a brief autobiographical sketch and several poems. His own poetry sometimes tends toward the academic, but it is so convincing and honest in its sincerity that the concern for form passes unnoticed. His vision of the poetic world is as follows: "Poetry is man's divine and luminous shadow. Without him it would not exist, yet it precedes him and to a degree also creates him. To believe what we never did see, they say is Faith. To believe what we will never see, this is poetry."[49]

Ballad of the Duero

O, Duero River, O Duero.
No one comes down to be with you,
No one even stops to listen
To the eternal song of your water.

Indifferent or cowardly
The city turns its back
Not wanting to see in your mirror
Its toothless walls.

You, ancient Duero, you smile
Behind your beard of silver,
Milling with your ballads
The ill-gathered harvests.

And among the saints of stone
And the magic poplars
You pass by taking as you flow
Words of love, soft words.

Who could ever, like you,
Still and quiet, yet flowing,
Always sing the same poem,
But with different water.

O Duero River, O Duero:
No one comes down to you,
Nobody wants to heed
Your eternal forgotten poetry.

Except those in love
Who ask about their hearts
And sow on your passing foam
Words of love, soft words.

JOHN A. CROW

Romance del Duero

Río Duero, río Duero,
nadie a acompañarte baja,
nadie se detiene a oir
tu eterna estrofa de agua.

Indiferente o cobarde
la ciudad vuelve la espalda.
No quiere ver en tu espejo
su muralla desdentada.

Tú, viejo Duero, sonríes
entre tus barbas de plata,
moliendo con tus romances
las cosechas mal logradas.

Y entre los santos de piedra
y los álamos de magia
pasas llevando en tus ondas
palabras de amor, palabras.

Quién pudiera como tú
a la vez quieto y en marcha,
cantar siempre el mismo verso
pero con distinta agua.

Río Duero, río Duero,
nadie a estar contigo baja,
ya nadie quiere atender
tu eterna estrofa olvidada,

sino los enamorados
que preguntan por sus almas
y siembran en tus espumas
palabras de amor, palabras.

Woman of Absence

Woman of absence,
Sculpture of music in time,
When I model the bust
The feet are missing and the face crumbled,
Nor does the portrait fix for me with its chemistry
The precise moment.
It is a dead silence
In the infinite melody.
Woman of absence, statue
Of dissolving salt, and the torment
Of immaterial form.

JOHN A. CROW

Mujer de ausencia

Mujer de ausencia,
escultura de música en el tiempo.
Cuando modelo el busto
faltan los pies y el rostro se deshizo.
Ni el retrato me fija con su química
el momento justo.
Es un silencio muerto
en la infinita melodía.
Mujer de ausencia, estatua
de sal que se disuelve, y la tortura
de forma sin materia.

49. *Ibid.,* 265.

Rafael Alberti

Spain, 1902–

Alberti began writing poetry that followed the traditional patterns, but he later composed in starkly realistic and surrealistic ways. He found special inspiration in the ancient folk songs and ballads of Spain and was also a great admirer of the poetry of Gil Vicente, Góngora, Lope de Vega, and Bécquer. He strove to become a part of the "collective unconscious" of his country by taking certain phrases from familiar old poems and incorporating these in compositions embodying his own private sensibility. During the Spanish Civil War (1936–1939) Alberti was a staunch defender of the Republican cause, often appearing at public gatherings in Madrid to deliver impassioned speeches. He became strongly politicized during this period and entered the Communist party. When the war ended he went into exile in Buenos Aires, where he spent many years before finally establishing himself in Rome.

Alberti holds no college degree, so he has not been a university professor like so many of his contemporaries. However, he has written and lectured widely on Spanish literature and for the motion pictures. His poetry has been much translated in France and Italy, and recently Ben Belitt made a good selection of it available in English. Alberti has often been linked with Lorca because of their close friendship and their mutual love of the popular poetry of Spain; but Lorca is intuitive, spontaneous, and incandescent in his expression, whereas Alberti is restrained, almost cold at times. Yet Alberti's mastery of technique implies ease and naturalness. His form is impeccable, whether he is writing in the traditional style or in one of the new styles.

Song of the Unlucky Angel

It was you, then, coming this way—
on the breaker that carried me in
and cast me away.

Look for me in the wave.

You who go with no thought of return:
a wind in the alternate dark
that blows itself out and burns itself back in a spark.

Look for me in the snow.

That presence whom nothing can know
yet tears at the world in its dearth
and converses with nothing on earth.

Look for me in the air.

BEN BELITT

Canción del ángel sin suerte

Tú eres lo que va,
agua que me lleva,
que me dejará.

    Buscadme en la nieve.

Lo que va y no vuelve:
viento que en la sombra
se apaga y se enciende.

    Buscadme en la nieve.

Lo que nadie sabe:
tierra movediza
que no habla con nadie.

    Buscadme en el aire.

Angel Undeceived

Blazing out of the frost
I was seized by your voice:
"Come to my kingdom!

My cities wait for you there—
neither living nor dead,
with a wreath for your head."

"No one dreams of my coming.
I sleep soundly," I said.

BEN BELITT

El ángel desengañado

Quemando los fríos,
tu voz prendió en mí:
ven a mi país.

Te esperan ciudades,
sin vivos ni muertos,
para coronarte.

—Me duermo.
No me espera nadie.

Lying Angel

And so, I was broken,
Yes I, without violence,
With honey, with words.

All alone, in a place
Of wind and of sand,
With no man, a prisoner.

And, somebody's shadow,
A hundred doors to time
Slammed on my blood.

O light! Stay with me!

For I was broken,
Yes I, without violence,
With honey, with words.

JOHN A. CROW

Paradise Lost

Across centuries
and the void of a world,
sleepless, I seek you.

Behind me, invisibly,
never grazing my shoulders,
my dead angel stands guard.

Where is that Paradise,
shadow, lately your home?
Ask it in stillness.

Unanswering cities,
mute rivers, peaks
of no echo, inarticulate seas.

Nobody knows. Men
tranced and upright on the beaches
at the stilled grave's verge,

with no thought for my presence. Wan birds
in a petrified singing, blind,
on their rapturous way,

knowing nothing,
sunless and stopped,
old winds make their circuit

of leagues, lift up the ash
of their passing and rain down
on our shoulders, having little to say.

All Heaven dissolves:
the truth that it bound in its being
turns shapeless and shuns me.

Here at earth's end,
at the ultimate margin,
my eyes fix on nothing.

I search in the death

El ángel mentiroso

Y, fui derrotada
yo, sin violencia,
con miel y palabras.

Y, sola, en provincias
de arena y de viento,
sin hombre, cautiva.

Y, sombra de alguien,
cien puertas de siglos
tapiaron mi sangre.

¡Ay luces! ¡Conmigo!

Que fui derrotada
yo, sin violencia,
con miel y palabras.

Paraíso perdido

A través de los siglos,
por la nada del mundo,
yo, sin sueño, buscándote.

Tras de mí, imperceptible,
sin rozarme los hombros,
mi ángel muerto, vigía.

¿Adónde el Paraíso,
sombra, tú que has estado?
Pregunta con silencio.

Ciudades sin respuesta,
ríos sin habla, cumbres
sin ecos, mares mudos.

Nadie lo sabe. Hombres
fijos, de pie, a la orilla
parada de las tumbas,

me ignoran. Aves tristes,
cantos petrificados,
en éxtasis el rumbo,

ciegas. No sabe nada.
Sin sol, vientos antiguos,
inertes, en las leguas

por andar, levantándose
calcinados, cayéndose
de espaldas, poco dicen.

Diluídos, sin forma
la verdad que en sí ocultan,
huyen de mí los cielos.

Ya en el fin de la Tierra,
sobre el último filo,
resbalando los ojos,

muerta en mí la esperanza,

of my hopes for a portico's
green in the blackened abysses.

O shadowy threshold!
Caldron and spate of a world!
What a riot of centuries!

Away! Away with them all! What unspeakable
panic of shadows!
What collapses of spirit!

—Dead angel, arise
where you are! Light the way
home with your blazon!

Silence; ever more silence,
as eternity's pulsebeat
fails in the night.

Ah, Paradise, lost!
Seeking you here I am lost in myself
and my night is forever.

BEN BELITT

Dream

> *Oarsmen, to the oars!*
> Gil Vincente

NIGHT.
The moon, a green snail.
On all the terraces
The white forms of naked girls.

Oarsmen, row! One, two three!
From the earth emerges the globe
That is to die in the sea.

DAWN.
Go to sleep, you naked girls,
Until the globe no longer falls
In the arm of the surf.

Oarsmen, row! One, two, three!
Until the globe no longer sleeps
On the breast of the sea!

JOHN A. CROW

My Voice

If here on earth my voice should die
Take it down to the level sea
And on the shore there let it lie.

Take it down to the level sea
And make it the Captain be
Of a great white ship of war.

Oh, my voice, your medals cry
These sailor badges are:

---

ese pórtico verde
busco en las negras simas.

¡Oh boquete de sombras!
¡Hervidero del mundo!
¡Qué confusión de siglos!

¡Atrás! ¡Atrás! ¡Qué espanto
de tinieblas sin voces!
¿Qué perdida mi alma!

—Ángel muerto, despierta.
¿Dónde estás? Ilumina
con tu rayo el retorno.

Silencio. Más silencio.
Inmóviles los pulsos
del sinfín de la noche.

¡Paraíso perdido!
Perdido por buscarte,
yo, sin luz para siempre.

Sueño

> *¡A los remos, remadores!*
> Gil Vicente

NOCHE.
Verde caracol, la luna.
Sobre todas las terrazas.
blancas doncellas desnudas.

¡Remadores, a remar!
De la tierra emerge el globo
que ha de morir en el mar.

ALBA.
Dormíos, blancas concellas,
hasta que el globo no caiga
en brazos de la marea.

¡Remadores, a remar,
hasta que el globo no duerma
entre los senos del mar!

Mi voz

Si mi voz muriera en tierra,
llevadla al nivel del mar
y dejadla en la ribera.

Llevadla al nivel del mar
y nombradla capitana
de un blanco bajel de guerra.

¡Oh mi voz condecorada
con la insignia marinera:

On my heart an anchor,
On my anchor a star,
On my star the wind,
And a sail on wind and sky.

sobre el corazón un ancla
y sobre el ancla una estrella
y sobre la estrella el viento
y sobre el viento la vela!

JOHN A. CROW

Luis Cernuda

Spain, 1904–1963

Luis Cernuda, like Salinas, Aleixandre, García Lorca, and Alberti, was born in Andalusia. At the beginning of his poetic career he was strongly influenced by Jorge Guillén, but later he moved into the area of surrealism and eventually found his own style. He was an intellectual poet with a romantic heart, and he wrote in an intense, highly colored, often cryptic poetic manner. After the Spanish Civil War he left Spain and lived the remainder of his life in Mexico, from time to time coming to the United States to serve as a visiting professor in various universities. He was a shy, soft-spoken, retiring man who lived primarily for his inner world, a world of torment and isolation.

When asked by Gerardo Diego to define poetry for his introductory sketch in an anthology, Cernuda skirted the question by replying: "It would hardly be worth the pain to go on forgetting reality so that I might now remember it, and before what people! I detest reality so as I detest all things that belong to it: my friends, my family, my country. I know nothing, I want nothing, I hope for nothing. And if I could hope for one thing only, it would be to die some place where this grotesque civilization which makes men conceited has not penetrated." [50]

That Recent Wind

That recent wind,
Gracefully moving,
Opening in the leaves
Only a spring.

Through the absolute clarity
Of the unblemished sky,
Birds in the hand:
The first swallow fly.

A tree quietly assumes
The brief space it knows,
So does fervor awaken
This present repose.

The leaves are green,
The twilight disappears,
Already shadows lean
On the fugitive lights.

In its peace the window
Each day redeems
The stars, the wind,
And the one who dreams.

Esa brisa reciente

¡Esa brisa reciente
en el espacio esbelta!
En las hojas, abriendo,
sólo una primavera.

Por el raso absoluto
del cielo sin divisa,
pájaros en la mano;
primeras golondrinas.

Un árbol quieto asume
la distancia tan breve.
Así el fervor alerta
la indolencia presente.

Verdes están las hojas.
El crepúsculo huye.
Ya las sombras alcanzan
las fugitivas luces.

En su paz, la ventana
restituye a diario
las estrellas, el aire
y el que estaba soñando.

JOHN A. CROW

50. *Ibid.*, 423.

How Tender the Station

How tender the station
Only a nest of passage
Opening a flight of trains
Toward the distant air.

Already the hand leads
To the sound-filled car:
Tenderness and dreams
Its lyrical baggage.

The rose of the winds
On the platform commands
A perfume of waves
And of virgin lands.

When the earth flows
Along the rails of time,
How far away goes
The handkerchief, the good-bye?

Does quietude not wish
To follow the new star?
Two longings embrace
On the window of the car.

JOHN A. CROW

Cuán tierna la estación

¡Cuán tierna la estación,
sólo nido de tránsito
abre un vuelo de trenes
hacia el aire lejano!

Ya la mano conduce
al vagón resonante,
la ternura, los sueños:
su lírico equipaje.

La rosa de los vientos
en el andén levanta
un perfume de olas
y de tierras intactas.

Cuando vaya el paisaje
por las vías del tiempo,
¡qué lejos quedarán
el adiós, el pañuelo!

¿Y la quietud no quiere
seguir la nueva estrella?
Dos anhelos cruzados
en el cristal se besan.

Hidden Between the Walls

Hidden between the walls
The garden gives to me
Its branches and its water
Of secret delight.

What silence! Is the world
Like that? It crosses the sky
Marking off landscapes
With smiles toward the horizon.

Indolent earth, in vain
Your destiny glitters;
Beside the still water
I dream, thinking that I live.

But time is restraining
The strength of this hour.
Its measure full blown,
It escapes with its roses.

And the fresh air returns
With accompanying night,
Its smooth flow forgetting
The branches and the waters.

JOHN A. CROW

Escondido en los muros

Escondido en los muros
este jardín me brinda
sus ramas y sus aguas
de secreta delicia.

¡Qué silencio! ¿Es así
el mundo?... Cruza el cielo,
desfilando paisajes,
risueño, hacia lo lejos.

¡Tierra indolente! En vano
resplandece el destino.
Junto a las aguas quietas,
sueño y pienso que vivo.

Mas el tiempo ya tasa
el poder de esta hora:
madura su medida,
escapa con sus rosas.

Y el aire fresco vuelve
con la noche cercana,
su tersura olvidando
las ramas y las aguas.

The Walls, Nothing More

The walls, nothing more,
Life is lying inert,

Los muros, nada más

Los muros, nada más.
Yace la vida inerte,

Without breath, soundless,
Without cruel words.

Livid, escapes the light,
The windowpane affirms itself
On the tenuous night
Of scattering rains.

Rising up, revived, the house
Came back into being.
Times are the same,
Different the seeing.

Have I closed the door?
Forgetfulness opens for me
Its emptied store,
Gray, white, and windless.

But nobody sighs.
A sob between the hands,
Nothing more. Nothing... silence:
The darkness is trembling.

sin vida, sin ruido,
sin palabras crueles.

La luz, lívida, escapa,
y el cristal ya se afirma
contra la noche incierta
de arrebatadas lluvias.

Alzada, resucita
tal otra vez la casa:
los tiempos son idénticos,
distintas las miradas.

¿He cerrado la puerta?
El olvido me abre
sus desnudas estancias
grises, blancas, sin aire.

Pero nadie suspira.
Un llanto entre las manos,
sólo. Silencio, nada:
la oscuridad temblando.

JOHN A. CROW

Vicente Aleixandre

Spain, 1900–

Aleixandre is a Sevillian who came to live in Madrid, where he absorbed many Castilian and cosmopolitan influences. Among the Spanish American poets who appealed to him profoundly were Herrera y Reissig, Nervo, and Darío. Among the Spaniards, Góngora, Jiménez, and Guillén were the three who perhaps meant most to him. Aleixandre writes poetry, he says, "because it is my necessity. But I do not know what poetry is. And I profoundly distrust every poet's judgment concerning the eternally inexplicable. However, I come closer and closer to the certainty of that final frustration which poetry means."[51] Frustration and even shame that it is never achieved as it is felt.

Much of Aleixandre's poetry suggests French surrealism, but there is always an emotional intensity and clarity to his vision that defies classification. His style and images are as brilliant and delicate as the scenes of a graphic dream. Love, nature, mystical union, the fleeting quality of life, something eternal—these things flow through his poems. Disintegration itself is continuity eternalized when expressed in an art form, and it becomes the basis of an exalted pantheism.

In October, 1977, when Aleixandre was notified that he had been awarded the Nobel Prize for literature, he said: "The communication from the Academy did not mention The Generation of 1927, but I, in receiving it, invoke my memory and my affectionate thoughts for my comrades of this generation, with whom, at this moment, I feel in complete solidarity."[52]

The Swedish Academy, in announcing the award, cited Aleixandre for "half a century of creative poetic writing, which, with roots in the traditions of Spanish lyric verse and in modern currents, illuminates man's condition in present day society, and in the cosmos."[53]

51. *Ibid.*, 402.
52. Stanley Meisler, "Nobel Prize Won by Aleixandre," Los Angeles *Times*, October 7, 1977, p. 1.
53. *Ibid.*, 8.

Possession

Black, black shadow. A tide
Of slowness. Impatiently
The moon struggles to raise
Its bridge across the darkness.

(Of silver? They are drawbridges
When, bizarre, headfirst,
Loosened from its moorings
Day slips across.)

Now the rays tear apart
The thick shadow. Suddenly
The whole landscape reveals itself
Open, mute, unmistakable.

Moist beams of light touch
The surfaces, they flit by
Nimble and brilliant; bursting
In relief like flowers.

The landscape is stretched out.
Its spacious mantle
Offers unto the air
The flowers and fruits of night.

Night, now ripening
Gravitates across spun snow.
What warm life juices
Will it yield in my hand?

Its swelling breaks the clamp
Precisely, and the red pulp
Spangled with shining
Seeds, pours out.

My red lips taste it.
I sink my teeth into its soft flesh.
My whole mouth is filled
With love, with a consuming fire.

Drunk with light, with darkness,
With shining, my body stretches out
Its members. Walking on stars?
Tiptoe across a tremulous sky.

The night in me. I the night.
My eyes burning, Tenuous,
Upon my tongue is being born
A savor of approaching dawn.

Posesión

NEGROS de sombra. Caudales
de lentitud. Impaciente
se esfuerza en armar la luna
sobre la sombra sus puentes.

(¿De plata? Son levadizos
cuando, bizarro, de frente,
de sus puertos despegado
cruzar el día se siente).
Ahora los rayos desgarran
la sombra espesa. Reciente,
todo el paisaje se muestra,
abierto y mudo, evidente.

Húmedos pinceles tocan
las superficies, se mueven
ágiles, brillantes; tensos
brotan a flor los relieves.

Extendido ya el paisaje
está. Su mantel, no breve,
flores y frutos de noche,
en dulce peso, sostiene.

La noche, madura toda,
gravita sobre la nieve
hilada. ¿Qué zumos densos
dará en mi mano caliente?

Su pompa rompe la cárcel
exacta, y la pulpa ardiente,
constelada de pepitas
iluminadas, se vierte.

Mis rojos labios la sorben.
Hundo en su yema mis dientes.
Todo mi boca se llena
de amor, de fuegos presentes.

Ebrio de luces, de noche,
de brillos, mi cuerpo extiende
sus miembros, ¿pisando estrellas?,
temblor pisando celeste.

La noche en mí. Yo la noche.
Mis ojos ardiendo. Tenue,
sobre mi lengua naciendo
un sabor a alba creciente.

JOHN A. CROW

Poem of Love

I love you dream of the wind
You flow into my fingertips forgotten by the north star
In the world's sweet mornings with head bending
When it is easy to smile because the rain is soft.

On the bosom of a river to travel is a delight
Oh friendly fish, tell me the secret of the open eyes

Poema de Amor

Te amo sueño del viento
confluyes con mis dedos olvidado del norte
en las dulces mañanas del mundo cabeza abajo
cuando es fácil sonreír porque la lluvia es blanda

En el seno de un río viajar es delicia
oh peces amigos decidme el secreto de los ojos abiertos

Of my own glances which will flow into the sea
Sustaining the keels of remote ships.
I love you—travelers of the world—you who sleep upon
   the water
Men who cross the seas seeking their raiment
Those who leave their painful nakedness upon the sands
And on the decks of the ship they draw the moonlight.
To travel expectantly is a smiling joy, is beautiful,
The silver and the gold are unchanged at heart,
They skip over the scaly crest of the waves
And make music or dreams for the brightest hair.
In the depths of a river my desire takes leave of
Numberless towns I have held in my fingers
Those darknesses that I draped in black
Have already left far behind.

Hope is the earth, is the cheek,
Is an immense eyelid in which I know that I exist
"Do you remember?" I was born for the world one night
Whose sum and residue were the key to dreams.

Fish, trees, stones, hearts, medals
Over your concentric waves, yes, motionless,
I move and if I whirl I am seeking, O center, O center,
My way—toilers of the earth—to the future that lies
Beyond the seas in the swift pulsing of my blood.

JOHN A. CROW

At the Bottom of the Well

There at the bottom of the well where the little flowers
Where the pretty daisies do not quiver
Where no wind blows and there is no scent of man
Where the sea never reaches to threaten
There, there exists that absolute quiet
Born like a sound stifled in a closed hand.

If a bee, if a winging bird
If that never anticipated error
Should be made
The cold remains
The upright dream sank into the earth
And now the air is free.

Perhaps a voice, a hand now loose,
An impulse toward the sky aspires to the moon,
To peace, to warmth, to that venom
Of a pillow that snuffs the breath from a mouth

But to sleep is always so serene!
Over the cold, over the ice, over the shadow of a cheek,
Over a stiffened word already spoken,
Over the very same and always virgin earth

A slab of wood at the bottom, Oh numberless well,
That illustrious smoothness which proves
That a human back is contact, is dry cold,
Is always a dream, even if the face is rubbed away.

Clouds may pass. No one knows

---

de las miradas mías que van a dar en la mar
sosteniendo la quilla de los barcos lejanos
Yo os amo—viajadores del mundo—los que dormís sobre
   el agua
hombres que van a América en busca de sus vestidos
los que dejan en la playa su desnudez dolida
y sobre las cubiertas del barco atraen el rayo de luna
Caminar esperando es risueño es hermoso
la plata y el oro no han cambiado de fondo
botan sobre las ondas sobre el lomo escamado
y hacen música o sueño para los pelos más rubios

Por el fondo de un río mi deseo se marcha
de los pueblos innúmeros que he tenido en las yemas
esas oscuridades que vestido de negro
he dejado ya lejos dibujadas en espalda

La esperanza es la tierra es la mejilla
es un inmenso párpado donde yo sé que existo
¿Te acuerdas? Para el mundo he nacido una noche
en que era suma y resta la clave de los sueños

Peces árboles piedras corazones medallas
sobre vuestras concéntricas ondas—sí—detenidas
yo me muevo y si giro me busco oh centro oh centro
camino—viajadores del mundo—del futuro existente
más allá de los mares en mis pulsos que laten.

En el fondo del pozo

Allá en el fondo del pozo donde las florecillas
donde las lindas margaritas no vacilan
donde no hay viento o perfume de hombre
donde jamás el mar impone su amenaza
allí, allí está quedo ese silencio
hecho como un rumor ahogado con un puño

Si una abeja si un ave voladora
si ese error que no se espera nunca
se produce
el frío permanece
El sueño en vertical hundió la tierra
y ya el aire está libre

Acaso una voz una mano y suelta
un impulso hacia arriba aspira a luna
a calma a tibieza a ese veneno
de una almohada en la boca que se ahoga

¡Pero dormir es tan sereno siempre!
Sobre el frío sobre el hielo sobre una sombra de mejilla
sobre una palabra yerta y más ya ida
sobre la misma tierra siempre virgen

Una tabla en el fondo oh pozo innúmero
esa lisura ilustre que comprueba
que una espalda es contacto es frío seco
es sueño siempre aunque la frente esté borrada

Pueden pasar ya nubes. Nadie sabe

That sound. Do bells exist?
I remember that the color white or the shape
I remember that the lips, yes, were even speaking

It was the hot summer season. Immolating light
It was then when the sudden flash of lightning
Was caught in suspension—wrought of iron—
Time of sighs or of worship me
When the birds never lost their feathers

Time of softness and permanence
The galloping feet did not tread the breast
The hooves did not remain, they were not waxen.
Tears ran like kisses
And in the ear the echo was solidified

Thus eternity was the passing moment
Time was only a tremendous hand
Clasping the long strands of hair

Oh, yes. In that deep silence or dampness
Beneath the seven mantles of the sky, I do not know
The music congealed into sudden ice
The throat that collapses across the eyes
The intimate curl that disintegrates upon the lips

Asleep like a piece of cloth
I feel the little herbs growing, the soft green
That uselessly awaits its upward curve

A hand of steel over the grasses,
A heart, a forgotten plaything,
A spring, a file, a kiss, a piece of glass

A crystal flower which thus impassively
Sucks from the earth a silence or a memory

JOHN A. CROW

Ese clamor ¿Existen las campanas?
Recuerdo que el color blanco o las formas
recuerdo que los labios, sí, hasta hablaban

Era el tiempo caliente. Luz inmólame
Era entonces cuando el relámpago de pronto
quedaba suspendido hecho de hierro
Tiempo de los suspiros o de adórame
cuando nunca las aves perdían plumas

Tiempo de suavidad y permanencia
Los galopes no daban sobre el pecho
no quedaban los cascos, no eran cera
Las lágrimas rodaban como besos
Y en el oído el eco era ya sólido

Así la eternidad era el minuto
El tiempo sólo una tremenda mano
sobre el cabello largo detenida

Oh sí, En este hondo silencio o humedades
bajo las siete capas de cielo azul yo ignoro
la música cuajada en hielo súbito
la garganta que se derrumba sobre los ojos
la íntima onda que se anega sobre los labios

Dormido como una tela
siento crecer la hierba el verde suave
que inútilmente aguarda ser curvado

Una mano de acero sobre el césped
un corazón un juguete olvidado
un resorte una lima un beso un vidrio

Una flor de cristal que así impasible
chupa de tierra un silencio o memoria

Song for a Dead Girl

Tell me, tell me the secret of your virgin heart;
Tell me the secret of your body beneath the earth;
I want to know why you are now turned to water,
Those fresh swirls where naked feet are bathed with
   foam.

Tell me why over your flowing hair,
Over your softly caressed grasses,
Falls, skips, touches tenderly, disappears,
A burning or solemn sun that touches you
Like a wind that bears only a bird or a hand.

Tell me why your heart like a tiny forest
Waits beneath the earth for impossible birds,
That total song which is made by dreams
When they pass noiselessly over the eyes.

Oh, you, song that to a dead or a live body,
That to a beautiful being who sleeps under the ground
You are singing with the color of stone, of lips or kisses,
You are singing as if mother-of-pearl were sleeping or
   dreaming.

Canción a una muchacha muerta

Dime, dime el secreto de tu corazón virgen;
dime el secreto de tu cuerpo bajo tierra;
quiero saber por qué ahora eres un agua,
esas orillas frescas donde unos pies desnudos se bañan
   con espuma.

Dime por qué sobre tu pelo suelto,
sobre tu dulce hierba acariciada,
cae, resbala, acaricia, se va
un sol ardiente o reposado que te toca
como un viento que lleva sólo un pájaro o mano.

Dime por qué tu corazón como una selva diminuta
espera bajo tierra los imposibles pájaros,
esa canción total que por encima de los ojos
hacen los sueños cuando pasan sin ruido.

Oh tú, canción que a un cuerpo muerto o vivo,
que a un ser hermoso que bajo el suelo duerme
cantas color de piedra, color de beso o labio,
cantas como si el nácar durmiera o respirara.

That waist, that frail curve of a sad breast,
Those ringlets of hair untouched by the wind,
Those eyes where only silence now resides,
Those teeth of well defended ivory,
That breeze which does not move the ungreen leaves . . .

Oh, you, laughing sky, you pass like a cloud;
Oh happy bird, laughing upon a shoulder;
Fountain that, fresh spurt of water, entwining you with
    the moon:
Soft grasses walked upon by two adorable feet!

JOHN A. CROW

The Old Man and the Sun

He had lived a long time,
He often leaned there, a very old man, on the trunk of a
    tree,
on a very thick trunk in the late afternoon when the sun
    was going down,
I used to pass by at that time and would stop to observe
    him.
He was old, he had a wrinkled face, and his eyes were
    lifeless,
rather than sad.
He would lean against the tree, and the sun would first
    reach him
softly biting his feet,
and it would stay there for a while as if in a huddle.
Then it would climb and slowly submerge him,
    immersing him,
gently tugging at him, making him one with its sweet
    light.
Oh, that living, enduring oldness, how it would dissolve!
All that eagerness, the story of his sadness, the traces of
    his wrinkles,
the misery of his eroded skin,
how it would slowly be filed away in little fragments, and
    then vanish!
Like a rock that softly crumbles in the destructive torrent
surrendering to love's loud cry,
the old man, in that silence, was slowly being consumed,
    slowly giving himself.
And I saw the powerful sun slowly bite him with a great
    love
and lull him to sleep
so as to take him bit by bit, so as to gently dissolve him
in its light,
like a mother who tenderly lifts her child back to her
    breast.
I passed there and saw him. But at times I saw only a
    trace.
Scarcely a frail thread of being.
What remained afterwards of that loving old man,
that sweet old man, had already become pure light,
and very slowly it too was carried away by the last rays of
    the sun,
like so many other invisible things of this world.

JOHN A. CROW

Esa cintura, ese débil volumen de un pecho triste,
ese rizo voluble que ignora el viento,
esos ojos por donde sólo boga el silencio,
esos dientes que son de marfil resguardado,
ese aire que no mueve unas hojas no verdes . . .

¡Oh tú, cielo riente, que pasas como nube;
oh pájaro feliz, que sobre un hombro ríes;
fuente que, chorro fresco, te enredas con la luna;
césped blando que pisan unos pies adorados!

El viejo y el sol

Había vivido mucho.
Se apoyaba allí, viejo, en un tronco, en un gruesísimo
    tronco, muchas tardes cuando el sol caía.
Yo pasaba por allí a aquellas horas y me detenía a
    observarle.
Era viejo y tenía la faz arrugada, apagados, más que
    tristes, los ojos.
Se apoyaba en el tronco, y el sol se le acercaba primero, le
    mordía suavemente los pies
y allí se quedaba unos momentos como acurrucado.
Después ascendía e iba sumergiéndole, anegándole,
tirando suavemente de él, unificándole en su dulce luz.
¡Oh el viejo vivir, el viejo quedar, cómo se desleía!
Toda la quemazón, la historia de la tristeza, el resto de las
    arrugas, la miseria de la piel roída,
¡cómo iba lentamente limándose, deshaciéndose!
Como una roca que en el torrente devastador se va
    dulcemente desmoronando,
rindiéndose a un amor sonorísimo,
así, en aquel silencio, el viejo se iba lentamente anulando,
    lentamente entregando.
Y yo veía el poderoso sol lentamente morderle con mucho
    amor y adormirle
para así poco a poco tomarle, para así poquito a poco
    disolverle en su luz,
como una madre que a su niño suavísimamente en su
    seno lo reinstalase.

Yo pasaba y lo veía. Pero a veces no veía sino un sutilísimo
    resto. Apenas un lévisimo encaje del ser.
Lo que quedaba después que el viejo amoroso, el viejo
    dulce, había pasado ya a ser la luz
y despaciosísimamente era arrastrado en los rayos
    postreros del sol,
como tantas otras invisibles cosas del mundo.

Jorge Carrera Andrade
Ecuador, 1903–

Carrera Andrade lived and studied for extensive periods in Europe (France, Germany, Spain) and has served as a counselor representative of his country in many foreign cities. In San Francisco he was consul general of Ecuador for several years. Góngora, Neruda, and the French poet, Francis Jammes, have all influenced his style, but his primary poetic view is Indianist. Mistral characterized him as "Indo-futurist," for it is his insight rather than his subject matter that reflects the Indian concept of the world. In his poetry objects and images flash before us as if they were called forth to take part in a secret rite.

Biography

The window was born of a desire for sky
And stationed itself in the black wall like an angel.
It is a friend to man
And a carrier of air.

It talks with pools of the earth
With the child mirrors of habitations
And with roofs in repose.

From their heights, the windows,
With their diaphanous harangues,
Are a landmark to the multitudes.

The window, master of science,
Diffuses its light in the night.
It extracts the square root of a meteor,
Totals the columns of constellations.

The window is the gunwale of the ship of the earth,
A surf of clouds surrounds it.
Captain Spirit seeks the island of God
And his eyes are washed by blue tempests.

To call men the window distributes
A quart of light, a bucket of air.
Plowed by the clouds,
It is the small property of the sky.

H. R. HAYS

Biografía

La ventana nació de un deseo de cielo
y en la muralla negra se posó como un ángel.
Es amiga del hombre
y portera del aire.

Conversa con los charcos de la tierra,
con los espejos niños de las habitaciones
y con los tejados en huelga.

Desde su altura, las ventanas
orientan a las multitudes
con sus arengas diáfanas.

La ventana maestra
difunde sus luces en la noche.
Extrae la raíz cuadrada de un meteoro,
suma columnas de constelaciones.

La ventana es la borda del barco de la tierra,
la ciñe mansamente un oleaje de nubes.
El capitán Espíritu busca la isla de Dios
y los ojos se lavan en tormentas azules.

La ventana reparte entre todos los hombres
una cuarta de luz y un cubo de aire.
Ella es, arada de nubes,
la pequeña propiedad del cielo.

Dust, Corpse of Time

You are the spirit of the earth, impalpable dust.
Omnipresent, impregnated, riding upon the air,
You cover sea miles and terrestrial distances
With your load of fantoms and blurred faces.

O subtle visitor of habitations!
Locked wardrobes know you.
Corpse of time or innumerable plunder,
Your ruin drops to the ground like a dog.

Universal miser, in holes and cellars
Endlessly you pile up your filmy, useless gold.
Vain collector of footsteps and of shapes,
You take the fingerprints of the leaves.

Polvo, cadáver del tiempo

Espíritu de la tierra eres: polvo impalpable.
Omnipresente, ingrávido, cabalgando en el aire
cubres millas marítimas y terrestres distancias
con tu carga de rostros borrados y de larvas.

Oh sutil visitante de las habitaciones.
Los cerrados armarios te conocen.
Despojo innumerable o cadáver del tiempo,
tu ruina se desploma como un perro.

Avaro universal, en huecos y en bodegas
tu oro ligero, inútil, amontonas sin tregua.
Coleccionista vano de huellas y de formas,
les tomas la impresión digital a las hojas.

Upon furniture, and nailed-up doors and corners,	Sobre muebles y puertas condenadas y esquinas,
Upon pianos, empty hats, and tableware,	sobre pianos, vacíos sombreros y vajillas
Your mortal wave or shadow	tu sombra o mortal ola
Extends its yellow banner of victory.	extiende su cetrina bandera de victoria.
Upon the earth you encamp like a master	Sobre la tierra acampas como dueño
With the pale legions of your scattered empire.	con las legiones pálidas de tu imperio disperso.
O rodent, your infinite teeth devour	Oh roedor, tus dientes infinitos devoran
The color and shape of everything.	el color, la presencia de las cosas.
Even the light is dressed in silence	Hasta la luz se viste de silencio
With your gray swaddlings, tailor of mirrors.	con tu envoltura gris, sastre de los espejos.
Final inheritor of defunct objects,	Heredero final de las cosas difuntas,
All shall be stored up in your moving tomb.	todo lo vas guardando en tu ambulante tumba.

H. R. HAYS

Eugenio Florit
Spain and Cuba, 1903–

Eugenio Florit moved from his native Spain to Cuba when he was fifteen years old, and he is usually regarded as a Cuban writer. His mother was Cuban, and he became a citizen of that country in 1922. In 1940 he came to the United States, where he was attached to the staff of the Cuban consulate in New York City. Shortly thereafter he also began to teach Hispanic literature at Columbia University. He has published many books in this country. Florit knew Jiménez and was profoundly moved by his poetry. However, he developed his own terse, mystical, symbolist style to a point of near perfection. The first poem that follows, "Elegy for Your Absence," written after the death of his father, is a statement of transfigured anguish in symbolic images of great beauty and feeling.

Few poets of this century have equaled Florit in capturing essence or in intensity of expression. The North American poet, H. R. Hays, who has beautifully translated so many Hispanic poets, points out that Florit is a neosymbolist "in the sense that he is preoccupied with subtle spiritual values," and that he is "filled with a burning desire to penetrate to the essence of experience." Hays sees Florit's poetry as varying "from classical simplicity to an almost baroque complication of detail," while a "dreamlike ecstatic mood indicates his debt to the English romantics, especially Keats and Shelley."[54]

Elegy for Your Absence

> *Peace, peace, he is not dead, he doth not sleep.*
> *He hath awakened from the dream of life.*
> Shelley

You went away that moment for all death
To travel on deep seas where silence seems
A long highway of eyes that are asleep,
A flock of doves all fastened to your dreams.

You live now in the beams of absent moonlight
More your own self than in time's golden hands and
  springs
On which so many borderless moments recorded
The thirst that burned your shoulders' budding wings.

Elegía para tu ausencia

> *Peace, peace, he is not dead, he doth not sleep.*
> *He hath awakened from the dream of life.*
> Shelley.

Te fuiste aquel minuto para toda la muerte
a navegar en hondos océanos de silencio
con un largo camino de pupilas dormidas
y un bando de palomas prendido a tus
  ensueños.

Ya estarás por ausentes claridades de luna,
más tuyo que en las flechas de tu reloj de oro,
donde contabas tanto minuto sin orillas
para la sed de alas que quemaba tus hombros.

54. H. R. Hayes (ed.), *Twelve Spanish American Poets* (Boston: Beacon Press, 1972), 94.

You will have moved beyond the seas' wild reckoning,
Abysses in your timid solitude now lost;
At night you will become a tenuous warm breeze
Beside that loving mound that holds your ghost.

Long held embrace of breaths over red poppies,
Laughter and wordless song, sans music, sans refrain,
A joyful "here I am" of many sleepless hours,
A warm "forever" on the cold and distant plain.

And since you went pressed in the arms of silence,
Your words of light will now more clearly sound,
Wings will be born for you in each butterfly,
And for each verse of air an accent will be found.

I live in joy for that eternal day
To find you in the water, grass, and sky,
Among the clouds you make crêches of silver,
And in a tree of stars your nest will lie.

JOHN A. CROW

Y habrás saltado mares que la inquietud
   miraba,
abismos en la tímida soledad de tu ausencia;
y en la noche habrás sido tenue brisa caliente
junto a aquel pedacito de tu amorosa tierra.

Largo abrazo de alientos sobre las amapolas
y una risa, y un canto sin palabras ni música;
y un aquí estoy gozoso de pasados insomnios,
y un para siempre cálido en la fría llanura.

Como partiste en brazos del silencio apretado,
resonará más viva la luz de tus palabras;
y en cada estrofa de aire se enredará un
   acento,
y en cada mariposa te nacerán más alas.

Gozo de estar ya vivo para el eterno día,
de saberte en el agua, y en el sol, y en la
   hierba.
Harás entre las nubes Nacimientos de plata
y encontrarás tu nido en un árbol de estrellas.

Nocturne

Above the smouldering coals
of memories and pleasures
the pulse of my night takes form:
a heart without words or measure.

Buried deep in a desert
of shifting wind-swept sands
with faintly yellowed waters
in a dreamy arid land.

To know that I go naked
beneath a thousand stars
and feel the painful trembling
of a world with open scars.

I make my way through hours
that suffer from the cold
of a landscape I once knew
beyond things faded and old.

To flee in the stream of night
that runs through a part of my soul
seeking to approach the white
unquietness of this death.

What strange rivers run through me
with cold waters from afar!
And how the rippling laughter
is falling into stars!

KATHARINE E. STRATHDEE

Nocturno

Corazón de mis noches:
desnudo de palabras,
hecho sobre las ascuas
de recuerdos y goces.

Hundido en el desierto
de arenas indecisas,
con aguas amarillas
en oasis de sueños.

Saber que voy desnudo
bajo miles de estrellas
y sentir cómo tiembla
el dolor en el mundo.

Navego por las horas
que más sufren el frío
de un paisaje vivido
más allá de estas cosas.

Huir en la corriente
por la mitad del alma,
que se acerca en la blanca
inquietud de esta muerte.

Qué ríos me atraviesan
de frías aguas tímidas,
y cómo va la risa
cayéndose en estrellas.

The Present Evening

Between me and the sunset, the whole of life.
As if time, arrested,
Were falling

Tarde presente

Entre el ocaso y yo, toda la vida.
Como si detenido
el tiempo se cayera

To blossom in a drop of water.
As if God in his lofty meditation
Were drying the tears of his sons;
And She, the colorless one, were sleeping on the
    flowering border
Of her innumerable tombs.
As if yesterday were to come with its written memory
And tomorrow were already in its prison of letters;
As if today were an enormous rose
Of millions of petals, united
In a single corner of the revealed world.
Or better still; as if all lovers' kisses
Had burst from their seedbed
And were raising in the twilight wind
Their liberated wings.
                        Like the compact flight
Of armies of angels
In their highest sphere.
Like the ascension of a thought at liberty
Toward the source
Where light is born and the core of sorrow,
The germ of a cry and a first tear
Have taken form under the sky.
As if all this together suddenly
Intervened between man and his destiny.
As if a sunflower were opening its yellow petals
In front of the red west.
As if the hand of yesterday
Were sprinkling blue lilies
And the sea beneath the hand
Were a dovecote of wounded petals.
And as if ships were emerging
From their dead iron, from their dream of fishes,
From their oblivion
To stretch their immortal sails
In the winds and the sun.
                        As if the cold
Bones of the earth,
Reddened by immaterial fire,
Were returning to the white heat of the soul
To ponder, to tremble,
To laugh, and to weep, with laughter and tears
Of truth, in the beating
Of an actual breast, in clean eyes,
In sinless mouths, in the warm
Caress of its flesh.
                        These words,
Facing the west, from sea to sky,
With tenderness close to me.
                        The heart,
Dressed in gray humility, rejoices.

a florecer en una gota de agua.
Como si Dios es su alto pensamiento
secara el llanto de sus hijos;
y Ella, la sin color, durmiera al borde florecido
de sus innumerables tumbas.
Como si ayer llegara con su recuerdo escrito
y mañana estuviera ya en su cárcel de letras;
como si hoy fuera una enorme rosa
de millones de pétalos unidos
en una sola esquina del mundo revelado.
O aún mejor: como si todo beso
de amante hubiera roto su semilla
y se alzaran al viento del crepúsculo
sus alas libres.
                Como el vuelo
apretado de ejércitos de ángeles
en su más alto círculo.
Como ascensión de un pensamiento libre
hasta el principio
donde nació la luz y se formaron
entraña de dolor, gérmen de grito
y lágrima primera bajo el cielo.
Como si todo junto de repente
se pusiera entre el hombre y su destino.
Como si ante el ocaso rojo abriera
un girasol sus rayos amarillos.
Como si aquella mano
de ayer regara azules lirios
y fuera el mar bajo la mano
un palomar de pétalos heridos.
Y como si los barcos emergieran
de su muerte de hierros, de su sueño
de peces, de su olvido,
para tender sus velas inmortales
a los vientos y al sol.
                Como si fríos
los huesos de la tierra,
por fuego inmaterial enrojecidos
hasta el blanco del alma
volvieran a pesar, a estremecerse,
a reír y a llorar, en risa y llanto
de verdad, en latidos
de pecho verdadero, en ojos limpios,
en bocas sin pecado, en tibia
caricia de sus carnes.
                Así dicho
frente al ocaso, desde la tierra al mar,
con la ternura junto a mí.
                Se alegra
el corazón de manso gris vestido.

H. R. HAYS

Miguel Hernández
Spain, 1910–1942

This gifted poet, who is extremely popular among the young people in Spain today, was of poor peasant stock and worked as a goatherd during his early years. He received only a limited education but was an avid reader with a strong literary bent. Juan Ramón Jiménez and Antonio Machado admired his first verses and encouraged him to continue writing poetry. Among the classical authors that Hernández liked were Góngora, Lope de Vega, Garcilaso, and San Juan de la Cruz. Among the contemporaries, Aleixandre and Neruda were his favorites. His own poetry fuses the classical with the contemporary, the artistic with the unpolished folk spirit. A rude and unique flavor of the earth, a kind of primitive essence, permeates his best work, which shows a remarkable spontaneity, directness, and economy of language. Hernández fought for the Republic during the Spanish Civil War; he was put into prison after the war (many of his finest poems were written there), and three years later he died there, of tuberculosis and pulmonary complications, at the age of thirty-two.

Death, All Riddled with Holes

Death, all riddled with holes
And gorings from your very self,
In the hide of a bull you walk and graze
On a bullfighter's shining meadow.

He gives volcanic roars in sudden flashes,
And then streams with the fierce smoke
Of a love for everything that is born
As he kills the quiet rancheros.

Wild, hungry, loving beast, you can
Feed on my heart, on tragic grass,
If you like its bitter flavor.

A love for everything torments me now
As it does you, and towards it all
My heart spills out dressed in its burial clothes.

JOHN A. CROW

La muerte, toda llena de agujeros

La muerte, toda llena de agujeros
y cuernos de su mismo desenlace,
bajo una piel de toro pisa y pace
un luminoso prado de toreros.

Volcánicos bramidos, humos fieros
de general amor por cuanto nace,
a llamaradas echa mientras hace
morir a los tranquilos ganaderos.

Ya puedes, amorosa fiera hambrienta,
pastar mi corazón, trágica grama,
si te gusta lo amargo de su asunto.

Un amor hacia todo me atormenta
como a ti, y hacia todo se derrama
mi corazón vestido de difunto.

Love Rose Between Us

Love rose between us like the moon
Between the two tall palms
That never kissed.

The intimate sound of our two bodies
Was like a secret lullaby,
But the hoarse voice was tortured.
The lips were cold as stone.

Flesh longed for flesh in a warm clasp.
It set a flame within the kindled bones,
But when the arms reached out
They died on other arms.

Love passed between us like the moon
And devoured our lonely bodies.
Now we are two ghosts who seek each other
But always with a distance between us.

JOHN A. CROW

El amor ascendía entre nosotros

El amor ascendía entre nosotros
como la luna entre las dos palmeras
que nunca se abrazaron.

El íntimo rumor de los dos cuerpos
hacia el arrullo un oleaje trajo,
pero la ronca voz fue atenazada.
Fueron pétreos los labios.

El ansia de ceñir movió la carne,
esclareció los huesos inflamados,
pero los brazos al querer tenderse
murieron en los brazos.

Pasó el amor, la luna, entre nosotros
y devoró los cuerpos solitarios,
y somos dos fantasmas que se buscan
y se encuentran lejanos.